Speaking of the Moor

Speaking of the Moor

From Alcazar *to* Othello

Emily C. Bartels

PENN

UNIVERSITY OF PENNSYLVANIA PRESS

PHILADELPHIA

Published by
University of Pennsylvania Press
Philadelphia, Pennsylvania 19104–4112

Printed in the United States of America on acid-free paper

10 9 8 7 6 5 4 3 2 1

A Cataloging-in-Publication record is available from the Library of Congress
ISBN 978-0-8122-4076-4

For Emma Smith

CONTENTS

INTRODUCTION
On Sitting Down to Read *Othello* Once Again   1

CHAPTER ONE
Enter Barbary: *The Battle of Alcazar* and "the World"   21

CHAPTER TWO
Imperialist Beginnings: Hakluyt's *Navigations* and the Place
and Displacement of Africa   45

CHAPTER THREE
"Incorporate in Rome": *Titus Andronicus* and the
Consequence of Conquest   65

CHAPTER FOUR
Too Many Blackamoors: Deportation, Discrimination, and Elizabeth I   100

CHAPTER FIVE
Banishing "all the Moors": *Lust's Dominion* and the Story of Spain   118

CHAPTER SIX
Cultural Traffic: *The History and Description of Africa*
and the Unmooring of the Moor   138

CHAPTER SEVEN
The "stranger of here and everywhere": *Othello* and the Moor of Venice   155

CONCLUSION
A Brave New World 191

NOTES 195
BIBLIOGRAPHY 227
INDEX 243
ACKNOWLEDGMENTS 251

On Sitting Down to Read *Othello* Once Again

"SPEAK OF ME as I am; nothing extenuate, / Nor aught set down in malice" (*Oth.* 5.2.341–42).[1] This is the instruction that Shakespeare's "valiant Moor" Othello offers to his audience at the end of the play that bears his name (1.3.48). Yet, as this book—and, I will argue, that play—attempt to show, to speak of Othello, of a "Moor of Venice," as he is is not as easy or straightforward as it sounds. Othello himself goes on to supply a number of divergent images, each with a different cultural edge. He is, he implies, a proper if erring lover—"one that loved not wisely, but too well," "one not easily jealous, but being wrought, / Perplexed in the extreme" (5.2.343–45)—and "one" generic or "Venetian" enough that he requires no qualification before the representatives of Venice. He is also, however, an "Indian" who "threw a pearl away / Richer than all his tribe," and possibly (though less likely) a "Judean" (5.2.346–47).[2] His "subdued eyes" become "Arabian trees," his "tears" their "medicinable gum" (5.2.347–50). All "this," he orders Lodovico, "set you down" (5.2.350). But "this" is not all. In addition, Lodovico must *say besides* that in Aleppo once," Othello "took by th' throat" "a malignant and a turbaned Turk" (who "beat a Venetian and traduced the state") and "smote him," just as Othello now stabs himself with an unnoticed weapon (5.2.351–54; emphasis added).

As these images mount up, it is hard to tell whether, where, or how to draw the line between them. Othello's directive, "set you down this; / And say besides," which is meaningfully enjambed in the script, at once breaks and bridges the figures that come before and after. It teases us with the illusion of closure and difference—an end to "this" and a start to what "besides"—where there may be none. Before "this" lies the (Venetian) lover, an Indian, maybe Judean, and Arabian trees; after lies the pat dichotomy, Venetian against Turk, done and undone by the Moor's claim to be both the Turk and the Turk-killing defender of the Venetians. The images get increasingly detailed, vivid, and physically immediate as Othello goes along, climaxing when he not only describes but actually enacts his startling suicide. At this, his darkest, most self-destructive moment, he might well be setting aside the exotically sugges-tive figures of the East and confining himself within the more readable, po-tentially incriminating opposition between Venetians and Turks, which has authorized his political, if not domestic, place in Venice. Even so, it is impos-sible to tell whether Othello's self-representation is continuous or discontinu-ous, a collage or a progression, impossible to tell whether the figures augment, supplant, or, in a Derridean sense, supplement each other. Is Othello, like Hamlet, improvising his way through a number of identities, across the rubs, until he gets it right? Or is he picturing himself as an amalgamated, multicul-tural subject, whose identity extends provocatively beyond any preordained geographical boundaries or any ready-made tensions or elisions between Venetian, Turk, and Moor?

More important than the answers, which will in any case be indetermi-nate, is the fact that at the very moment Othello hands his story over, he re-sists settling its terms. "Set you down this" is not the be-all and end-all here, either for him or for the play. Within the dramatic fiction, the prospect of setting down "this," the Moor's story, appears somehow unsettling, unsatisfy-ing, and untenable—even, if not especially, to the Moor himself. Othello be-gins, in fact, by asserting and immediately dismissing a bold self-evaluation: "I have done the state some service, and they know't—/ No more of that" (5.2.338–39). Shakespeare may be pointing to a "fact" of Venetian history, that foreigners could become citizens on the basis of "service" to the state—a fact that could clarify how Othello occupies the place of "Moor of Venice" in the first place.[3] "That," however, provides a false and fleeting start, its absolutes ("I have done" and "they know't") absolutely rejected as the sum of his part: "no more of that." Before suggesting more elusive and exotic models, Othello adds a preemptive caution: Lodovico is to "extenuate," to minimize or excuse, "nothing," nor alternatively, to say anything ("aught") "in malice."[4] Although Othello anticipates being judged, for better or for worse, he positions his case between the extremes of exoneration and condemnation. To speak of him as he is to imagine an indefinite middle ground, for which there are no words, between a series of different, not exactly oppositional poles—the wisely and the excessively loving, the "easily jealous" and the "extremely perplexed," the Turk and the non-Turk.

In the final moments, the play itself leaves its own "bloody period," the response to the Moor's "unlucky deeds," somewhat open-ended (5.2.356, 340). Othello closes his performance with a literal kiss of death. But if the wheel comes full circle appropriately on the lover, who first kissed then killed his wife, Lodovico, Gratiano, and Cassio are left struggling to put closure on a tragedy which, along with "all that's spoke," is inexorably but, to us, unfathomably "marred" (5.2.356). How exactly has Othello's self-destruction "marred" what has been spoken? The Venetians can readily codify, blame, and sentence Iago, the "hellish villain" and "Spartan dog, / More fell than anguish, hunger, or the sea" (5.2.360–61, 368). But in the case of Othello, their censure is mixed with certain, ultimately immeasurable degrees of sympathy. Lodovico directs Gratiano to "keep the house / And seize upon the fortunes of the Moor" (5.2.365–66). If the categorical reference to "the Moor" demeans or alienates Othello (and for me, the assumption that "the Moor" is automatically discriminatory is an "if"), Lodovico's insistence that the Moor's possessions "succeed on" Gratiano, Brabantio's brother, simultaneously underscores Othello's propertied place within a Venetian family (5.2.367). The Moor's fortune is not simply randomly "seized," though the word carries the force of usurpation; it is legitimately inherited—an outcome that Brabantio's otherwise dramatically incidental death makes room for. Lodovico will "straight aboard, and to the state / This heavy act with heavy heart relate" (5.2.370–71). As he projects his own "heavy" condition onto the fatal act, one thing is clear: even in the face of Othello's prompts, speaking of the Moor as he is will have to wait.

So what is Othello's, or Shakespeare's, problem? Or what, we might better ask, is ours? As critics who have seen and read *Othello* through and through, who have looked long and hard beyond the play and its performances to a broad history of dramatic and nondramatic representations of Moors, we'd like to assume that we have the advantage, at least over the characters, whose views are circumscribed and whose capacity to view is always only a fiction. "What [we] know, [we] know," to borrow dangerously from Iago (5.2.301)—and we hope that we can know enough to speak of both Othello and "the Moor" as they are. Yet from the time that Eldred Jones initiated a serious discussion of "Othello's countrymen" in 1965, promoting "Africans" as an important subject on the English Renaissance stage and "the idea of Africa" as an important part of England's global consciousness, we have not been able to say fully or finally what "the Moor" represents.[5] Every critic from Jones on has had to somehow confront the "notorious indeterminacy" of the term—which, as Michael Neill so aptly summarized in 1998, "could refer quite specifically to the Berber-Arab people of the part of North Africa then rather vaguely dominated as 'Morocco,' 'Mauritania,' or 'Barbary'; . . . could be used to embrace the inhabitants of the whole North African littoral; . . . might be extended to refer to Africans generally (whether 'white,' 'black,' or 'tawny' Moors); or, by an even more promiscuous extension, . . . might be applied (like 'Indian') to almost any darker-skinned peoples—even, on occasion, those of the New World."[6] Not always an ethnic type, "Moor" might also indicate a religion (usually Mohammedanism), a color (usually "black"), or "some vague amalgam of the two."[7] Early modern scholars have been less alone with the problem since Henry Louis Gates brought new attention to the instability of "race" as a term and concept in our own, more recent history.[8] Even so, in speaking of the Moor we have always had to ferret the subject out from a seemingly endless set of diverse, divergent, and sometimes overdetermined images, to decide who our Moors will be.

* * *

Perhaps the first question we should ask, though, is why speak of "the Moor" at all? The term has by now lost its currency as a designation of a racial or ethnic population. So why write (or read) a book in the early twenty-first century on England's staging of the Moor at the turn of the sixteenth century, especially a book centered on only four plays: one, *The Battle of Alcazar* (1588–89), so generically quirky that critics have been hard pressed to see the coherence between its "tangled" historical and political "web," its antiquated chorus, and its erratic revenge play;[9] one, *Lust's Dominion* (ca. 1599), that reads like a "frantic perversion of history" and feels like a "mere nightmare" and that, like *Alcazar*, has rarely been performed or edited;[10] one, *Titus Andronicus* (1593–94), which seems like a ghastly caricature in its excessive, outrageous, even gratuitous violence; and finally—but only—one, *Othello* (ca. 1604), that has commanded widespread critical respect and theatrical attention? Why sit down to read and rethink *Othello*, along with its unusually ragged dramatic peers, and the unaccommodating subject of the Moor once again?

The answer, in large part, is related to the very problem I—and I think, Shakespeare—started with: the difficulty of speaking of the Moor "as he is" in any single set of terms (and in the plays I am focusing on, it is "he"). The "notorious indeterminacy" that seems to mar the Moor's story is, in fact, essential to its core, not because, as a signifier, "Moor" is unstable and unreadable but because, as a subject, "the Moor" does not have a single or pure, culturally or racially bounded identity. Within early modern representations, I hope to show, the Moor is first and foremost a figure of uncodified and uncodifiable diversity. Though shadowed by evolving vocabularies of discrimination and practices and policies of prejudice, between and within each incarnation that figure nonetheless takes definition from a number of histories, geographies, and ideologies, all with their own racial and cultural markers, and all necessarily contingent on the immediate circumstances of their articulation. In fact, the early modern Moor uniquely represents the intersection of European and non-European cultures. And if his dark- skinned presence calls into being discrete and discriminatory inscriptions of history, race, and ethnicity, segregating Europe from other cultures (or rather, other cultures from Europe), the Moor's complex position between worlds also calls those inscriptions into question.

If we look, just in outline, at where and how Moorish characters take their bearings on the English stage in the short period between *Alcazar* and *Othello*, the complicating intersections are clear. In *Alcazar*, a "negro" Moor stands against his Barbarian uncle on the fields of Morocco, both of Arabian descent, one allied with the Turks, the other with Portuguese, Spanish, Italian, and even English defenders (*Alcazar* 1Pro.7).[11] *Titus*'s Moor Aaron is a prisoner of war, captured by the Romans and absorbed into their society with the Goths—to the point that he fathers a mixed-breed offspring with Rome's new empress, the Gothic queen, and embeds that son, at least temporarily, in Rome, the deadly giveaway of the child's dark skin notwithstanding. In *Lust's Dominion*, Eleazar is at once the son of a conquered Barbarian king and the husband to a Spanish noblewoman as well as the lover of the Spanish queen and, for a brief but incredible moment, the Spanish king himself. And Othello, as we have seen, is a worldly "Moor of Venice," a Venetian his wife, the military his life, and the images of Egypt, Arabia, India, and Africa his discursive legacy. What's more, the dramatic heritage of these marquee Moors derives directly and indirectly from the extravagant figures of both Jew and Turk in Christopher Marlowe's *Jew of Malta* (ca. 1589). Notably, too, even as secondary characters, Moors occupy and define similar kinds of cultural intersections. Shakespeare's Prince of Morocco is modeled on a Turk, Brusor, from *The Tragedie of Solimon and Perseda* (ca. 1590), as Jonathan Gil Harris has noted, and stands in Belmont beside a group of noble Europeans, no more or less likely a match for the wealthy Portia than they.[12] In the final episode of Thomas Heywood's *Fair Maid of the West, Part I* (1600–1603), Mullisheg, the Moorish king of Fez, provides the material and figurative (and if he could have it, erotic) means for the ever English Bess to prove herself climactically "a girl worth gold" (*Fair Maid, I* 5.2.153).[13] In Marlowe's *Tamburlaine* plays (1587), Moors are seamlessly enmeshed in the multicultural forces of the Turks, fighting alongside Arabians, Jews, Grecians, Albanese, Sicilians, Natolians, Sorians, black Egyptians, Illyrians, Thracians, and Bithynians.[14] Even in outline, striking here are not simply the differences *between* these Moors, who appear in Venice, Morocco, Belmont, Spain, and Rome, but also the differences— the multilayered dramatic and cultural histories—invoked *within* the representation of any given Moor.

To be sure, across dramatic and nondramatic depictions in this period, what we would call "racist" articulations are clearly taking shape and obscuring the particulars that make any one Moor's story culturally and ideologically complex.[15] In letters dated from 1596 to 1601, Queen Elizabeth, now famously, turns the presence of "blackamoors" within her realm into an urgent national problem and promotes their deportation as a natural and possible solution. Within the landscapes of Africa in Richard Hakluyt's globe-trotting *Principal Navigations* (1589, 1598–1600), the "cruel hands of the Moores" appear out of nowhere and out of context, to "long detain" "English gentlemen" "in miserable servitude," as if that is just what Moors are wont to do (6:294).[16] In a translation of *The History and Description of Africa* (1600), John Pory emphatically associates Moors with the "accursed religion" of Islam and frames the text with an edgy apologia for the "Mahumetan" past of its author, "John Leo."[17] On the stage, *Alcazar* links barbarity to blackness in the figure of its "barbarous Moor," Muly Mahamet, who seems not coincidentally to be both "black in his look, and bloody in his deeds," his face "full of fraud and villainy" providing a readable sign of his malignancy (1Pro.6, 16; 5.1.70). In *Titus*, Aaron presents himself as similarly transparent, insisting that his "cloudy melancholy" and "fleece of woolly hair," among other things, can only mean one thing (2.2.33–34): "Vengeance is in my heart, death in my hand, / Blood and revenge are hammering in my head" (2.2.38–39).[18] As *Lust's Dominion* plays with fantasies (soon to be historical realities) of deporting all Moors from Spain, it comes as close as I think early modern drama ever does to articulating a clearly cut racist ideology. Within its dramatic fiction, the "perfect villainy" of the leading Moor (5.5.3794), the self-styled "black Prince of

Divels" Eleazar (1.1.126), provides the official rationale for the incrimination and banishment of *all* Moors. And while Othello has obvious clout in the high circles of the Venetian court as "the valiant Moor" (1.3.48), a battery of racially suggestive, color-coded, and sexually loaded slurs precedes and surrounds his appearance, bringing a debilitating discourse of blackness into form as something even he will use to condemn his allegedly promiscuous wife, the fair-skinned "black weed" (4.2.67).

If we start and end with these as the cruxes of the Moor's story, however, if we set down these impressions without saying besides, we will, I think, miss what is equally crucial: within early modern representations, the Moor serves as a site where competing, always provisional axes of identity come dynamically into play, disrupting our ability, if not also our desire, to assign the Moor a color, religion, ethnicity, or any homogenizing trait. It is, in fact, the complexity and variability of these cultural and racial inscriptions that make turning or returning to the Moor, and understanding England's short but serious preoccupation with that subject in all its particulars, so pertinent and pressing now. For the uncodified diversity that *is* the Moor's story constantly demands negotiation and so draws attention inevitably—in early modern plays quite consciously—to how and where we draw the line on difference. Because of course we do. We are at a historical moment when globalization is still somewhat embryonic, when political and economic relations are organized increasingly around an expansive and expanding "world"—a moment which, in that regard, parallels the early modern. At just such moments, the danger is that the unaccommodating particulars, the differences within differences, that would otherwise define a cultural history, space, or subject will disappear under the pressure to accommodate, if not also to conquer or commodify, a vast and unfamiliar global terrain. The danger is, that is, that in coming to terms with an overwhelmingly diverse, always changing and expanding set of unfamiliar subjects, we will either obscure their heterogeneity with homogenizing generalizations or select our differences out, targeting some and not others as what matters.

The danger has perhaps been especially great in the case of Africa and Africans, whose multiplex histories have long been blurred together in an undifferentiated bias against "blacks." Consider what happened when the British government declared 2005 "the year of Africa" and, armed with "indigenous resolve and cash from Western governments," dedicated its international outreach to "a new assault on the roots of poverty in *the continent*."[19] Instead of developing strategies specific to the needs and problems of individual African states and populations, Tony Blair's Commission for Africa "impose[d] . . . a general explanation, on the whole place," as John Ryle has protested, compressing its many nations, peoples, languages, identities into "a single reality," as if there were one Africa and one overarching problem that could be fixed simply by "stimulating trade, increasing aid, tackling corruption, cancelling debt."[20] Or consider the U.S. response to the crisis in Darfur at the beginning of the twenty-first century. In a *New York Times* editorial (August 8, 2006), Nicholas Kristof presents that history comparatively as "the tale of two military interventions, of which one happened and the other didn't."[21] "Three weeks ago," he writes:

> with President Bush supplying the weaponry and moral support, Israel began bombarding Lebanon. The war has killed hundreds of people, galvanized international attention and may lead to an international force of perhaps 20,000 peacekeepers. Three years ago, Sudan began a genocide against African tribes in its Darfur region. That war has killed hundreds of thousands of people, and it is now spreading. There is talk of U.N. peacekeepers someday, but none are anywhere in sight. The moral of the story? Never, ever be born to a tribe that is victim to genocide in Africa.[22]

In Britain's case the sweep, and in America's, the selectivity, of the government's putatively global vision has obscured the distinctive histories of "African" subjects, skewing or erasing their importance in a crisis-ridden world.

Or, to turn to literary terrains, consider what Celia Daileader has tagged "Othellophilia," a long-standing Anglo-American obsession with "the *Othello* myth," with the disturbing play of the "black male" against the white female he "tups."[23] This fixation, as Daileader charts it, registers a color-based racial (and gendered) difference as *the* source of contention. But when Shakespeare plays and replays the *Othello* myth himself, culture trumps color as what gives potentially deadly unions their twist of difference: in *Much Ado About Nothing* (1598–99) Claudio is a Florentine, his betrothed, a daughter of Messina; in *The Winter's Tale* (1610–11) Leontes is Sicilian, his wife, daughter of a Muscovite. In *Cymbeline* (1609–10), the embedded *Othello* story of a noble husband ingeniously coerced into doubting his wife's chastity plays out across the tensions of family, with Imogen, the heir apparent of Britain, made vulnerable by her choice to marry Posthumus, himself displaced and replaced as the king's favorite by the repulsive royal stepson, Cloten. In the early modern period lineages such as these also fell under the umbrella of "race," and that these stories have not ushered in their own obsessions is a telling sign that not all racial and cultural differences carry the same weight or garner the same interest in or across time periods. Nor do they hold the same meanings. Is Othello really a "black male" in his first incarnation (or second, if we count Cinthio)? Or, what's different, is he a Moor, called "black" by some (including himself), not others, when it serves their turns, his skin color only one of his distinguishing and demonized features? In summing up his story, can we assign him a "black ethnicity" when he and his audiences do not?[24] And in the aftermath of 9–11, were we to revive the morally freighted dichotomy between African and Arabian embodiments of Othello, the one (African) long imagined by critics, actors, and producers as the more savage, the other (Arabian) the more noble, would the Arabian Moor still come out on top?[25]

These examples remind us how vulnerable "African" subjects, in particular, still are to codification and obfuscation within globally oriented and transhistorical narratives, even after more obvious discriminations have come under decades of critique. As our political, historical, and literary frames expand, so too may the impulse to classify whatever may otherwise seem to be an endlessly proliferating set of variables. It is all the more important, then, to understand the complexities that define and disturb early modern representations of Moors. Whatever else we may learn, to sit down to read the Moor once again in an era of globalization is at once to recover a particular and peculiar history of difference and to remember difference as always particularly and peculiarly historical.

* * *

From the start, studies of the Moor, along with the related topics of Africa and race, have served to challenge, if not in some cases dismantle, some of the institutional, political, intellectual, and textual boundaries limiting our views of the early modern period. To take on these subjects, with all their indeterminacy, as the defining matter of English literature has been to acknowledge the diversity of England's material and imaginative interests, the centrality of its cross-cultural relations, and the tentativeness of its—and finally any—"world picture." It has been to open up both what and how we read and teach, to call attention to identities and differences that authorizing narratives have effectively obscured in and long after the early modern period. Even so, in coming to terms with the historical and literary figure of the Moor, each generation of critics, from Eldred Jones on, has framed that interrogation along limited axes of difference, necessary in their own moments but needing review and revision in ours.

Initially, the Moor came into scholarly discussion as an "African," not coincidentally in the era of the civil rights movement, when "Africa" was providing an empowering collective base for black power and pride. In attempting to prove that "Othello's countrymen" and "the Elizabethan idea of Africa" were important subjects for literary study, Jones was the first to challenge an otherwise whitewashed Elizabethan world picture—one which had yet to acknowledge the extent and significance of England's interactions in Barbary and West Africa. Though still in 1978 G. K. Hunter was basing his assessments of "colour prejudice" on the assumption that England had little firsthand knowledge of Moors, Jones's work went a long way in showing that England's imaginative engagement with figures such as Othello actually derived from historical encounters.[26] Interestingly, Jones's critical agenda of introducing the subject of Africa into a scholarly discourse to which it had been strange is reflected in his critical narrative. For within his work, it is Africa's "strangeness," its sensationalism, exoticism, and "novelty," to the English that becomes its "most interesting aspect."[27] While this emphasis on the differentness of Africa to Renaissance England served to restore the historical edge, and edginess, of the subject, it nonetheless obscured the differences *within* Africa: in Jones, Moors become indistinct within a general category of "Africans," with figures such as Othello labeled at once a Moor, "black Moor," and "Negro."[28] To be sure, by the early modern period Africa had been mapped, literally and figuratively, as a continent. But as texts such as *The History and Description of Africa* make clear, "Africa" indicated neither a single nor an homogenous place. Nor was "Moor" synonymous with "African." None of Shakespeare's Moors bears that denotation: "African" appears only once, and only in *The Tempest* (1611), where Sebastian criticizes Alonso for "los[ing]" his daughter "to an African" (*Temp.* 2.1.123).[29] Jones acknowledges the distinction between western and northern peoples, which is key within early modern representations (he has, in fact, gone on to become the chairman of the Sierra Leonean Writers Series, a project established in 2001 with the specific mission of drawing attention to the writers of and writings on Sierra Leone and introducing these into West Africa's academic curricula).[30] Still, in establishing the importance of "Africa" both to the historical moment and to the studies of it, he merges Moors into a generalized African population, glossing over the fact that not all Moors were Africans and not all Africans, Moors.

The association of Moors with Africa remained a critical starting point in the decades after Jones, yet with an important difference: evolving conceptions of what and how Africa signified no longer hinged on its strangeness or novelty but rather on its connection to American history and the acts and the ideologies of oppression which that history ushered in. Edward Said's revolutionary *Orientalism* (1978) had by then exposed the imperialist underpinnings of exoticizing cultural discourses.[31] Scholars after Said saw in England's depiction of African subjects a politically self-serving racial prejudice, which helped propel and which could help explain the emergence of New World slavery in the early modern period and the persistence of a racism against blacks in the centuries after. In *The Popular Image of the Black Man in English Drama, 1550–1688* (1982), for example, Elliot Tokson correlates the response of English playwrights to "a black African who was a stranger to their land and their consciousness" with the actions of English entrepreneurs who "were beginning to exploit that same black man as the most suitable material for slave labor."[32] He sets "tawny" Moors therefore indistinguishably beside Ethiopians, Negros, and other Africans as representatives of a "black" race, subject to an "antiblack" sentiment that helped catalyze the development of the Atlantic slave trade.[33] In *Black Face, Maligned Race: The Representation of Blacks in English Drama from Shakespeare to Southern* (1987), it is the assumption that "blacks are different and that the black on their faces, when not thought to signify the Moors' kinship to the devil, reveals . . . their separation from the community" that Anthony Barthelemy examines in order to understand and underscore the racism of his own era.[34] He distinguishes "Moor" from "Negro" and "African" only at the level of language, as the term English writers may have preferred "because it helped to distinguish in a more precise way something supposed to be essential about blacks"—something implicitly alien and negative, if not altogether evil.[35] This emphasis on "blacks" was clearly useful in introducing racial politics into the critical picture, since initially blackness *was* race. But the interpretative frame simultaneously obscured the complicating particulars. Atlantic slavery, after all, would not significantly define England's relation to Africa until well into the seventeenth century. And although in the sixteenth century Moors were being drawn into a discriminatory discourse on blackness along with the "Negros" from Africa's western ("slave") coast, Moors were never New World slaves.

If the conception of "blacks" put in place by Tokson and Barthelemy reproduced the homogeneity of Jones's Africa, however, their emphasis on "race" and "racism" prepared the ground for a more incisive interrogation of those terms and for a direct confrontation of the uncertainties surrounding the denotation and depiction of Moors.[36] In the mid-1980s, African-Americanists began to question the meaningfulness of "race" as a "category in the study of literature and the shaping of critical theory," to expose the arbitrariness and instability of its articulation, and to unravel the discourses that were giving it form.[37] Positing imperialism and colonialism as the political cornerstones of the early modern English state, new historicists and cultural materialists were simultaneously deconstructing the dichotomies of self and other that enabled the inscription of state power, domestically as well as cross-culturally.[38] And in efforts to bring gender into this new historical picture, feminist critics exposed the crucial intersections of gender and race.[39] Early postcolonial critiques built on these advances by recovering otherwise silenced voices of resistance and hybrid subject formations that exposed the other's effect on the self.[40] As a result, by the 1990s the exclusive association of the Moor with blackness, and of blackness with the Moor, was broken apart and conceptions of race, racialized subjects, and England's early "racism" were complicated by intersections with gender, religion, ethnicity, whiteness, genre, and performance.

Nonetheless, through the end of the twentieth century, Africa remained the preeminent geography of the Moor's cultural definition. Indeed, when I first conceptualized this project in the early 1990s, my own intention was to treat the staging of the Moor in terms of a broader staging of Africa—until I realized that Moors were the only "African" subjects featured on the early modern stage and that they were not necessarily connected to Africa, ethnically or geographically.[41] Moreover, although England's preoccupation with the Moor preceded the colonial moment and exceeded the ideologies of oppression that came into force with colonialist and imperialist activities, as I have argued elsewhere, the specter of New World slavery and its legacy of racial prejudice continued to define the politics that early modern scholars imposed backward onto representations of the Moor.[42] Even in Kim Hall's historically rigorous *Things of Darkness* (1995), which locates a pervasive, gender-based "poetics of color" within England's domestic representations, the starting point is a "'self' and 'other'" divide "so well known in Anglo-American racial discourses."[43] Acknowledging "Moor" as a "multivalent designation," Hall uses it nonetheless as a "general term for the ethnically, culturally, and religiously 'strange,'" a signpost of "the idea of African difference."[44] For the first wave of critics who, like Hall, exposed the complexity of "race," "blackness" was not simply (and not a simple) provenance of the Moor, but an alien status resulting from colonialism was.

This opening up of conceptions of race ultimately prompted changes in the segregated world picture that, among other things, assigned Africa a stable and unified shape and laid the ground for a second wave of interrogations, ongoing now, that are looking again at England's cross-cultural relations. In turning to religion (Islam, especially), scholars such as Ania Loomba brought into view a new set of cultural sites and subjects, with India, the Ottoman East, and the Mediterranean supplementing Africa and the New World as pivot points for emergent constructions of race.[45] The result has been a major shift in critical orientation from the national to the transnational, the cultural to the multicultural, the local to the global. Where before the organizing cornerstones of our interpretations of cross-cultural contact were self-authorizing *nations* mapping their boundaries against "other" cultures, now we think in terms of "worlds," charted more loosely across bodies of waters and boundaries of nation-states, configured dynamically as transnational and international economies, and defined by mixed and ethnically intermixed populations. For Anglo-Americanists, the centerpiece of global politics has been a variously circumscribed transatlantic network; for early modernists, it is the Mediterranean.[46] This renovated geopolitics has fostered unusually malleable conceptions of race and ethnicity. Within its frames, Gil Harris, for example, has drawn our attention to "new, protean forms of identity and affiliation" that were evolving with a globally oriented mercantilism and instantiated vividly by the figure of the Jew, a "transnational stranger" of "undecideable" country, poised between the foreign and the domestic.[47] Mary Floyd-Wilson has used geohumoral theory to ally England's "northern" people with their southern neighbors in Africa, arguing against the terms and tenability of an English fantasy of racial superiority.[48] Daniel Vitkus has established "turning," and especially "turning Turk," as important signs and symptoms of the cultural and ideological flexibility essential to Mediterranean exchange.[49]

Scholars such as Michael Neill have begun to place Moors lucratively within this Mediterranean world picture and to understand the multicultural edges of their identity.[50] Yet while approaches to the Moor are no longer limited to and by the legacy of Africa, they are constrained by elisions of Moors with other subjects—especially with Turks, who have dominated studies of the Mediterranean just as they once dominated its early modern histories.[51] Turks have, in fact, become the primary model for Mediterranean identities, and critics now tend to treat Moors and Turks interchangeably under the umbrella of "a generalized Islamic identity."[52] As a consequence, even a figure such as Othello, who merely *imagines* himself to be a circumcised Turk but bears no other or actual traces of a Muslim past, is nonetheless assigned one.[53] Not only does the elision of Moor and Turk thus risk implanting religion squarely into representations where its relation to the Moor may be, at best, uncertain and oblique; it also risks inflecting our new vision of the Moor, and therefore of the Mediterranean, with a new kind of estrangement. We no longer read England reading either the Turks or Islam simply as the ultimate in evil; rather, conceptions of that threat have been mollified by our and early modern England's awareness of the inclusiveness of the Turks' cultural politics and practices, the permeability of their image, the variability of their heritage, and the all too realizable prospect that, with a switch of a blade and a religion, almost anyone could "turn Turk." Nonetheless, critics have understood that very openness—and with it, the multiculturalism of the Mediterranean, its Moors and Turks—as a source of anxiety for a contrastingly provincial England.[54]

Yet as this book will stress, what is crucial to the Moor's (and so to the Mediterranean's) story—and what has been long submerged in conceptions of England's cross-cultural outreach but what we are now in a position to see—is its close, ameliorating, and complicating connection to Europe.[55] Europeans were no strangers to Morocco, as *The History and Description of Africa* attests. Nor were Moors strangers within Europe. The very Moor who wrote *The History* ("John Leo Africanus") did so from Rome, after being baptized by Pope Leo X. Moreover, by the sixteenth century, Moors had been subjects of Spain for so long that their history and Spain's were effectively inextricable, as Barbara Fuchs has argued.[56] Even after Spanish Inquisitors began (in 1492) to condemn their Muslim beliefs, it would take over a hundred years for Moors to be officially banished from Spain.[57] We need only look again to the stage to see how interested England was in these intersections. It is no coincidence, as I have suggested, that in each of the plays I am treating here, either Europeans come to Morocco to further their political fortunes (as is the case in *Alcazar*) or Moors appear in Europe to further theirs (Aaron in Rome, Eleazar in Spain, Othello in Venice).

Such is not ordinarily the case within representations of other "non-Europeans." Consider the innovative "tyrant plays" that chose "Eastern" despots, in lieu of English monarchs, to tell cautionary tales of disastrous rule. Thomas Preston's *Cambyses, King of Persia* (ca. 1569–70) concentrates myopically on the Persian king's incestuous manipulation of a Persian "race," his people and his kin; and even his notably unstaged conquest of Egypt provides fodder for a *Measure for Measure*-like substitution of rule *within* the Persian state (6.18).[58] Marlowe's Scythian Tamburlaine is determined to make himself "monarch of the East," scourge of god, and lord of all the earth (*Tamb. I* 1.2.185). But when he maps his astounding imperial ambitions across the globe, taking over Persia, Greece, western Africa, Arabia, and Egypt in the play's first part alone, his campaign stops tellingly short of Europe, reaching only the seas around Portugal and Venice. *Selimus, Emperor of the East* (1594) recycles significant parts of Tamburlaine's story, including the Turkish emperor Bajazet, who claims as his domain "all the world" "from the south pole unto the northern," "from East to Western shore" (1.13–15).[59] Yet while the Turkish empire is at stake, the focal point of the play is a historically based civil struggle for the Turkish crown, played out as a family romance between the Turkish emperor and his catastrophically disloyal sons.[60] In the end, however much these plays and players may revel in unbounded fantasies of empire, Europe remains out of the reach of their actions, if not also of their desires.

Indeed, set the Moor against the multicultural Turk or the ubiquitous Jew and what emerges on the early modern stage is a dramatic subject uniquely poised to negotiate, mediate, even transform the terms of European culture. Where the "renowned Turke" Bursor is a bombastic Muslim crusader determined to stain "the desert plaines of Affricke" "with blood of Moores" (*Solimon* B1r), his dramatic descendant, the Prince of Morocco, is a suitor, who swears by a "scimitar / That slew the Sophy, and a Persian prince" but whose imperialist histrionics are circumscribed by a romantic conquest that starts and ends in Belmont (*MV* 2.1.24–25).[61] What finally distinguishes and defeats him is neither his scimitar nor, for that matter, his "complexion" (*MV* 2.1.1), but his privileging of gold over silver and lead as a measure of his, and Portia's, worth—a measure he appropriates from an English "coin that bears the figure of an angel / Stampèd in gold" (*MV* 2.7.56–57). Or consider the contrast between Shakespeare's Moor and Jew of Venice. Where Shylock celebrates his distance and difference from the Venetians, Othello actively embeds himself within Venice's political and domestic spheres. The Jew's sole and signal "bond" is a hideously vengeful arrangement to cut, if not symbolically to circumcise, a Christian merchant's flesh, the Moor's, a military commission and a marriage. Where Shylock rejects all things Christian, Othello embraces the terms, if not the beliefs, of Christianity. And where laws against the "alien"

panies.[64] And not only was English activity across the Mediterranean, in general, at a peak, with factors stationed prominently in Italy, Egypt, Syria, and Turkey as well as in North Africa; English interest in Barbary, in particular, was especially vibrant and visible. The English had been involved in the Barbary trades since the 1550s; but Queen Elizabeth's negotiations with Morocco escalated notably in the 1580s, after a civil war (which climaxed with the "battle of Alcazar" in 1578) put a new regime in place there and required new diplomatic arrangements.[65] As Nabil Matar and others have pointed out, Moorish ambassadors came to London for publicized state visits in 1589, 1595, and 1601.[66]

For Matar, the introduction of Moors on the English stage was "a direct result" of "the negotiations and collusions" between England and Morocco.[67] I think instead, though, that the impulse behind that staging was much broader, catalyzed not only by England's specific dealings with its Moroccan trading partners but also by the desire to come to terms with a more reaching and emergent globalization. England's overseas interventions had no established terminologies, ideologies, or geographies, though discourses of the national and transnational as well as of imperialism and colonialism would evolve through them. If this period prefaced or predicted the high colonialism that would take shape—and give shape to "black" subjects—in the New World, England had not yet found its colonial footing.[68] Indeed, how telling that when Shakespeare staged colonialist domination in the "brave new world" of *The Tempest* in 1611, he could only imagine bringing his European colonizers home. Nor, as historians have emphasized, was the English state decidedly imperialist, despite Hakluyt's best efforts to have it otherwise.[69] Even the idea of "culture"—a term which has enabled critics (and which I use here) to think beyond the politically freighted constructs of "nation" and "state" and socially freighted construct of "society"—invoked a fairly provincial conception of land-based cultivation, not coming to indicate a distinctive population group or community until the nineteenth century.[70] Hence, at the turn of the sixteenth century, the English needed to figure out the politics and parameters of a new globally oriented environment—to explore the permeability of geographic boundaries, to decode and encode an expansive network of cultural identities and differences, to develop vocabularies for the accommodation and alienation of mixed populations, mixed marriages, and mixed blood, and to otherwise negotiate the extraordinary volatility of cultural change and exchange.

In this, the early modern moment was like our own—but with significance differences. While we have come into a global era after New World colonialism and slavery had institutionalized racial prejudice, after British imperialism had orientalized the East and assigned Africa the lasting legacy of a "dark continent," after terms of oppression, assimilation, segregation, and integration had formed around a number of collective subjects, the early moderns came into their global era *before*. Where our world is in these ways "old," theirs was relatively "new." In effect, we are writing our evolving multicultural geographies *against* a long history of cultural differentiation that the early moderns were just beginning to write *in*. This is not to say that some terms of racial and cultural difference were not already in place in the sixteenth century. As I have suggested above, they obviously were—though the continued scholarly debate about when exactly blackness became race underscores their tentative hold.[71] It is rather to emphasize that in the sphere of global relations, England's slate, though not clean, was sketchy, the indelible writing on the wall not yet clear.

Enter, then, the Moor, center stage. In *Othello*, when Desdemona asks Emilia whether she would commit adultery "for all the world," Emilia takes her phrase literally, insisting that "the world's a huge thing" and a "great price / For a small vice" (*Oth*. 4.3.63–65). The "world" was indeed a "huge thing" at the turn of the sixteenth century. And it seems no coincidence that references to "all the world" surface repeatedly in plays that feature Moors. For there was perhaps no figure better suited to an exploration of that world and the ideological adjustments it required than the Moor, who took his bearings from multiple Mediterranean and European geographies, who stood out from and in for a number of other subjects, and who drew and defied discrimination. Nor was there, for that matter, a better medium than drama, which depends on improvisation, on the illusion that actions and reactions within dramatic fictions are unscripted, evolving always in and at the moment of their articulation. If to write the Moor into history was to produce the figure's identity, however conceived, as a matter of "truth," to stage the Moor was at once to bring that figure into form and draw attention to the process of forming, to construct a Moorish character and expose that character as constructed, out of the needs, desires, and biases of a particular moment. It was, that is, to expose cultural identity and cross-cultural exchange as a dynamic work in progress, always contingent on the unpredictable intricacies of circumstance and always therefore vulnerable to change, a thing perpetually in the making and never quite the thing made.[72]

To be sure, the danger in coming at these plays in the twenty-first cen-

tury, out of a desire to unseat homogenizing assumptions of cultural difference, lies in looking too far in that direction, to the exclusion of the "other."
I may err on the side of wanting early modern drama and culture to be more
radical, more liberal than it finally was. As essential as the complicating particulars that open representations of the Moor up are, no doubt, the classifi-
cations and codifications that would close such complexities down. There is
no Othello story, after all, without Iago and the nasty stream of racist epithets
he hurls (and prompts others to hurl) in the Moor's direction. Nor is the
restoration and institution of a globally oriented Moroccan regime in *Alcazar*
meaningful without the challenge of a vengefully myopic Moorish challenger.
And even if *Titus* and *Lust's Dominion* situate the Moor within a European
mainstream, as I will argue, as a subject who is almost impossible to write off
or out, the Moors in question are nonetheless archvillains. This is part of the
stuff that Moors on the early modern stage are inexorably made on. And it
stands beside incriminating histories—beside the "cruel hands" of Hakluyt's
Moors, beside John Pory's apology for Africanus's "Mahumetan" past, beside
Queen Elizabeth's proclamations against "blackamoors." But even in the face
of a "perfect villainy" that is executed by a Moor, a "black" "look" that augurs
"bloody" "deeds," or a "fleece of woolly hair" that speaks revenge, we cannot
know to what extent England's production of the Moor was encumbered by
"anxiety"—a word, though currently ubiquitous within our critical lexicon,
that projects our own anxiety-ridden times and psyches backward. Nor can
we evaluate England's take on the Moor in terms of moral distinctions, separating "Princes of Darkness" from "white" Moors "of the nonvillainous type,"
as preceding surveys of dramatic Moors have done.[73] For what seems to me
crucial to early modern representations of the Moor is their ability to have it
both ways (at least), to distance complex cultural and cross-cultural politics
from simplifying moralities, to imagine the embrace and the exclusion of the
Moor as constantly competing impulses, and to insist on complicating differences in the face of an ostensibly all-consuming difference.

In order to expose the diversity between and within England's representations of the Moor and the importance of that diversity to England's negotiation of a global environment, I want to look closely at the brief but crucial
moment at the turn of the sixteenth century, when the Moor seems to have
captured England's imagination newly and urgently. It is then that Hakluyt's
Navigations construct a determined and overdetermined expansionist terrain,
then that *The History and Description of Africa* brings the voice of a "real"
Moor to life, then that Queen Elizabeth protests the presence of "black-

amoors" in her realm. And it is congruently then that Moors become a featured subject on the stage, in *Alcazar, Titus, Lust's Dominion,* and *Othello.* Moors figured, of course, in such contemporaneous plays as *The Fair Maid of the West, Part I* and *The Merchant of Venice,* as I've mentioned, and also in plays that came after, among them Webster's *White Devil* (1611), Heywood's *Fair Maid, Part II* (1630), Behn's remake of *Lust's Dominion, The Moor's Revenge* (1677), and Ravenscroft's *Titus Andronicus* (1686). The numbers are not large: Elliot Tokson identifies only twenty-nine plays and masques "containing black characters or characters disguised as blacks" (not all of them Moors) that emerged between 1588 and 1687.[74] Prior books on the Moor have surveyed this broader field, overlooking the unusual concentration on Moors that begins with *Alcazar* and ends with *Othello* and making little distinction between featured Moors and those in minor roles, which allow and demand less scrutiny.[75] What gets lost within these panoramas is the particular relevance of the figure and the moment: the fact that, just before New World colonization began to set the terms of expansion, England's accommodation of a global economy pivoted uniquely around the culturally complex Moor.

By focusing on the dramatic and historical representations that characterize the Moor in the decades from *Alcazar* to *Othello,* this book attempts, then, to define an important local period in England's imaginative engagement with "all the world" and with the Moor, whose position between worlds suggests the malleability and multiplicity of cultural bounds and histories. In the subsequent decades, the New World would become increasingly central to England's cross-cultural plans and dreams, and the Atlantic slave trade would at once justify and be justified by an increasingly recognizable racism. It is perhaps all the more important then to understand what came before: a provocative unmooring of cultural identity that happens around the Moor, between and within the dramatic texts that feature that "extravagant . . . stranger" (*Oth.* 1.1.135) as well as between them and the historical record, whose constructions they directly and indirectly amplify, expose, and critique. In the chapters that follow, what I will set down is a story not of endless indeterminacy but of contingency, complication, and change, hoping to make clear that in speaking of the Moor "as he is" we must always "say besides."

CHAPTER ONE

Enter Barbary

The Battle of Alcazar and "the World"

IN THE SUMMER of 1578, in the North African town of El-Ksar el-Kebir, two Moors and their accumulated factions fought for rule over the domains surrounding Marrakech and Fez, the regions early modern England would designate as Morocco or Barbary.[1] The current ruler, Abd el-Malek, was the legitimate head of state, next in line after his brother (since succession traveled through all the males of one generation before passing on to the next). He was challenged by his brother's son, Mulai Mohammed el-Meslokh, "the Black Sultan," who had usurped the reign in 1574, had been ousted from power in 1576, and was now, in 1578, fighting to regain control. As the conflict unfolded, Abd el-Malek enlisted the support of the Turks; meanwhile, Mulai Mohammed sought aid from the Portuguese king, Don Sebastian, who was additionally backed by Spain, Rome, and a wayward Englishman, Thomas Stukeley. The culminating battle—what the early modern period would know (and critics come to know) as "the battle of Alcazar"—restored the legitimate line, although Abd el-Malek died from illness during the fight. His brother, Ahmed el-Mansur, succeeded, ruling from 1578 to 1603, when he succumbed to plague and his family's dynastic control over Morocco was disrupted, diminished, and dispersed. Sebastian and Stukeley were killed at Alcazar, the dispossessed Mulai Mohammed drowned on the battlefield, and his recovered body was flayed, stuffed, and displayed as part of the triumphant progress of the restored regime.[2]

In England, Alcazar was news from almost the moment it happened.

Anonymous tracts, namely "A Dolorous Discourse of a most terrible and bloudy Battel fought in Barbarie" (1579) and "Strange newes out of Affrick" (referenced by Gosson in 1586, but lost), sensationalized the event, drawing on eyewitness accounts (available on the continent) written by Portuguese and Spanish survivors.[3] George Whetstone's *English Myrror* (1586) and John Polemon's *Second part of the booke of Battailes* (1587) wrote Alcazar into history—in Whetstone's case, exemplary English history. John Florio's translation of Montaigne's essay "Against Idlenesse, or Doing Nothing" (1600) sanctified Abd el-Malek as a moral champion who "stoutly" and "vigorously" made "use" of his "undanted [*sic*] courage," and who "caused himselfe to be carried and haled, where-ever neede called for him" while "he was even dying," "lest the souldiers hearing of his death, might fall into dispaire."[4] Thomas Stukeley became something of a cult figure, appearing in a number of English ballads, chapbooks, pamphlets, and tracts.[5] For decades after Alcazar, as well, a devoted cadre of "Sebastianists" in Portugal, Spain, and England resurrected the Portuguese king in tracts such as "The Strangest Adventure that Ever Happened" (translated by Anthony Munday, 1601) and "A Continuation of the Lamentable and Admirable Adventures of Don Sebastian" (1603).[6] And as late as 1633, the English would still be reading Abd el-Malek's story in John Harrison's *The Tragicall Life and Death of Muley Abdala Melek*, the hero of the Moroccan civil war persisting as a marketable topic of English discourse, outliving the local circumstances that defined his life and immediate textual afterlife.[7]

The events at Alcazar also provided the ground for the very first representation of Moors on the early modern English stage. As best we can tell, in 1588–89, just after Marlowe had astounded English audiences with his inimitable Tamburlaine, George Peele produced *The Battle of Alcazar*, featuring the conflict between the "barbarous Moor," the "negro Muly Hamet" (or "Muly Mahamet"), and Abdelmelec, the "brave Barbarian lord" (1Pro.6–7, 12).[8] Peele's play might have been preceded or followed by another on the same subject, *Muly Molocco* (ca. 1580–90)—the name Peele and others give to Abd el-Malek—which is listed in Henslowe's *Diary* and which might be either Peele's play under a different name or another Alcazar play altogether.[9] And not only did *Alcazar* provide the dramatic precursors for Aaron, Eleazar, and Othello; after Peele, the battle and its non-Moorish characters continued to be reanimated or invoked on the early modern stage. *The Famous History of Captain Thomas Stukeley* (1605) traces the fortunes of the Englishman Stukeley, from their highly questionable beginnings in England to their redemptive end at Alcazar.[10] And in the second part of *If You Know Not Me, You Know Nobody* (ca. 1606), Thomas Heywood interrupts the two focal points of the dramatic action, the building of England's Royal Exchange and Elizabeth's defeat of the Spanish armada, two signal acts of English nation building, to announce the results of "that renowned battell / Swift fame desires to carry through the world" (293).[11]

"That renowned battell / Swift fame desires to carry through the world." The obvious question is *why*? Why would early modern audiences desire to hear about a "civill mutinie" between two Moors over the disposition of Moroccan rule (*Famous History* 1565)? Why would Heywood interrupt representations of foundational moments in the evolution of English nationhood to direct attention to Alcazar? And why would the conflict at Alcazar prompt early modern dramatists to embrace a new dramatic subject, the Moor? Officially, Alcazar was not England's war. The one Englishman who achieved fame through the battle, Thomas Stukeley, had been planning instead to invade Ireland, with the forces and backing of the pope, and it was only because he took temporary harbor in Lisbon (a port in the storm) and was enlisted by Sebastian that he joined the campaign in Morocco, fighting there for Portugal, not for England. Other English soldiers were involved in the battle, but their contributions were "so insignificant," as Nabil Matar contends, that they are not mentioned in contemporary Moroccan records or in Polemon's *Booke of Battailes*.[12] In Hakluyt's *Navigations*, a brief account of Sebastian's forces (translated from a Latin history of that king) ends with the insertion "It is further to be remembered, that divers other English gentlemen were in this battell, whereof the most part were slaine" (6:294). The document names one English survivor, M. Christopher Lyster, but gives no details about his role in the conflict, focusing instead on his subsequent fate. As that record tells it, he was "taken captive" and "long detained in miserable servitude" at "the cruel hands of the Moores" (6:294). After an escape, he became "Viceadmirall" of a voyage "for the South sea," served in other posts "of speciall command and credite," and finally was "miserably drowned in a great and rich Spanish prize upon the coast of Cornwall" (6:294). Almost before it can be articulated, his involvement at Alcazar, along with England's, thus appears (or disappears) as an incongruous trace, and the account presses forward to document signs of England's outreach elsewhere and the ubiquitous conflict with Spain. What then was Alcazar to England, England to Alcazar?

* * *

In the decades surrounding the Moroccan crisis and the emergence of Peele's
play, Queen Elizabeth was carrying on negotiations with each of the Alcazar
Moors—Mulai Mohammed, Abd el-Malek, and Ahmed el-Mansur.[13] For by
the time of Alcazar, the lucrative Barbary trade, especially in sugar, had already become important to the English. James Alday, traveling with Thomas
Wyndham, professed "himselfe to have bene the first inventer" of the "traffique into the kingdom of Marocco in Barbarie, begun in the yeere 1551,"
though undocumented ventures may have preceeded (Hakluyt, 6:136); Alday
claims that "in the first voyage to Barbary" "two Moores," were "convayed"
"into their Countrey out of England" (Hakluyt, 6:137). Wyndham captained
a second voyage in 1552, its gains "Sugar, Dates, Almonds, and Malassos or
sugar Syrrope" (Hakluyt, 6:139). By 1559, English factors had established
themselves in Morocco.[14] And in the 1570s, through the efforts of one of them
(John Williams), the trade expanded to include saltpeter, an ingredient England needed for the making of gunpowder.[15] When Edmund Hogan set out
for Morocco in 1577, the year before Alcazar, his extended negotiations with
Abd el-Malek climaxed and concluded with the acquisition of that prize.
After Alcazar, relations between England and Morocco seem to have slowed;
but just as Peele was bringing the Moor to the English stage for the very first
time, el-Mansur was sending his own ambassadors to the queen, establishing
an economic and political alliance which lasted until the end of both their
reigns.[16] Matar has speculated that, as far as England was concerned, "as long
as there was profitable trade with the Barbary region, there was no need to sail
far and wide in dangerous search of colonial conquest and settlement."[17] "If
Elizabethan England wondered where its economic future was going to lie,"
he argues, it would look first to Barbary.[18] Barbary may not have been the
only "future" England could foresee, but it was there that England gained an
important foothold in the Mediterranean and entered the global marketplace
that was shaping "the world."

England's relations with Barbary were no simple or local matter, politically or economically; from the start, they were inextricably triangulated with
by the competing presence of Catholic Iberia.[19] Well before the English
started exchanging armor, ammunition, timber (for ships), metal (for
canons), and such for the much desired Moroccan sugar, a papal bull authorized a Portuguese monopoly over trade in Barbary as well as Guinea and a
papal ban outlawed trade of weapons by Christians to the "infidel." England's

violations of these dictates increased when saltpeter was introduced into the exchange, since Mulai Mohammed, who was in power at the time, insisted that the English pay with ammunition. Initially Elizabeth complied, arousing the ire of the Iberian powers, who pressured England to honor the papal ban. Though in 1574 the queen officially conceded, behind the scenes the trade continued through the reign of el-Mansur, under the auspices either of her own clandestine orders or of the clandestine activities of her own, independently motivated agents. These developments did not go unattended. A letter sent from a Spanish ambassador in London to the Grand Commander of Castile in 1574 expresses dismay "that the King [of Portugal] will allow English heretics to . . . trade with the Moors, carrying there, as they constantly do, great quantities of arms, to the prejudice of the King [of Spain] and his subjects."[20] And a Portuguese ambassador had Hogan hauled before the Privy Council to answer charges that he had broken the weapons ban.[21]

In pursuing their goals in Morocco, the English needed to walk gingerly around Spain and Portugal and attempted therefore to hide these controversial deals, as E. W. Bovill long ago suggested. Bovill likely goes too far in arguing that the queen, rather than her agents, directly authorized the covert activities.[22] But in any case, as he has shown, traces of the trade and cover-up appear in public records. So, for example, Hogan's account of his negotiations with "Mully Abdelmelech," which is published in Hakluyt's *Navigations* and which provides the fullest view of Barbary there, is filled with loaded digressions and silences obscuring the details of the very trade it lays out (Hakluyt, 6:285). Hogan repeatedly diverts attention from the substance of the bargaining by focusing rather on exchanged gifts and entertainments—among them "musicke," "a Morris dance, and a play" (6:291). Where Hogan details the mercantile transactions, he emphasizes Abdelmelech's promise to allow English ships "good securitie" within "his ports and dominions," "in trade of marchandize, as for victuall & water," and to grant them "safe conduct" for their ventures into the Levant (6:290). At the end of the narrative, he does admit that the English also sought and acquired saltpeter. But while it is clear that the necessary bargaining was more extended and more vexed (a meeting for Tuesday was put off until Thursday and not settled for five days, the question of saltpeter brought up at least twice), Hogan does not indicate why. Hints of the arms deal appear only through telling denials. Abdelmelech, he reports, did not want "to urge her Majestie with any demaundes, more then conveniently shee might willingly consent unto" (6:288). Reciprocally, the queen (Hogan claims to have declared) was prepared to "pleasure" the Moor "with such commodities as he should have need of, to furnish the necessities and wants of his countrey in trade of marchandize, so as he required nothing contrarie to her honour and law, and the breach of league with the Christian princes her neighbours" (6:290–91). Renouncing "demaundes" that might "breach" the "league," Hogan's Moor and queen seem to protest a bit too much. In the years after Alcazar, the trade—and the evasions—continue. The "letters patent" of 1585 establishing the Barbary Company explain only that "divers Marchandize" from the region "are very necessary and convenient for the use and defence of this our Realme of England" (Hakluyt, 6:420). And in 1587, when Elizabeth writes to "the Emperour of Marocco," Ahmed el-Mansur, she speaks (without speaking) of "certaine things which you desire to bee sent unto you from hence" (6:433).[23]

Colonialist discourse analysis once taught us to read these kinds of narrative gaps (with what Myra Jehlen has critiqued as "excessive certainty") as coded incriminations of the "other," and I, for one, have done just that—interpreting Hogan's lapses as attempts to make the Moor look bad (uncooperative, unreliable, erratic, crafty) and the English agents, good (tolerant, patient, trustworthy, and so on).[24] In assuming that the only issue here is a clandestine arms deal, we do not want to replace one kind of excessive certainty with another. Still, the historical records do seem to bear out an awareness on the part of the English that their dealings in Morocco could compromise their relations with "Christian princes" in Europe, who were evidently scrutinizing the exchange.

And with good reason. If the English were trying to avoid a direct confrontation with the Spanish and Portuguese in bargaining with the Moors, the Moroccan rulers themselves seemed intent, from England's side, on using the alliance with England against Iberia. When Abd el-Malek came to power in 1576, he pushed for a significant increase in the arms trade, insisting that the English not sell the saltpeter they acquired in Morocco to Portugal or Spain. Whatever his intentions, in Hogan Abdelmelech sets the English explicitly against the Spanish, displaying his embrace of the one to register his antipathy toward the other. As Hogan tells it, the Moorish leader

> gave me to understand, that the king of Spaine had sent unto him for a licence, that an Ambassadour of his might come into his countrey, and had made great meanes that if the Queenes majesty of England sent any unto him, that he would not give him any credit or intertainment, albeit (said he) I know what the king of Spaine is, and what the

Queene of England and her Realme is: for I neither like of him nor of his religion, being so governed by the Inquisition that he can doe nothing of himselfe.

Therefore when he commeth upon the licence which I have granted, he shall well see how litle account I will make of him and Spaine, and how greatly I will extoll you for the Queenes majestie of England. (Hakluyt, 6:288–89)

We must take Hogan's words, his emphasis on the Moor's preference for the English, with a grain of salt (or, dare I say, saltpeter), especially since Hogan makes clear that, although he was getting better treatment than the Spanish ambassador, Abdelmelech nonetheless intended to receive the Spanish. Still, the account raises the possibility that the Moor was working the triangulation to Morocco's advantage, whether by actually antagonizing the Spanish or by displaying a pretended antagonism in order to court the English. Ten years after Alcazar, el-Mansur upped the ante on these tensions by proposing that England join him in a joint attack against Spain—with England supplying naval equipment and labor and Morocco financing the whole venture.[25] Matar notes that el-Mansur's interest in reviving Morocco's fallow relations with the English followed immediately on England's defeat of the Spanish armada and argues that it was, in fact, grounded on the hope of an alliance against Spain.[26] Be that as may be, England's historical record, in what it says and silences, presents England's interactions with Barbary and Barbary's with England as inevitably contingent on the contending presence of the Spanish and the Portuguese.

It was during these decades that the crisis within the Moroccan dynasty erupted, resulting in a successive change of leadership (from Mulai Mohammed to Abd el-Malek to Ahmed el-Mansur)—though, because of Elizabeth's willingness to deal with whoever was in power, *not* in an interruption of England's negotiations with Barbary. The battle of Alcazar marked the climax of the local conflict, but the impact was strikingly global—drawing attention to the complex political environment in which England was trying to advance economically. As the Portuguese, the Spanish, and, even on the sidelines, the Turks joined the fray to support one or the other Moorish faction, they simultaneously fortified their own imperialist agendas. The Turks sent aid to Abd el-Malek with the understanding (never fulfilled) that he would, in turn, assist them against the Spanish.[27] The Portuguese king, Sebastian, allied himself with Mulai Mohammed with the hope of furthering Portugal's crusade against Islam. And the Spanish king, Philip II, in sending only limited troops to bolster Portugal's arguably reckless cause, not only positioned himself against the Turks; his tepid support had the side effect of leaving the Portuguese—and ultimately the Portuguese state—vulnerable.[28] Backed by insufficient forces and foresight, Sebastian risked and lost his life in Morocco. Because he had no heir, his death opened Portugal up to takeover by Spain, whose king had a strong claim to the throne. After Alcazar, all that stood between Philip II and Portugal's autonomy were Sebastian's sixty-six-year-old uncle, Cardinal Henry, who ruled for two years (1578–80) and then died without an heir, and Don Antonio, who had been captured in Morocco but who was ransomed in time to succeed. Still, within a week of his investiture in 1580, Spanish forces invaded, and within four months, the crown belonged to Philip, Portugal to Spain. Ultimately, then, the events at Alcazar determined not simply the allocation of rule within Morocco, but the balance of power across Europe and the Mediterranean.

Although England was not militarily invested in the battle in any significant way, perhaps what made the "renowned" event so marketable to English audiences was that it underscored Barbary's centrality as a site for global change and exchange. In France, in immortalizing the "notable" battle in 1580, Montaigne not only valorizes the exemplary behavior of Abd el-Malek and emphasizes its immediate outcome, the remarkable death of "three Kings" (Abd el-Malek, Mulai Mohammed, and the Portuguese Sebastian); he also laments its political aftereffect, the "transmission of so great a Kingdome [Portugal] to the crowne of *Castile*" (405).[29] In Portugal, anti-Spanish propaganda presented Alcazar and Philip's limited backing of Sebastian there to display the Spanish king's "unmesurable ambition & insatiable desire to have dominion" over Portugal, as A. R. Braunmuller as noted.[30] And it may be, as D'Amico has suggested, that Portugal's failure "to reassert dominion in Morocco" increased England's interest in and access to the Barbary trade—at least until Spain's absorption of Portugal heightened "Anglo-Spanish tension over, among other things, that very Moroccan trade."[31] Yet while these material consequences certainly registered within England, for an English state that was just beginning to come to terms with an evolving "world" economy, the implications were, I think, much broader. If England stood on the margins of Alcazar, Alcazar was not marginal to England. For the event and its aftermath exposed Morocco as a place whose cross-cultural connections not only carried "through the world" but, indeed, defined it.

* * *

It is no small point, and no coincidence, that the very first representation of Moors on the early modern stage takes its bearing from this complex, globally oriented history. Othello, the Moor of Venice, is no anomaly. From *Alcazar* to *Othello*, the Moor stands pivotally at the intersection of European and non-European cultures. *The Battle of Alcazar* is, to be sure, a creaky and erratic play; the earliest text we have (a 1594 quarto) may even be a shortened performance script.[32] A choric Presenter introduces—and imposes moral judgments upon—each act. In preparing the way for the first, he scrolls through Muly Mahamet's murderous usurpation of Moroccan throne and, with the aid of two dumb shows, sets the stage for a classical revenge play, insisting that "Nemesis, high mistress of revenge" calls for vengeance against the "traitor-king" (1Pro.35, 42). Accordingly, the first act starts with Abdelmelec's campaign to avenge his wrongs and "re-obtain [his] right" (1.1.83) and ends with his triumph and Muly's angry retreat to a "blasted grove," where he self-indulgently licks his political wounds (1.2.81). With Act Two, however, the dramatic terrain shifts radically into what G. K. Hunter has termed a "tangled web of *Realpolitik*."[33] While Abdelmelec celebrates his victory, Muly Mahamet decides to garner new forces and fight back, enlisting the aid of the Portuguese king Sebastian, who enlists the aid of the English venturer Thomas Stukeley, who is leading Catholic troops to Ireland. With the Presenter's announcement, "now begins the game" (2Pro.52), the action that unfolds is at once a political history, tracing the second triumph of Abdelmelec and the rise of Muly Mahamet Seth (el-Mansur), and a moral tragedy, centered on Sebastian (whom the Presenter glorifies) and his tragic entanglement in the "wily" Muly's "dangerous war" (5Pro.3–4). And within the interstices of these dramas erupt the outlandish actions of Thomas Stukeley, who temporarily steals the show in its—and his—final moments, recounting the full "story of [his] life" while "brave Sebastian's breathless corse" lies unattended (5.1.178, 72).

The unorthodox mix of genres, convoluted display of Moroccan history, and repeated shifts in focus from one main character to the next have baffled critics, with the result that analyses of the play have tended to distill select nationally and racially edged preoccupations from the dramatic chaos, to emphasize *Alcazar*'s (and Alcazar's) story as Stukeley's, Sebastian's, or Muly's. Thorlief Larsen, who initially set the terms for the criticism on Peele's play in 1939, valorized the real and imagined Stukeley as a "man of dare-devil courage, of boundless energy, and of magnanimous temper," and he also read Peele's—

and England's—interest in Alcazar as an interest in him.[34] Joseph Candido, after him, proposed *Alcazar*'s representation of the "charismatic and controversial" Stukeley as the starting point for "Tudor 'biographical' drama," and the surrounding Moroccan history, merely the "panoramic backdrop against which [his] life . . . is brought into relief."[35] Scholars have treated Sebastian similarly, as a signpost for the playing out of England's national politics, underscoring Sebastian's ties to "the English house of Lancaster" and understanding Peele's invocation of Moroccan history as "exotic" or incidental.[36] Criticism on *Alcazar*'s racial dimensions brought attention to the Moor, but it has focused primarily on Muly, reading him in isolation from Morocco's complex history. In Barthelemy, for example, the "mimetic historical drama" that embeds the allegorically demonized Muly only works to validate, in a "real" world, the association of Moors and blacks with "the devil."[37] Even while Matar places England's interactions in Barbary in the foreground of *Alcazar*, he singles out "the evil Muly Mahamet" as "the formative Moor in English dramatic imagination," arguing that this "Negroid, evil, anti-Christian and ruthless" figurehead, alongside "the dangerous Muly Mahamet Seth" and Stukeley, "bring[s] . . . home" to England "the danger of political and military entanglement with Moors."[38]

Yet although *Alcazar* starts provincially, with a locally grounded and dramatically archaic revenge play, and although it produces a provocative series of nationally embraceable heroes, as its political geography expands the play presses significantly against the bounds of history, genre, race, and nation. On Peele's stage, Barbary provides a setting where not only Moors but also Turks, Spaniards, Portuguese, and an Englishman "perform, in view of all the world" (*Alcazar* 1.1.27). And as they do, the play explores the dynamic, if unpredictable, interconnections that were shaping the Mediterranean. Within the space of Barbary, the ideals of nationalism necessarily give way, and what emerges in their stead is not a "tangled web" but an evolving cross-cultural environment, contingent on political alliances and exchange, with the Moor providing the central model and means.

In dramatizing the Moroccan conflict, Peele seems initially to define the competing Moors through an easily readable, color-coded, moral divide. On the one side is the "black" and "barbarous" "negro" Moor, Muly Mahamet, who has usurped the Moroccan throne; on the other is the rightful king, the "brave Barbarian lord," Abdelmelec, defined by class and country rather than skin color, who is set (and sure) to reclaim his politically anointed place. Before the play proper begins, the Presenter underscores the difference between them by vigorously condemning Muly for being "black in his look, and bloody in his deeds," guilty of "ambitious tyranny," "cruel," and "unbelieving" (1Pro.34, 10, 32). While acknowledging that Muly's father installed his son on the throne, the Presenter stresses that Muly's "passage to the crown" was "by murder made" (1Pro.13) and calls up two dumb shows to enforce the point. In the first, Muly puts his two "younger brethen" to bed, "like poor lambs pre-pared for sacrifice" (24, 26); in the second, Muly and "two murderers," "dev-ils coated in the shapes of men" (20), bring his uncle Abdelmunen to the scene, smother the princes before him, and then strangle him (the last, a mur-der which Mulai Mohammed did not commit). At the end of these specta-cles, the Presenter turns responsibility over to Nemesis, who, he says, "calls the Furies from Avernus' crags, / To range and rage, and vengeance to inflict, / Vengeance on this accursed Moor"—Muly—"for sin" (38–40).[39] If Peele's staging of this "modern [i.e., commonplace] matter full of blood and ruth" is not quite the "classical confrontation of good and evil" which Barthelemy has argued for, it does bear the signs of a morally freighted revenge play (1Pro.50).[40] Abdelmelec takes arms against the usurping Muly, imploring the gods to "pour down showers of sharp revenge" upon the "traitor-king" (1.1.88). Muly stands his ground, embracing "blood" as "the theme whereon our time shall tread" (1.2.54). And when Abdelmelec triumphs, requisite ghosts urge the retreating Muly to continue the cycle, echoing the stock re-frain "*Vindicta!*" (S.D.2Pro.8).

Instead of setting the prevailing terms for *Alcazar*, however, this saga of revenge takes shape rather as a dramatically outmoded backstory, signaled es-pecially by its dumb shows, if not also by the Presenter's absolute moral dif-ferentiation of bad Moor from good, the "barbarous" from the "Barbarian." Signs of a more complex political and racial geography, in fact, perforate its fictions. Not only is Abdelmelec, arguably, as vengeful as Muly.[41] In addition, try as the Presenter might to incriminate Muly as Negro, to correlate his "black" "looks" with his "bloody" "deeds," and to set him apart from his "brave Barbarian" rival, these distinctions are undone by the glaring fact that the two Moors share a single bloodline. In the opening chorus, the Presenter notes in passing that Muly is "sprung from th' Arabian Moor" (1Pro.15), and his uncle Abdelmelec echoes these terms as he lays out his own right to suc-cession, claiming that he and his followers are "sprung from the true Arabian Muly Xarif, / The loadstar and honour of our line" (1.1.50–51). According to Abdelmelec, Muly Xarif "descended from the line / Of Mahomet," left Arabia, and "strongly plant[ed] himself in Barbary" (1.1.64–67). Even this genealogy is too clean, for Xarif's historical prototype was, in fact, a Turk, Moulay Mohammed el-Kaim bi amer Allah; and Abd el-Malek had himself been raised by Turks.[42] So much for black versus white, Negro versus Moor, Moor versus Arabian, Arabian versus Turk.

Alcazar, which does not expose the Turkish edge of the Moors' ancestry, does not therefore go as far as the history behind it does in mixing cultural identities. But Peele does complicate the revenge plot and the Presenter's moral codification of the Moors by emphasizing Abdelmelec's crucial connection to the Turks—one which contrasts with Muly's self-imposed isolation and which suggests political orientation, in lieu of moral or racial markers, as the defining axis of difference. In the opening act, what sets Abdelmelec apart from Muly as the Moor most likely to succeed in the pre-*Alcazar* conflict is his involvement in a worldly politics, instantiated by his long-standing alliance with the Turks and their leader "Great Amurath," "Emperor of the East" (1Pro.44). In introducing the act, the Presenter has already explained that "in flying the fury" of Muly's father who "wrong'd his brethren to install his son," Abdelmelec "served in field" under the "colours" of the Amurath's father, the "Sultan Solimon" (1Pro.45–48). When Abdelmelec appears, he announces his intent to "bear witness to the world" how he "adore[s] / The sacred name of Amurath the Great" (1.1.10–11). Reciprocally, a Turkish Bassa professes that he and his men have come to Morocco, under Amurath's orders, not as "mercenary men" but as "friends"—"to gratify and remunerate" Abdelmelec's "service in his father's dangerous war," "to perform, in view of all the world, / The true office of right and royalty," and to "make" Abdelmelec "Emperor of this Barbary" (1.1.22–24, 26–28, 31).

Though the Moor and the Turk—and, I would argue, the play—imagine the alliance as something that "all the world" would not only watch but endorse, editors and critics of the play have tended to take a darker view of this interaction, portraying Amurath as a "cruel voluptuary" and Abdelmelec's relation to him as "slavish deference."[43] In the 1590s, Amurath's reputation did come under fire for waging what Leeds Barroll has called "a major land offensive in central Europe."[44] In Shakespeare's *2 Henry IV* (1590–91), for example, Hal assures his brothers that, as the new king, he will "bear [their] cares" (5.2.58), proclaiming, "This is the English, not the Turkish court, / Not Amurath an Amurath succeeds, / But Harry Harry" (5.2.46–48).[45] In the years before *Alcazar*, however, Elizabeth had herself engaged in sustained negotiations with this "great Turke" ("Zuldan Murad Can"), gaining authorization for the Levant Company to traffic in his "Imperiall dominions" (Hakluyt, 5:178, 183,

185).[46] And whereas in Marlowe's *Jew of Malta* the Turkish Calymath is ominously poised for conquest when he collects tribute from the Christian governor, in Peele there is no sign of impending Turkish domination.[47] The Turks' intervention before Alcazar restores Abdelmelec's regime and leads to an extended chain of reciprocity and remuneration: Abdelmelec's sister-in-law (Abdelmunen's widow) offers Amurath her son, and another Moorish queen offers herself, along with "the gold of Barbary" (2.1.38); in turn, the Turk leaves the "chosen guard of Amurath's janizaries" to "honour and attend" on the Moor (2.1.48–49). And not only does Abdelmelec rule Morocco without interference (as Muly's son will complain) "in eye of all the world" (3.4.42), he "intitle[s]" his brother, Muly Mahamet Seth "true heir unto the crown" (2.1.19), declaring his "due and duty" "to heaven and earth, gods and Amurath" thereby done (2.1.22–23). It is only the discredited Muly and his son who fear that the Turk will, like "Tamburlaine," "invade," "chástise," and "menace" Africa's "lawful kings" and "right and royal realm" (1.2.22, 33–34). Even so, they envy "that brave guard of sturdy janizaries / That Amurath to Abdelmelec gave" and that keeps their hated enemy "as safe / As if he slept within a walled town" (1.2.40–43).

Abdelmelec's efforts to "perform" his legitimacy and his loyalty to the Turks "in view of all the world" set him meaningfully apart from Muly Mahamet, who embraces rather what appears to be a naive and atavistic isolationism. Indeed, the more isolated he becomes within the dramatic fiction, the more exaggerated and outmoded his characterization seems.[48] Before his first attempt to usurp the throne, Muly boasts that his gold will provide "the glue, sinews, and strength of war" (1.2.8), and he bolsters his campaign only with the support of his wife Calipolis, his son, and his guard. The consequences are dire: Muly is quickly overthrown, and he immediately withdraws to the "shade / Of some unhaunted place, some blasted grove, / Of deadly yew or dismal cypress-tree," where he means to "pine with thought and terror of mishaps" (1.2.80–82, 86). Dramatically and politically, what threatens is stagnation, alienation, and annihilation. There, in a space of "cursèd solitaries" (2.3.38), the objective correlative of his despair, Muly "lives"—and imagines he will always live—"forlorn among the mountain-shrubs, / And makes his food the flesh of savage beasts" (2Pro.34–35), with the Furies seeking revenge against him. His only recourse consists of lamenting his fortunes in "huge exclaims," which his starving wife underscores as pointless (2.3.16). It is only with the announcement that he has sent word to Sebastian, "the good and harmless King of Portugal," promising "to resign the royalty / And kingdom of Morocco to his hands" (2.2.48–50), that the play can proceed, that Muly's small cadre of supporters can grasp onto "the slenderest hair" of opportunity and see an end to "this miserable life" (2.2.55–56).

In staging the prehistory of Alcazar, Peele thus uses a revenge frame to articulate, complicate, and ultimately displace the categorical differentiation of its Moors. As false plays against true, "barbarian" against "Barbarian," so does isolation against alliance, the local against the global. The Moor who triumphs understands that "all the world" is watching. And though he reaches out materially only to the Turks, his gesture nonetheless permeates the ideological and dramatic barriers that would otherwise limit Moroccan history to Morocco, prove the Turk a Turk, and reduce a provocative politics to an overdetermined morality. As the opening act outlines the complex genealogies that define and rupture the Moorish regime, it makes clear that to succeed in the world is necessarily to succeed *in the world,* which extends beyond Barbary and its blasted groves.

* * *

Starting with the second act, the civil war escalates almost to the point of its own erasure, inflecting but not dominating the action. It is here that the Presenter announces "now begins the game," here that European interests and alliances become crucial, here that "Sebastian's tragedy in this tragic war" emerges centrally, ushering in Thomas Stukeley's vainglorious rise and fall (2Pro.53). It is here, too, that the claustrophobic revenge play is displaced and replaced by a complex Mediterranean history, Hunter's "tangled web," and here that the Presenter's moral frames seem increasingly out of sync with the enactments they introduce.[49] As the scope and staging of Moroccan politics expand to include European subjects, the tensions between the local and the global that fracture the easy dichotomies in the opening act become clearer, as well as more clearly relevant to England. As the uneasy alliance between Muly Mahamet, Sebastian, and Stukeley takes shape, Morocco provides a staging ground for both Portugal and England. And though the European campaign pivots on the promotion of a fervent nationalism, suggestively shadowed by Muly's isolationism, what prevails with Abdelmelec's regime is a global politics which challenges the ideologies of nation.[50]

Now begins the game: Sebastian's tragedy within this tragic war. In advocating for the Portuguese king, the Presenter stresses the moral edges of that tragedy, ultimately placing the blame on Muly, the "foul ambitious

Moor, / Whose wily trains with smoothest course of speech / Have tied and tanged in a dangerous war / The fierce and manly King of Portugal" (5Pro.2–5). Muly does, of course, deceive and coerce Sebastian, using false promises to "set these Portugals a-work / To hew a way for me unto the crown" (4.2.70–71).[51] Yet it is Abdelmelec, not Muly, who is Sebastian's political opponent, as the title to the 1594 quarto—*The Battell of Alcazar, fought in Barbarie, betweene Sebastian king of Portugall, and Abdelmelec king of Marocco. With the death of Captaine Stukeley*—stresses.[52] In scapegoating Muly, the Presenter obscures the problem which the competing action underscores: Sebastian's own imperialist agenda, which has nation written all over it. Sebastian markets his campaign in Morocco as a "holy Christian war," designed "to plant the Christian faith in Africa" (2.4.66, 165), and his evangelical zeal is inextricably coupled to his overbearing intent: to make "Abdelmelec and great Amurath" "tremble at" Portugal's "strength" (2.4.48–49) and to "propagate the fame of Portugal" (3.1.7). Even the Presenter admits that, while "honour was object of [Sebastian's] thoughts," "ambition was his ground" (4Pro.13)—and ground, we might add, his ambition. Not only do Muly's promises to "surrender up the kingdom of Moroccus" and to render the "realm of Fess" "contributary" to Portugal lure the ambitious king into war (2.4.14–17); when the legate from Spain assures Sebastian that the Spanish king will support his campaign by sending "aid of arms," offering his daughter in marriage as well as title to "the Islands of Moloccus" (3.1.40, 26), Sebastian immediately takes the bait.

Clearly here, Sebastian's mission to increase Portugal's fame and territory represents a political liability, blinding him to the competing aspirations of his own ostensible allies. While he is sure that the king of Spain, like the would-be king of Morocco, will give up terrain in order to "honour and enlarge" Portugal's "name," as the Spanish legate suggests (3.1.21), others, better in tune with the volatile ways of the world, are more skeptical and foresighted. Stukeley, who has joined with Portugal by this point, surmises that Philip is "disguising with a double face" and "flatter[ing] [Sebastian's] youth and forwardness" while arming for a conquest of Flanders (3.1.50–51). More importantly, Abdelmelec rightly anticipates that, even if Spain's promises are real, its loyalties are negotiable: he sends a letter to the Spanish king to "crave that in a quarrel so unjust, / He that entitlèd is the Catholic king, / Would not assist a careless Christian prince" (3.2.14–16) and sways Philip to his side by offering up "seven holds" [i.e., holdings] (3.2.18). As well, although Abdelmelec is happy to let the Portuguese self-destruct, leaving him "guiltless" of

their "blood" (3.2.30), he nonetheless, "in pity to the Portugal," appoints "secret messengers to counsel" that misguided king (3.2.10–11). These efforts apparently go unattended (we hear no further of them), but the Moor's
diplomacy and perspicacity underscore the limits of Sebastian's—and the limits of Sebastian's, the extent and expediency of the Moor's. Focused only on
his own advancement, the Portuguese king waits futilely in Cadiz for support,
while Philip (who did assist, historically) "pretends a sudden fear and care to
keep / His own from Amurath's fierce invasion"—one which, if it has threatened at all, has already been circumvented by Spain's alliance with Abdelmelec
(3.3.36–37). Some fifteen years after *Alcazar*, *The Famous History* builds this
invented military abstention into a devious and decisive plot: there, Philip
promises troops only to set his Portuguese rival up for the kill, withdrawing
at the last minute and leaving Sebastian in Barbary and in danger, without ad-
equate arms.[53] In Peele, however, Philip never appears; the emphasis is rather
on Sebastian, who, because of his "ambitious wiles," "poison'd eyes" (3Pro.20)
and, as Abdelmelec puts it, "deceiving hope" (3.2.1) for power, overlooks the
political agendas of his rivals, and on Abdelmelec, who, in contrast, does not.

It is, not coincidentally, when Sebastian coerces Stukeley to abort his invasion of Ireland and join the Portuguese campaign in Morocco that the play
challenges the logic and integrity of nationalism most explicitly, linking it to
an imperialist platform that is at once self-serving and self-defeating. In a gesture that can only be ironic, Sebastian pressures the Englishman to change
course by glorifying the supreme right of the English queen and the invulnerability of her kingdom (which includes Ireland). Presenting Elizabeth's "seat"
as "sacred, imperial, and holy," "shining with wisdom, love, and mightiness"
(2.4.109–10), he insists that neither "nature that everything imperfect made"
nor "fortune that never yet was constant found" nor "time that defaceth every
golden show" can "decay, remove, or her impair," but rather "bless and serve
her royal majesty" (2.4.111–16). On every side, England is supported by natural defenses—by "wallowing oceans" and "raging floods" which "swallow up
her foes, / And on the rocks their ships in pieces split," by "the narrow Britain-
sea," "where Neptune sits in triumph to direct / Their course to hell that aim
at her disgrace," by "the German seas," "where Venus banquets all her water-
nymphs" (2.4.117–19, 123–27)—with the important consequence that "danger,
death, and hell" will "follow" "all that seek to danger" this blessed island or
blessed queen (2.4.132–33). "Were every ship ten thousand on the seas, /
Mann'd with the strength of all the eastern kings, / Conveying all the monarchs of the world," Sebastian argues, "T'invade the island where her highness

reigns, / 'Twere all in vain, for heavens and destinies / Attend and wait upon her majesty" (2.4.103–8).

Although this passage speaks to "the condition of England" in an overtly conventional form, English audiences are to take no more—and maybe less—stock in Sebastian's encomium, I think, than they are in John of Gaunt's vacantly nostalgic idealization of the "sceptred isle" (*R2* 2.1.40) in Shakespeare's *Richard II* (1595), both which seem strangely out of touch with the political realities unsettling the imagined nation.[54] Indeed, Sebastian's vision of an inviolate, impenetrable England should give pause to spectators who have just seen where isolation leads Muly Mahamet: to a debilitating despair, impotence, regression, and retreat. In any case, in playing up England's strength, Sebastian's point is solely to play down Stukeley's, to prove his forces "far too weak" for the invasion of Ireland that would otherwise keep him from Morocco (2.4.100). These forces are stronger in Peele than they were historically, adding up to seven ships and six thousand troops rather than the three ships and six hundred soldiers of the "real" faction.[55] The difference may work to amplify the threat that Stukeley poses to Ireland and so to England—a threat that Queen Elizabeth apparently feared, worrying that Sebastian and Stukeley would head there instead of Morocco.[56] But if the troop increase makes Sebastian's derailment of the Irish campaign a welcome side effect of his self-promotion, his ostensible idealization of England's natural and national sovereignty betrays itself nonetheless as what it is: self-serving propaganda, designed to advance Portugal's, not England's, fame. Though Stukeley acquiesces, pausing to "admire [Sebastian's] words" (2.4.137), the Catholic leaders who accompany him do neither, "willingly" agreeing "to be commanded" only because the king has "made [them] captives at [his] royal will" (2.4.158–60).

Ultimately, Sebastian's alliance with Stukeley does not speak well for either Portugal or England, or for a nationalist cause. Though he asks Stukeley to follow him to "fruitful Barbary" "in honour of thy country's fame" (2.4.85, 87), the "Englishman" defines himself as fervently against the bounds of nation as the Portuguese king defines himself through them. The "real" Stukeley was infamous for being a renegade expatriate, if also a "bubble of emptiness, and meteor of ostentation."[57] A known Catholic, he was alternately embraced and spurned (even imprisoned) within England, with the result that he spent substantial portions of his career in Catholic Europe.[58] In the 1550s, for example, he fled to France and allied himself with Henri II after participating in a potentially treasonous plot against the English state. He returned to England thereafter (to betray Henri's plans of invading England), and though he was temporarily imprisoned in the Tower, under Elizabeth's auspices he subsequently became a privateer. Those activities elicited such protest from Portugal, Spain, and France that Stukeley again lost the queen's favor and left the country, garnering support rather from powerful Catholic leaders: from Shane O'Neill, a prominent Irish nationalist; Philip II, who made Stukeley a knight in the Order of Calatrava; and Pope Gregory XIII, who made him "Marquis of Leinster." In a history I have already outlined, Stukeley's career took its final turn in Portugal, where Sebastian coerced or convinced him to fight in Morocco, on Mulai Mohammed's behalf.[59] And in the end, it is likely that his forces turned against him, killing him at Alcazar for abandoning the invasion of Ireland, betraying them and their Catholic crusade.

Because of this globe-trotting track record, critics have valorized the real and imagined Stukeley as a self-actualized "citizen of the world" and have located in Peele's characterization a newly compelling stage personality, full of the "expansiveness of spirit that typifies the Marlovian hero at his overween-ing best."[60] It is he, rather than Abdelmelec, who gets credit for going global. Within *Alcazar*, Stukeley himself provides the passion and the cues for such a reading. When he first appears in Lisbon, the Portuguese governor welcomes him and his faction as "brave Englishmen" (2.2.2) and objects to their plan to invade Ireland, protesting: "are ye not all Englishmen, / And 'longs not Ireland to that kingdom?" (2.2.20–21). In response, Stukeley defines himself rather as one who "may at liberty make choice / Of all the continents that bounds [*sic*] the world," insisting that although he is an Englishman, so also is he a man, destined "to follow rule, honour, and empery, / Not to be bent so strictly to the place / Wherein at first I blew the fire of life" (2.2.29–33). According to his philosophies, "to be begot or born in any place" is "not so great desert," "sith that's a thing of pleasure and of ease / That might have been perform'd else-where as well" (2.2.34–37). This is not the breaking apart of an English "fan-tasy of ethnic coherence," though, as John Drakakis has suggested, that would happen elsewhere.[61] Birth is neither culturally impure or intermixed; it is ran-dom, at least as far as political loyalties are concerned.

Yet despite its appearances, Stukeley's antinationalist posture actually instantiates a national, not a global, perspective, its negation reinforcing rather than upending the boundaries of state. His driving ambition is noth-ing more, and nothing less, than "to win a crown," as he reiterates in his first soliloquy, proclaiming, "There shall no action pass my hand or sword, /

That cannot make a step to gain a crown; / No word shall pass the office of my tongue, / That sounds not of affection to a crown"—and so on, and doggedly on (2.2.69–74). Here is Tamburlaine's signal fetishization of "the sweet fruition of an earthly crown," his "perfect bliss and sole felicity," writ in bold redundancy (*Tamb. I* 2.6.68–69).[62] But, as Peele's parodic invocation of Marlowe's imperializing superconqueror emphasizes, Stukeley is not Tamburlaine, who also "love[s] to live at liberty" (*Tamb. I* 1.2.26) but who, by absorbing or annihilating every party in his path, means to be "monarch" not of any single kingdom but of all kingdoms. Before Stukeley is rerouted to Africa, his defining ambition is—simply, provincially, in contrast to Tamburlaine's—to be the "King of Ireland" (2.2.80–81). His explanation for his choice—"king of a mole-hill had I rather be, / Than the richest subject of a monarchy" (2.2.81–82)—is telling. For while he makes a distinction here between a mole-hill and a monarchy, the major boundary he imagines crossing is of class. There is little difference between one state, one crown, one monarchy, and another; the difference that signifies lies between subject and king.

It is perhaps not so surprising then that, after *Alcazar*, Stukeley's reputation as a worldly renegade is tempered notably by representations that mold him into an English national hero. In *If You Know Not Me*, Heywood praises him in passing as "that renowned Englishman, / That had a spirit equal with a king" and "in warlike strife, / Honord his country, and concluded life" (293). Although *The Famous History* begins with Stukeley's troubled start as a "lewd misordred villaine" (279), it ends with his redemption as one of England's finest. There, in what is largely domestic comedy, Stukeley competes for a wife against his English rival Vernon in order to gain access, everyone rightly fears, to her father's wealth. Though both he and Vernon leave the country and tour the world, the humor and the hitch revolve around the constant coincidence of their paths. The play climaxes on the fields of Alcazar, where the two join in a ritual of forgiveness, with Stukeley declaring them of "one selfe heart" and "one country" (2938–39), and their "English bloud," the last of its kind spent in Barbary (29–45). At the end, Stukeley's followers kill him, but not before Vernon sacrifices himself in an attempt to save his countryman— their deaths together demonstrating an English solidarity, which melodramatically redeems all. In addition, decades later, Fuller's *History of the Worthies of England* (1662) will write Stukeley's monarchical ambitions into an apocryphal English anecdote. Clearly echoing Peele, Fuller explains that Stukeley was "so confident" in "his ambition"

> that he blushed not to tell queen Elizabeth, "that he preferred rather to
> be sovereign of a mole-hill, than the highest subject to the greatest king
> in Chistendom [*sic*];" adding moreover, "that he was assured he should
> be a prince before his death." "I hope," said queen Elizabeth, "I shall
> hear from you, when you are stated in your principality." "I will write
> unto you," quoth Stukeley. "In what language?" said the queen. He
> returned, "In the style of princes; To our dear Sister." (1:414)

In Fuller, the "mole-hill" is not Ireland but Florida, a place of special interest in the mid-seventeenth century, when England began to see a profitable future in the New World.[63] The substitution only reiterates the irrelevance of which "principality" is at stake. The punch line turns on turning a question about a different nation ("what language?") into an answer about a different class ("the style of princes")—a class which aligns Stukeley familiarly with "our dear Sister," the English queen.

If these representations take their cues from Peele, however, in nationalizing Stukeley's story they must (and do) extract it from the complications and implications that come with *Alcazar*'s larger, cultural picture. For to read Stukeley in the context of *Alcazar* is to see neither a self-actualized worldly citizen nor a valorous English hero, but an antinationalist Englishman who is as out of place within Morocco's political theater as are Sebastian and Muly Mahamet. In his final hour Stukeley, "slain with many a deadly stab" at the hands of his followers, appropriates the occasion of Alcazar to retrace his spectacular tracks—to "tell the story of [his] life" on "the desert fields of Africa" in order to "beguile the torment of [his] death" (5.1.132–35). In a lengthy soliloquy, he details his extravagant history—from his "golden days" of youth in London (5.1.138), to his advancement in Spain, where he lived "like a lord" and "glitter[ed] all in gold" (5.1.149, 146), to his "royal welcomes" in Rome, where he was "graced by Gregory the Great" and "created" "Marquis of Ireland" (5.1.155–57), to his arrival in Lisbon and his rerouting to Morocco, the "discontented humour," "strife," and banishment that prompted his many moves appearing in the gaps between them (5.1.142, 152). Coming *after* Stukeley has been stabbed, this attempt to bring his worldly past to life is as ironic and empty as Hamlet's triumphant self-profession, "This is I, Hamlet the Dane," which, as Catherine Belsey has suggested, covers a void, at a moment when all is irredeemably lost and Hamlet has no place "to be" (*Ham.* 5.1.257–58).[64] Stukeley's performance not only interrupts the progression of plot, eclipsing the staging of both Muly's and Sebastian's deaths and delaying the new Moroccan regime's impending rise. Because he addresses his speech to "friends" and "lordings" in the audience, it also breaks the frame of the dramatic illusion, momentarily undoing the history that is *Alcazar* (5.1.134, 136). Ironically too, with "the story of [his] life" told, as Stukeley prepares to die "in that bed of honour" "where brave Sebastian's corse doth lie," he expresses the hope that "thy [i.e., his] "country" will "kindly ring thy [i.e., his] knell" (5.1.176–78). In thus reclaiming his English roots, he wrests himself from the global scene—from Africa's "desert fields" and "barbarous Moors" (as well as from the "proud malicious dogs of Italy")—that embeds him (5.1.123, 126), and puts closure on his part, and Sebastian's, with a discordant note of hardcore national bias.

* * *

Although the "careless Christian prince" of Portugal has imagined that he, with Stukeley in tow, could write Portugal's name over Morocco (not to mention, literally over parts of Spain and figuratively over England), in the end it is neither Sebastian nor Stukeley but the new Moroccan regime that gets the final say (3.2.16). For ultimately in *Alcazar*, it is not Portugal's or England's history that frames Barbary's, but Barbary's that frames Portugal's and England's. The Presenter looks ever forward to that moment of tragic recognition and release when Sebastian will realize that he has been duped by the "false-hearted Mahamet" and when someone (it will be Muly Mahamet Seth) will take revenge on Muly, predictably too late to save Sebastian. Sebastian's moment of truth indeed comes on the fields of Alcazar, where he finally is able to "see [his] oversight," to realize the "treachery" of the "false-hearted Mahamet," to remember warnings he tragically ignored "to beware / A face so full of fraud and villainy" (5.1.67–70). However much the Presenter tries to redeem the Portuguese crusader and make Alcazar's story his, the potential catharsis of this moment is quickly diminished by the displacement of Sebastian's death (which happens offstage) and of his body (which is lost!) as well as by a disjunctive shift in focus to Muly, who retreats once again into the vengeful solipsism that has already proven politically and dramatically deadly. His defeat imminent, the Moor can only think to retire again to "some uncouth walk" where he can "curse [his] fill," blaming fate, "my stars, my dam, my planets, and my nurse" (5.1.76–77). In lines that Shakespeare will echo in *Richard III* (1592–93), Muly stands before the river that will drown him and calls for "a horse, a horse, villain, a horse!" so that he can "take the river straight and fly" (5.1.96–97). But instead of flying or fighting, he reiterates his hope for vengeance, imagining now that he will meet the newly dead Abdelmelec in hell and take revenge finally on his soul. If Muly's final moment displaces Sebastian's, Stukeley's disassociated autobiographical outburst displaces both, with the result that the moral tragedy loses its focus and its edge.

As the contenders' saga ends thus with a spectacular, internally vexed, thud, what prevails in its stead is Morocco's political theater, where Muly Mahamet Seth, like Abdelmelec before him, deftly negotiates lines of difference and, unlike his opponents, actively accommodates "all the world." In the final scenes, instead of closing Morocco's borders or invading Portugal's, the victorious Moor orders his Portuguese prisoners to recover Sebastian's body, and when they bring it forth, he seizes the moment to honor the "earth and clay / Of him that erst was mighty King of Portugal" (5.1.222–23). His eulogy anticipates similarly climactic moments, such as Marc Antony's public adulation of Brutus as that "noblest Roman of them all" in *Julius Caesar* (5.5.68), and Fortinbras's arguably dubious reconstruction of Hamlet as one who would "have prov'd most royal" "had he been put on" (*Hamlet* 5.2.397–98). In Shakespeare, the opportunism of these gestures, which come only when the valorized subjects can no longer flex their political muscles, is glaring: after the adulation is done, Antony obliterates Brutus's dreams of a managed republic by supporting an insidious oligarchy (which he hopes to head), and Fortinbras claims Denmark for Norway. Here is power using subversion to advance itself. In honoring "the mighty king of Portugal," however, Muly Seth undoes the terms of antagonism that Sebastian's "holy Christian wars" have imposed and establishes new grounds for connection, if not alliance (2.4.135). Where Sebastian, in repeatedly announcing his aim to "fight for Christ," codes the Moors as misbelievers (3.1.31), Muly Seth gives the conquered Portuguese Christians apparently due place: he not only allows them to "return from hence to Christendom" (5.1.225); he also orders his lords to "tread a solemn march, / Trailing their pikes and ensigns on the ground, / So to perform the . . . funerals" of "this Christian king" (5.1.256, 258–69). To be sure, Peele's representation of the Moors' religious affiliation is inconsistent throughout. Abdelmelec, for one, explicitly gives "God" "due thanks" and acts "in sight of heaven" in some places (1.1.5, 62) while invoking implicitly pagan "gods of heaven" (2.1.20) in others. Still, Muly Seth's valorization of Sebastian's Christian body creates an important political bridge, emphasizing the compatibility between Barbary and Christendom, the Moroccans and the Portuguese.

This integrating tribute to the defeated king of Portugal is, in fact, sandwiched between and contrasted by Muly's Seth derogation and ostracization of Muly Mahamet, "the traitorous Moor" (5.1.203). With Sebastian's recovered body lying newly before him, Muly Seth receives two peasants, who throw Muly's body at his feet. Declaring the traitor "beastly, unarmèd, slavish, [and] full of shame," Muly Seth asserts that death by drowning is "too good for such a damnèd wretch" (5.1.236, 246). He then calls for a spectacle of retaliation that will embody the "rage and rigour of revenge" (5.1.247): he orders that Muly's skin "be parted from his flesh," "stiffen'd out and stuff'd with straw," "so to deter and fear the lookers-on / From any such foul fact or bad attempt" (5.1.251–54). In excoriating Muly's "bad attempt," Muly Seth separates the Moor's actions from Sebastian's, suggesting usurpation from within a greater threat than occupation from without. While Sebastian will be honored by public obsequies, Muly will be flayed; and while both will become objects of politicized spectacles, it is Muly who will be on permanent, if not also ghoulish, display before the "lookers-on."

Yet tellingly, even as Muly Seth distinguishes the soon-to-be stuffed and stiffened body of the "beastly" Moor from the honored body of the Portuguese king, he also takes into account the political connection between the two. Instead of producing Muly simply as a didactic prop, a punishable embodiment of a "foul fact," clearly and cleanly separated from his European ally, and instead of treating Muly's "bad attempt" as an exclusively internal problem, Muly Seth expressly puts the Moor forward "that all the world may learn by him t'avoid / To hale on princes to injurious war" (5.1.249–50). Not only is the spectacle designed for "all the world"; it is designed in terms of it, the moral of its story, not local but global. For it is not Muly's unsuccessful attempt to usurp the Moroccan throne that must be punished and its like prevented, but his successful move to lure the Portuguese prince into "injurious war." Between the lines of Muly Seth's official sentence lies anticipation and regulation of further cross-cultural exchange.

As a theatrical text, *Alcazar* is unquestionably quirky, uneven, and disjunct, having no single focal point but a series of several competing foci. And yet what brings order and meaning to the ostensible chaos is a depiction of Moroccan politics, which is as crucial to Muly's, Sebastian's, and Stukeley's individual tragedies as the story of Fortinbras is to Hamlet's. In setting Moor against Moor, "Barbarian" against "barbarian," *Alcazar* presses its spectators to look beyond the bounds of race, religion, and nation, to see a Mediterranean "world" improvised from the unpredictable intersections of Europeans and non-Europeans, of Moors, Arabians, Turks, Portuguese, Spanish, Italians, and at least one Englishman. Here, on the staging ground of Morocco, where history takes form "in view of all the world," not only does cultural integration trump isolation; cultural identity is neither pure nor stable. As *Alcazar* speaks of the Moor in terms that will carry through to *Othello*, it speaks thus across assumptions of difference, asserting all the complicated distinctions and connections between "Barbarian" and "barbarian" while making clear that lineage and morality, ethnicity and attitude, color and behavior do not always, though they may sometimes, go hand in hand. The plays that immediately follow and absorb *Alcazar* will take a darker turn as they position the Moor within Europe. *Titus Andronicus* and *Lust's Dominion* build primarily on the model of Muly Mahamet, centering almost exclusively on Moors who seem to be as black in their looks and bloody in their deeds as he. Yet as these plays produce terms—and reasons—for racial and cultural discrimination, their starting point is close to Peele's. For even within the spaces of Europe, as Shakespeare and Dekker will suggest, the alienation of the Moor is not only not assumed; it is also not assured.

CHAPTER TWO

Imperialist Beginnings

Hakluyt's *Navigations* and the Place and Displacement of Africa

ROUGHLY FIVE YEARS after *Alcazar*, Peele collaborated with William Shakespeare on *Titus Andronicus* (1593–94), the second early modern play to feature the Moor as a primary subject.[1] The "execrable wretch" Aaron (5.3.176) bears clear traces of the "barbarian" Muly Mahamet, but otherwise *Titus* seems to have come a long way from *Alcazar*—from its dramatization of contemporary history and its imaginative construction of a Moroccan regime which determines its own civil and global destiny, letting in "all the world" on its own terms.[2] The later play embeds the Moor in the classical past, in the history of imperial conquest, presenting that figure as what Rome takes in and ultimately must cast out if it is to insist on its cultural purity. Like *Alcazar*, however, in staging the Moor *Titus* touches directly on England's negotiation of global change and exchange and especially on its fantasies of cross-cultural domination.

Before turning to that play, I want to look first at the one text that, probably more than any other, was giving such fantasies shape at just the moment when the Moor was becoming a prominent theatrical subject: Richard Hakluyt's *Principal Navigations, Voyages, Traffiques & Discoveries of the English Nation* (1589, 1598–1600). Hakluyt's agenda, most scholars agree, was to push the English court toward an imperialist future, and he did so by crafting England's spotty record of "navigations" into an extensive and progressive history of expansion.[3] However the narratives themselves complicate that project, showing traces of uncertainty and ambivalence within the cross-cultural mission, of mutuality and mimicry within exchange relations, or of hybridity, intermixing, or the blurring of boundaries between or within encountered cultures (and I have taken on some of this elsewhere), Hakluyt's hope was to give England the license and the leeway to establish its dominance across the world, especially in newly "discovered" domains.[4] Hence, if there is any place that we expect to find an ideology of English domination producing an identifiable Other, to find Moors racialized and codified in relatively consistent terms, or to find Africa transformed into an homogeneous "heart of darkness" in need of England's light, it is here, in Hakluyt's propagandistic documentation of England's "principal navigations, voyages, traffiques [and] discoveries."

Yet while the *Navigations* "would live on as the founding text of the British Empire," it was not because the England of Hakluyt's era had an imperialist agenda, but in spite of the fact that it did not, as David Armitage has argued.[5] For if the English were already dreaming of empire by the late sixteenth century, those dreams had neither a definitive shape nor a discernible purchase on reality, which was being improvised overseas, venture by venture. The New World, where Hakluyt pinned his expansionist hopes, would gradually become a viable site for colonization. Signal developments there, however, were only the tenuous starting points of uncertain, uneven, and not inevitable "progress." Years after the founding of Jamestown in 1607, for example, William Strachey and John Smith continued to anticipate its failure, with Strachey advocating in 1610 for stricter governance of unruly colonists and Smith in 1622 for the institution of a "running Army" against ever-growing Indian aggression.[6] Moreover, and more important to my focus here, the continent of Africa was no more the unified object of clearly cut imperialist ambitions than England was an imperialist state. However much England may have been anticipating an "economic future" in Barbary, that future was unquestionably sketchy.[7] Although English ventures to Barbary started in the 1550s, there was no attempt to regulate the trade officially until the 1580s, when the Barbary Company was chartered (in 1585), and when the charter expired (in 1597) after little more than a decade, there was no attempt to renew it.[8] Indeed, its powerful leader, the Earl of Leicester, was more interested in the Low Countries, and he meant to route the Barbary profits into expeditions there.

Try as Hakluyt might to craft the records of English exploits overseas into persuasive testimony that England "excelled all the nations and people of the earth," historically and currently, "in compassing the vaste globe of the world," ultimately the *Navigations* exposes the unevenness of England's efforts and the uncertainty of its aims. And importantly, the representation of Africa is especially fragmented and unfocused, its landscape not only split between north and west but also embedded within other defining geographies. Here, in a text that aims to prove and promote England's superiority as a global presence, Africa lies tellingly in the margins, its pertinence to England's overseas explorations subordinated by other priorities. Moors, though neither the only nor the primary "African" subjects within the *Navigations*, come into its story explicitly in accounts of Barbary. To look across Hakluyt's narratives on Africa, west as well as north, is to see Africa's displacement within England's imperialist fantasies and the Moor's place outside them.

* * *

The dark continent. In 1878, Henry Stanley (of Stanley and Livingstone) entitled an account of his African expedition *Through the Dark Continent*, and his coinage has been commonly appropriated to give Africa a black face much earlier. And with good reason. If the designation of the "dark continent" did not explicitly enter the public discourse until the nineteenth century, the idea of Africa as the great, unfathomable icon of darkness surfaced long before.[9] Up to the fifteenth century, rumor had it that "any Christian who passed [Cape] Bojador"—the farthest south explorers had gone on the West African coast—"would infallibly be changed into a black, and would carry to his end this mark of God's vengeance on his insolent prying."[10] The "insolent prying" continued nonetheless, and step by step, from 1415 onward, Portuguese mariners made it beyond that first awesome obstacle and around the next, the Cape of Good Hope, presumably in much the same color they started in. But European exploration of Africa's interiors and some parts of the coast was substantially limited well into the eighteenth century. We need only look at the maps Europe produced in the mid-sixteenth century, which demarcate myriads of coastal ports but leave the rest of the continent blank, filling it in only with black and white figurines of generic warriors and kings that convey no geographic or ethnographic information.[11]

Yet significantly, when the English began their expeditions to Africa in the mid-sixteenth century, they were not sailing in the dark. Nor did they set out with a scheme to colonize or civilize a "dark continent." Rather, they were following the unpredictable, economically oriented lead of the Portuguese, who had claimed a veritable monopoly over the trades there by the 1490s, with the backing of papal bulls, but whose primary interests lay elsewhere, in the ever-alluring East.[12] To be sure, Prince Henry the Navigator, who authorized the first wave of activity, was interested in finding Christian allies in Africa, including the legendary Christian emperor, Prester John.[13] But while the Portuguese established a number of trading posts and forts on the African coasts, the latter largely to fend off encroaching Europeans, their goal was neither to colonize occupied nor settle in unoccupied African territories. Nor was it, at least at first, to develop new economies there. Their initial aim was to tap into the well-established—and they hoped, easily accessed—trades in North Africa, sub-Saharan gold its much-sought prize. When the North African traders proved unwilling to cede control of their operation or their profits, the Portuguese expediently changed course: they sold their shipping services to African merchants and transported goods (including slaves) from one part of the continent to the other, acting as middlemen rather than as independent traders.[14] They also became involved in the gold and slave trades of Guinea, and established sugar plantations on the island of São Tomé, just off Africa's western coast, developing a lucrative model of production and slavery that they would eventually transport to Brazil and expand substantially there.[15]

If in theory these projects bear the signs of colonial domination, in practice they generally did not. More often than not, instead of conquering the local people where their outposts lay, the Portuguese relied on the natives for provisions, water rights, and aid.[16] As well, these missions and ambitions were both coupled and secondary to one thing vastly greater: the overwhelming desire to reach the East, with its fabulously fabled store of spices, silks, and precious stones.[17] From the start, Portuguese mariners were looking for a direct sea route to the East. Once they made it around the Cape of Good Hope (in the late fifteenth century) and within reach of India, their activities escalated: they launched an unprecedented series of annual expeditions and constructed just enough outposts on Africa's east coast to allow them command of the Indian Ocean and so, of the Eastern trade—outposts which they held until the next century, when the Dutch moved in and forced them out.

England's African ventures were, to a substantial degree, improvised around this history, having themselves no single or definitive focus, beyond, of course, expedient economic gain. It was only after, if not because, the Portuguese redirected their efforts from Barbary to Guinea, that Thomas Wyndham initiated the Barbary trade, with his two voyages to Morocco in 1551 and 1552.[18] In the years immediately after, the English began to explore Africa's

western coast: Wyndham led an expedition to Guinea in 1553, John Lok another in 1554, and William Towerson several, in 1555–58.[19] During this period,
Turkish advances in the Mediterranean were temporarily obstructing England's access to North Africa as well as to the Levant. But if the Turkish presence necessitated the move toward Guinea, the Portuguese provided both the
model, and, in some cases, the means—the pilots, captains, routes, and even
ships. The Portuguese were the first to discover how Atlantic winds and cur-
rents moved; and though the English were already fairly able to sail south-
wards, this new navigational information allowed them to negotiate the more
forbidding and treacherous return north.[20] In fact, the Portuguese seaman
Francisco Rodrigues piloted Wyndham's first Guinea voyage, and the Portuguese Antonio Pinteado, "one of the foremost commanders in Atlantic
trade," served as co-commander.[21] One record in Hakluyt actually credits the
"expert Pilot" and "politike captaine" Pinteado with "perswad[ing] [English]
marchants to attempt the said voyages to Guinea" in the first place (Hakluyt,
6:145, 152).[22]

Moreover, although Queen Elizabeth maintained the Barbary trade
throughout her reign, English expeditions to Africa—like those of the Portuguese—were nonetheless shadowed if not driven by hopes to reach the East.
It was there, after all, "in the eastern rocks" and not in Africa, that Marlowe's
gold-hungry Jew of Malta imagines a "wealthy Moor" who could "without
control" "pick his riches up, / And in his house heap pearl like pebble-stones"
(*Jew of Malta* 1.1.21–23). On Marlowe's globally materialist stage, the prospect
of acquiring of "infinite riches"—"bags of fiery opals, sapphires, amethysts,
/ Jacinths, hard topaz, grass-green emeralds, / Beauteous rubies, sparkling dia-
monds, / And seld-seen costly stones of so great price"—lies not with the
Moors or other Africans (*Jew of Malta* 1.1.37, 25–28), but with "the Arabians,
who so richly pay / The things they traffic for with wedge of gold / Whereof a
man may easily in a day / Tell that which may maintain him all his life"
(1.1.8–11); with "the merchants of the Indian mines, / That trade in metal of
the purest mold" (1.1.19–20); with "Persian ships" and argosies "from Alexan-
dria," "laden with riches and exceeding store / Of Persian silks, of gold, and
orient pearl" (1.1.2, 84, 86–87).

However these fantasies took hold, the English press eastward may well
have been predicated on the practical reality that the African trades were already monopolized by the Portuguese—not to mention, frequently plundered
by the Spanish.[23] Still, prospects in Africa never had the draw of those to the
East. The first of England's merchant companies, the Merchant Adventurers

of London (initially authorized during the reign of Henry IV) was revived and chartered in 1552, just as the first sustained wave of African expeditions was under way, but its primary purpose was to find a northeast route to Asia.[24] And while the Barbary trade would eventually be managed through a chartered company, the West African expeditions never would. Instead, the Guinea ventures were financed one by one by temporary syndicates, many of their backers becoming members of the Muscovy Company (chartered in 1555).[25] Because the Portuguese effectively held "their" ground in the region, England's initiatives stalled out within less than two decades, ending with George Fenner's voyage to Guinea in 1567. Although the English did undertake a couple of missions to Benin at the end of the century, once the Turks were defeated at Lepanto in 1571 and access to the Levant and the East Indies reopened, England lost its interest in West Africa almost entirely. Not until James's reign did an African company organize—the Company of Adventurers of London (chartered in 1618)—but even then without much sustained success.[26] And not until 1631 did the English establish their first permanent African outpost.[27] Under Charles I, the English intervened in the African trades and had some success with sugar plantations. African projects really did not gain footing, however, until after the Restoration, when they fell, tellingly, under the wing of the East India Company.[28]

The Atlantic slave trade would, of course, put Africa distinctly on the map. But, as I have suggested, this part of Africa's and England's history did not develop substantially until the mid-seventeenth century, its implications neither predictable nor certain when English venturers first set out for Barbary and Guinea or when English playwrights brought the Moor to center stage a few decades later.[29] The Portuguese began transporting African slaves to Europe, São Tomé, the Atlantic Islands, New Spain, and Brazil in the fifteenth century.[30] But it was only at the end of the sixteenth century, and with the burgeoning of the sugar plantations in Brazil, that Portuguese involvement in Atlantic slaving escalated, creating an "Atlantic plantation complex" that would ultimately revolutionize Europe's view of Africa as well as of the New World, though not for some time.[31] Granted, William Hawkins had tested a three-pronged trade between England, West Africa, and Brazil in the 1530s, following the early model of the Portuguese, and his son John revived these efforts and headed three slaving voyages in the 1560s.[32] The prospects and promise of these initiatives were so limited and uncertain, however, that no one followed up for almost a century.[33] Even when the English began to develop colonial projects in the New World, initially these efforts were not setting the foundation for "true transplantation," as Karen Kupperman has argued.[34] If Carole Shammas is right, only during James's reign, and only after the first wave of African ventures had ceased, did colonization start to become "commercialized"—and the English, to place their bets on the development of the new commodities, new markets, and new networks of exchange that would eventually "require" a massive (slave) labor force.[35]

In the broadest outlines, then these are the events and impulses that laid the ground for Hakluyt's representation of Africa as well as, in part, for the staging of the Moor. What is particularly striking is the improvisational nature, the political and ideological openness and uncertainty of these early approaches, which had no established scheme for colonial domination or for economic development behind them. For clearly, English venturers did not take on Africa as a "dark continent" in need of their (or Portugal's) civilizing light or even as a literal or figurative gold mine, there for their exploitation or excavation. In fact, the English did not take on Africa as a continent at all. Rather, when they headed first to Barbary and then to the Guinea coast, they did so erratically and sporadically, with one eye on the Portuguese as well as, in a different way, the Turks, and the other on the legendary trades and traffic of the East—their exploits always contingent on the broader network of global relations and prospects that surrounded, and so defined, Africa.

* * *

When Richard Hakluyt brings this history into his expansive vision of England's imperial power and promise in the *Principal Navigations*, he positions Africa as a touchstone of Europe's greatest achievements. In the preface to the second edition (1598), he asks:

> Wil it not in all posteritie be as great a renowme unto our English nation, to have bene the first discoverers of a Sea beyond the North cape (never certainly knowen before) and of a convenient passage into the huge Empire of Russia . . . ; as for the Portugales to have found a Sea *beyond the Cape of Buona Esperanza*, and so consequently a passage by sea into the East Indies . . . ? Be it granted that the renowmed Portugale Vasques de Gama traversed the maine Ocean *Southward of Africke*: Did not Richard Chanceler and his mates performe the like Northward of Europe? Suppose that Columbus that noble and high-spirited Genuois escried unknowen landes to the *Westward of Europe*

and Africke: Did not the Valiant English knight sir Hugh Willoughby; did not the famous Pilots . . . accoast Nova Zembla, Colgoieve, and Vaigatz to the North of Europe and Asia? (1:xl; emphasis added)

Strikingly, however, the touchstone of "Africke" marks advances in other directions. In this list of accomplishments (which goes on), it is the continent that the Portuguese have bypassed and surpassed to reach eastern lands and seas, that Columbus has bypassed and surpassed to reach the West, and that the English have, even more impressively, bypassed and surpassed by to head north. Within the body of his collection, Hakluyt does, of course, include the African expeditions as a subject in themselves, though he chose only some of the accounts of Africa that he had collected and so limited an already relatively limited set of materials.[36] But importantly, throughout the *Navigations*— and especially in the prefacing, selection, and arrangement of materials, where Hakluyt's hand shows most—Africa figures as a place of passage, a place to go *through*, literally and figuratively, rather than *to*, en route to greater gains. To engage in traffic there, the narratives themselves suggest, is to enter a network of exchange framed and mediated not simply by Africa's own people but also by the Portuguese, Turks, and Spanish.[37]

To look at the structural layout of the *Navigations* is to notice that, rather than having a coherent space to themselves, the narratives on Africa are embedded in other geographies and other stories. In both the first and second edition, Hakluyt arranges his records chronologically and geographically: he begins with England's early past (with the travels, in the first edition, of "Helena, the Empresse, daughter of Coelus, King of Britaine and mother of Constantine the great" in 337 and, in the second, of King Arthur in 517) and moves toward the present, dividing what follows into three expansive regions, partitioned relative to England: the South and Southeast; the North and Northeast; and the West, Southwest, and Northwest.[38] Before the publication of the *Navigations*, Hakluyt had been preoccupied with New World projects and had already produced two texts devoted to them, *Divers voyages touching the discoverie of America and the Ilands adjacent to the same* (1582) and the *Discourse concerning western planting* (1584). In both editions of the *Navigations*, he gives the New World narratives a similar priority, setting them apart at the very end, as the culmination of a move through time and space, from past to present, East to West, the Old World to the New.[39] In the case of Africa, however, he not only does not assign the narratives their own section; he also disperses them between two sections. The main cluster appears in the section on the South and Southeast, which charts the evolving engagement with the East, and these accounts stand separate from the depictions of stops in Guinea, which were part of the English travels to the West and which emerge in the section on the West, as part of the New World's story.

Though accounts of Barbary and Guinea do comprise a substantial block within the section on the South and Southeast, narratives on the Levant, East Indies, and Far East take precedence there. The Levant trade was heating up just as the *Navigations* was coming out: the Turkey Company got its charter in 1581, shortly before the appearance of Hakluyt's first edition (1589), and was rechartered in 1592 as the more powerful Levant Company, shortly before the appearance of the second edition (1598–1600).[40] In the second edition, Hakluyt prefaces the section with a dedicatory epistle to Robert Cecil, praising and promoting "the happie renuing and much increasing of our interrupted trade in all the Levant" (I:lxix). Moors figure in the epistle, but only as an example that helps justify new relations with the Turks. Aware that the new trade might not be universally embraced since the Turks were "misbeleevers" (1:lxix), Hakluyt asks:

> Who can deny that the Emperor of Christendome hath had league with the Turke, and payd him a long while a pension for a part of Hungarie? And who doth not acknowledge, that either hath travailed the remote parts of the world, or read the Histories of this later age, that the Spaniards and Portugales in Barbarie, in the Indies, and elsewhere, have ordinarie confederacie and traffike with the Moores, and many kindes of Gentiles and Pagans, and that which is more, doe pay them pensions, and use them in their service and warres? Why then should that be blamed in us, which is usuall and common to the most part of other Christian nations? (1:lxx)

Here "confederacie and traffike with the Moores," implicated as "misbeleevers," provides a useful precedent for trading with Turks (and the involvement of the Spanish and Portuguese, for the involvement of the English), and not the other way around. In the second edition as well, Hakluyt places several newly available documents on the Turks just before the narratives on Africa, including one (on a voyage to Constantinople and Syria in 1593–95) that describes an exchange of gifts between Queen Elizabeth and the emperor of Turkey and then details the power and pervasiveness of the Turks at length, tallying up their available forces, their sites of conquest, and their ability to "[glory] in the taking of all Christendome" (6:107–8). While this emphasis on the Levant frames the materials on Africa most immediately, they are also preceded by accounts of the East Indies, including a provocative inventory of all the commodities to be had there and a useful calendar of "monsons" to be avoided, and succeeded by extensive "reports of the province of China."[41]

It is not only this framing and organization of materials, however, which eclipses Africa's importance to the evolution of a global economy but the African narratives themselves—even those that trace England's attempts to access the promising Barbary trade. In the letter that documents the inauguration of that trade, James Alday at once excuses his absence from the first Barbary venture (claiming an attack of "the great sweate") and expresses his eager commitment to "the olde intermitted discoverie for Catia [Cathay]" (6:136–37), the East's "unspeakably rich" paradise (2:481). And if in the *Navigations* the East beckons on the other side of Barbary's borders, the Portuguese loom within them, complicating if not determining England's actions, much more, in some cases, than do the Moors. Interestingly, the very first record on Barbary which Hakluyt chooses to include points to Portugal's conquest of Ceuta—of "the Moores in the dominion of the king of Barbary"—in 1415, emphasizing the fact that "John the first king of Portugall" was "principally assisted" in this endeavor "by the helpe of the English Marchants, and Almaines" (6:121). The second (from a Portuguese chronicle), which describes the efforts of John II to keep the English out of Guinea in 1481, exposes the tenuousness of the Anglo-Portuguese alliance.[42] As the *Navigations* then jumps forward to England's contemporary negotiations with Barbary, the vexing presence of the Portuguese surfaces as their biggest impediment. The account of the second Barbary voyage (1552), for example, represents the trade between the English and the Moors with a notable nonchalance. The first port of call ("Zafia, or Asafi") appears as a reliable anchoring spot: there the English "put on land" the "marchandise" which was "to be conveied," and was conveyed, "by land to the citie of Marocco" (6:138). After "refresh[ing] [them]selves with victuals and water," they moved on to Santa Cruz, where they "discharged the rest of [their] goods" with equal aplomb, their "linnen and woollen cloth, corall, amber, Jet, and divers other things" all "well accepted by the Moores" (6:138). From what we see (and this is really all we see), the commercial traffic proceeded smoothly; and it stands in striking contrast to the sailing, which did not. On the way out, the English scuffled briefly with the French (who did not know that England and France were no longer at war); on the way back, they engaged in a more serious conflict with the Spanish, which, though it included casualties, reached a peaceful, if not equitable, resolution. Much more problematic was, it seems, an encounter with the Portuguese, who were themselves heading toward Barbary and who, when they spied the English, "shot off their great ordinance in [the English venturers'] hearing" (6:140). The English "escaped their handes" "by God and good providence," but the message of the encounter and the narrative is clear: "here by the way it is to bee understood that the Portugals were much offended with this our new trade into Barbarie, and both in our voiage the yeere before, as also in this they gave out in England by their marchants, that if they tooke us in those partes, they would use us as their mortall enemies, with great threates and menaces" (6:140). Adding insult to injury, the unmentioned irony of this episode is the fact that one of the English ships was actually "a Portugall Caravel bought of certaine Portugals in Newport in Wales" (6:138).[43]

The accounts of West African ventures are similarly overshadowed by a preoccupation with the "Portugals," who have already left their marks on the landscape before the English ever arrive.[44] In Richard Eden's record of a "second voyage" to Guinea in 1554, for example, the landmark Cape de las Barbas takes its bearings from the fact that "there use many Spaniardes and Portugals to trade for fishing" (6:157); and, in this case as in others, the place name itself betrays Iberian roots. During that venture too, the English also stopped to trade their cloth at the well-known "Castello de mina," headed at that time by the Portuguese captain "Don John" (6:160). A subsequent narrative on William Towerson's first venture down the Guinea coast (1555–56) suggests that, in negotiating with the "Negroes" (one who spoke Portuguese) in the "towne of Don John," the English had to undo the damaging precedent set by "the Portugals" who previously "took away a man from them," "spoiled their boates," and "destroyed" "halfe of their towne" (6:196). Similarly, the account of Towerson's second voyage (in 1557) pivots on the reiterated contrast between the Negroes' fear of "the Portugals" "who did much harme to their Countrey" and their embrace of the English, who promised to—and then did—"defend them from the Portugals" (6:218).

Even more telling is the earliest and most widely known of the Guinea narratives, Richard Eden's record of the first (1555) voyage, which circulated first as an appendix to his translation of Peter Martyr's *Decades of the new worlde* (1555) and which includes "A briefe description of Africke." Although that "description" purports to give Africa its due, the account's focal point nonetheless is the unavoidable, if also uncontainable, presence of the Portuguese, for whom Eden becomes a somewhat ambivalent advocate. In prefacing his account, Eden asserts that the English can only get to Africa, and so beyond it, through the Portuguese, the "Lordes of halfe the world," whose "voyages to Calicut" have opened up Africa's eastern shores (6:141, 144). While on the one hand he acknowledges that those who did the work of "discovering and conquering . . . such landes ought by good reason to have certaine privileges, preheminences, and tributes for the same," on the other he argues that it is "agaynst good reason and conscience," "agaynst the charitie that ought to be among Christian men, that such as invade the dominions of other [sic] should not permit other friendly to use the trade of marchandise in places neerer, or seldome frequented of them, whereby their trade is not hindered in such places" (6:141). Notably, here the Guineans drop out of the picture: it is the traffic of the Portuguese that the English mean to share, and Eden's strong, if not defensive, insistence that any obstruction to this "use" goes against good reason, conscience, and Christian charity suggests that the Portuguese have stood in England's way.

In detailing the voyage itself, Eden casts an accepting but wary eye on England's dependence on these rivals. His hero is the "expert Pilot" Antonio Pinteado who had been one of Portugal's top naval commanders but who had defected to England in 1552. Eden not only praises Pinteado as "a wise, discreet, and sober man" (6:145); he also contrasts him to the English co-captain, Thomas Wyndham, "a terrible Hydra" and "an unequal companion," "with vertues few or none adorned" (6:146–47). The conflict between them, in fact, defines and derails the venture, with Wyndham first flattering Pinteado and then denying him his due command. According to Eden, when the mariners reached their destination, the problem escalated to the point that Wyndham, not satisfied with the amount of gold his men had collected, overrode Pinteado's urging that, with intemperate weather approaching, the English should return home. Calling Pinteado a "whoreson Jew" and threatening to "cut off his eares and nail them to the maste," Wyndham demanded that the company press on to Benin (6:148). Pinteado acquiesced, but while he and a small party were on shore there, negotiating with the king ("a blacke Moore" who spoke Portuguese "which he had learned of a child"), Wyndham "brake open" all of Pinteado's "chestes, spoiled such provision of cold stilled waters and suckets as he had provided for his health, and left him nothing, neither of his instruments to saile by, nor yet of his apparell" (6:149, 151).[45] Wyndham died before Pinteado returned, but "certaine of the mariners and other officers" aboard continued to oppose and demean their Portuguese captain, "spit[ting] in his face, some calling him Jewe," holding him aboard ship "against his will, thrust among the boyes of the ship, not used like a man, nor yet like an honest boy" (6:151). His spirit and his honor battered, Pinteado himself then died, Eden writes, "for very pensivenesse & thought that stroke him to the heart" (6:151). While Pinteado is clearly the tragic hero here, the account ends with a crucial twist. For Eden presents Pinteado finally as "a man worthy to serve any prince, and most vilely used" not only by England but also, unconscionably, by Portugal (6:151). For support, Eden appends a number of documents exposing the treachery of the Portuguese at home, who "intended to slay [Pinteado], if time and place might have served their wicked intent" (6:154). Hence, if a Portuguese pilot in the hand is worth two Englishmen in the bush, "the Portugals his countrey men" are decidedly not (6:154).

What the West Africans are worth is surprisingly unclear. For even within accounts ostensibly centered on African ventures, the most extended descriptions of Africa's lands and peoples appear as narrative digressions, based not on the explorations at hand but on secondary, largely textual evidence. Eden's "briefe desciption of Afrike," which was obviously written before the English had ventured much down the coast, provides little more than a categorical outline—in circuitously random order—of Africa's parts "knowen in old time" (6:144). In it, Eden distinguishes North Africa ("Africa the lesse") from the south, emphasizes Barbarie as the "best" of the northern domains, separates the Moors there, all of "the sect of Mahomet," from the inhabitants of Guinea, themselves "pure Gentiles, and idolatrous, without profession of any religion, or other knowledge of God, then by the law of nature" (6:143–44). But, as these examples attest, his differentiations are general to an extreme. And if the fact that he, like others before him, locates "the great and mighty Emperour and Christian king Prester John" in eastern Africa does not strain his credibility, his admission that this information is "well knowen to the Portugales" suggests the tenuousness of his authority, as well as, again, the omnipresence of the Portuguese (6:144).

Similarly, in his account of the second Guinea voyage, Eden interrupts the report of "the voyage, as it was described by the . . . Pilot," to "speake somewhat of the countrey and people, and of such things as are brought from thence" (6:163), producing what critics have often cited in defining the terms of early modern England's view of Africa. Yet here too fiction clashes with fact, myths with realities, the textual with the actual. In prefacing the venture, Eden emphasizes the authority of his eyewitness, remarking that the pilot was "one of the chiefe in this voyage" and that what he saw was "so well observed" (6:154–55). When Eden then breaks in with his own description, he resurrects some of the most exotic—probably already cliched—myths and figures commonly ascribed to Africa in classical texts (and prominently invoked in Othello's travel history): among them, the Guineans "in old time called Æthiopes and Nigritae, which we now call Moores, Moorens, or Negroes, a people of beastly living, without a God, lawe, religion, or common wealth, and so scorched and vexed with the heat of the sunne, that in many places they curse it when it riseth"; the Troglodytica, who dwell in caves, eat snake meat, and "have no speech, but rather a grinning and chattering"; the Anthropophagi, who "are accustomed to eat mans flesh"; the Blemines, who have "their eyes and mouth in their breast"; and the Satyrs, "which have nothing of men but onely shape," along with Prester John, who seems in this context relatively real (6:167–70). If the marvelousness of these figures does not give their veracity away, Eden admits that much of his knowledge, which "is to be understood," comes from someone or somewhere else—an anonymous "they" or classical texts written (and he stresses written) by Pliny, Solinus, Gemma Phrysius, and others (6:167). In this, the exotic Africans are much like America's "Savages," who, as Karen Kupperman has argued, are at their "cultureless" savage worst in accounts by armchair, and not actual, travelers.[46] Even so, within accounts of New World travels, there is rarely such a gap between details of the venture and depictions of the indigenous people.[47] In Eden, the myths not only supplement but also displace the "real" natives, as if knowledge of the West Africans is ultimately tangential to England's exploits.[48]

Even in accounts where English forays into West Africa are embedded within New World enterprises as a pit-and-provisions stop for the way west, representations of the natives appear ancillary, although eventually, as slaves, these "Negroes" would become central to England's colonial "success." England's principal competitor in the New World was, of course, Spain, and the group of narratives on the West is as preoccupied with the Spanish as the group on the South and Southeast is with the Turks and Portuguese. The *Navigations* contains an especially large number of records on John Hawkins's experimental slaving ventures, including three reports on his third expedition (of 1567–68), one written by Hawkins himself, and one each by Miles Philips and Job Hortop, two men who were "set on land by sir John Hawkins in 1568 in the bay of Mexico" and who then lived in captivity under the Spanish.[49] These narratives do describe the forceful "taking" of "Negroes," quite often maneuvered around conflicts with the Portuguese. But even in these accounts, which James Williamson has taken to be "propaganda, written with an eye to English relations with Spain and Portugal," the focus is on the New World endpoint, where Negroes seem unusually like Indians and the status of both obscured by narrative scrutiny of the Spanish.[50] Miles Philips, for example, centers on the unhappy afterlife of Hawkins's final expedition, when he, Job Hortop, and others were forced "to serve as slaves to sundry gentlemen Spaniards" (9:416). Philips does draw attention to the Negro slaves who were also serving under the Spanish, distinguishing their enslavement from the servitude of the Indians: the Spaniards, he declares, "are all of them attended and served by Indians weekely, and by Negroes which be their slaves during their life" (9:422–23). These distinctions fall by the wayside, however, as he emphasizes rather the "cruell handling" and "persecution" effected by the Spanish and the Spanish Inquisition, his main preoccupation. Specifically, he presses "Indians and Negroes" into a single group of subjects, kept "in such subjection and servitude" and abused by such "horrible crueltics" that they alike "doe daily lie in waite to practise their deliverance out of that thraldome and bondage, that the Spaniardes doe keepe them in" (9:423, 430). And in describing his own appointment as "overseer" to a group of "Negroes and Indians" working in the mines, he overlooks the differences between them to stress the difference between the English and the Spanish, explaining that while the Indians and Negroes would, if they could, flee the Spanish, they work overtime for the English because of "our well using & intreating of them" (9:423). It is the Spanish who become the distinctive bogeymen, and as they do, Negroes "which be slaves during their life" are merged with Indians who serve "weekely." Philips's narrative is as long as it is ideologically complex, but what is particularly striking here is that even in an account which involves African slaving, not only is the place of African subjects neither stable nor distinctive; it is also not (yet) central.

There was another available record of the venture, which Hakluyt likely knew but did not include—an account probably written by one of Hawkins's officers and containing at least four times as much description of the activity in Guinea as the other three accounts combined.[51] In it, the Guinea natives exhibit a particularly vicious cannibalism, which might "justify" their capture and enslavement. Not only are they accused of eating "[*very barbarously each*] other"; the narrator also reports that

among these negros there is a greate [*feast whenever*] the soldiers have taken any of them, eve[n *one man*. They] binde him to a stake and make a fyre hard [by and rou]nd abowt it, and the miserable creature [*while he is yet*] alive they will with their knives cutt of his . . . laces and roste it, eating his owne fleshe by p[*urpose* before h]is eyes, a terrible kinde of death. The others [in other places] doe not thus eate them, but kill them owte of h[and at the] first and cutt them of by the loynes and eat the[ir flesh as] we wolde befe or mutton, the which oure owne menne [did witness] as hereafter I will declare.[52]

We cannot be sure, of course, why Hakluyt chose the other documents over this. The account details a fight that broke out during the expedition, between the likely author, one of Hawkins's officers, and a third officer, whom Hawkins almost then put to death, and Hakluyt may have been hesitant to expose this internal violence.[53] Still, though we can only speculate, it is possible, and significant, that the imperialistically minded Hakluyt may have bypassed an ideological opportunity to produce the subjects targeted for slavery in their darkest light, choosing rather to expose the "horrible cruelities" of the Spanish who seem to matter more.

To be sure, within these New World records (more than in the African narratives in the section on the South and Southeast), specters of disease and blackness darken the Guinea coast. But these figures work as contrast to make the New World seem a comparatively habitable and desirable place. We know, of course, that disease was a real concern for the venturers traveling to Africa as well as to the Americas, where such "African" diseases as malaria and yellow fever would be transported and would threaten England's efforts to maintain a New World labor force.[54] In the accounts where Guinea is the destination (and not the pit stop), disease does figure; but it is Africa's heat, rather than its contagion, that appears to be the biggest health risk. Indeed, part of what makes Wyndham impatient with Pinteado's extended stay in Benin is that the men waiting on shore were dying "sometimes three & sometimes 4 or 5 in a day" (6:150). According to Eden, the English died because they, "partly having no rule of themselves, but eating without measure of the fruits of the countrey, and drinking the wine of the Palme trees, . . . and in such extreme heate running continually into the water, *not used before* to such sudden and vehement alterations (then the which nothing is more dangerous) were thereby brought into swellings and agues" (6:150; emphasis added). Here, as elsewhere, the problem is not inherent to the place, but to the English outsiders, who have not acclimated to Africa's heat.

The New World narratives, in contrast, associate West Africa with disease, but in a way that effectively disinfects the New World landscape.[55] Consider, for example, the account of Anthony Shirley's ill-fated voyage of

1596. According to that record, disaster and disease struck almost the moment the English reached Cape Verde: there, their "General fell exceeding sicke" "most unfortunately," while the men, in seeking water, "had many skirmishes with the barbarous Negros" (10:267). With what sounds ominously like his last breath, Shirley advocated moving on, not because he feared the Negros but because, "finding the cost of Guynea most tempestuous, hee saw in reason that the bay of Æthiopia would be [their] utter overthrow, and infect [the company] all to death" (10:268). After "departing from [that] contagious filthy place," the English went only as far as São Tomé (10:268). Again they "were enforced to beare up & take some other course," the narrator explains, because the "men fell sicke, and the coast was contagious alwayes raging & tempestuous"; as well, "the water falling from the heavens did stinke, and did in 6 hours turne into maggots where it fell" (10:268). Once the party leave West Africa and head for the West Indies, however, their troubles seem to be over. Admittedly, a stay on the island of "Fuego" "yeelded [them] nothing but miserable infection" (10:271); and while they were en route to Dominica, everyone on board "fell generally downe" with a "disease . . . so vile that men grew lothsome unto themselves, franticke and desperately raving" (10:272). Yet the account nonetheless codes the turn to the west as a trajectory from extraordinary sickness to extraordinary health. Not only did Shirley "[begin] to recover strength" almost the moment the ships "were departed from this vile coast of Guyny" (10:269). As well, when the English landed "at Dominica," "with all our men sicke and feeble," the narrator reports, "wee found there two hote bathes, wherein our weake men washing themselves were greatly comforted: and the Indians of this place used us with great kindnesse, so that we were all perfectly well before we departed from this place" (10:272). In Jamaica too, the narrator adds, the company found unparalleled fertility and healthfulness, with no other stop in the Indies proving "a more pleasant and holsome place" (10:274). Where Africa brings disease, the New World brings the cure—ironically, even in Dominica, "an Island of the Canybals" (10:25). The comparison, it seems, reveals and conceals all.

Notably too, the blackness that would become Africa's distinctive trademark takes it most explicit definition in the New World accounts—in what has become an important signpost for scholarship on race, George Best's "true discourse" on the search for the Northwest Passage (and ultimately for Cathay).[56] Just as the emphasis on West Africa's contagion serves to disinfect the New World's terrains, so does Best's inscription of blackness work to whiten the West. In explaining why Africans are black, Best recounts the story of Noah's (here Noe's) "wicked sonne Cham," who "used company with his wife" on the Ark, against his father's orders, and whose offspring were therefore cursed with blackness (7:264).[57] Best concludes "that the cause of the Ethiopians blacknesse is the curse and naturall infection of blood, and not the distemperature of the Climate" (7:264). Yet his purpose is to show that blackness is *not* caused by the climate of "the middle Zone," which covers both these cursed inhabitants and "our people" of the the West, the "Meta Incognita," "of whom and for whom this discourse is taken in hande" (7:262). Best enforces the same point with a related story, which has also been pivotal to critical treatments of race and gender, of "an Ethiopian as blacke as a cole brought into England, who taking a faire English woman to wife, begat a sonne in all respects as blacke as the father was, although England were his native countrey" (7:262).[58] As he himself asserts, this example speaks to "a more fresh example, [of] our people of Meta Incognita," who are colored in ways that climate cannot explain (7:262), and it counters the false impression, created by "some there be that thinke" and "others [who] againe imagine," that in the New World the white-skinned English might turn black (7:260–61). Best's use of these stories does not undo their codification of blackness as the thing that is—or should be—not, not at least in the West. But what is nevertheless significant, if not also surprising, here is that the representational priority, which colors Africa's features, is first and foremost the West.

Hakluyt's representation of the New World "remained resolutely the history of transitory voyages, traffics, and discoveries, not of permanent plantations, colonies, and empire," as Armitage has argued, themselves initially catalyzed by the search for the Northwest Passage to Cathay.[59] Still, their story is unified in the *Navigations* by an overriding theme of discovery and acquisition, by a sense that the parts all contribute to a new world whole upon which England could and should leave its mark—even if neither Hakluyt nor England had a clear idea of quite what that mark would be. From the very first document onward, "possession," which Stephen Greenblatt has distinguished as a New World trope, is literally everywhere: from Henry VII's "letters patents" to John Cabot and sons, licensing them to "subdue, occupy and possesse all . . . townes, cities, castles and isles of them found" (7:143); to Hakluyt's "Notes" to the Frobisher company, directing them to choose a "seat" where they "may possesse alwayes sweete water, wood, seacoles or turfe, with fish, flesh, graine, fruites, herbes and rootes" and not to worry about "possessing of mines of golde, of silver, copper, quicksilver, or of any such precious

thing" which may be "supplyed from some other place by sea" (7:244–45); to
Queen Elizabeth's letters patent to Ralegh, licensing him to "discover, search,
finde out, and view such remote, heathen and barbarous lands, countreis, and
territories, not actually possessed of any Christian prince" (8:290) and to "subdue," "possess," and colonize them (8:291); to Ralegh's earnest fantasy, expressed in his "discoverie of . . . Guiana," that "whatsoever prince shall
possesse it [Guiana], that Prince shall be Lord of more golde, and of a more
beautifull Empire, and of more Cities and people, then either the King of
Spain, or the great Turke" (10:355).[60] Take us to whatever part of the mainland
or islands they will, the narratives give England an urgently reiterable, and
distinctively American, mission: to discover and claim.

To view the accounts of Barbary and Guinea next to these New World
stories is to notice how comparatively unfocused and undirected Hakluyt's
representation of Africa is—how open-ended the place and how uncertain the
prospects of this inconsistently "dark continent" even in the face of New
World ventures that would determine and overdetermine England's future
there. Clearly, within the *Navigations*, Africa is neither unified nor commod-
ified for material or ideological consumption; rather its landscapes appear in
the margins of the imperialist drive through which Hakluyt would construct
a globally engaged and empowered England. It may well be the nature and
ease of negotiations with the English that, in places, determines whether
Moors figure synecdochally as "cruel hands" holding captive English in "miserable servitude," or as "emperors" and "kings" treating their English trading
partners with "great honour and speciall countenance" (6:293, 294). It may
well be that blackness here codifies "Negroes" as accursed. But if these representational strategies betray the imperialist vision that underlies and pervades
the collection, they, along with the other matter of Africa, inhabit only the
peripheries of that vision, whose focus is decidedly elsewhere—on the Portuguese, Turks, and Spanish and the enticing prospects to the east and west.

If we turn back to the stage, to *Titus* and its story of Roman conquest,
with Africa's displacement within England's imperialist history in mind, we
may be better able to understand the Moor's otherwise surprising but signal
invisibility. *Titus* comes at imperialist politics through a classical past that England sometimes embraced as its own. But if Shakespeare's dramatic fiction
stands at a distance from contemporary developments, from the "navigations
and discoveries" that Hakluyt was promoting as a cornerstone of an imperial
English nation, its interest in the consequences of conquest do not. Though
Hakluyt partitions the world into discrete, differently valued domains, press-

CHAPTER THREE

"Incorporate in Rome"

Titus Andronicus and the Consequence of Conquest

AT THE END of *Titus Andronicus* (1593–94), after most members of the ruling Roman and Gothic families have been mutilated, killed, or eaten, a Roman calls for the state to "give sentence" on the Moor Aaron, an "execrable wretch / That hath been breeder of these dire events" (5.3.176–77). Lucius, now the head of state, takes the lead, ordering:

> Set him breast-deep in earth and famish him;
> There let him stand and rave and cry for food.
> If anyone relieves or pities him,
> For the offense he dies. This is our doom;
> Some stay to see him fastened in the earth. (5.3.178–82)

This final sentence accentuates the Moor's depravity. In contrast to the honored Andronici, whose ceremonial interment in the family tomb opens the play, Aaron is "fastened in the earth" as a subject unworthy of food, pity, and the ultimate sign of honor and respect in this play, due burial.[1]

Here, then, is the apparent institution of an absolute cultural discrimination, a state-authorized excoriation of the Moor as Other—*the* Other to outdo and undo all others. Lucius will insist that the body of the "ravenous" and "beastly" Gothic queen, Tamora, be "throw[n] forth to beasts and birds to prey," she like Aaron committed to the wild, deprived of the "funeral rite," "mourning weed," and "mournful bell" that seem to mark civilized society (5.3.194–98).

Still, the anticipated torture of the Moor promises to be physically more extreme, visually more sustained, and ideologically more potent. It is, after all, the Romans' second attempt to impose on Aaron "some direful slaughtering death / As punishment for his most wicked life" (5.3.143–44). Lucius has already ordered a hanging. But when Aaron boasts of having happily executed a series of "heinous deeds" (5.1.123), Lucius commands his men to "bring down the devil, for he must not die / So sweet a death as hanging presently" (5.1.145–46). While Tamora is literally eating her poisonous sons, the Romans hold Aaron without "sustenance" until he can testify against her (5.3.6). And when her death obviates the need for his testimony, Lucius constructs a doom that will turn the Moor's voice and body into a dehumanizing public spectacle—burying him alive, so that he will "rave and cry for food" while "some" "stay to see." Part of Lucius's efforts to rebuild the walls of Rome and Romanness, to "heal Rome's harms and wipe away her woe" (5.3.148), this radical sentence serves to distance Aaron from both the Romans and the Goths, to codify him ineradicably as a "barbarous Moor," a "ravenous tiger," an "accursed devil," an "inhuman dog," and an "unhallowed slave" (5.3.4–5, 14).

By this point in the play, the Moor's characterization seems to have fallen into stereotype.[2] In front of his Roman captors, Aaron exaggerates his villainy to a point that strains the credibility of his statements and his characterization. He not only lays claim to a "thousand dreadful things" that he has done but also augments his criminal record with myriad things he regrets not doing (5.1.141). He "curse[s] the day," which he counts as rare, "wherein [he] did not some notorious ill, / As kill a man or else devise his death, / Ravish a maid or plot the way to do it, / Accuse some innocent and forswear [himself]," and so on and on and on (5.1.125–30). His only regret is that he "cannot do ten thousand more" notorious ills (5.1.144) as well as "ten thousand worse" (5.3.186). Aaron's confessional set piece points obviously back to Marlowe, as scholars have noted: to the self-incrimination of Barabas, the Jew of Malta, who markets himself similarly through a panoply of false crimes, and of his Turkish slave, Ithamore, who applauds and mimics them.[3] *Titus* points obviously back, that is, to a play (*The Jew of Malta*), a playwright, and a passage which capitalize self-consciously on the production and performance of stereotypes. Moreover, *Titus*'s coding of the Moor as a subject deserving a fate worse than death also directly invokes *Alcazar*'s: hanging seems too "sweet a death" for Aaron just as drowning seems "too good for such a damnèd wretch" as Muly Mahamet (*Alcazar* 5.1.246). Increasingly, scholars and editors are tending to ascribe at least the first act of *Titus* to Peele.[4] And clearly, whether under

Peele's hand or influence, Aaron's characterization resembles Muly's in appearing unusually stylized, potentially retrograde, historically out of fashion, and dramatically out of date, especially at the play's end. These precedents in turn anticipate *Lust's Dominion*, where Eleazar's "perfect villainy" will result in a state-sanctioned act of racially based discrimination.[5] Stuffed, tortured, or appropriated as the prompt for the expulsion of a race, Muly Mahamet, Aaron, and Eleazar become the durable signposts of an excessive villainy that requires and justifies extraordinary gestures of public retaliation.

But if *Titus Andronicus* ends with an inscription which seems to insist that the Moor be written permanently out of mainstream culture and into a detachable, indictable type, that is not where the play begins. Already critics have understood that Aaron's appearance within Rome disturbs the assumption of cultural purity, clarity, and "civility" of the Roman—and by extension, English—state. The specter of barbarism emerges immediately within the political chaos of the opening scenes, raising the question, in Ian Smith's words, of "who is, really, the barbarian here?"[6] For Smith and others who have come at the issue from the angles of language, race, and culture, the Moor gives the lie away, signaling the pervasive presence of the "alien within," Rome's "guilty secret."[7] In such readings Aaron, the Moor in Rome, represents what Michael Neill sees as Roderigo's take on Othello, the Moor of Venice: "a principle of wild disorder lodged in the very heart of metropolitan civilization."[8] If Rome is to remain the seat of culture, to preserve the illusion of its sanctity as a civilized state, it must cordon off all signs of internal violation and eliminate the "detritus" that is both its other and its own.[9] Conveniently, but not coincidentally, the Moor's distinctive blackness supplies a sinister touchstone—both as a thing in itself, which, if Neill and others are right, was becoming England's "most important criterion for defining otherness," as well as a thing that could invade Roman and Gothic bloodlines, producing a miscegenous mess.[10] So while the Gothic Tamora has, as it were, her day in court, Aaron the Moor provides the more visible and viable subject for strategic derogation.

Or does he? The problem with reading Aaron as the sign that Rome (or England) is itself a "wilderness of tigers" (3.1.54) is that we start therefore with the assumption that Aaron is necessarily out of place in Rome. We start with a Rome and an England anxious about the penetration of cultural borders and populations, unused to the consequences of conquest, and uncomfortable with the prospect of cultural intermixing and exchange—a Rome and an England that are, in current terms, metropolitan more than they are cosmopolitan. We start with a Moor whose barbarous behavior, though it may reflect the inherent violence and defining chaos of Rome, is signally different, enough that he can serve as an open dumping ground for displaced and disturbing disorders. His menacing presence may expose the darker side of Rome and, by extension, England. Still, as the outsider within, he is always part of the problem, a symptom as much as a sign of catastrophic cultural breakdown.

But suppose we begin where *Alcazar* ends—not just with the stuffed and stymied Muly Mahamet, but with the triumphant Muly Seth and his strategic embrace of the defeated Christian king of Portugal. Suppose, that is, we begin with a stage and a society where Moors stand beside Europeans, Englishmen, and Turks, and against each other, unscripted partners in a volatile history of conquest and consent. Shakespeare will provide glimpses of that kind of environment not only in *Othello*, where Othello is set to defend the Venetians against the Turks, but also in *The Tempest* (1611), where the Neopolitan Claribel weds the King of Tunis.[11] Although Muly Mahamet creates and fulfills unseemly expectations of "the Moor" in *Alcazar*'s space of "all the world," his self-defeating solipsism is challenged by the pressures of a political scene where interaction, alliance, and exchange are key to survival. If this is one of the dramatic starting points of *Titus*'s representation of the Moor, then Aaron's story is complexly more than the sum of Muly's part. And what is especially surprising, dramatically risky, and crucial in *Titus* is not that an attempt to codify and discriminate against the Moor happens, along with the expected tragic recognition, *too late*; what is remarkable is that it happens *at all*.

I want to argue that the association of the Moor with the alien is not what is given here, but what must be made—and made against the odds of a society that takes its very definition from conquest and so depends, even thrives, on the cultural intermixing that is the predictable result. Crisis occurs not because Rome is or becomes unbounded, its assumed sanctity undone by the presence or exposure of the alien within. Crisis occurs because at an arbitrary moment in history Rome attempts to lay down the law and postulate an idea and ideal of cultural purity as crucial to its core. That the ideal is acted out on and over the body of one embedded Moor is neither inevitable nor even entirely plausible within the dramatic fiction; from where we sit in the theater, that choice is at least partly, provocatively ironic.

*   *   *

In the opening scene of *Titus*, Titus Andronicus enters fresh from war, "re-salute[s] his country with his tears" of "true joy," and celebrates both his newest victory over the Goths and his triumphant "return to Rome" (1.1.78–79). The captain who prepares the stage for this grand entrance introduces the return-ing hero as "Rome's best champion" and "patron of virtue," invariably "success-ful in the battles that he fights" and now responsible for having "circumscribed with his sword / And brought to yoke the enemies of Rome" (1.1.68–72). Titus himself further elides his story with Rome's: though saddled with the "poor re-mains" of "five-and-twenty valiant sons" ("half of the number," he is careful to point out, "that King Priam had"), he "hail[s]" Rome as "victorious," projects his "mourning weeds" onto Rome, and invokes the "defender of this Capitol"— implicitly Jupiter—in an apostrophe that could as well point to himself (1.1.73, 80, 82–84).[12] Embedded within these glorifications is the assumption not only of Rome's superiority over the Goths but also of its purity and permanence as a clearly bounded state, one which has claim on the ur-past of Troy.[13] Although Titus's victory has meant returning with both Gothic prisoners and a Moor, for him there is only one "culture" and it is Rome's.[14]

Critics have endorsed Titus's presumptions as Rome's starting ideal, how-ever it may be punctured by the all too telling presence of a Moorish "alien within."[15] Yet as the first act traces the incorporation of the Goths and the Moor into Roman society, it exposes that ideal as Titus's own atavistic fantasy, one clearly unsuited to the politics and cultures of conquest. One of the first signs of Rome's own breakdown comes when Lucius demands that "the proudest prisoner of the Goths," Alarbus, be sacrificed, his limbs "hew[ed]" (1.1.99–100). The Gothic queen declares the sacrifice "cruel, irreligious piety," her son Chiron insisting as well that Scythia (the origin of Marlowe's contro-versial conqueror, Tamburlaine) was "never . . . half so barbarous" as Rome (1.1.133, 134)—both charges, which critics have taken up, challenging Rome's vaunted virtue. Importantly too, however, in lamenting Alarbus's fate, his brother Demetrius calls for "sharp revenge" while simultaneously recalling the glory days "when Goths were Goths" (1.1.140, 143). As the play thus raises the possibility that something may be rotten in the city-state of Rome, it also un-dercuts the discriminatory fantasy of cultural purity that his revenge and Titus's Rome are built on, coding as dangerously reactionary the inscription of a world where Romans are Romans, Goths are Goths—and, we might add, Moors are Moors. The representation of Aaron is embedded within this cri-tique, not as its vehicle but as its evidence, a realized subject whose inevitable presence within Rome requires accommodation. To see him for what he is here, the opening act suggests, we must first see Rome for what it is: a place where the crossing of cultures is not the exception but the rule.

Even before the sacrifice, Titus's valorization of all things Roman appears curiously strained by the situation which is its prompt. His triumphant entrance into Rome coincides purposefully with an internal political crisis, the uneasy selection of a Roman emperor, for which he provides the perfect solution. While Saturninus implores the "noble patricians" to support his "successive title" of "first-born son" of the last emperor (1.1.1, 4–5), his younger brother, Bassianus, turns instead to the people, his "friends, followers, [and] favourers of [his] right," urging them to "fight for freedom" and endorse "pure election," which he hopes, of course, to win (1.1.9, 16–17). Before anything can be resolved, Marcus enters with a crown and circumvents the conflict with the announcement that "the people of Rome," "have by common voice / In election for the Roman empery / Chosen Andronicus" and that Titus "by the senate is accited home / From weary wars against the barbarous Goths" (1.1.20–23, 27–28). Being at once the "noble" Titus's brother (1.1.53) and a tribune, "a special party" who "stand[s]" for "the people," Marcus is usefully poised between the two factions that Saturninus and Bassianus have set at odds, and, he makes clear, his resolution comes with the support of both the "common voice" and the senate (1.1.20–21). Accordingly, the election of "the good Andronicus" seems to resolve all tensions (1.1.40), prompting both Saturninus and Bassianus to dismiss their claims, disband their supporters, and at least profess a loyalty to the new state.[16]

The circumstances surrounding Titus's recall, however, raise serious questions about the status of Rome's war with the Goths and the integrity both of the Roman triumph and of the exaltations that adorn it. For despite all the pomp and circumstance, there is no guarantee that the war is actually over. Titus, after all, has been "accited home" by the senate, explicitly because he won the *election*, not the war. It could be little more than a happy coincidence that he is able to return to Rome "laden with honour's spoils" (1.1.39). Even Titus does not fully suppress the contingency of the victory, admitting that the Goths "have given me leave to sheathe my sword" (1.1.89).[17] To be sure, when Marcus justifies the outcome of the election, he cites Titus's "many good and great deserts to Rome" (1.1.24) and, echoing the captain, singles out the fact that Titus has "yoked a nation"—the Gothic nation—"strong" (1.1.30). But Marcus's rendering of the military backstory leading to this politically welcome and unusually well-timed climax leaves significant room for doubt. For ten years, Marcus testifies, Titus has been fighting for "this cause of

Rome," and, in fact, *five times* he hath returned / Bleeding to Rome, bearing his valiant sons / In coffins from the field" (1.1.32–35; emphasis added). That Titus has returned from the war four (or five) times before, doing exactly what he is doing now, can only make us wonder whether what we witness is another in a continuous series of false stops or, once and for all, the real thing.[18] At the end of the play, Lucius will ally himself with an army of Goths, and although the resulting siege is under his command, we are left nonetheless with an instance of Goths once again advancing against a Roman regime.

If we turn to history in an attempt to nail Titus's victory down, to locate his war with the Goths in time, and to verify or refute his claims to closure, we will find an open end. Indeed, among Shakespeare's Roman plays, *Titus* is anomalous not only because, within the dramatic fiction, the lopping of limbs risks becoming a horrifying quotidian gesture; outside the script, there seems to be no single source behind its representation of the past.[19] To date critics have been able only to piece together that history from a set of chronologically, generically, and geographically disparate texts—prominent among them an English translation of Herodian's *De imperatorum Romanorum*, entitled *The History of Herodian* (ca. 1550); a chronicle "conteyning the lives of tenne Emperours of Rome" (1577), translated from Antonio de Guevara's *Decada* but probably drawn as well from *Herodian*; and a chapbook, *The History of Titus Andronicus, The Renowned Roman General*, translated from Italian and published between 1736 and 1764, its materials possibly circulating early enough to reach Shakespeare.[20] These records suggest notably different chronologies. Where the chapbook has prompted scholars to elide *Titus's* Saturninus with the emperor Theodosius, who ruled "during the last years of the Empire, just before one of the early Gothic invasions in 410 A.D.," Herodian points rather to the tortuous period between 180–238 A.D., when Rome was controlled and internally fractured by "an Afro-Asiatic dynasty" and a brutal ruler Bassianus.[21]

It may well be that we misread the play's agenda in searching for a definitive text or history that would situate the dramatic action in time and establish, from the outside, the legitimacy of Titus's assumed triumph.[22] Throughout, *Titus* repeatedly jars its spectators into viewing the past through competing textual frames, mingling myth and allegory with classical history, for example, and, through the imaginative texts, realizing the carnage that the political story glamorizes as appropriate to war. Indeed, when fictional stories such as Ovid's tale of Philomel become fleshed out in actors' bodies, textual determinacy translates theatrically as terror. In any case, whether the play evades or draws eclectically on one or more potential sources, it effectively dislocates its story in time and underscores the uncertainty of any given historical markers. Congruently, the histories it seems to engage tell an open story, raising the possibility that Rome's conquest of the Goths is no more a fait accompli than was George Bush's invasion of Iraq when he declared his "mission accomplished" in May of 2003. The chronicle reports that Titus "was styled the deliverer of his country" after a "signal victory" in which he killed the Gothic emperor and captured the Gothic queen, but also acknowledges that "those barbarous people still increas[ed] in their numbers" and, implicitly, in their aggression against the Romans.[23] It was, in fact, to secure the unstable "peace" that the Roman emperor decided to marry the enemy queen.[24] In Herodian too, Rome appears constantly under siege by "barbarian" invaders—who are also, as abstractly, termed "Goths."[25]

Whether we look within the text or outside it, then, when Titus returns for the fifth or sixth time, "bleeding to Rome," "bearing" and burying "his valiant sons," and "resaluting his country with his tears," his attempt to glorify the moment edges on emptiness—as does his production of a purely bounded Rome. In his pomposity, Titus seems much like the easily critiqued Othello that Iago will at first construct and condemn—a warrior who "lov[es] his own pride and purposes," "evades" the realities of the moment "with a bombast circumstance," and is "horribly stuffed with epithets of war" (*Oth.* 1.1.11–13). Moreover, Titus's exuberant patriotism is tarnished by a bizarre political necrophilia that renders his politics, and his promotion of a purely Roman Rome, questionably eccentric.[26] In an odd move that blurs triumph into obsequy, Titus—who groups his surviving and deceased sons together as "poor remains, alive and dead" (1.1.84)—turns the tomb, the "sweet cell of virtue and nobility" and "sacred receptacle of [his] joys," into the preeminent measure of Roman honor and value (1.1.95–96). That is, instead of valorizing the act of conquest, he memorializes its losses, celebrating the tomb as the ideologic repository of an unchangeable and impenetrable Rome, leaving his sons, "Rome's readiest champions," to rest there immutably "in peace and honour" (1.1.153–54).

Even if "proper burial" "provides the sign of [Roman] culture," against which the torture of Aaron gets "counterposed" as deviant, the play codes Titus's macabre dance of death as perversely and problematically his—not Rome's.[27] The Andronici who applaud his return look beyond the tomb to other sites of meaning and action. Reading the tomb as an "earthly prison," Lucius, for one, insists that proper burial is not enough and that the ritual sacrifice of an enemy Goth is necessary to appease the "shadows" and prevent disturbing "prodigies on earth" (1.1.102–4). Lavinia pays due "tributary tears" to her "brethren's obsequies," but her own ceremonial theatrics emphasize life over death, triumph over mourning, the future over the past (1.1.162–63). Kneeling at Titus's feet with "tears of joy" and exhorting him to "live Lord Titus long," "live in fame!," she asks that he bless her with his "victorious hand, / Whose fortunes Rome's best citizens applaud" (1.1.164, 160–61, 166–67). In response and contrast, Titus, true to form, stresses his mortality, his "age and feebleness," and enjoins her to "outlive thy father's days / And fame's eternal date, for virtue's praise" (1.1.191, 170–71). Even Marcus, who finds "safer triumph in this funeral pomp" than in the wars, immediately turns attention to the urgent matter of rule, imploring Titus to "help set a head on headless Rome" (1.1.179, 189).

Glaringly here, in fact, Titus's attempts to immortalize an ideal Rome come at a significant political cost, limiting his comprehension and apprehension of the present, his ability to head a headless, or multiheaded, state. For in so fetishizing the tomb, Titus neither acknowledges nor negotiates the cultural complexity that his own acts of conquest have created.[28] On the stage, that complexity is obvious: standing with the Romans, in living, possibly startling color, are the ultrawhite Goths and the "raven-coloured" Moor (2.2.83), prisoners of war who are now, necessarily, Rome's subjects.[29] Instead of scripting his triumph over their distinctive bodies, the self over the necessary Other, as new historicism would dictate that he should, or in some less divisive way acknowledging and installing their presence, Titus effectively looks the other way—at the corpses of his sons.[30] In fixating on their funeral rites, he immortalizes a conquest and conqueror quite apart from the conquered, displaying the Roman victory as if it were spontaneously generated exclusively from the matter of a sui generis Rome. Although Lucius will ask for the sacrifice of a Gothic prince, prior to that point Titus explicitly references the enemy Goths only when he credits them with giving him "leave to sheathe [his] sword," and he does not refer to the Moor at all.

Moreover, when Lucius's demand for a sacrificial Goth forces Titus to address the fates of Rome's new captives, he does so in self-reflexive terms, making no allowances and no space for alternatives to his monolithic "Roman" view. In selecting the victim, he automatically follows the code of primogeniture which he will valorize when he appoints the next Roman emperor and which, in that case, overrides the will of his people: his choice of Saturninus, the "first-born son that was the last / That wore the imperial diadem" (1.1.5–6), gives precedence to inherited Roman rights, to the emperor "that held [the rule] last" and, according to Titus, held it "upright" (1.1.202–3).[31] In the case of the sacrifice, Titus's adherence to primogeniture absolutely closes out Tamora's voice. Still a queen, the Goth reaches out to the "Roman brethen" as a mother whose "passion for her son" should translate across cultures, urging the "gracious conqueror" to understand her plight through his and imploring: "if thy sons were ever dear to thee, / O, think my son to be as dear to me" (1.1.107, 109–11).[32] She further underlines the political advantage Titus has already achieved through the display of captive Goths. "Sufficeth not that we are brought to Rome," she asks, "To beautify thy triumphs, and return / Captive to thee and to thy Roman yoke?" (1.1.111–14). Whether we take her words as devious or sincere and the sacrifice as "cruel" or pious, Titus's response shows how immovably entrenched he is in the Rome of his own making.[33] First, he refocuses the gaze on his sons' bodies, the "brethren whom your Goths beheld / *Alive and dead*," using the same language he has used before to exalt his offspring (1.1.125–26; emphasis added). For them, Alarbus must die; there is no space for negotiation. And after the deed has been done, though Tamora and her sons express their outrage openly, Titus averts his gaze from these warnings of impending disaster, retreats to the obsequies he cherishes, and idealizes the impenetrable safety of the tomb, emphasizing how "secure" it is "from worldly chances and mishaps" (1.1.155): "Here lurks no treason," he asserts, "here no envy swells, / Here grow no damned drugs, here are no storms, / No noise, but silence and eternal sleep" (1.1.156–59). In thus bounding off the tomb, Titus simultaneously bounds himself off from "worldly chances and mishaps," recognizing only their most abstract embodiments (storms, noise, treason, envy) and ignoring the more pressing and apparent threats of the Goths.

Within these opening ceremonies, the only space Titus makes for the Goths and Moor is one that, instead of accommodating their domestic position, reaffirms his. Ceding the place of emperor to Saturninus, he asks for "a staff of honour for mine age, / But not a sceptre to control the world" (1.1.201–2). When Saturninus, in turn and in gratitude, selects Lavinia for his empress, Titus reciprocates by turning over his "sword," "chariot," and "prisoners," "consecrat[ing]" them as "presents well worthy Rome's imperious lord," "the tribute that I owe, / Mine honour's ensigns humbled at thy feet" (1.1.252–56). These gestures set the stage for a major political upheaval: Bassianus will claim Lavinia as his own and Saturninus will reject her—and with her, Titus and Titus's Rome—in favor of Tamora, the Gothic queen. Yet at the moment, Titus imagines the transfer of prisoners as a complement to the new emperor's "motion" to "advance" the Andronici "name and honourable family" (1.1.242–43). Accordingly, he assures the Gothic queen that she is "prisoner to an emperor, / To him that for your honour and your state / Will use you nobly and your followers" (1.1.262–64)—sure that Saturninus will uphold the "Roman" standards of order and honor that he himself defines.

Titus is not the only one setting the terms here, however. The play not only critiques the Rome he would create as dangerously self-centered but also juxtaposes it to a contrasting reality, which increasingly displaces and replaces Titus's untenable ideals. Recent interrogations of *Titus*'s colonial politics have tended to focus on the colonized subjects—Aaron, predominantly, and Tamora, secondarily.[34] Yet installed with Saturninus's regime is an accommodation of "outsiders" that suits the situation of conquest in a way that Titus's myopic and nostalgic politics do not. Saturninus is, of course, no prize. It is not without reason that scholars have singled him out as distinctively "wicked" or "vicious," even when they notice the pervasive corruption within Rome, and not without reason that Julie Taymor's *Titus* casts a smarmy Alan Cummings in the role.[35] Within criticism on the play, Saturninus's marriage to the Gothic queen emerges as especially problematic, since it "places the enemies of Rome too near the heart of its power."[36] That liaison does prove dangerous, creating an opportunity for both the Goths and the Moor to take revenge against their Roman conquerors and enact an Ovidian nightmare of appalling proportions. Yet to blame Rome's downfall on Saturninus's incorporation of "enemies" is, I think, to miss the complexity of the cultural picture here: it is to think of Rome, as Titus does, through an insular model of state, and to overlook the presence and pressures of internally colonized subjects. For Saturninus acts on and through the side effects of empire, the inevitable cross-cultural connections, which Titus denies. Within the dramatic fiction, whatever hideous outcome the marriage of the Roman emperor and Gothic queen ultimately brings, as a dramatic device it signposts an important openness that, instead of Titus's fantasies, define the Roman state.

As we think about *Titus*'s take on racial and cultural crossing, we should not be too quick to condemn Saturninus's unlooked-for liaison with the Gothic queen. Ania Loomba has argued provocatively that "as a white though foreign queen, [Tamora's] marriage to the Emperor Saturninus is *not unthinkable* in a feudal dynastic world in which both war and intermarriage between different groups and kingdoms were widespread."[37] As the double negative suggests, Loomba is hesitant to consider the bond inherently unproblematic. In her reading, race, gender, and class do set limits: what makes the marriage initially acceptable is that it "preserve[s] existing hierarchies of gender and rank" as well as the appearance of "racial purity," which Tamora's "whiteness" allows.[38] Loomba concedes that ultimately "the marriage *is* considered inappropriate because it reveals Tamora's ability to manipulate her way to power," underscoring her "status as alien."[39] Yet if we consider the bond in the context of a Rome habituated to the consequences of conquest, the marriage of Roman and Goth seems not only "not unthinkable," but rather imperatively thinkable.

It is not that, after all, that ignites the initial chaos, but Bassianus's assertion of a prior claim to Lavinia—which Titus declares "treason" (1.1.288).[40] In attempting to "bear his betrothed from all the world away," Bassianus effectively shatters the illusion of Titus's homogenized Roman order, setting one set standard against another, the rites of betrothal against the law of the Father (1.1.290). Marcus attempts to resolve the conflict with an absolute statement of the Roman way: "*Suum cuique* is our Roman justice" (1.1.284). But although he thereby means to prove that "the prince in justice seizeth but his own" (1.1.285), his efforts leave open the determinates of rightful ownership, which, coded thus ("to each his own"), could apply as easily to either "prince." In the end, the Andronici sons turn against their father, with Mutius literally, figuratively, and fatally obstructing Titus's "way in Rome" (1.1.295), while Bassianus flees with Lavinia, leaving the Andronici family in ruins.

Saturninus stands at a notable remove from this chaos, to the point that he seems to be the last to know that—and "by whom"—"Lavinia is surprised" (1.1.288–89). Although his "sudden choice" of Tamora is arguably as startling as Bassianus's seizure of Lavinia, within the dramatic fiction it appears to be both less contested and less contestable (1.1.323). We may denounce Saturninus for allowing his "sexual attraction to Tamora" to "obscur[e] his sense of duty to the Roman people," bringing Rome's "enemies" too close to home and catalyzing a "barbarous infiltration" of aliens into the Roman body politic.[41] We may fault the Gothic queen for "her behavior as an ambitious woman" and set her beside the "chaste Roman matron," Lavinia, as contrastingly "assertive, deceptive, and lascivious."[42] But tellingly, within the dramatic fiction, no one protests the marriage between the Roman emperor and the Gothic queen as a problem in and of itself. While Saturninus is still betrothed to Lavinia, he declares Tamora "a goodly lady . . . of the hue / That I would choose were I to choose anew"—apparently in front of a listening court (1.1.265–66). Although the impertinence of these remarks has caused editors to mark the couplet as an aside, in the play the only response comes from Lavinia, who praises the emperor's treatment of the Gothic queen as a sign of "true nobility" and "princely courtesy" (1.1. 275–76).[43] When Saturninus then stages his imperious change of heart, Titus does protest, yet not because the emperor chooses Tamora but because he rejects Lavinia—separate acts which, though they happen almost simultaneously, are decidedly not the same. Cutting off Titus's efforts to "restore Lavinia to the emperor," Saturninus asserts that "the emperor needs her not, / Nor her, nor thee, nor any of thy stock" and insists that Titus "go give that changing piece" to Bassianus (1.1.301, 304–5, 314). These alone are the "monstrous" and "reproachful" words that Titus declares "razors" to his "wounded heart" (1.1.313, 319). When the emperor subsequently announces his intentions to "create [Tamora] empress of Rome" and exits with her to "consummate [their] spousal rites," Titus objects only that he is "not bid to wait upon this bride" and instead must "walk alone," "dishonoured" and "challenged" (i.e., accused) "of wrongs" (1.1.343–45). Despite his own valorization of a Roman Rome, in both cases what worries him is not the connection between Roman and Goth but his disconnection from the Roman court.

Similarly, the other Andronici, who come on stage to sift through the wreckage, make no mention of the impending intermarriage, being preoccupied rather with the crises that have divided their family from within and caused their own political displacement. Directing Titus to "see what thou hast done," "in a bad quarrel slain a virtuous son," Marcus ignites a family argument over whether that (in Titus's mind, treasonous) son, Mutius, should be honorably interred (1.1.346–47). Marcus eventually questions "how comes it that the subtle queen of Goths / Is of a sudden thus advanced in Rome," but only after the matter of burial is settled and only in order, he says, "to step out of these dreary dumps" (1.1.396–98). If, in his case, the subject of the Gothic queen's advance serves as a useful distraction, in Titus's it provides a site where he can project and address his own dejected status. Unable to tell whether Tamora's rise has come "by device or no," he leaves that question to "the heavens" and asks rather: "Is she not then beholden to the man / That brought her for this high good turn so far?" (1.1.400–402). Caught up, like Lear, in his own narrative of "filial ingratitude," the Roman patriarch is less interested in whether the Gothic queen has manipulated her way into power than he is in whether she will show her new husband the due gratitude that Saturninus did not show to him (*Lear* 3.4.14).

The liaison between the queen of Goths and the Roman emperor, of course, proves to be hideously malignant. Yet nonetheless, the play suggests, it has an important political advantage, giving Saturninus leverage to distance himself from the confining provincialism that Titus would otherwise impose on him and on Rome. Skirting on impropriety, Saturninus's unorthodox praise for the Gothic queen's "goodly hue" immediately follows and publicly belies Titus's prescriptive prediction that the emperor will use her "nobly." Moreover, his admittedly "sudden" embrace of Tamora coincides meaningfully with his explicit rejection of Titus's dominance. Just before turning to her, Saturninus accuses the Andronici of mocking him and excoriates Titus for voicing the "proud brag . . . / That saidst I begged the empire at thy hands" (1.1.311–12). In Act Four, he will reiterate these charges and present Titus as a "sly frantic wretch that holp'st to make me great / In hope thyself should govern Rome and me" (4.4.58–59). Whatever the validity of these indictments and the veracity of Saturninus's desire, it seems no coincidence that his embrace of Tamora follows on his rejection of Titus, opening the possibility that these actions are of a piece. We might compare his public staging of his union with the Gothic queen to Edward II's similarly public staging of his reunion with Gaveston in Marlowe's *Edward II* (ca. 1590), the latter serving Edward as a means to contest the oppressive control of the nobility, however sincere his sexual desire.[44] In any case, by installing Tamora as his empress, Saturninus not only marks his distance from Titus, and Titus's Rome, but also institutes a new Roman and a new kind of Romanness, which is culturally mixed instead of pure. He sets Tamora beside Phoebe (i.e., Diana) and "the gallant'st dames of Rome" whom she "overshine[s]" (1.1.322), distinguishing the Gothic queen through a resonantly "Roman" term ("overshines") from *The Aeneid*.[45] In addition, he swears "by all the Roman gods," and, recycling Titus's words, vows not to "*resalute* the streets of Rome" until he and Tamora have married (1.1.327, 331). Now it is union with the Goths, in lieu of conquest over them, that ushers in a return to Rome—improvised across cultural boundaries in response to political challenge and change. The immediate result is not anarchy, but effective, if temporary, accommodation.

In fact, until the moment, deep in the opening scene, when Tamora directs Saturninus to "be ruled by me" and vows to "find a day to massacre" all the Andronici, the Roman/Gothic bond appears to provide an acceptable and accepted alternative to Titus's stagnant and insular nationalism (1.1.447, 455). In seeking to remedy their own alienation, the Andronici themselves welcome the mediation of the Gothic queen, who stages and directs a performance of public reconciliation: she urges Bassianus to "be more mild and tractable," warns Titus to pay heed that "this day all quarrel dies," and advises the Andronici to kneel and seek pardon (1.1.475, 471). In response, Titus initiates a celebration, a hunt, which begins the literal and figurative "dawning" of a new day and, to Titus's mind, a "new comfort" (2.1.10). With the Andronici's blessings, Tamora declares herself "*incorporate* in Rome, / A Roman now *adopted* happily" (1.1.467–68; emphasis added). These words have broader resonances, beyond the situation (of intermarriage) that they here describe: "incorporate" means "formally admitted, by legal procedure," or more loosely, being "admitted to fellowship with others," and "united in" "one body"; "adopted" indicates a legal but "voluntary taking of someone into a relationship as heir, friend, citizen."[46] In deploying these terms, the Gothic queen assumes—and raises the provocative possibility—that the Romans share with her a technical vocabulary not just for her own case of intermarriage, but for cross-cultural integration of a more inclusive, if less determinate, nature. Though she will turn against the Andronici, they, notably, do not turn against her, and for a moment what we glimpse is a state defined not by exclusion but by inclusion.

Perhaps the critical problem that *Titus*'s opening act sets up, then, is not that a bond between the Romans and the Goths *forms* but that, because of the devious personalities of the involved players, it *fails*. After all, the play's resolution will depend significantly on a crucial alliance between Romans and Goths—one (Goth 2) who supplies the Romans absolutely crucial *insider* information, bringing Aaron's and Tamora's miscegenous affair to light. And although the marriage of Saturninus and Tamora becomes neither productive nor reproductive, the latter always a bad sign in Shakespeare (witness, for instance, *Macbeth*, where the unsuckled and unsexed maternal body breeds bloody murder), it is not their mixed union that sets the revenge play in motion, but Titus's inability to read and reach across cultures, to recognize the problem of the Gothic sacrifice and the potential of the Gothic threat. In *Titus*, there is no room for Romans to be Romans, Goths to be Goths, or Moors to be Moors. For in its world of empire, these cultures not only inevitably clash but also, as inevitably, intersect.

* * *

Enter Aaron. If Rome's cultural boundaries really are negotiable, how then do we—and they—accommodate the unsettling presence of the "barbarous," "accursed," and "misbelieving" Moor? While the initial tensions play out,

Aaron is onstage, embedded in the newly conquered and colonized Gothic population, silent but distinctive in his color and in his prominence beside the Gothic queen. Before he ever speaks, the "raven-coloured" Moor appears to be a self-contained, self-incriminating sign system—a darkness that seems undeniably visible. He himself will later articulate the negative connotations of his blackness and acknowledge, indeed celebrate, the potential congruity of having (he says "Aaron will have") "his soul black like his face" and of therefore standing in bold-faced contrast to "fair men" who "call for grace" (3.1.205–6). He does not take that congruity for granted; he actively "wills" it into being. But *Titus* clearly draws on a colored opposition that is already loaded, already lethal, already in circulation in England. When Aaron finally does speak, after the vexing political ruptures have come and ostensibly gone and the Romans and Goths have agreed to a conciliatory hunt, he voices a readable malignancy that seems neither motivated nor mitigated by the complications of conquest.[47] He admits that he is hell-bent on "mount[ing] aloft with [his] imperial mistress," who he knows will "charm Rome's Saturnine / And see his shipwreck and his commonweal's" (1.1.512, 522–23). His illicit liaison with the Gothic queen provides an exposing antitype of her legitimating marriage to the Roman emperor, and the parallel draws attention to the fact that the incorporation possible for her seems to be contrastingly impossible for him.[48] Aaron is in some ways, then, the test or limit case for Rome's ostensible cosmopolitanism. For if the evidence of toleration and accommodation begins with the ultrawhite Gothic queen, we expect it to end with the darkly coded Moor.

Yet notably, although Aaron's dark exterior may seem automatically to give his malignancy away, within the dramatic fiction it does not. Conquered with the Goths, Aaron is freed with the Goths, and, for the Romans, who initially pay no further attention to his presence, that seems to be the end of the story. For us, however, it is the beginning of a critique that complicates the revenge plotline—the "shipwreck" of "Rome's Saturnine" and of Saturninus's Rome—that Aaron dictates and that finally is too simple to define or contain him. For despite the "dreadful things" that Aaron will soon set in motion, what is most striking as the play unfolds is that he is taken in by the Romans, even as they are taken in, in another sense, by him. When his horrors do come out, the Moor must be brought into visibility and meaning, his darkness given a significance which it does not otherwise seem to hold. The stakes, then, are higher, the choices harder, in the "real" world of conquest than they are in an ideologically overdetermined world staked on good versus evil, a culturally pure self versus an easily demarcated and disenfranchised Other. And if on the one hand the incorporation of Aaron exposes the dangers of writing the colonial subject in, on the other it underscores the impossibility of writing the colonial subject out.

From the start, Aaron figures as a Moor without a country, his history inextricably entwined with that of the Goths. In *Lust's Dominion*, the Spanish Moor Eleazar will identify himself as a prince of Barbary, left "Captive to a Spanish Tyrant" when Spain conquered his father's empire (1.2.236). But in *Titus* there is no competing place or story of origins to explain the Moor's presence in a European culture that is ostensibly not his own—just as there is no colonial backstory for Muly, a Moor in this play quietly inhabiting the outskirts of Rome, interbreeding with, it seems, a Roman wife. Given the early, still persuasive tenets of colonialist discourse analysis and the construction, evident especially in nineteenth-century French discourse, of Africa as a "peculiar empty profile" filled in by the terms and desires of European colonizers, we may be inclined to interpret that dramatic omission as a discriminating erasure of identity, acted out routinely, if not uniquely, on the colonial Other, here the Moor.[49] Yet to imagine a suppressed past is to eclipse the present expressed and modeled in this play: a cross-cultural "incorporation" which, though it may begin with conquest, defeat, and domination (as it does in Tamora's case), unsettles the defining lines of both culture and power. In *Titus*, Tamora is the only one to declare herself "incorporate," but that term may be as close as we can come in the play's own vocabulary to describing Aaron's place within Gothic society—closer surely than the concepts of integration and assimilation which neither Peele nor Shakespeare uses and which anachronistic histories of racial oppression have given form. For the starting point of Aaron's story is not an unstated precolonial, pre-Goth past but an explicit, open-ended "uniting" into the "one body" of Goths, with whom he is literally and figuratively embedded.

It is, in fact, quite telling that in this play there is no fixed term to describe Aaron's "incorporation," only a similar but not entirely equivalent model—and telling too that in early modern society there is no fixed vocabulary to define such cultural intermixing. Because we come at cross-cultural encounters (especially those involving African subjects) from a postcolonial perspective, we have a political investment in distinguishing various positions of domination and subordination precisely. But *Titus* apparently does not, not even as it imagines the place and power of the Moor. What references there are to Aaron's established connection to the Goths' past accords him a notably flexible social position—one that defies easy colonialist codification, the relative license and limit of his power and agency both unclear and unfixed. Once in Rome, he acknowledges the Gothic queen as his "imperial mistress," presenting her advance as the necessary vehicle for his own (1.1.512). But before we take his words as a sign of an ingested, ideological if not actual subjugation, as critics have done, we have to notice that his metaphorical self-positioning shifts, the language of conquest calling attention to the improvisational nature of his speech and vision.[50] Where at one point he presents Tamora as his current "mistress," at another he claims to have held her "prisoner" in their erotic past, "fettered in amorous chains / And faster bound to Aaron's charming eyes / Than is Prometheus tied to Caucasus" (1.1.514–16). At another he casts—and emphasizes that he *can* cast—her aside with his "servile weeds and slavish thoughts," replacing the decision to "wait upon" the queen with the choice to "wanton with" her instead (1.1.517, 520). Tamora herself depicts him as the epic Aeneas, the "wandering prince," to her Dido, their cross-cultural liaison pivoting seductively on an ever-changing performance of power (2.2.22).

In thus assigning the Moor a history which is already, inextricably, and inexplicably merged with that of the Goths, the play insists on the openness not only of Gothic society but also of Aaron's cultural place and past, and it establishes a crucial precedent for his present and presence in Rome. Despite his declared dependence on Rome's "new-made empress," Aaron's insinuation into the Roman body politic does not stop with the Gothic queen's body (1.1.519). For indeed, instead of being bounded off as alien, he penetrates the inner circles of Rome, to the point that it becomes difficult to tell when his plots and power end and the Roman court's begin. In that, he stands notably apart from the self-authorizing stage villains whose lineage he shares. In *The Jew of Malta*, Barabas sets the terms of his own deceptions and dictates their performance without the backing or backdrop of the Christian court. In *Othello*, Iago effects his destruction from a position well outside the Venetian senate—in the dark streets of the city and in the colonial outpost of Cyprus, the one as hard to see as the other is hard to reach. There is no question in the case of either the Jew or the Venetian under whose auspices these villains operate; their initiatives are undeniably their own. At the end of *Titus*, Aaron will claim, and indeed celebrate, a similar autonomy: he will resist Rome's attempts to silence and subdue him by confessing exuberantly and excessively like Barabas, even laying claim to crimes he has not actually (but would like to have) committed. Yet until the end, his plots take shape suggestively in the domains, if not under the authority, of the Roman court.

Granted, when Aaron begins his reign of terror, he engineers the inaugural crimes—the murder of Bassianus and the rape and mutilation of Lavinia—in the "ruthless, dreadful" and "unfrequented" forest that he declares fit "by kind" for "rape and villainy," its deadly pit providing an ominous parallel to the Andronici tomb (1.1.628, 615–16). In taking Aaron's incorporation as the sign that Rome itself has devolved into a "wilderness of tigers," critics have associated the Moor with a beastly wild, endorsing images certain characters pointedly invoke as they defame Aaron for being a "ravenous tiger" or "inhuman dog." Yet even as the play gives Aaron rein and domain in Rome's unsettled outskirts, it also emphasizes his physical and figurative proximity to the court. For starters, he improvises his very first conspiracy practically in the emperor's backyard. Just after, and in the same space that, the Romans have installed their new regime, Aaron stands alone, there imagining how Tamora will "charm" Saturninus into "shipwreck." When Chiron and Demetrius then enter, dueling over "Lavinia's love" (1.1.535), he rebukes them for "maintain[ing] such a quarrel openly" "so near the emperor's palace," and then uses their "storm" to invent a rape plot that will better "serve [their] turns" as well, of course, as his own (1.1. 545–46, 524, 596). His insistence on the perils of transgressing "so near the emperor's palace" exposes how near he himself is, in both physical place and cultural fluency. Speaking with the authority of an insider, the Moor informs the Goths "how dangerous / It is to jet upon a prince's right" and "in Rome / How furious and impatient they be, / And cannot brook competitors in love" (1.1.562–63, 574–76); witness Saturninus and Bassianus. In a not too subtle play on the idea of "ground," the scene here urges a contrast between the centrality of the position that Aaron inhabits and articulates and the eccentricity of the Goths' intentions. As he asserts, "the ground of all [their] grudge," "this discord's ground," would both defame and displease the Gothic queen (1.1.547, 569). The "path" he finds to solve the Goth boys' problem leads them to the forest (1.1.611), but it is no small matter that he directs their progress from the court, with a keen eye to Roman ways and values.

It is not just the Goths but also the Romans who look to Aaron for direction. The primary victims of his schemes are, of course, the Andronici, and if their insouciant disregard for signs of trouble undermines their credibility, it nonetheless underlines his. Bestowing upon Aaron "an absolute trust" as naive as Duncan's upon Cawdor (*Macbeth* 1.4.14), Titus's sons Quintus and Martius follow the Moor to the "loathsome pit" where, he insists, a "panther" (really, the newly made corpse of Bassianus) lies (2.2.193–94). Neither we nor they have to wait for Freud in order to understand that a "subtle hole" "covered with rude-growing briers" is a foreboding and "fatal place" (2.2.198–99, 202), any more than Hamlet has to wait for Freud in order to accost his mother Oedipally.[51] The Andronici notice that their "sight is very dull," a term implying apprehension, and when Martius falls into the pit, Quintus is "surprised with an uncouth fear," "a chilling sweat," and "trembling joints" (2.2.195, 211–12).[52] Even so, both continue to turn to Aaron for guidance, even after he has exited the scene—we might think, as they apparently do not, inauspiciously.

More remarkably, as the plot plays out, the Roman emperor not only follows Aaron's lead but further builds his own authority upon it. After "fetch[ing] the king," Aaron encourages him toward a "likely guess" that the entrapped Andronici, both now in the pit, "were they that made away his brother," Bassianus (2.2.206–8). When Saturninus comes upon the scene, it takes only the bodies in the pit, a letter crafted by Aaron and conveyed by Tamora, and a bag of gold produced by Aaron to lead him to the conclusion that Quintus and Martius are guilty and deserve "some never-heard-of torturing pain," which he means to devise (2.2.285). Although the emperor plays easily into Aaron's play-within-the-play, this is not Hamlet setting a public mousetrap for Claudius, or Don John producing a pornographic spectacle for Claudio. In an immediate reversal, Saturninus re-presents the act of following the Moor into an act of leading. Approaching the scene of the crime, he orders, "Along with me! I'll see what hole is here" (2.2.246). In his anxious attempts to get the w/hole story, he makes no acknowledgment of Aaron's part in the discovery. When Aaron brings forward the bag of gold (uttering his only line here, "My gracious lord, here is the bag of gold"), Saturninus turns instead, and not necessarily consequently, to Titus, at that point pronouncing the Andronici's guilt (2.2.280). And when Titus then hints at the prematurity of such sentencing (begging a favor "if the fault be proved in them"), in order to reconfirm his own case Saturninus defers to Tamora and to the anonymous letter, not to the Moor or the gold, seeking to know, once and for all, "who found this letter?"—as if knowing that is to know the truth (2.2.291, 293).

We could read this eclipse of Aaron's interventions simply as a sign of his subordination within the court, but to do so is to overlook the indeterminacy that surrounds the crucial prop here, the "fatal writ" which Saturninus himself takes as the clincher, the sign that the Andronici's "guilt is plain" (2.2.264, 301). For the letter not only carries Aaron's imprint; it simultaneously enlists and encodes Saturninus's venality, putting the Moor's false writing on a plane of culpability with the emperor's false reading. As Aaron scripts it, the unsigned letter relies on—and encourages false—inference and induction. Hardly transparent, its incrimination requires complicity in the constitution of blame. The letter's text mentions only Bassianus (not his murderers) by name and introduces a superfluous "*huntsman*" who is to "*dig the grave*" for Bassianus if the unnamed author(s) of the letter "*miss to meet him handsomely*" (2.2.268–70). Its pronouncement, "*Thou know'st our meaning,*" cagily invites conspiracy (2.2.271). Picking up Aaron's cues, Saturninus orders his men to seek the huntsman out. He then chooses what for him are the more convenient and pertinent targets, Quintus and Martius, literally and figuratively letting the fabricated third party go. In using the prop to condemn the Andronici, Saturninus acts on his own vengeful score, with the result that his and Aaron's actions and agendas therefore merge, the Moor's voice and vision not displaced as much as they are extended.

There is, we have to note, a significant textual problem in this scene, one that raises questions about the transmission of the very letter that is its crux. Aaron directs Tamora to "take [the letter] up" and give it to Saturninus, as she does (2.2.46). But when Saturninus attempts to verify its validity by tracing its course, Tamora declares, in an echo of Aaron, that Titus did "take it up" (2.2.294). Titus confirms the "fact" on the spot, seizing the chance to plead simultaneously for his sons' "bail" (2.2.295); and Aaron confirms the story later, in one of his final self-aggrandizing confessions. But if these testimonies are true, where and why did Titus get the letter? For what strategic or dramatic end? It may well be that the discrepancy is a textual glitch, as editors have suggested, deriving from error or another (no longer extant) version of the play.[53] But even if the textual mishandling of the prop is an accident, it is not, I would argue, a coincidence. Given the grounds of "incorporation" from which Aaron and the play operate, it makes sense that the letter, in which the Moor impersonates a Roman, would get inexplicably diverted into Roman hands. The confusion follows almost too coherently from the play's concerted insistence that the boundaries between the Moor and the Romans are penetrable—so coherently that it seems as if the text has fallen into a plot, a logic, of its own design.

This is not the only instance where the faultline between Roman and Moor, Aaron and the emperor, blurs. Take the gruesome exchange of promises and body parts between Aaron and the Andronici, after the unwarranted imprisonment of Quintus and Martius. Aaron invites the Andronici to ransom the brothers with a severed hand, assuring Titus that "my lord the emperor / Sends thee this word" and that "the king" "will send thee hither both thy sons alive" (3.1.151–52, 155–56). Without hesitation, the Andronici take him at his word as the conduit for the emperor's authority and voice. Titus praises the "gracious emperor" and "gentle Aaron" in one breath, unaware that his own expression of relief—that the "raven" now "sing[s] so like a lark" (3.1.158–59)—associates Aaron rather with Tamora, the "raven" whom Lavinia has invoked in the face of her rapist Chiron, as one that "does not hatch a lark" (2.2.149). As well, the Andronici sons compete with each other over whose hand is best to "serve the turn" proposed, they assume, by the emperor, and instead of doubting Aaron's connection to the court, they unwittingly ingest the very idiom he has used to prompt Chiron and Demetrius to "serve their turns" on Lavinia. This ironic circulation of language emphasizes how readily, if also blindly, the Andronici accept the Moor's channeling of the emperor, with Titus ultimately enlisting Aaron to undo himself, to chop off his own hand, and to "deceive" his own sons (3.1.187). Even when a messenger returns thereafter with only the heads of Titus's "two noble sons" (3.1.237), the Andronici do not suspect Aaron of deceiving them. In the face of this horrific betrayal, Marcus rails against the abstract, Titus goes mad, and Lucius goes "to the Goths" to "raise a power, / To be revenged on Rome and Saturnine" (3.1.300–301)—notably not on the Moor.

But whose plot is it really? The play exposes as tragically naive the Andronici's trust in Aaron's claims to speak for Saturninus. And Aaron himself, in an address to the audience, claims the deception as his own. Taking the words right out of Titus's mouth, he promises that if what Titus does "be called deceit, I will be honest / And never whilst I live deceive men so. / But I'll deceive . . . in another sort" (3.1.189–91). The aside lends the Moor a unique authority, an ability to step outside the dramatic fiction, to speak exclusively to the spectators, and to enforce his "I" and his "will." When his own head is metaphorically on the block at the end of the play, he not only confesses to the plot, insisting that he "played the cheater" for Titus's "hand" (5.1.111); he also exaggerates his role, and his pleasure, by presenting himself as the sole spectator, enjoying with self-authorizing abandon the frisson of villainy. Blocking (with sets, props, and gestures) a performance we never see, he reports that he "drew [himself] apart," "pried [himself] through the crevice of a wall," and, when Titus "had his two sons' heads, / Beheld his tears and laughed so heartily / That both mine eyes were rainy like to his" (5.1.112–17). Aaron further admits using "this sport" in erotic play with the empress, eliciting from her a slight swoon and "twenty kisses" (5.1.118, 120).

Yet as I have suggested, Aaron's confessions are as notoriously suspect in their truth value as are those of Marlowe's self-stereotyping Jew. And although the Andronici's naïveté cautions us against taking Aaron's words as the emperor's, the plays offers provocative signs of some collusion or cooperation, or at least malign inattention, from the court. It is, after all, necessary as well as possible for Aaron to penetrate the prison, activate a messenger, and secure the heads of bodies, all under the emperor's imperious command. We know that Aaron's lover, Tamora, does not enable these actions, since she responds to his account of his "sport" with kisses of surprise, at least according to him. We are left to wonder, then, about the emperor's involvement. The messenger believes the "good hand" that Titus "sent'st the emperor" and that was "in scorn . . . sent back" came to and from the emperor (3.1.236, 238). In Act Four, Saturninus himself will claim responsibility for the execution of Titus's sons. Disturbed by the barrage of arrows that the aimless Titus levels at the gods and at the court, the emperor protests the "monstrous villainy," asking (rhetorically) whether the affront must "be borne as if his traitorous sons, / That died by law for murder of our brother, / Have by my means been butchered wrongfully?" (4.4.50, 52–54). His question has a pointed and pertinent double edge, leaving open what is wrongful, the butchering itself (have been *butchered* wrongfully) or only its application (have been butchered *wrongfully*). He will subsequently imagine himself a "slaughterman" (4.4.57), immediately after sentencing an innocuous clown to an arbitrary death by hanging.[54] We do not know where butchery and beheading fit under Saturninus's "law"; we only know that he has authorized an execution which Aaron can and does reuse. What the play thus insistently obscures here is the all important difference between the lawful and the wrongful, the actions of emperor and the plots of the Moor.

For Aaron, then, to be "incorporate" in Rome is for him to stand inscrutably between the legitimate and the illegitimate, between his own means and the law, an internally colonized subject who can move seamlessly from court to forest, forest to court. Instead of simply exposing Rome as a "wilderness of tigers," signing its repressed violence, or undermining its truths, his ability to decipher and penetrate Roman ways unsettles the bounds of cultural identity from all sides, rendering the cross-cultural relation ultimately indecipherable but nonetheless provocatively open. If that relation is also therefore corruptible, that cost does not cancel out the fact that we are in a world driven by the variable realities of *suum cuique*, read the phrase how one will. Nor does it cancel out the fact that it is the representation of the Moor that brings those variable realities out. If he is the exceptional test case for reading Rome against the grain of an expected discrimination, he is the exception that proves the rule of cross-cultural incorporation.

* * *

What, then, are we to make of the moments when the Moor is singled out, scripted into stereotype, and produced finally as an "execrable wretch"? If we really are in a world where cultural intermixing defines the status quo, where a Moor such as Muly can interbreed unnoticed on the sidelines of Rome, why then does the discovery of the "black" baby, fathered by Aaron and mothered by Tamora, provide the climax for the Moor's undoing? Is it not miscegenation that tests and establishes the limit here, becoming the thing itself, an unquestionable sign of an ultimately unaccommodating, would-be-impenetrable culture? If not, why then at the end of the play is a highly public "direful slaughtering death" reserved exclusively for the Moor?

Despite Aaron's ability to insinuate himself inscrutably into the structures of the Roman court, it is simultaneously, even ironically, clear that Rome is well-equipped for discrimination against the Moor—so equipped that negative associations emerge within the language as part of the culture's inherited, proverbial lore. Consider the exchange that follows Aaron's initial confession of his many crimes. A Goth asks how Aaron can "say all this and never blush" (5.1.121), invoking the commonplace "to blush like a black dog," which means to show a "brazen face."[55] Aaron himself completes the proverbial phrase with "like a black dog, as the saying is," and his addition calls attention not only to the embedded slur but also to the fact that it is so embedded that it can literally go *without* saying (5.1.122). Or consider the cryptic message that Titus sends to Chiron and Demetrius once he realizes their guilt: "*Integer vitae, scelerisque purus, / Not eget Mauri iaculis, nec arcu*"—"the man of upright life and free from crime does not need the javelins or bows of the Moor" (4.2.20–21).[56] Chiron misses the point entirely, not realizing that the lines are meant to incriminate him and his brother. He notes rather that the lines come from "a verse in Horace" which he read "in the grammar long ago" (4.2.22–23). Prejudice is masked along with pertinence by the assumed neutrality and remoteness of classical education that seems, even in this "Roman" world, almost quaint. It is not even clear that Titus intends the line literally; his reference to the "javelins or bows of the Moor" functions as a figure of speech, not necessarily as speech about a figure. Aaron, who calls the unseeing Chiron an "ass," is sure that "the old man hath found [the brothers'] guilt," but not his own (4.2.25–26). The image of the weaponed Moor is perhaps all the more insidious then because it circulates loosely within this culture—and within foundational texts of England's humanist schooling—to give definition to the crime-free "man of upright life."[57]

Yet in *Titus*, the embeddedness of derogatory terms is not the same as their pervasiveness, their availability not the same as their viability. If these references prove discrimination *possible*, they do not necessarily prove it *plausible*. To the contrary, Aaron's case sets the possible against the plausible, revealing the surety of the one to expose the uncertainty of the other. *Titus* offers a radical experiment in representation, a Julie Taymor dream come true, playing provocatively on the brink of parody, disenchantment, and disbelief by yoking images and bodies violently together at the same time that it pulls them violently apart. The Ovidian pre-text, for example, does not begin to tell Lavinia's story, does not begin to voice the horrors of the mutilated body on stage. Nor can the dramatic embodiment of that pre-text give sustaining voice or meaning to Lavinia's body, "Rome's rich ornament" and tragic "changing piece," which is abstractly more and physically less than the sum of its parts (1.1.55, 314). In Aaron's case, the relation between the figure, the prescriptive discourse, and the presumptively signifying body is similarly strained. The play certainly tempts us to draw a correlation, as Aaron does, between his "black" skin and "black" deeds or soul. Yet here black skin does not automatically incriminate any more than white skin exonerates or absolves; witness the innocuous, presumably black Muly or the deadly white Gothic queen. Even in a staged society where color prejudice finds expression, the feature that ought to be patently "non-negotiable" is, it turns out, essentially unfixed.[58] For within this context of a conquering and culturally mixed Rome, when discrimination against the Moor erupts, it appears at once marginal and provisional, surprisingly limited to and precisely licensed by the mode and moment of its articulation.

In fact, until the discovery of the baby, the most blatant excoriations of the Moor happen outside the political center, where Aaron has some leverage. During the conciliatory hunt, Bassianus and Lavinia come upon the Moor in the forest, "wantoning" with the Gothic queen. There Bassianus insists that Aaron's "hue" colors Tamora's implicitly white "honour," making it "spotted, detested and abominable" (2.2.73–74). He further declares her clandestine association with a "swart Cimmerian" a readable sign of "foul desire," loading his condemnation with two synonyms ("swart," which can mean "malignant," and "foul") for "black" and through them naturalizing the association of blackness with badness (2.2.72, 79).[59] In turn, Lavinia denounces Tamora for "horning" with her "raven-coloured love" (2.2.67, 83). If the impact of her imagery pales when she then calls the white queen a "raven" (2.2.149), the unprecedented vehemence and vulgarity of her language stands out against the courteous compliance that characterizes her speech at court.[60] The difference draws attention to contingency—to the fact that these attacks are spoken, and apparently speakable, only in the shadowy outskirts of Rome, where Tamora is "unfurnished of her well-beseeming troop" (2.2.56)—much in the same way that Iago's vituperations against Othello, as a "black ram" "tupping" Brabantio's "white ewe," are speakable only on the Venetian streets, out of the senate's hearing (*Oth.* 1.1.88–89).[61] Bassianus and Lavinia do threaten to tell the Emperor of the "foul desire," but their own disruptive desire has already prevented that possibility, alienating them from court. Separated from the hunting party, they themselves are out of range, their voices beyond reach—as it turns out, permanently.

If the forest scene thus encodes such racist derogations as unspoken, if not also unspeakable, within Rome, the bizarre fly-killing scene in Act Three presses them to the brink of absurdity, effectively denaturalizing their logic. In it, when Marcus kills a fly, Titus rails against the deed, first as tyrannous, then as inhumane. To calm Titus's frenzy, Marcus likens the "black illfavoured fly" "to the empress' Moor" (3.2.67–68). Satisfied and inspired, Titus "insult[s]" on the fly "as if it were the Moor / Come hither purposely to poison [him]" and declares the corpse a "likeness of a coal-black Moor" (3.2.72–74, 79). Marcus concludes (and who would not?) that the aggrieved Titus has gone mad, taking now "false shadows for true substances" (3.2.81). But if the plot is hard to take seriously, the imagery is not. We can only think of Donne's "The Flea," which may look back to *Titus*, and which takes perverse pleasure in, and poetic power from, the excessive overloading of image onto insect, metaphysics onto mite. In *Titus*, take away the uneasy superimposition of Moor onto fly and what remains, for English audiences, is a not unthinkable translation of "coal-black" into poisonously "ill-favoured."

Scholars and editors commonly view the episode, which appears in the Folio but not the earlier quarto, as an addition designed (probably by Shakespeare) to register Titus's wholehearted descent into madness.[62] Even so, we cannot but notice what the scene scripts as a sign of madness: a color-coded discrimination against the Moor. It is not just Titus's conflation of fly and Moor that registers falsely but also his equation of blackness and criminality.

Titus fantasizes that the "coal-black Moor" would naturally come to poison him. But to this point, not only have there been no signs of poison (though Aaron's ancestor, the Jew of Malta, has poisoned with a vengeance); there have also been no signs that Titus suspects Aaron of catalyzing any crimes. While he understands the Moor to be attendant on the Goths, to the end he insists that "Chiron and Demetrius" "ravished" his daughter and "did her all this wrong" (5.3.55–57).[63] What emerges thus in bold, if somewhat comic, relief is a jarring disjunction between the "true substance" of the Moor that Titus knows from experience and the "false shadow" of the Moor that he derogates from expectation.

If we look beyond these "false shadows" to the "true substance" of what blackness actually signifies when the Moor, the Goths, and the Romans bring it into visibility at the play's end, blackness encodes not villainy but race, understood as family line. With the birth of Aaron's "first-born son and heir" (4.2.94), the play explicitly raises the connection between lineage and color, in a way that it does not in the case of either the Romans (who seem to have no color) or the Goths (who have "hue" but who identify as Goths). Aaron has pressed the correlation between his "black" "face" and his villainous "soul," but with the appearance of his son, he emphasizes rather the power of that color to carry his imprint and mark his race.[64] He celebrates the fact that his own "seal" is "stamped" in the baby's face, that "the black slave smiles upon the father, / As who should say, 'Old lad, I am thine own'" (4.2.129, 122–23). The child may be the Goths' "brother by the surer side" (i.e., the female body), as Aaron admits (4.2.128). But blackness, which "scorns to bear another hue," gives Aaron an unusually firm claim to paternity, linking father to son as part of an indelible race (4.2.102). I do not think, as some critics do, that the effect is to draw our sympathies toward Aaron for his potentially humanizing "paternal" sentiments.[65] Aaron is already "in blood / Stepp'd in so far," too far, for that (Macbeth 3.4.135–36); and his tagging of his son as a "black slave," a "thick-lipped slave" (4.2.122, 177), and maybe (it is hearsay) a "'brat'" (5.1.28) has as much potential to convey antipathy as it does to convey affection. Less ambiguous and more persuasive than the paternal is paternity, which grounds the crucial racial relation.

Yet significantly, that race, though signed by blackness, is inherently heterogeneous. The baby, after all, embodies a fusion of black and white, Moor and Goth, and though his blackness does not show another hue, it indeed contains one. Black does not erase white here any more than white erases black.[66] Aaron assures Chiron and Demetrius that the child has been "sensibly fed / Of that self blood that first gave life to you, / And from that womb where you imprisoned were / He is enfranchised and come to light" (4.2.124–27). Even if we read these claims as Aaron's ploy to elicit sympathy for a baby that the brothers are set to kill, the lines nonetheless call attention to the Gothic blood that brings that baby "to light." Further, a Goth reports overhearing Aaron describe his son, in one and the same breath, as a "coal-black calf," who lacks its "mother's look," *and* as a "tawny slave," who is "half me and half [its] dame" (5.1.32, 29, 27). Neither the Goth nor (if we believe his report) the Moor registers any contradiction in declaring a baby with half-white, half-Goth roots "black" or "coal-black" as well as "tawny." Color obviously matters and means, but it is neither exclusive nor excluding. Aaron, in fact, expects his son ultimately to live successfully among both Goths and Romans. According to the overhearing Goth, he anticipates that a "trusty Goth" will "hold" the baby "dearly for [its] mother's sake" (5.1.34, 36). Although he recognizes that his black son cannot be emperor, he intends to "bring [him] up" "to be a warrior and command a camp" (4.2.181–82). That he does not specify what camp, whether of Goths, Romans, Moors, or some other, suggests that the limit he anticipates is not of race or culture but of class. Blackness distinguishes race, but in the incorporated world of conquest, it is a race predicated not on a sacrosanct purity but rather on cross-cultural intermixing and exchange.

Certainly, the discovery of the baby does prompt Rome's alienation and punishment of Aaron. Yet the "cause" is neither clearly nor simply anxiety about miscegenation or the consequent replication of blackness that the baby, as a racial icon, makes obvious. The play moves us beyond this kind of abstracting ideology, insisting instead that the baby's figuration and fate derive from pressing political contingencies, involving the support or subversion of the Roman regime.[67] For by coincidence not design, Aaron's son poses both a practical problem for the seated Goths who would secure that regime and a practical solution for the ascendant Romans who would instead undo it, and what makes the difference within his representation is not a generalized color prejudice but particularized political aim.

As much as the baby's color underlines the racial integrity of the emergent Moorish line, what the Goths are obviously worried about is the fact that the color betrays the empress's adultery and so undermines her place (and their places) in the court. Tamora has no trouble fornicating with the Moor, but to preserve her reputation, she orders, must order, the death of the child that bears Aaron's telling "stamp" and "seal" (4.2.71). Her Gothic sons are similarly preoccupied with the fact that while the baby lives, "our mother is for ever shamed" (4.2.114). Similarly, the attendant nurse wants to "hide [the baby] from heaven's eye" because, she emphasizes, it evidences "our empress' shame and stately Rome's disgrace" (4.2.60–61). For the Gothic contingent, blackness is not problematic in and of itself. Within the nurse's description of the "joyless, dismal, black and sorrowful issue," blackness, in fact, figures as one among several adjectives of melancholy (4.2.68). Nor is it problematic as a miscegenous product of black and white. Construct a plot (the substitution of Muly's "fair" child for Aaron's black one) that takes away the shameful evidence of adultery, produce an offspring (itself half Moor) who can "be received for the emperor's heir," and, as far as Chiron and Demetrius are concerned, the crisis is resolved (4.2.156, 160). But blackness is problematic— because impossible—when both partners within a breeding couple are supposed to be white. The nurse declares "the babe" "as loathsome as a toad / Amongst the fair-faced breeders of our clime" (4.2.69–70), the enjambment here at once teasing us toward an abstract proposition (the baby is loathsome) and then attaching a crucial condition (a community of fair breeders). As Aaron allegedly has stated before, "where the bull and cow are both milk-white, / They never do beget a coal-black calf" (5.1.31–32). In the confrontation over the baby, Aaron does press the question of color, defending and celebrating its representational power, asking whether "black" is "so base a hue" and insisting, on principle, that "coal-black is better than another hue" (4.2.73, 101). But his question receives no answer, his argument no response. What ultimately matters to the Goths is not what black, in the abstract, is but what, in the particular context of "fair-faced breeders," black *does*.

We might not be surprised by these reactions, since the Goths initially appear with the Moor incorporate among them. But if their reading of the colored offspring does not stand out as remarkably practical and provisional, the Romans' reading does. The revelation of the baby coincides, accidentally but significantly, with Lucius's return to reclaim Rome. His responses are therefore inextricably entwined both with his need to "signif[y]" "what hate" Rome "bear[s]" the current regime and with the desires of his new Gothic allies to "be avenged on cursed Tamora" (5.1.3, 16). In confronting the "issue," he condemns Tamora's sexual transgression (which he registers as hers) at least as much as he condemns the Moors' racial penetration.[68] Specifically, when Aaron's story comes out, Lucius excoriates him not only as "the incarnate devil / That robbed Andronicus of his good hand" but also as "the pearl that pleased [the] empress' eye" (5.1.40–42).[69] Though he clearly demonizes Aaron,

Who indeed. Though Saturninus seems to be the obvious answer, his embrace of Tamora and unleashing of Aaron, the obvious offense, it is actually Lucius who is on the spot here, Lucius who must defend himself and justify the "civil wound" he has created by overthrowing the legitimate regime—and for him the Moor and his child become key. To exonerate himself as the true champion of an embattled but unified Rome, Lucius deflects attention from the divisions between the Romans and lays the blame almost exclusively on the Goths, singling out Chiron and "the damned Demetrius" as the culprits who "murdered our emperor's brother" and "ravished our sister" (5.3.96–98). "For their fell faults," Lucius argues, "our brothers were beheaded, / Our father's tears despised and basely cozened / Of that true hand that fought Rome's quarrel out / And sent her enemies unto the grave" (5.3.99–102). Making no mention of the Andronici's alienation under Saturninus, he glorifies Titus as the true champion who "fought Rome's quarrel out" and himself as the next in this heroic line, as one who braved "the enemy's point" to "preserve [Rome's] welfare in my blood" (5.3.109–10). Lucius elides his family with the emperor's, placing "our emperor's brother" beside "our sister," "our brother," and "our father" as Roman victims of the Goths. He then represents his banishment from—and ostensible betrayal of—Rome in abstract, and so less indictable, terms: erasing the fact and the reason that Saturninus banished him, he admits simply that the "gates" of Rome were "shut on" him, that he, "the turned-forth," was "unkindly banished" and left "to beg relief among Rome's enemies" (5.3.103–5). He also validates and neutralizes his potentially treasonous alliance with the "enemy" Goths by personalizing the relation, crediting them with opening "their arms to embrace me as a friend" (5.3.107). As if overwhelmed by passion, he interrupts his "worthless praise" to, in fact, underscore it, explaining that "when no friends are by, men praise themselves" (5.3.116–17). And while he suggests that the Romans are indeed on his side, know that he is "no vaunter," and will believe that his report "is just and full of truth," his doubts come through clearly as he offers additional evidence, producing his "scars" which, he insists, "can witness, dumb although they are" (5.3.112–14). We can only think of Coriolanus, who also appropriates his exile and his enemy to authorize and even name himself, and to justify effective treason against the Roman state.

In *Titus* the strategy does not work any better than it works in *Coriolanus*. When Lucius interrupts himself, Marcus takes over, augmenting the argument before giving the "common" Roman "voice" opportunity to judge whether "the poor remainder of Andronici" have "done aught amiss" (5.3.139,

130, 128). Significantly, Marcus changes the terms, now and only now bringing forth Aaron and his offspring as a potent visual aid. To justify the Andronici's actions against "wrongs unspeakable," Marcus produces the baby, beseeching the still silent Romans to "behold the child," "the issue of an irreligious Moor, / Chief architect and plotter of these woes" (5.3.125, 118, 120–21). As he prompts Rome to "*hail*" Lucius as "Rome's royal emperor," he orders some attendant to "*hale* that misbelieving Moor," these gestures linked by the homonymic echo (5.3.140, 142; emphasis added). Bringing Aaron into visibility appears thus as a way to make invisible Lucius's politically unconscionable murder of the legitimate head of state. The climax of this strategy, and the climax of the play, becomes then the final sentence, the "direful slaughtering death," imposed on Aaron. Marcus and, following his lead, Lucius seem finally to have done their new historicist homework, producing the Moor as villain at just the right moment to validate and verify their reclamation of Rome.

This is neither a routine nor a successful scapegoating or invention of "the Other," however, which would instantiate and require a degree of cultural bias that, I have argued, *Titus*'s Rome does not show. For not only does Marcus's turn to the Moor happen as a sort of coda, an afterthought to Lucius's indictment of the Goths, a desperate supplement to the not yet settled or convincing restitution of state. His turn against the Moor arbitrarily introduces terms of "misbelief" that do not fit the picture we have seen or are seeing. With the discovery of the "black" baby, Lucius has condemned Aaron with, it seems, every stereotype in the book, declaring him a "barbarous Moor," a "ravenous tiger," an "accursed devil," an "inhuman dog," and an "unhallowed slave," all abstractions that could apply to any number of Others, Turks, Muscovites, Jews, Indians, and such and that, in this play, in fact, do: Lucius himself calls the Gothic Tamora a "ravenous tiger" (5.3.194). Alternatively, in invoking a religious marker, Marcus emphasizes a feature that was associated more distinctively (though not exclusively) with the Moor, an Islamic "infidel," like the Turk—notably, while pointing to Aaron's "child," the telling "issue" of blackness. We cannot here miss the fact that neither Marcus nor Lucius condemns the Moor through the color, the clearly available evidence that, we imagine, might absolutely clinch the case. Nor can we ignore the signs that Marcus's resort to faithlessness is both arbitrary and untenable. The difference belief or nonbelief marks must be taken, as it were, on faith. But in *Titus*'s Rome, pure faith is as hard to come by as it is hard to read. Tamora has charged the Andronici with their own brand of "cruel irreligious

piety," and Aaron has accused Lucius of observing "popish tricks and ceremonies" (5.1.76), anachronistically calling up the "Roman" religion which, for
Protestant England, was itself "misbelief." Too, it is clear from Aaron's last
speech act that he—and anyone—can speak the speech of Christianity, regardless of faith. "Repent[ing]" any good he did (if any) "from [his] very
soul," he puts religion on at the very moment he puts it off (5.3.189). At worst,
then, Marcus's denunciation of the "misbelieving" Moor is self-referential and
self-incriminating; at best, it is blatantly ideological, undeniably unrelated to
the "wrongs unspeakable" that the Moor is asked to speak as well as to political transgression that Lucius must defend and that incrimination of the
Moor obscures.

And significantly, if not consequently, the Roman audience is decidedly
quiet on both fronts, on the matter of Rome and the matter of the Moor. The
one named Roman, Emilius, assures Marcus, the "reverend man of Rome,"
that the "common voice" will support his story and Lucius's rule (5.3.136, 139).
Editors have amended a speech prefix, which in the early quarto is "Marcus,"
to have "All Romans" subsequently endorse the Andronici's actions by reiterating the refrain "Lucius, all hail, Rome's gracious governor!" (5.3.145).[71] Yet
we do not want to be too quick to put words in the mouth of the "common
voice," especially in light of Shakespeare's subsequent Roman plays, where the
appropriation and eclipse of that voice is constantly at stake and where representation itself, as a political process, is constantly under suspicion.[72] Lucius's
and Marcus's extended defenses of a politically indefensible coup suggests that
the public "uproar" is not so easily silenced. When "a Roman" finally does
speak, signs of skepticism remain. He dictates two actions, both which subtly
challenge the Andronici's stance. First, he directs the "sad Andronici," who
have become nostalgically, atavistically, caught in their "obsequious tears" for
the dead Titus, to "have done with woes" (5.3.175, 151). Then, he implores Lucius to "give sentence" on Aaron, the "execrable wretch / That hath been
breeder of these dire events" (5.3.176–77). Although he seeks the punishment
Marcus has prescribed, he changes and so challenges the terms of complaint.
Instead of stereotyping Aaron as a "misbelieving Moor," he indicts the
"wretch" for the "dire events" that Aaron has, in fact, committed. That is, he
turns the focus from who the Moor categorically is to what this particular
Moor has done, thus displacing and replacing *discrimination* with *incrimination*, the "misbeliever" with the criminal. Though the desired sentence is the
same, the terms of sentencing are radically different.

If Marcus does not understand the potential skepticism within the "common voice," Lucius, it seems, does. Laying down the law, he sentences the Moor to a "direful slaughtering death," outdoing the "never-heard-of torturing pain" that Saturninus promises to the doomed Andronici brothers. Though we do not see the execution of the Andronici, the play emphasizes the anticipated culmination of Aaron's story as something to see—something, according to Lucius, that "some *must* stay to see." Yet at this moment, instead of writing the Moor *out* of Roman society, Lucius effectively writes him *in*. For embedded within his mandate against the Moor is an anticipation—and significantly harsh regulation—of popular resistance. That is, attached to the order that Aaron be set in earth and left to "stand and rave and cry for food" is the additional provision "if anyone relives or pities him, / For the offense he dies." In the case of the deceased Goth queen, Lucius has no worries: though he insists that "no funeral rite, nor man in mourning weed, / No mournful bell shall ring her burial," he imagines that only birds will "pity" her (5.3.195–96, 199). In the case of the incorporate Aaron, however, there is no such guarantee. Hence, at the moment that the Moor becomes most visible as a target of discrimination, the possibility that the Romans will nonetheless embrace him comes into visibility under the law, his presence becoming therefore not only a public fact of life but a cause for public dissent.

When the story of Titus Andronicus is retold in a ballad, "Titus Andronicus' Complaint," first printed in 1620, the spectacular punishment of the Moor provides the culminating image for a didactic Christian closure:

> Then this revenge against their Moor was found:
> Alive they set him half into the ground,
> Whereas he stood until such time he starved;
> And so God send all murderers may be served.[73]

Here there is no question about the appropriateness of the sentence, no worry about the intervention of the public audience, no sense, finally, of contingencies: the Moor's punishment provides a timeless template for the treatment of "all murderers." At the end of *Titus*, we may want to stay and see the Moor, who has done so many "dreadful things," treated like an "execrable wretch," condemned to a "direful slaughtering death," and bounded off once and for all. Yet to look to that moment for unconditional dramatic, political, and cultural closure is to miss a crucial point: discrimination against the Moor is never here the end of the story but always only the beginning. Ultimately, we cannot know how the Goths or the Romans would react to the "black" baby if it were not a sign of the Gothic queen's adultery, or how Lucius and Marcus would react to the Moor were they not staging a precarious and indefensible political coup, any more than we can know how the Venetians would react to Othello if the Turks were not threatening Cyprus. Rome does not have an absolute stand on the Moor's reproduction of a blackness any more than Venice has an absolute stand on the Moor's marriage to a Venetian. There is, after all, no single Rome, just as there is no single Venice. In *Titus*, as in *Othello*, interpretations of the Moor happen *inside*, not *outside*, the cultural moment. Within the Roman world of conquest, discrimination against the Moor appears at once monumental and incidental as a political act. And if the Moor marks the breaking point between the "true substance" of a Rome in the making and the "false shadow" of a Rome already made, it is not because his image can be permanently fixed but because his "incorporation" within this signal space of Europe cannot.

CHAPTER FOUR

Too Many Blackamoors

Deportation, Discrimination, and Elizabeth I

IN THE SAME decade that *Titus* was bringing to center stage the problem of the invisible but indelible Moorish presence within classical Rome, Queen Elizabeth was attempting to make visible a similar "blackamoor" problem in England.[1] Where *Titus*'s imaginary Romans made the mistake of looking the other way, the English queen would not. In 1596, she issued what is by now a well-known "open letter" to the Lord Mayor of London, announcing that "there are of late divers blackmoores brought into this realme, of which kinde of people there are allready here to manie" and ordering that they be deported from the country.[2] One week later, she reiterated her "good pleasure to have those kinde of people sent out of the lande" and commissioned the merchant Casper van Senden to "take up" certain "blackamoores here in this realme and to transport them into Spaine and Portugall."[3] Finally, in 1601, she complained again about the "great numbers of Negars and Blackamoors which (as she is informed) are crept into this realm," defamed them as "infidels, having no understanding of Christ or his Gospel," and, one last time, authorized their deportation.[4] Although it is not clear whether these initiatives were successful, or even enacted, Elizabeth's letters give official voice to a kind of discrimination that had rarely been authorized before.

England was, of course, no stranger to strangers, nor to discrimination against them. As Laura Yungblut has shown, European immigrants constituted a noticeable part of the English population starting in the twelfth century.[5] Although they could gain certain rights of citizenship, the Crown also had a long history of taxing, regulating, or otherwise restricting resident foreigners whenever it was politically or economically expedient. This was not xenophobia as we have come to know it: within these policies economics were likely to trump ethnicity as a generating case. One need only look at the Dutch Church libel to see concerns about the national identity of "strangers" give way to worries about trades, rents, and coins, as Gil Harris has argued.[6] Nonetheless, during Elizabeth's reign, immigration increased markedly and so did the constraints: every year from 1571 to 1574, for example, the state expelled all immigrants, excepting only those who had come to England for religious reasons.[7]

Elizabeth's orders to deport "divers blackmoores" stand out within this context as unique. For they articulate and attempt to put into place a race-based cultural barrier of a sort England had not enforced since the expulsion of the Jews at the end of the thirteenth century. In mandating the geographical alienation of certain "Negars and Blackamoors," the queen sets them categorically apart from her "own liege people."[8] While she figures the English in terms of their national allegiance, she designates the "Negars and Blackamoors" as a "kind" of people, "those kinde," defined by skin color (the blackness suggestively stressed by "*Negars*" and "*Black*amoors") and associated, less inclusively, with a religion or lack of religion ("most . . . are infidels"). That is, against the contrasting *national* identity of her "own liege people," she depicts and condemns "Negars and Blackamoors" as a *race*—a *black* race.[9]

These documents have become pivotal to critical assessments of the material and ideological place of "blacks" within early modern England as well as of early constructions of racism and race. Scholars have tended to read these letters as "the visible signature of the imperial metropolis's nervous writing out of its marginalized other" and have taken this writing out of "blacks" as the writing in of a color-based race and racism.[10] There continues to be debate over when "the association of race and color" became "commonplace," when blackness supplanted religion as "the most important criterion for defining otherness," as I have suggested already, with early modern scholars locating this development at the end of the sixteenth century and eighteenth-century scholars, at the end of the eighteenth.[11] Even so, it is clear that a discourse of blackness was taking shape and getting use as a vehicle of discrimination at the time that English playwrights were featuring the Moor and that the English queen was declaring the "blacks" in her realm "to manie." Yet what complicates the inscription of racial identity and bias is the fact that constructions such as these emerged within a complex of social, economic, political, religious, and natural discourses—none existing in isolation and only some originally engineered to produce the national or racial boundaries that had to be made if they were to be.

In the case of Elizabeth's letters, in particular, if the clarification and codification of a racist ideology was the result, it was not alone "the cause." For although the queen presents the presence of "blackamoors" in England as an internal problem, prompted by the fact that "of late divers blackmoores" have been "brought into this realme" and added to a population that "allready" numbers "to manie," her efforts are framed by an external conflict: England's ongoing war with Spain, which been heightened more than it was mollified by the defeat of the Spanish armada in 1588. That war was playing itself out partly in privateering ventures, some which brought "blackamoors" into England.[12] Whatever its ideological bearings, Elizabeth's plan to reverse that immigration served as a practical means for reclaiming English prisoners from Spain: for from what we can tell in each case, the queen intended to exchange "blackamoors" for the captive English. From the start, then, not simply were the "Negars and Blackamoors" selected for deportation positioned in an oppositional relation to England's "own liege people"; that relation was itself defined by the dynamic between England and Spain—a dynamic that hinged on the practicalities of war and was, in many ways, inattentive to boundaries of race or color. As Elizabeth's letters publicly outline these transactions, they *do* expose a color-based racist discourse in the making. But significantly, that discourse takes shape largely in response to political and economic circumstances that themselves complicate and compromise its terms.

* * *

We need, then, to start with these political and economic circumstances and with the "blackamoors" who are caught in the middle. In an influential study on the "staying power" of "black people in Britain," Peter Fryer has argued that the queen's discriminatory project "failed completely" "*in so far* as [it] was a serious attempt to deport all black people from England."[13] Elizabeth's efforts extended only across the short period between 1596 and 1601 and did little to diminish the size of that population. Whatever their numbers (and there is little evidence on this), black subjects remained in England throughout the early modern period and by the middle of the eighteenth century composed somewhere between 1 and 3 percent of the London populace.[14] Yet to evaluate Elizabeth's policies in the ambitious terms of a full-scale deportation is misleading, even with qualification ("in so far as") of the sort that Fryer offers, since (as Fryer also admits) Elizabeth never attempted to deport "*all* black people from England," only certain "blackamoors." While her abstract language suggests that the problem of "to manie" blacks was widespread, her plan seems to have been limited to a relatively small and select number, at first ten, then eighty-nine.[15]

To date, critics have only speculated about the identity of these subjects—first called "blackmoores" and in the last letter "Negars and Blackamoors"—and, in efforts to underscore the racial politics significantly at issue here, have named them "blacks," "black servants," "Moors," and "Africans."[16] These terms are not interchangeable, as I have suggested here and as Nabil Matar has also cautioned.[17] While their use was indispensable in articulating race as a visible category for early modern as well as modern readers, we are now in a position to historicize these markers more carefully and to recognize their vagueness. In the seventeenth century, "blackamoor" gets somewhat codified in poetry (e.g., Henry King's "The Boyes answer to the Blackmoor") that, according to Kim Hall, "insists on the absolute difference between black and white."[18] Earlier, however, "blackamoor" is sometimes substituted for "Moor," and its resonances seem torn between ethnicity and color, especially on the stage.[19] In *Lust's Dominion*, for example, when (and only when) Eleazar is about to usurp the Spanish throne, his lover, the Queen Mother, declares him a "proud Blackamore" (3.4.1836). "Negars" was clearer: as my discussion of Hakluyt suggests, the equivalent "Negroes" usually indicates West Africans, separating them from North Africa's Moors. Yet while Elizabeth's conjunction of "Negars" with "Blackamoors" places a homogenizing emphasis on color, it does so at the expense of any regional or geographic distinction.

What gets notably—and, I would argue, strategically—lost in these inscriptions is the fact that the initial group targeted for deportation were "Negroes" captured from a Spanish colony in the West Indies. Specifically, the queen's first initiative proposes deporting ten "blackmoores" who had been recently brought into the country by Thomas Baskerville. In 1596, she explains to the Lord Mayor of London:

> Her Majestie understanding that there are of late divers blackmoores
> brought into this realme, of which kinde of people there are allready
> here to manie, consideringe howe God hath blessed this land with great
> increase of people of our owne nation as anie countrie in the world,
> whereof manie for want of service and meanes to sett them on worck

fall to idlenesse and to great extremytie. Her Majesty's pleasure
therefore ys that those kinde of people should be sent forth of the
lande, and for that purpose there ys direction given to this bearer
Edwarde Banes to take of *those blackmoores that in this last voyage under
Sir Thomas Baskervile were brought into this realme the nomber of tenn*, to
be transported by him out of the realme. Wherein wee require you to
be aydinge and assysting unto him as he shall have occacion, and
thereof not to faile.[20]

The voyage Elizabeth references, the "last [i.e., latest] voyage" of Thomas
Baskerville (of 1595–96), is now more often known as the final voyage of John
Hawkins and Francis Drake.[21] Both Hawkins and Drake died during the expedition, and Baskerville, who had been commissioned as colonel-general of
the land troops, ended up in charge.[22] Initially, the venture was designed to
recharge England's waning efforts against the Spanish. Drake and Hawkins
proposed sending ships to the isthmus of Panama to intercept the silver Spain
was bringing from Peru and so to cripple the Spanish economically and militarily.[23] Elizabeth, however, was troubled about rumors that the Spanish were
advancing on England and insisted on a project closer to home. As a compromise, Drake and Hawkins scaled back their plans, and the queen agreed to a
raid on a Spanish ship grounded in San Juan de Puerto Rico, loaded with "tow
myllyons and a hallf of tresure."[24]

Despite its limited aims, the mission in San Juan failed, and Hawkins, in
the meantime, died. Drake then turned to the coast of what early maps de-
picted as the West Indian mainland and waged an assault on the town of Rio
de la Hacha, "a pearl-fishing settlement consisting of about fifty houses," occupied by the Spanish.[25] According to the account in Hakluyt, the Spanish
governor, Manso de Contreras, tried to negotiate a ransom for the town, but
apparently not to Drake's liking.[26] As a result, while Baskerville stormed a
main outpost, "the Generall," Drake, "with some hundreth and fiftie men
went by water six leagues to the Eastward, and tooke the Rancheria a fisher
towne, where they drag for pearle. The people all fled except some sixteene or
twenty souldiers, which fought a little, but some were taken prisoners, *besides
many Negros*, with some store of pearles and other pillage" (10:234; emphasis
added). Again the Spanish governor attempted to set a ransom, as, he later admitted, a stalling tactic to buy time for other towns to prepare for the attacks
of the English. When he finally announced that "he cared not for the towne,
neither would he ransome it," Drake allowed the Spanish to clear out, and

then "the Rancheria, and the towne of Rio de la Hacha were burnt cleane downe to the ground, the Churches and a Ladies house onely excepted, which by her letters written to the Generall was preserved" (10:235). Drake's company departed, taking with them the captured Spanish and "Negros." According to an additional account, written by a Spanish captain (Miguel Ruiz Delduayen) who fought against Baskerville, the English also captured two Negroes at Nombre de Dios, where there were two Negro settlements, Santiago del Principe and Santa Cruz la Real.[27]

It seems highly likely that these two groups of Negroes were indeed the "blackmoores" Elizabeth originally selected for deportation. But if these are the facts of the Negroes' history at the moment that they become part of the Baskerville venture, the crucial question is not just why Elizabeth targeted "black" subjects for deportation in 1596, but why she chose *these particular* black subjects. Why deport ten West Africans who had just been brought or captured from Spanish domains in the New World? Why scapegoat as "blackmoores" figures designated as "Negroes" in the contemporary accounts that tell their story? Why, that is, select a target group so precisely and then represent them so obscurely?

To invoke the Baskerville expedition—which Kenneth Andrews has declared "one of the worst conceived and worst conducted major enterprises of the entire sea-war"—was not in and of itself especially advantageous.[28] Although the English repeatedly attacked Spanish holdings across the West Indies, these conflicts did little to tilt advantage one way or another. As Andrews argues, the "unfortunate voyage" neither signaled "the recovery by Spain of general control in the Caribbean" nor prompted "any significant decline in the numbers of English ships frequenting the West Indies after 1595."[29] The head of the Spanish fleet, Don Bernardino Delgadillo de Avellaneda, in fact, used the events as evidence of England's cowardice, accusing the English mariners of fleeing Spanish attacks at sea and attributing Drake's death to well-placed despair (and not to the dysentery that actually killed him).[30] This "Libel of Spanish Lies" was troubling enough to prompt one of the English captains, Henry Savile, to craft an exaggerated mistranslation of the Spanish text and to record his own version of the conflict, the one proving the Spanish liars and the other, the Spanish fleet ultimately "in greate distresse mightily beaten and torne."[31] Seconding Savile, Baskerville produced his own bombastic rebuttal, daring the Spanish general to meet him in "any indifferent kingdome of equall distance from either realme," since "the kingdomes wherein we abide are enemies" and "there is no meanes in either of them" for a fair challenge.[32] Even in its afterlife, "this last voyage of Sir Thomas Baskerville" does not appear to have been England's finest hour.

Significantly, however, the Negroes from the Baskerville campaign came to England as prisoners of the Anglo-Spanish war, and it was that political position, I would argue—more than, say, any presumed African identity, heritage, or history—that made them especially useful to the queen. For within accounts of the voyage, it is the dividing line of *war*, more than of culture, race, or color, that defines encountered Negroes—and defines them significantly as allies to the Spanish. Admittedly, this alliance may have been uneasy, if not also forced, at least for some Negroes who may have been "runaway slaves."[33] There was a settlement of "freed Negroes" living near Nombre de Dios, who, according to Spanish sources, had come "to serve [the Spanish] in this war under the banner of their captain Juan de Roales who is also one of them."[34] But the Spanish seem to have been nonetheless suspicious of their loyalty. Writing of the Negroes of Santa Cruz "imployed in your majesties service," the Spanish surveyor Juan Bautista Antoneli cautions that "there is no trust nor confidence in any of these Negroes, and therefore we must take heede and beware of them, for they are our mortall enemies."[35] In addition, both English and Spanish accounts raise the possibility that Negroes from these territories willingly left with Baskerville in order to escape Spanish rule. The Spanish governor, Contreras, writes to the Spanish king that Drake took "100 Negroes and Negresses from the pearl station, who for the most part joined him voluntarily."[36] In a narrative which was not published until the nineteenth century, Thomas Maynarde, who sailed with Drake, states that among their "many prisoners Spaniards & negroes" were "some slaves repairinge to us voluntarily."[37] Apparently, before the Baskerville venture, the English had considered forming an "alliance with the Negros."[38] That plan never materialized in any full-scale way, but the English do admit relying on the "intelligence of som negros" during the venture and, in one instance, include a Negro, along with "three English men" and "a Greeke," as their own military casualties.[39]

Yet whether the Negroes served the Spanish—or joined the English—voluntarily or by force, what matters above all else to both English and Spanish witnesses is the fact that Negroes, "subjugated" alongside "freed," by and large "rallied to [the Spanish] majesty's service with loyalty, hard work and energy" against the English.[40] The English captain John Troughton reports fighting against "some Spanyardes & negros" at Nombre de Dios.[41] English narrators otherwise pay little attention to the "negroe towne," whose labor force Spanish narrators survey pointedly.[42] Another account notes that "Negroes," along with "a few Spaniards" and "Indians," aimed "some 30 or 40 shot" at the Baskerville contingent at Santa Marta.[43] Moreover, once the Baskerville Negroes are taken, they figure as prisoners of war in one group *with* the Spanish. The account of the events at the Rancheria, for example, asserts that Spanish soldiers defending the settlement "were taken prisoners" "*besides many Negroes*" and that when the English later docked at Porto Belo, they "set ashore" "all our prisoners as Spaniards and Negros."[44] Maynard conjoins "many prisoners Spaniards & negroes" in one phrase, and Troughton reports that the Spanish at the Rancheria intended "to Ransom their houses, negros, and som spanyard*es* pr*i*soners."[45] In these representations, the tensions and differences between Negroes and Spaniards are leveled or muted out, and these figures are pressed together into a single category of captives.

In the letter of 1596, then, when Elizabeth proposes deporting "blackmoors" from the Baskerville expedition, she is choosing subjects who stand beside the Spanish and who have come to England as prisoners of the war against Spain. That status helps explain the timing and focus of her ambitions, which seem to have involved, if not to have been directly prompted by, a crisis developing over Spain's alleged mistreatment of English captives. During the voyage itself, Drake wrote to the governor of Puerto Rico, Pedro Suarez, insisting that "whenever I have had occasion to deal with those of the Spanish nation, I have always treated them with much honour and clemency, freeing not a few, but many of them," following "the honourable usage of war."[46] He further warns the Spanish governor that if the English "receive good and fair treatment" from their Spanish captors, "I shall be my usual self, but otherwise I shall be obliged to act against my nature."[47] Less than a month before Elizabeth first ordered the deportation of "blackmoores," she too apparently expressed concern that "Englishmen that have been taken prisoners and carried into Spain are used there with great rigour and cruelty, some in Seville and other places condemned to death, others put into the galleys or afflicted with great extremities which is far otherwise than any of the Spanish prisoners are used here in England."[48] In retaliation she threatened "that such Spanish prisoners as yet remain in England shall be restrained from their gentle usage."[49] Under the supervision of "Mr. Nicholas Owsley," those prisoners were to be "search[ed] out" and sent to "Bridewell or some such prison of severe punishment."[50] There are subtle signs as well that Elizabeth may have been planning to exchange these Spanish prisoners for English captives. She justifies Owsley's appointment on the grounds that he "hath heretofore brought prisoners from

Spain and carried Spanish prisoners back."[51] Moreover, she assures "any man that holdeth any prisoners for ransom" that cooperation would not curtail profit, that is, "that no prisoner shall be *sent out of the realm* without the knowledge and satisfaction of the party whose lawful prisoner he is."[52]

We do not know the outcome. But when the queen authorized the expulsion of "blackamoores" less than a month later, she may have had just this kind of arrangement in mind. The timing of her initiative raises the possibility that she decided ultimately to substitute Negro for Spanish prisoners, a change that, if true, creates a suggestive parity (almost) between two captive groups. In any case, it seems very likely that Elizabeth's proposal was catalyzed primarily by the worry over English captives and designed as a way to recompense Spain for their return. Negros had value in similar kinds of negotiations, enough that, according to Contreras, Drake offered "to restore all he had taken from me and the other citizens, to leave the Negroes to their masters, and to refrain from burning the settlement" at Rio de la Hacha in exchange for treasure there.[53] Contreras refused, preferring rather to "lose my head rather than see [the Spanish king's] treasure reduced by a single *real* for this purpose of ransoming the settlement."[54] But in other Spanish accounts, Negroes are returned for ransom. In one, a Portuguese mariner promises to pay two thousand ducats for "Ana Gomez, a free Negro," who was captured at Nombre de Dios (he is willing to pay four thousand ducats for one of his countrymen).[55] If Negroes could be ransomed *by* the English, they could also be ransomed *for* the English.

Admittedly, we will never know whether Elizabeth's first deportation plan was tied to an exchange for English prisoners, or whether her original target group had been Spaniards, however likely these scenarios seem. But roughly one week later, when she ordered another population of "blackamoores" out, she explicitly justified this move as a payback for the return of English prisoners held in Spain and Portugal.[56] Her "open warrant to the Lord Maiour of London and to all Vyce-Admyralles, Maiours and other publicke officers whatsoever to whom yt may appertaine" explains:

Whereas Casper van Senden, a merchant of Lubeck, did by his labor and travell procure 89 of her Majesty's subjectes that were detayned prisoners in Spaine and Portugall to be released, and brought them hither into this realme at his owne cost and charges, for the which his expences and declaration of his honest minde towardes those prizoners he only desireth to have lycense to take up so much blackamoores here

in this realme and to transport them into Spaine and Portugall. Her
Majesty in regard of the charitable affection the suppliant hathe
shewed, being a stranger, to worke the delivery of our contrymen that
were there in great misery and thraldom and to bring them home to
their native contry, and that the same could not be don without great
expense, and also considering the reasonablenes of his requestes to
transport so many blackamoores from hence, doth thincke yt a very
good exchange and that those kinde of people may well be spared in
this realme, being so populous and nombers of hable person the
subjectes of the land and Christian people that perishe for want of
service, wherby through their labor they might be mayntained. They
are therfore in their Lordships' name required to aide and assist him to
take up suche blackamores as he shall finde within this realme with the
consent of their masters, who we doubt not, considering her Majesty's
good pleasure to have those kinde of people sent out of the lande and
the good deserving of the stranger towardes her Majesty's subjectes,
and that they shall doe charitably and like Christians rather to be served
by their owne contrymen then with those kinde of people, will yielde
those in their possession to him.[57]

This document makes clear that Elizabeth planned to send eighty-nine
"blackamoores" to Iberian domains in exchange—"very good exchange"—for
the eighty-nine English prisoners that Van Senden had already recovered.
These new orders may not necessarily explain her initial proposals either to
deport the Baskerville Negroes or to detain the Spanish prisoners. Yet given
the timing and the context of Anglo-Spanish tensions, it seems quite likely
that these initiatives were related—and especially that the proposed expulsion
of "blackamoors" was, in the first case as in the second, part of a prisoner exchange with Spain.

This reading of the historical circumstances does not entirely answer the
question of why "blackamoors" became the targeted group in lieu of, say, imprisoned Spaniards. But it does begin to suggest how complicated that answer
is, and was, for an England engaged in a war against Spain. On both a practical and an ideological level, the proposed expulsion appears to further a nationalist cause and solve an internal economic crisis. We do not have enough
records to show what happened to Negroes who were brought back to England.[58] In her second letter Elizabeth does suggest that the "blackamoores"
were in the "possession" of "masters," but we do not want to take this as an

indication that they were enslaved, since medieval forms of slavery had been abolished from England and most of Europe by the sixteenth century.[59] As far as we can tell, imported Negroes occupied positions of service—positions that, the queen insists, the English themselves could fill.[60] According to her argument, the problem with so many "blackamoores" is, then, that they displace "nombers of hable person[s]" from jobs. To deport "those kinde of people" was to open up the labor market. It was also to encourage English "masters" to give preference to their own countrymen, who are "the subjectes of the land and Christian people" and who might otherwise (as the first letter asserts) "fall to idlenesse and to great extremytie," and even "perishe," "for want of service and meanes to sett them on worck."

Yet the internal, nationalist focus of this proposition is compounded by external, practical pressures that appear more urgent and compelling. In both sets of orders, the number of "blackamoors" to be expelled is obviously incommensurate with the magnitude of the articulated problem. The creation of ten, or even of eighty-nine, new jobs would do little to ease the situation Queen Elizabeth represents as resulting from a "great increase of people of our owne nation" and affecting "manie" in "want of service." In fact, in the second letter, the size of the population to be deported is determined *not* by the needs of the unemployed and idle English but by the needs of a "stranger," the "merchant of Lubeck," Casper van Senden. Van Senden, "at his owne cost and charges," brought eighty-nine "of her Majesty's subjectes" "home to their native contry"—something, Elizabeth stresses, that "could not be don without great expense." His "requestes to transport so many blackamoores from hence" in recompense comes first. The desire to repay him determines and trumps the justification that follows: that "those kinde of people may well be spared," "being so populous," and that the English need their jobs. In justifying her schemes, the queen puts Van Senden's "labor and travell" tellingly before the lack of "labor" faced by England's idle poor, the "great misery and thraldom" of the English he saves tellingly before the "perishing" of the unemployed English at home, and even his nationalism, his respect for their "native contry," tellingly before theirs. Represented thus, remunerating the merchant seems more urgent than relieving the poor or, indeed, ostracizing unwanted blacks, and it takes precedence as the central problem for which the deportation is the "reasonable" solution. It is *because*—and within the document, *after*—the "blackamoores" figure as a "very good exchange" for Van Senden (and indirectly for the men he rescued) that they become a people who "may well be spared in this realme."

Ideologically, the exchange actually challenges the national and racial boundaries Elizabeth invokes in its defense. While she promotes the strength of her "own nation" over "anie countrie in the world," her ability to negotiate with Spain over the treatment and release of English prisoners depends, ironically, on the mediation of a Dutch "stranger." Moreover, the proposed substitution of "blackamoores" for the English in Spain and the consequential substitution of unemployed English for "blackamoores" in England undermine the divide between the Negroes, who are invisibly embedded in the English economy, and the English. "Those kinde of people" may be unwelcome and unwanted in England, but they also occupy positions Elizabeth's "own liege people" do or might hold. And if they are suspect as subjects once in service to the Spanish, their presence in England, like Van Senden's, gives the queen leverage in working out relations with Spain. Thus if, on the one hand, Elizabeth's rhetoric suggests and supports a provincial nationalism, on the other, what she proposes relies on the complex connection between England and the various "strangers" who serve England's international interests.

In fact, those international interests take precedence over the national. Despite her insistence that the deportation would improve the demographic and economic situation within England, she anticipates internal loss and internal resistance to that loss. Her second letter is written with an eye to those "masters" who would rather hold Negroes as servants than employ the English (presumably at a cost, or greater cost) in their stead. Although the letters patent were officially "open" to the public, they were intended primarily for the public officials to whom they were addressed and who were to "aide and assist" in the rounding up of the targeted population.[61] Accordingly, these documents provide a rationale that will not only persuade those officials to do their duty but also gain the "consent" (which Elizabeth admittedly wants) of those in "possession" of the needed "blackamoors." The queen insists, of course, that she "doubts not" the willingness of the masters to comply. But she does seem to protest too much, providing a loaded valorization of Van Senden that too obviously serves to argue for the necessary economic sacrifices that make the exchange problematic. She emphasizes that Van Senden has worked for the "delivery" of English prisoners with a "*charitable* affection" at his own sizeable expense, and she presents his economic sacrifice as a model for her own subjects. As a "suppliant," he becomes the exemplary Christian, "delivering" her people with a Christlike charity and self-sacrifice as well as reverence for a supreme authority (hers). Just as Van Senden relieved Englishmen suffering abroad so should the English "doe *charitably*," "like Christians," and relieve the English suffering at home; and just as he did so "at his own cost and charges," so implicitly should they. The queen underscores the "reasonableness" of this request by insisting that she asks no more from her people than Van Senden has already given voluntarily. He is to "have lycense to take up so much blackamoores"—and *only* so many "blackamoores"—as he needs to be repaid via a one-for-one exchange. That exchange, Elizabeth assures her subjects, will prove "very good." In stressing that "those kinde of people may well be spared in this realme" because they are "so populous," she may as well be hinting that there will still be plenty of "blackamoores" to go around after the deportation. Indeed, her first pronouncement (in 1596) that "there are allready here to manie" may itself imply that there will always be enough.

Despite itself, Elizabeth's second letter makes clear that while unemployed English citizens stand to gain from the deportation, then, English "masters" stand to lose. In the face of this economic double edge, what begins to emerge in the second letter, and what will get an even bolder iteration in the third, is an important shift from a practical argument based on economic expediency to an ideological argument grounded on innate difference. Elizabeth draws here a unifying boundary around England, one that can at once accommodate the service of the Dutch mediator and at the same time rationalize the expulsion of the serving blacks. In promoting the Protestant Van Senden as a model for English Christians, the queen defines her people as part of a Protestant community that selectively exceeds the bounds of nation. That community is unified and identified by its charity to "insiders," and it includes the Dutch Protestant, Van Senden, whose status as "stranger" she highlights. And it excludes, of course, "blackamoores," some who have served the Spanish/Catholic foe. Within this Protestant framework, their deportation comes to answer an indisputable moral imperative, trumping the economic losses of English masters. Insisting that "God hath blessed" the increase of the English people, she implicates the burdensome increase of "blackamoores" as a recent development that works against this providential design. Notably, although this letter is more explicit than the first about where those "blackamoores" are being sent (Iberia) and why, it is less explicit about their identity. Elizabeth notes that they have been brought "of late" into the country, but she gives no indication of when or by whom, as she did before. Rather, she distinguishes the group mainly by their increased numbers, which make them expendably unlike the English, whose increase "God hath blessed." In contrast with Christians, they begin to emerge as a problem and a race in their own right, a "kinde" of people without a country, homeland, or history, and also without a blessed soul. For the moment, that incrimination comes by implication only—in part because the document puts such an emphasis on economic concerns. Elizabeth obviously does imagine that there is enough antipathy toward "blackamoors" that she can market them as a deportable "kinde of people," who "may well be spared." But she does not count on that base of ideological prejudice, whatever its strength, to overcome the practical utility and profitability of harboring Negroes within the realm, not at least within the class of masters who stand to lose materially from the deportation.

We do not know how well her argument worked or whether the exchange ever took place. Yet five years later, when Elizabeth tries one last time to deport a group of black subjects, her worries about her own citizens' resistance have increased and so—consequently, I would argue—have her efforts to code "blacks" as a separate race. In 1601 she writes:

> After our hearty commendations; whereas the Queen's Majesty, tendering the good and welfare of her own natural subjects greatly distressed in these hard times of dearth, is highly discontented to understand the great numbers of Negars and Blackamoors which (as she is informed) are crept into this realm since the troubles between Her Highness and the King of Spain, who are fostered and relieved here to the great annoyance of her own liege people that want the relief which those people consume; as also for that the most of them are infidels, having no understanding of Christ or his Gospel, hath given especial commandment that the said kind of people should be with all speed avoided and discharged out of this Her Majesty's dominions. And to that end and purpose hath appointed Caspar van Zenden, merchant of Lübeck for their speedy transportation, a man that hath very well deserved of this realm in respect that by his own labor and charge he hath relieved and brought from Spain divers of our English nation who otherwise would have perished there. This shall therefore be to will and require you and every of you to aid and assist the said Caspar van Zenden or his assigns to take up such Negars and Blackamoors to be transported as aforesaid, as he shall find within the realm of England. And if there shall be any person or persons which are possessed of any such Blackamoors that refuse to deliver them in sort as aforesaid, then we require you to call them before you and to advise and persuade them by all good means to satisfy Her Majesty's pleasure therein, which if they shall eftsoons willfully and

obstinately refuse, we pray you then to certify their names unto us, to the end Her Majesty may take such further course therein as it shall seem best in her princely wisdom.[62]

Where before Elizabeth pretends that she "doubts not" that the English masters possessing "blackamoors" will follow Van Senden's lead and deliver those subjects up, now she admits directly that some of her subjects might "willfully and obstinately refuse." She therefore prescribes more aggressive action against any noncompliant citizens. She directs her public officials, if they know of anyone "possessed of" "Negars and Blackamoors," to "advise and persuade" that citizen "to satisfy Her Majesty's pleasure." If that pressure fails, the officers are to "certify their names unto" the Crown "to the end Her Majesty may take such further course therein."

In trying to counter willful domestic resistance, the queen couples these practical measures to a developing ideological argument—enforcing a more limited conception of nationalism and a more absolute conception of race than had appeared in the earlier letter and strategically widening the divide between the national and the racial, the English and the blacks. Now, instead of scripting the English into a wider Protestant community, with a Dutchman at its helm, Elizabeth closes England's borders and stresses the primacy and priority of her "own natural subjects." The need for action comes this time from her, from "the Queen's Majesty," whose main worry is the situation of the English who suffer—and suffer more extensively, as this version tells it—from "hard times of dearth." While she again praises Van Senden as "a man that hath very well deserved of this realm," he appears as her appointee rather than, as before, the one dictating the conditions of the exchange. The queen herself gives the "especial commandment" that blacks be deported because they take jobs from England's poor. In the background are "the troubles between Her Highness and the King of Spain," which demand attention to nation, an assertion of "Her Majesty's dominions," and the protection of her "own liege people." But notably here, it is the unemployed underclass, and not English masters, who become the citizens whose problems define her moves and her state, they who "want the relief which those [black] people consume," they who (like herself) are "greatly annoyed" that blacks are "fostered and relieved" by English masters, whom she implicates through the passive voice. If those masters are to be, like the poor, loyal representatives of the realm, troubled as it is by Spain, they must hand over the blacks in their possession and hire their countrymen. National allegiance takes precedence over Christian duty, economics, and class.

As this more guarded and insular nationalism surfaces in this last proposal, so does a more insistent racism. In this final letter, Elizabeth abstracts the targeted blacks even further than before from the historical circumstances that explain their presence in—and justify their deportation from—England. An ameliorating Anglo-Spanish exchange of prisoners still shadows the document as a motivating factor: Van Senden once again seems to be the man for the job, for the "transportation," because he "hath relieved and brought from Spain divers of our English nation who otherwise would have perished there." But this time Elizabeth does not situate Van Senden's accomplishment in time, does not specify whether the prisoner crisis is current, recent, or past, does not distinguish it either as a new initiative or as the event she referenced in 1596. Hence, if the suffering of the English in Spain appears more serious (the imprisoned English here "would have perished"), it also seems less urgent, less compelling as a motive for action. With the need to bring English prisoners home obscured and abstracted thus, the need to get the black population out takes its place newly as "the thing itself"—the propelling problem rather than an expedient solution to other crises.

That problem is inscribed and abstracted in racial and ultimately racist terms. Now the targeted subjects themselves are responsible for their presence in the realm: where before Elizabeth states that the "blackamoors" had been "brought" into England, implicitly under the auspices of the venturing English, this time she implies that they have "crept" into the realm, in worrisome numbers, both independently and secretly (she must be "informed"). And who they are becomes more inclusive and less clear. Here for the first time she names the subjects in question "Negars." But she simultaneously conflates that more historically meaningful designation with the more elusive "Blackamoors," creating a composite category of "blacks" that pivots on the apparently binding trait of color to the occlusion and exclusion of the included subjects' history, heritage, political status, or place. To this color coding, she adds the accusation that "most of them are infidels, having no understanding of Christ or his Gospel." Where before "blackamoores" appeared as non-Christian only via a contrast with the constructed Protestant community from which they were, and were to be, excluded, here the incriminated group has its own self-defining feature: a probable lack of faith. Even if only "most" are infidels, *all* are nonetheless automatically suspect for an infidelity that no one could see literally and so would see figuratively. Hence, while nation (in lieu of Christianity) becomes the primary term to distinguish the English here, religion (in its absence) becomes an additional term to distinguish the black race. And in this document, as not in the prior letters, blacks acquire their own negative attributes as a "kinde of people." It is no longer expediency and circumstance that make their deportation from England "reasonable" at a particular historical moment. They, by virtue of their innate and collective characteristics, their blackness and their probable faithlessness, are a race, a people, that "should be with all speed avoided and discharged out of . . . Her Majesty's dominions." If the current "hard times of dearth" within the nation make such an action particularly urgent in 1601, Elizabeth's rationale extends across time, producing a population—the idea of a population—that could and should be repeatedly constructed and condemned as the infidel "black."

The official letters Queen Elizabeth issued between 1596 and 1601 move then from the contingent to the absolute, the practical to the ideological, the economic to the racial, ultimately coming as close as contemporary texts will come to categorically defining a "black" race. The proposal to deport "blackamoors" begins, in its first manifestation, as an expedient solution to crises resulting from the Anglo-Spanish war; in its last incarnation, it produces the infiltration of "blacks" as a threat to England's economy and to its national unity and "natural" identity. Yet the story these documents tell is not simply of a growing English racism or the stabilizing of an association between color, "blacks," and race. Rather, the letters evidence how pressured that ideological trajectory was by practical circumstances that were divisive to any single way of seeing. Together, the letters expose the tensions not just between the English and the Spanish, but between the queen and her "own liege people," whose interests were themselves not one. These documents do not provide a representative measure of the racist sentiment within England at the turn of the century. They show us, rather, how seriously Queen Elizabeth's attempts to activate that sentiment were molded and challenged by competing political and economic circumstances that themselves pointed in conflicting directions, both for and against the deportation of blacks. If her more explicitly "racist" language suggests that England's subjects had themselves grown *more* inclined *ideologically* toward discrimination against blacks as a racial group, the new vehemence and new threats coupled to that language suggest as well that England's citizens were nonetheless *less* inclined *practically* toward the deportation of particular "blacks" in their possession. And if we can trace in

Elizabeth's open letters a subtle change in attitudes toward the accommodation as well as the alienation of a black population, it is a change that we must understand as always under revision, inevitably contingent on the practical, political, and economic needs of the moment and inevitably framed and fractured by those needs.

CHAPTER FIVE

Banishing "all the Moors"

Lust's Dominion and the Story of Spain

WHILE ELIZABETH WAS scripting proposals to delineate and deport "black-amoors" as an unwelcome, unwanted, and unfaithful "kinde of people," in Spain a related history was taking shape around the figure of the Moor. At the turn of the century, the situation of Moors in Spain was reaching a point of crisis that would climax in 1609, when Philip III ordered their expulsion. Until the conquest of Granada in 1492, Moors lived within Spain's borders and colonies as practicing Muslims, their history, culture, and heritage an indelible part of Spain's, as Barbara Fuchs has argued.[1] When the Spanish Inquisition started policing the purity of the Catholic state, and Spanish imperialists, publicizing Spain's national supremacy, however, church and state reinscribed the Moorish presence as a problem—according to Deborah Root, ostracizing Moors first as "infidels," then forcing them to convert to Catholicism and assimilate.[2] Yet ironically, these "Moriscos" were subject to increased suspicion and regulation. Conversion did not guarantee belief, and the state could only legislate the performance, not the presence, of faith. Moreover, the likelihood that Moors were simply "passing" raised the unsettling possibility that Catholic practitioners might be passing too. Hence, from 1520 on, Moriscos were targeted as Christian "heretics" in an increasingly hostile Spain, until their expulsion ostensibly solved the problem.

It was very likely in the period between Queen Elizabeth's propositions to deport certain "blackamoors" and Spain's official banishment of its Moors that *Lust's Dominion; or, the Lascivious Queen* emerged. Although the text, written by Thomas Dekker, probably in collaboration with other playwrights, was not published until 1657, a reference to *The Spanish Moor's Tragedy* appears in Henslowe in 1599–1600, and critics tend to take that play as *Lust's Dominion*.[3] If it was, its appearance was especially timely. For its story of the Spanish Moor, Eleazar, takes the issue of discrimination to its limits, playing seriously with the possibility that Moors could be officially expelled from Spain. At the end of the play, Philip (III) reclaims his rightful place on the "Royall Spanish throne" from the usurping Eleazar (5.5.3798) and then closes down that "perfect villainy" by equating and eradicating the individual and collective body of the Moor (5.5.3794). In the text that we have, Philip commands: "for this Barbarous *Moor*, and his black train, / Let all the *Moors* be banished from Spain" (5.5.3812–14).[4] There is clearly no equivocation or limitation in this couplet. All Moors, not just some, are to be banished. The reason is clear: the "Barbarous" Eleazar and his "black train" have violated Spain, and their violation justifies the expulsion of the Moors they thus are made to represent. This is a moment, then, of straightforward racial discrimination, an official targeting and banishing of Moors, grounded on the assumption that if one Moor is evil, all Moors must be. This is, that is, the active construction and authorization of a stereotype, a prejudice, an ideology. Like Queen Elizabeth's proposal of 1601 and Philip III's policy of 1609, this dramatic pronouncement defines Moors as a justifiably expendable population.

Lust's Dominion provides an important bridge, ideologically if not chronologically, between *Titus*, where ruling Romans demand the "direful slaughtering death" of the "execrable" Aaron, and *Othello*, where ruling Venetians lament the social displacement, psychological dissolution, and physical self-destruction of the "valiant" Othello. As bold as *Lust's Dominion* is in its casting out of the Moor, its starting point is a place and past in which Moors were obviously embedded, and its leading Moor is a figure who stands with one foot outside and the other inside the European domain which he inhabits. Like Aaron, Eleazar works his way to power from a position of illegitimacy, "wantoning" with the Queen Mother of Spain just as Aaron wantons with the empress of Rome, acting inscrutably, if centrally, behind the scenes to destroy the court. But like Othello, he is also legitimately installed and embraced within European society: his wife, Maria, is a Spanish noblewoman, and her father, Alvero, and other prominent members of the court are his loyal supporters. If the tragic irony of *Titus* is that a villainous Moor is indelibly written into Europe, do what it may to cast him out, and (as I will argue) the tragic irony of *Othello*, that a valiant Moor is ultimately written out of

Europe, do what it may to draw him in, in *Lust's Dominion* these two trajectories collapse into each other. For here as the racist coding and elimination of the Spanish Moor come into play as the ultimate fantasy, the longed for apex of desire, that fantasy betrays its own implausibility, exposing the potentially alienable Spanish *Moor* as an essentially inalienable *Spanish* Moor.

* * *

The moment in *Lust's Dominion* when Philip orders "all the *Moors*" from Spain is indeed unprecedented within early modern stagings of the Moor; none of the related plays imagines such a full-scale racial cleansing.[5] We cannot be entirely certain that this was the original end envisioned by Dekker and his collaborators. For as critics have posited, these final lines (along with oblique references to the Gunpowder Plot) may have been the product of a subsequent revision, constructed sometime after (and with an eye to) the 1609 expulsion.[6] It did not take the actual event itself, of course, to make clear that the Moriscos were in line for such a fate: by the end of the sixteenth century Spain's restrictions against its Moors had already tightened so much, according to Root, that the eventual expulsion may have been a predictable outcome of "more than a century of inquisitorial repression."[7] If Dekker and his collaborators were looking to Spain in 1599, they may well have been able to see this eventuality coming. Yet whether the play's last lines were invented in 1599 or written later, whether they imaginatively anticipate or record an actual historical event, in *Lust's Dominion* the prospect of banishing the Moor—especially the one Moor, Eleazar, whose particular "evils" come to define "all the Moors" categorically (5.5.3774)—emerges as a pervasive but problematic cultural fantasy.

When the play opens, Eleazar appears with the Spanish queen, engaging in an illicit but not entirely unnoticed affair, which marks Spain as "lust's dominion," his lover as a "lascivious queen," and himself, he says, as "the Minion of the Spanish Queen," who "makes a Cuckold of our King" (1.1.124–25). His purposes are questionable, if also somewhat unfathomable. While the queen lavishes her desires upon him, he castigates her for having "melted all [his] spirits, / Ravish'd his youth" and "deflour'd [his] lovely cheeks" in order, he says, to "try" her "love" (1.1.159, 109–11). In addition, after she exits, he anticipates "shutt[ing]" his "dear love" "up in hell" (1.1.213–15). Still, this dangerous liaison goes unpunished (for two scenes) until the king dies and his putative heir, Prince Philip, returns from Portugal. By then, the late king's brother, Fernando, has become king and Cardinal Mendoza has become the Protector, in a succession that departs radically from the historical record. While they "all" "stand . . . still, yet let this divell [Eleazar] stand here" (1.3.507–8), the disenfranchised prince impugns Eleazar as a "Divell" (1.3.480), indicts the queen as "a Moor's Concubine" (1.3.499), and accuses both of "rip[ping] up the entrails of [Spain's] treasury: / With Masques and antick Revellings" (1.3.501–2). Claiming the "consent / Of all these peers," Mendoza consequently orders that Eleazar be "uterly deprive[d]" "of all those Royalties [he] hold'st in Spain" (1.3.512–14). Although the queen (now the queen mother) questions his "Commission," asking that Eleazar be "try'd" (1.3.516, 524), the cardinal shuts down her request with a cataclysmic pro-nouncement. Insisting that the Moor's "treasons" are "too plain" to "need . . . tryal," he warns Eleazar: "Come not within the Court, for if you do, / To beg with Indian slaves I'le banish you" (1.3.525–28).

Eleazar is not banished, either from the court or to the domains of "In-dian slaves," but neither are the cardinal's words an empty or insignificant threat. Mendoza's order catalyzes a serious breach within the court and presses Spain to the brink of civil war. Notably, it is not the "lascivious" behavior of the Moor but the proposal to ostracize him that is the disturbing source of contention here. For starters, Fernando, who secretly lusts after Eleazar's wife and hopes to keep her in range, pledges therefore to overrule the Moor's "late receiv'd disgrace" with his own kingly "grace" (1.3.631, 641) and challenges the cardinal's "authority, / To banish [Eleazar] the Court without our leav" [sic] (2.1.701–2). Eleazar himself protests that "the Cardinal / (Oh! rare) would bandy me away from Spain, / And banish me to beg; I, beg with slaves" (1.4.544–47), and his noble father-in-law takes his and the king's side, ques-tioning "why should my sonne be banished?" (1.4.531–32). Meanwhile, Philip joins forces with Mendoza, objecting to the fact that "this Divell" Eleazar re-mains in their presence after the cardinal's "sacred mouth" "pronounc'd the sentence of his banishment" (2.1.662, 667–68). Both Mendoza and the king declare their own words "laws," the one in asserting and the other in repeal-ing the Moor's banishment (2.1.685, 687). As tensions escalate, the king cries treason, the rebelling peers cry tyrant, and the cardinal cries pope, and the showdown expands quickly into a more abstract contest for power between the newly appointed king and his faction (which includes the Moor) on one side and the disenfranchised prince and his faction (which includes the cardi-nal) on the other. The Queen Mother temporarily resolves the crisis, induc-ing both sides to "leave these arms" and "embrace" (2.1.774–75, 777) by promising Mendoza, who lusts after her, that she will "reward" his "love" (2.1.788–90) and Eleazar, that she will kill Mendoza. Though Philip says nothing, the cardinal pretends to "lay by [his] / Hostile intendments, and return again / To the fair circle of obedience" for "love" of his "Country" (2.1.798–800). Even so, the unseating of the Moor remains the precarious proposition that can make or break the state.

Remarkably here, even in the face of a Moor whose transgressions are all "too plain," a local exile appears as a vexed, not natural, solution. To be sure, lustful ambitions drive both the king's resistance to the order and the cardinal's acquiescence to its repeal. But if Alvero's loyalty to Eleazar does not raise questions about the advisability of banning the Moor from court, the political chaos that results from such an attempt does. Indeed, in creating a space to represent the crisis of banishment, the play distorts the history at its base: it disrupts the otherwise smooth transition between Philip II (who died in 1598) and Philip III (who succeeded immediately), filling in the gap with the controversy over Eleazar and creating what one editor has called "a mere nightmare," a "frantic perversion of history."[8] If the result is to incriminate Spain as "lust's dominion," we should not take its perversions therefore to be unique, a sign that what is imaginable there would not be believed in England. For within the invented space between the death of Philip II and the accession of Philip III, the play suggestively invokes the precedent of Marlowe's *Edward II* (ca. 1590), where the forced exile of the English king's "minion," Gaveston, catalyzes similar controversy and catastrophe (*Ed. II* 1.4.87).[9] Though *Edward II* seems to have been "publiquely acted" only sporadically, starting in 1592, the text was published in 1594 and reprinted in 1598, just before *Lust's Dominion* was likely to have come out.[10] And while there is no guarantee that the spectators would have seen Marlowe's play, *Lust's Dominion* is nonetheless saturated with parallels in plot and language, which critics have noticed though not theorized and which quietly insist that the prospect of banishment (like the dominion of lust) is neither peculiar to the Spanish Moor's tragedy nor simply cued or warranted by the Spanish Moor.[11]

Like Eleazar, Gaveston is "minion" to a royal head of state and is heavily persecuted for his sodomitical transgressions. Gaveston's story starts, in fact, with a prior exile. As the play opens, he is just returning—and reading Edward II's letter commanding that he return—to England from his native France, where he has been ousted by the previous king (Edward I) for a questionable erotic attachment to the then crown prince.[12] It will not be long after the reunion between Gaveston and Edward II before the English peers accuse them of "draw[ing] the treasury dry" with "the idle triumphs, masques, lascivious shows / And prodigal gifts bestowed on Gaveston" (2.2.157–59), just as it will not be long after the Spanish king's death before Prince Philip accuses Eleazar and the Queen Mother of "ripping up" England's treasury "with masques and antick Revellings." Nor is it long before the nobles and the leaders of the Catholic Church demand that the "wicked Gaveston" be forced again from England for his sexual transgressions (1.1.176), just as it is not long before the cardinal and Philip demand that the devilish Eleazar be banished from Spain for his. In *Edward II* as in *Lust's Dominion*, since illicit desire provides unmitigated access to power, the imposition of a geographical exile seems to be the only way, short of murder, to write the "other" out.

In embedding *Edward II*'s story so prominently within its own, *Lust's Dominion* underscores the fact that such a solution is itself a problem, a challenge rather than a complement to the stability of the state. In both plays, the demand for exile expands into a potentially treasonous play for power, with the nobility using their case against the targeted subject to take a rebellious "stand against [their] king" (*Ed. II* 1.1.96). Both kings fight that fire with fire: Fernando displays his support of Eleazar to overrule the nobles' revolt, condemning these "Subjects" for attempting to "counter-check their Soveraigns will" (*L.D.* 2.1.720–21), while Edward displays his embrace of Gaveston to chastize and constrain the peers, refusing to "brook these haughty menaces" and answering the broader political question—"Am I a king and must be overruled?"—with a resounding no (*Ed. II* 1.1.134–35). But where *Lust's Dominion* stops short of having the crisis over banishment result in an immediate civil war, *Edward II* does not: armed with thinly veiled allegations of sodomy (or "baseness"), the nobles not only expel, recall, and then kill Gaveston; they also depose and kill the king.[13] Hence, as this dramatic history shadows *Lust's Dominion*, it amplifies not only how ubiquitous the proposal of banishment is to the mapping of political contention but also how dangerous it is to the assertion of political order.

At the end of Marlowe's play there is no cry for the banishment of all sodomites as there is at the end of at least one version of *Lust's Dominion* for banishment of all Moors. Nor, ultimately, can there be. For the England of *Edward II* is a place where the king himself is a sodomite and where his nobles and "minions" alike vie for his "love" (1.1.79).[14] The peers do succeed in ousting and destroying Gaveston, as well as the Younger Spenser who follows him as the king's political, though apparently not sexual, favorite. But as the substitution of Spenser for Gaveston itself suggests, political and sexual favor blur together here. In the end, the play condemns the nobles—and particularly the Younger Mortimer—for displacing the demarcated "others" only finally to replace them. When the tragic wheel comes full circle, Mortimer has committed adultery with the English queen, usurped the reign as self-proclaimed protector of the prince, and authorized the murder of the deposed but nonetheless legitimate king. It is Mortimer, then, who takes, must take, the final fall, with Edward III claiming his rightful place on the English throne and restoring his father's legitimacy. In this play, to banish all the sodomites would be to banish all the world, at least the world of England, where sexual and political favor lose their distinction in the name and play of power.

In *Lust's Dominion*, then, the incorporation of *Edward II* creates a provocative overlay of England onto Spain, sodomite onto Moor—one that plays against the peculiarities of type and emphasizes resemblances where characters within the dramatic fictions mark difference. In Marlowe, because the contested difference, sodomitical desire, is itself invisible, the unsettling resemblances between Gaveston, Spenser, the king, and the peers are therefore easier to see.[15] In *Lust's Dominion*, however, although it is not Eleazar's "gloomy" complexion but his "lascivious" activity that explicitly prompts the call for banishment, that complexion nonetheless sets him visibly apart—making his lust especially suspect as an innate racial trait, a sign of a deviant identity not just a deviant behavior, and making his relocation to a domain of "Indian slaves" appear somehow uniquely appropriate (3.2.1500). Yet in suggesting a parallel between Eleazar and Gaveston, *Lust's Dominion* effectively denaturalizes such discrimination, prompting us to think across the bounds of race, to recognize that the "treasons" of the Moor are equally characteristic of the Spanish (as of the English). The subtitle, after all, declares the Spanish queen "lascivious," presenting her and not the Moor as the representative of "lust's dominion," and, we quickly see, the Spanish king and cardinal prominently share the fault. The point is not, then, that Spain's incorporation of the Moor signs its corruption, but that the Moor's corruption is already, pervasively (though not necessarily uniquely) Spain's. If the Moor is to Spain what the sodomite is to England, even if his "treasons" "need no tryal," the attempts to write him out of the country into a separable race, in another sense, do. For in both plays to "subscribe" to exile is not only to undermine monarchical authority (*Ed. II* 1.4.53); it is also to impose a geographic distance when ideological difference will not hold.

It is not the intertextual parallel alone that unsettles the ideological boundaries of banishment and makes a legal separation between the Moor and the Spanish seem implausible if not also impossible. In an important reversal of terms and players, *Lust's Dominion* restages Mendoza's discriminatory gesture in a way that renders both its particular imposition and its underlying logic highly questionable. This time it is the Spanish king, Fernando, who imagines ousting Eleazar, changing his original loyalties but acting once again on lust. Though Fernando's initial defense of Eleazar has the useful side effect of keeping Maria near both court and king, it also puts the Moor in the way of the seduction that was an important part of its point. In acting on his lustful desires, the Spanish king invokes and expands the cardinal's controversial precedent. Entering Maria's bedchamber (armed for rape, we might notice, in case his persuasions fail), he insists that, if she does not succumb to his advances, he will send Eleazar to war to die "nobly" (3.2.1529), "call a Parlament / And banish by a law all *Moors* from Spain" (3.2.1532–34), and finally make it "death for any *Negroes* hand, / To touch the beauty of a Spanish dame" (3.2.1537–38).

If the reversal, as well as the illicit circumstances that condition both his embrace and his rejection of the Moor, betray the instability of Fernando's particular politics, his propositions simultaneously undermine the logic of racial discrimination more broadly. These fantasies come, tellingly, not at the beginning of his seduction but the end, and his threat to impose a physical separation between Spaniard and Moor derives from (and emphasizes) his repeated failure to create a social, sexual, emotional, or ideological distance. In beginning his persuasions, Fernando tries first to appeal to Maria's Spanishness, asserting:

> Thy husband is no Spaniard, thou art one,
> So is *Fernando*, then for countries sake
> Let mee not spare thee, on thy husbands face
> Eternall night in gloomy shades doth dwel;
> But I'le look on thee like the guilded Sun. (3.2.1495–1501)

Using definitive differences in color and nation to suggest undesirable differences in race, he contends (and pretends) that, for her "countries sake," she should prefer the sunny Spaniard to her husband, who is "no Spaniard," his "gloomy" countenance marking him subtly as also not white.[16] Maria resists these attempts to exhibit and exploit racial differences by turning Fernando's overused imagery against him and rejecting his "Sun-set eyes" (3.2.1504). In response, he appeals to her national pride, adding station to ethnicity and color and promising that "in pride *Maria* shall through Spain be born" (3.2.1508): if she agrees to "love" him, he declares, he will "circle [her] white forehead with the Crown / Of Castile, Portugall, and Arragon, / And all those petty Kingdoms which do bow / Their tributarie knees to *Philip*'s heir" (3.2.1519–24). It is only because these efforts are unsuccessful that he translates racial and cultural difference into geography and turns prejudice into law.

Significantly, that law evolves here uneasily as the unwarranted extension of a specific example. As Fernando's threats move from military conscription of Eleazar, who could die "nobly," to the banishment of all Moors, whose offenses are assumed rather than explained, to the death of any Negroes who are incriminated as sexual predators, the king blurs the convenient disposition of a particular Moor into legal and social imperatives against all Moors and Negroes, turning Eleazar into the natural representative of a necessarily alienable (black) race. Yet as these terms get more general, they also get less tenable. That is, the harder Fernando tries to distance the Moor as a racially marked Other, the clearer he makes the Moors' (and Negroes') penetration of Spain. Fernando's audience, after all, is the Moor's own Spanish wife, and the unrelenting obstacle to his lust is a marriage that gives Eleazar legitimacy within Spain. Maria, in fact, thinks that Fernando might spare her "for [her husband's] sake" (3.2.1493–94). Moreover, though the king imagines that he could send Eleazar to war, he acknowledges that it would take an act of parliament to rid the realm officially of Moors. Even that seems inadequate. For as he elides Eleazar's particular case into a more easily incriminated general race of Moors and Negroes, he suggests that Maria might not be the only Spanish dame to be "touched" by a Negro—that the contact between black and white is neither an anomaly nor an aberration, but a fact of Spanish life. Otherwise, why would it take an official threat of death to restrict Negroes from "touching" Spanish dames, if not Spanish dames to be "touched" by them? (We can think back to *Titus* here, to Lucius's declaration that any one who relieves or pities the starving Moor must die.)

Fernando's persuasions ultimately fail, and although he resorts to force within the bedchamber, his threats come quickly to naught. Maria has not only anticipated his coming but also informed Eleazar, who arms her with a poison to fend off the lustful king. Fend him off she does, by poisoning him into a deathlike sleep right out of *Romeo and Juliet* (1595–96). In an even more incredible dramatic twist, "Oberon, and Fairyes" (3.2.1583 S.D.) come out of nowhere—disjunctively invoking *A Midsummer Night's Dream* (1595–96)—to warn Maria that the Queen Mother will kill her, as indeed she does, "think-ing her own son is done to death" and hoping "to be thy husbands wife" (3.2.1594, 1596). If this dizzying cacophony of dramatic plots takes the focus off Eleazar, it nonetheless brings the racist discriminations that Fernando has articulated to a certain if outrageous end: his illicit desire for the Moor's wife is finally undone and outdone by the Spanish queen who would herself have the Moor. In a world where Negroes' hands have easy access to Spanish beauty, and it seems, Spanish beauty to Moorish hands, ideology needs geog-raphy to create a distance, and that distance simply is not (yet) there, even if a fantasy of banishment is.

Ultimately, then, however much the impulse to expel the Moor might be reiterated, recycled, or replayed, the move to banish Eleazar in *Lust's Dominion*—like the move to exile Gaveston in *Edward II*—marks the vexed beginning of a political crisis, not simply an ameliorating end. The official im-position of that collective cultural fantasy may indeed mark the culmination of the Spanish Moor's history and the cathartic consummation of the specta-tors' own desires. But as *Lust's Dominion* presses the Moor—and the idea of expelling the Moor—to the brink of its own dramatic reality, the dialogue within this play (as well as between it and *Edward II*) indicts the translation of one bad Moor into a constructed race of banished Moors as neither as plau-sible nor as possible as its reiteration might make it seem. If the irrepressible, even irresistible fantasy ultimately becomes the ubiquitous sign of Spain at its best, it starts as the ubiquitous symptom of Spain at its worst.

* * *

While this vexed and complex writing out defines the Moor's place in *Lust's Dominion*, so also does the equally vexed and complex writing in. For if the desire to banish the Moor drives the play's fantasies, the Moor's ability both to penetrate and to represent Spain constitutes its realities. In *Lust's Domin-ion*, Spain's demarcation of the Moor is significantly coupled to the Moor's de-marcation of Spain. The result will eventually be civil war—one predicated by Eleazar's ascension to the highest reaches of court, rather than by talk of his expulsion, evidencing his invulnerability, rather than his vulnerability, as a Spanish subject. Though in the end he will undoubtedly fall, what falls stun-ningly with him is the very stuff that Spain is made on—the sanctifying be-lief in *limpieza de sangre*, in the "purity" of Spanish blood.[17]

Like Aaron before him (and unlike Othello after him), Eleazar's presence within Europe derives from a history of conquest. As the Queen Mother tells it, the "deceast King," Philip (II), "made warr in *Barbarie*, / Won *Tunis*, conquered *Fesse*, and hand to hand, / Slew great *Abdela*, King of *Fesse*, and father / To that *Barbarian* Prince," Eleazar (5.1.2968–72). Consequently, according to Eleazar, when the Barbarian king "with his Empire, lost his life," he "left [Eleazar] Captive to a Spanish Tyrant" (1.2.235–36). Contextually, what lies behind these events is a long history of conquest, extending from the eighth century to 1492, between Moors (the Umayyads), who conquered large parts of Hispania, and the Iberian Christians, who orchestrated what they justified as a "*reconquista*" to get those domains back. Though we might therefore read Eleazar's coming in story as an extenuated after-effect of a prior contention, the Moor himself does not. Rather, he translates the past of conquest into a peculiar present of oppression, depicting himself as uniquely and unjustly alienated within Spain. He "cannot ride through the Castilian streets," he asserts,

> But thousand eies through windows, and through doors
> Throw killing looks at me, and every slave
> At *Eleazar* darts a finger out,
> And every hissing tongue cries, There's the Moor,
> That's he that makes a Cuckold of our King,
> there go's the Minion of the Spanish Queen;
> That's the black Prince of Divels, there go's hee
> That on smooth boies, on Masks and Revellings
> Spends the Revenues of the King of Spain. (1.1.116–30)

Asking how one could "loose a kingdom and not rave," he indeed raves— especially against Spain's "silken Courtiers" who, he says, "christen" him "a *Moore*, a Devill, / A slave of *Barbary*, a dog" (1.2.239, 227–30).

If *Titus* has taught us anything, it is that the legacy of conquest can rarely be codified along such clearly cut political axes that separate insiders from outsiders, Europeans from Moors. To be sure, very soon in *Lust's Dominion*, the contest over banishment will bring out the racist terms—for example, the charge of "Devill"—that Eleazar says affronts him now. But, as I have argued, their articulation becomes a vehicle for a power play that is less about the Moor than it is about the monarchy. Moreover, as Eleazar emphasizes his cross-cultural oppression, he lays the ground for his own unprecedented rise. When he brings up his abuse on the Castilian streets, it is to accuse the Spanish queen of ruining his reputation with her lust—of "arm[ing]" the "many headed beast" of Spanish street talk and fueling Spain's disdain for the Moorish "minion" in its midst (1.1.131). Although his purposes are not transparent, his allegations manipulate the Queen Mother's sympathies and desires, putting this increasingly crucial ally defensively under his command. When he again brings up the scene of conquest, it is to distract his father-in-law from connecting the dots between himself and the queen (whom Alvero seeks in his presence). Accusing Alvero of "grow[ing] Jealous" and suspicious of his relations with the Spanish queen (1.2.226), Eleazar glorifies his own (implicitly better) father, who "lost his life" "with his empire." He simultaneously uses the example to exonerate himself. Proving the injustice of his resulting captivity under the Spanish tyrant, he argues: "Although my flesh be tawny, in my veines, / Runs blood as red, and royal as the best / And proud'st in Spain" (1.2.231–33). Within Eleazar's constructions, royalty prevails across the bounds of culture, conquest, and captivity, outdoing and undoing the variables of history, ethnicity, and race. And with the question of the queen thus displaced and replaced, Alvero can do nothing but urge Eleazar to "think on" these "wrongs" in "fitter hours," to now "take leave" of the dying king, "halfe of his body" already lying "within a grave" (1.1.245–46, 249, 253).

Try as Eleazar might to narrate himself into a precarious position as a captive forced by a tyrant king into an unwilling and unwelcoming Spain, however, in producing himself as a wronged but rightful subject, he emphasizes rather his uncontested domestic position.[18] From the start, it is clear that, despite its interracial edges, his marriage to Maria gives him substantial leverage at court. If the specter of miscegenation haunts Mendoza's protests against the Moor's illicit dealings with the Spanish queen (for example, in the elision of the Moor with Indian slaves), it does not haunt responses to the Eleazar's marriage.[19] Fernando will, of course, attempt to prove to Maria that Spaniards should not be with Moors, but his efforts fail completely. In *Lust's Dominion*, there is no angry father making a public issue of the fact that a "black ram" may be "tupping [his] white ewe" or demanding that the Moor answer charges of bewitching one of Europe's fairest daughters, as there will be in *Othello* (*Oth*. 1.1.88–89). To the contrary, Alvero embraces Eleazar as his "sonne," even at the expense of his real son, Hortenso, who has no clout at court until Philip joins with him at the end of the play. Indeed, in choosing sides against the potentially ascendant Philip and Mendoza, Alvero self-consciously stakes his own political standing on the Moor's. When talk of Eleazar's banishment emerges, he worries that if the nobles "triumph o're" the

Moor, they will then "spurn me down" (1.4.593–94). In addition, the dying King Philip receives Eleazar as "*Don Alvero's* son," commending him to the court as "a man / Both wise and warlike (1.3.387, 391)." If father supplants daughter here as Eleazar's ennobling link to Spain, the interracial marriage nonetheless provides the vehicle. Although the king cautions the court to "beware of him, / Ambition wings his spirit, keep him down; / What wil not men attempt to win a crown" (1.3.392–94), the caution suggests how far Eleazar might go not only *against* Spain but more so *within* it.

Though it is unclear whether Eleazar's display of his marital bond predicates or is predicated on Spain's endorsement of intermarriage, he uses the domestic connection to stage his own radical rise to power and ultimately to change the terms of Spanishness. Unlike Aaron, who asserts control illicitly behind the scenes—even if in the proximity and with the authority—of the court, with no hope of claiming the rule, Eleazar uses his legitimacy as a Spanish husband to openly challenge (and kill) a sitting monarch. After the Spanish queen "discovers" and kills Maria for poisoning the Spanish king, it turns out (as the queen knows) that Fernando is not dead. Eleazar seizes the occasion for his own play-within-the-play and stabs Fernando in front of a watching court, confidently condemning "the unchast blood of that lecher King, / That threw my wife in untimely grave" (3.4.1746–47). Extrapolating a policy and politics from those particulars and insisting that revenge is due, he explains: "Were he ten thousand Kings that slew my love, / Thus shou'd my hand (plum'd with revenges wings) / Requite mine own dishonour, and her death" (3.4.1734–39). One of the onlooking nobles (Roderigo) does "crie treason," damning "this black feind" for his actions, but Eleazar holds his ground (3.4.1755–56). Not only does he seize the castle with his own armed "slaves" (3.4.1772); he continues to argue the legitimacy of his cause, putting the claims of marital dishonor above the alleged crime of treason. "The King is murdred," he argues, "and I'le answer it; / I am dishonour'd, and I will revenge it" (3.4.1762–63). Eleazar, of course, distorts and manipulates the facts, accusing the lascivious king of actions authored (with his own assistance) by the lascivious queen. Yet what is especially striking here is how astoundingly effective his domestic cover is—so effective that, in front of friend and foe, the dishonored husband can announce his intentions to acquire "A Kingdom, Castiles crown" (3.4.1815).

A kingdom, Castile's crown? Far outdoing Thomas Stukeley, the man who would be, but could never be, king, the Moor imagines that he could be king, even within a kingdom which has already ordered his expulsion. And

what is even more remarkable is that he can make his dream come true by re-
constructing the terms of Spanish identity and Spanish rule. Immediately
after Fernando's murder, the Queen Mother urges the court to "choose a new
Soveraign," and "all" automatically endorse the ostensible heir apparent,
"Prince Philip" (3.4.1783–84). Yet Eleazar makes his own claim to the crown
(with the blood of this regicide at least metaphorically on his hands), and in
the process, not only takes charge of the Spanish bloodline but also undermines its stability and its significance. While on the one hand he declares
Philip a "bastard," on the other he promotes behavior over birth as the deter-
minant of rule (3.4.1788). Positioning himself next to Philip as a Spanish insider and not a Moorish outsider, he implores the courtiers and public to
"look well on *Eleazar*," to

> Value me not by my sun-burnt
> Cheek, but by my birth; nor by
> My birth, but by my losse of blood,
> Which I have sacrificed in Spains defence. (3.4.1794–98)

Here, he explains his skin color as the product of the sun and distances himself from his Barbarian birth, aligning his "blood" rather with defense of
Spain. Letting blood sacrificed *for* Spain trump the blood *of* Spain, he gives
political action precedence over genealogy. With inheritance rendered therefore secondary, he then directs the audience to "look on *Philip*, and the
Cardinall," and to compare him to these "gaping currs," who would (as he
himself implicitly would not) "swallow you, your country, children, wives"
(3.4.1799–1800, 1804–5). The Queen Mother clinches the case by emphasizing Eleazar's racial difference only to underplay its significance. Pretending to
see "horror on each side," she deems it "miserie" "when Indian slaves thirst
after Empery" (3.4.1821, 1818–19), but declares setting "the Crown / Upon a
bastards head" the greater "disgrace" to "fair Spain" (3.4.1832–35). Since
"Spains bright glory" has already been dimmed by the shame of Philip's bastardy, she argues, Spain might as well put its stock in "that proud Blackamore," who, if he is not a perfect choice, is comparably the best choice for
an already compromised Spain (3.4.1836–38). In playing thus into the potential prejudices of the "Princes and Peers of Spain," she plays against them,
minimizing the significance, but not the signs, of racial difference (3.4.1820).
With the Queen Mother behind him, Eleazar succeeds: he not only gains the
endorsement of the anonymous "all" who first championed Philip; he also,

more insidiously, changes the measure and meaning of race, turning Spanish identity and lineage into negotiable terms, their value dependent on deeds, not fixed innately by blood.

There is, indeed, some protest. Alvero himself objects to the royal investiture of one "that slew [the] King" (3.4.1846–47), and while one Spanish nobleman declares Eleazar "a villain and a base born fugitive," another calls him "a bloody tyrant, [and] an usurping slave" (3.4.1866–69). As well, before too long, Philip's Portuguese ally, the king Emmanuel, resorts to demonizing fictions to comprehend the Moor's otherwise incomprehensible success. Asserting that "the *Moor's* a Devill," he argues,

> never did horrid feind
> Compel'd by som Magicians mighty charm,
> Break through the prisons of the solid earth,
> With more strange horror, then this Prince of hell,
> This damned Negro Lyon-like doth rush,
> Through all, and spite of all knit opposition. (4.2.2215–24)

The play goes out of its way to bring Emmanuel in, since his historical prototype, Manoel the Fortunate, died before Philip was born.[20] Manoel was known for attempting to expel Portugal's Jews and unconverted Moors in the early sixteenth century. But before we endorse the polymorphic racist prejudices of his dramatic descendant as the play's, as at least one critic has done, we should notice that Philip himself casts them immediately aside, to locate the fault rather in his own faction's "cowardise" and in the deceptions of the Spanish cardinal, now a culpable "slave" (4.3.2228–29).[21] Eleazar is, of course, a villain (though neither a Negro nor a prince of hell), but the "strange horror" that allows him to break into a position of power in "spite of all knit opposition" is not some devilish enchantment, but Spain itself. Within a single scene, although Eleazar loses the support of his father-in-law, he sways other Spanish nobles to his side, with promises to "divide" the "Empery" among them (3.4.1873). As civil war breaks out, Eleazar defends his place as "Castiles Royall King" from the center of the Spanish court, while Philip must retreat to Portugal, to clear his name of bastardy and treason from the outskirts of Spain (3.4.1865). Though the Moor is obviously not in the right, he stands nonetheless in the position of king, with the backing, if not quite the blessing, of Spain.

As Eleazar thus changes the standards of Spanish identity, he is able not only to secure his rise but also to determine Philip's fall. Almost the moment the rumor of Philip's bastardy hits the Castilian streets, his standing is at least as much in question Eleazar's, with action challenging blood as the means and measure of right. As Eleazar's cronies, Friars Crab and Cole, circulate in the Spanish marketplace, they instruct the public to "set that bastard and *Eleazar* together" and "compare them" (3.5.2015–16, 2018), producing Philip as not just a "bastard" but also a "dastard," a man "that kill'd your King," "onely to make himself King" (3.5.1979–82), and Eleazar as "a valiant Gentleman," "a Noble Gentleman," even "a fair black Gentleman," as well as "a Champion for Castilians" who is "fit to be King" (3.5.1996–99, 2001–2). Eleazar's hired Moorish guns shoot the friars, and the scene breaks into riot, leaving "every man" to "shift for himself" (3.5.2024–25). Still, the confusion of standards results in a telling confusion of response—the citizens of Spain running "up and down," "some crying kill the bastard, some the *Moor*; / Some cry[ing], God save King *Philip*; and some cry[ing], / God save the *Moor*; some others, he shall die" (3.6.2050–55). Philip himself takes the challenge seriously, acting on the battlefield to clear his name by exchanging blood for blood, behavior for birthright. Since lineage does guarantee legitimacy under Eleazar's regime, the prince's only hope is to "let out blood enough" to "quench" his "Fathers wrongs, [his] brothers wounds, / [His] mothers infamie, [and] Spains miserie" (4.3.2329, 2325–27).

Blood for blood. Philip will defeat and kill Eleazar, and regain the crown, but not before the Moor has compromised the very "purity of blood" that has served as the linchpin of Spanish nationalism. After promoting his new Spain as a place of glorious light, where "vice Roys" "Shine about our bright Castilian crown, / As stars about the Sun" (3.4.1877–81), Eleazar puts Spain's whiteness on trial, implicating it as an unreliable measure of national or cultural purity and turning the line between Spaniard and Moor into a matter for debate. In a remarkable deception, he sets his own newly gained crown up for grabs and heads a fallacious public attempt to identify, and either punish or redeem, the bastardizing father of the bastard prince. He first argues that, if the offender is "noble & a Spaniard born," "the white hand of marriage" will hide "the apparent scarrs of their infamies," and he urges the court not to let that cover "eat the blemish off" (5.1.2919–23). Mendoza, unfortunately, takes the bait, insisting that justice (or revenge) must be done, that "Spaniard or *Moor*, the saucy slave shall dye" (5.1.2925–26). Eleazar seizes this refrain, reiterating "Spaniard or *Moor*, the saucy slave shall dye" (5.1.2928–29), "Spaniard or *Moor*, that saucy slave shall dye" (5.1.2986–87), keeping Spaniard and Moor

poised on the precarious edge of accusation in a way—like Portia's now famous question, "Which is the merchant here? and which the Jew?" (*MV*
4.1.174)—that undermines rather than underlines their difference.[22] Though
Mendoza offers the declaration rhetorically, to incriminate the Moor, in *Lust's
Dominion*, it takes only one more shove for the incrimination of Spaniard *or*
Moor to become the incrimination of Spaniard *not* Moor. Following Eleazar's
cues, the Queen Mother recalls Spain's conquest of Barbary and locates in it
the telling moment of adultery. "Twice ten years" ago, while Philip (II) was at
war in Barbary, she testifies, Cardinal Mendoza "threaten[ed] my death if I
deni'd his lust" and "by force" "abus'd the bed of Spain," in that act fathering
the bastard prince (5.1.2966–67, 2982–83, 2985). Once again appropriating the
scene of conquest to his own ends, Eleazar condemns the cardinal for "abus-
ing the bed" he himself has enjoyed. Unfathomably, Mendoza accedes, pro-
fessing his innocence only when he is dragged off to prison to await trial, with
Eleazar still reiterating the now dangerous refrain "Spaniard or *Moor*, the
saucy slave shall die." What results is an astounding substitution of Spaniard
for Moor, Eleazar here not only making the Spaniard over in the incriminating image he has sported as his own but, in the process, calling into question
the readability of Spanishness itself.

There is one final twist. For not only does Eleazar take control of the
Spanish state by bastardizing the prince and incriminating the cardinal, displacing the political legitimacy of the one and projecting his illegitimate sexual doings onto the other; he also takes control of the Spanish race by
displacing and replacing the Queen Mother. There is no danger here, as there
is in *Titus*, that the Moor will reproduce himself. Neither Maria nor the
Queen Mother will give birth to a "blackamoor" baby and so, in Maria's case,
undo the supremacy of white over black or, in the Queen Mother's, expose
her own "lasciviousness" (which she has already publicized). Yet if Eleazar
does not literally reproduce his race, he does take figurative control over the
Spanish queen's womb. As the Queen Mother watches Eleazar pacing, pon-
dering, and preparing for (we know but she does not) the cardinal's demise,
she herself begins to worry: "What shape will this *prodigious womb* bring
forth, / Which groans with such *strange labour*" (4.4.2604–6; emphasis
added). Eleazar himself speaks of his scheme as something "breeding in the
brain" and looks forward to "the hour wherein 'tis born" (4.4.2622, 2637). And
at just the moment that the queen is preparing to betray him, he turns his
own "strange labour" against her: subsuming and assuming her power to produce a legitimate heir, he offers the Spanish crown to the princess Isabella,

whom he plans to win for himself. If his actions are seeded with lust, they are also seeded with power.[23] In advancing Isabella, he advances and possesses her hereditary right, which he traces through the father, instead of the mother. Denying the Queen Mother's royal body its determining place and power, he insists that "all may doubt the fruits of such a Womb" as hers (5.2.3093–94). And while he directs the Spanish lords to "be deaf, be blind, hear not, behold her not" (5.2.3103), he prompts them rather to "look . . . upon your Sovereign *Isabel,*" to consider whether she "is . . . not like King *Philip*" (5.2.3092, 3095). With the male, not the female, setting the terms here, legitimacy is now in the eye of the beholder, and the beholding eye that matters, that dictates the succession of Spanish royalty and sets the terms of the Spanish race, is the Moor's.

Ultimately Philip does return to restore the boundaries that would permanently delimit the Moor, but his triumph is only partial. He first must escape the imprisonment the Moor has authorized, and in order to do so, he and his ally Hortenso must impersonate the Moors who hold them— "put[ting] the *Moors* habits on, and paint[ing] [their] faces with the oil of hell" (5.5.3584–86). Only in this guise—and only through a play-within-the-play, which Eleazar directs and in which he plays the cardinal and has Philip and Hortenzo, whom he thinks are Moors, imitate themselves—can Philip then change places with Eleazar, constraining him physically with manacles and containing him ideologically, as if once and for all, as "the actor . . . of evils" (5.5.3773–74). In hoisting Eleazar with his own petard, Philip's actions replay the final substitution of Marlowe's *Jew of Malta,* where the Christian governor traps the Jew in the "deep pit past recovery" (*Jew of Malta* 5.5.36) that the Jew has constructed to trap the Turks.[24] Eleazar himself emphasizes that he is "betray'd and cozen'd in [his] own designs" (5.6.3763–64). If in Marlowe the ironic reversals are still to come, with the Spanish, who resemble the Turks, waiting ominously in the wings to claim and control the island, in *Lust's Dominion* they reside in the very moment of the Spaniard impersonating a Moor, performing and installing himself in what Isabella calls "the mold of Hell" (5.5.3558).

What becomes clear in the final scene, however, is that it is easier to put on the "oil of hell" than it is to take it off. As the play works to its close, Philip and Hortenzo remain in Moorish drag—their disguise so convincing that they must discover themselves not only to the unsuspecting Eleazar but also to the Queen Mother. In reclaiming his own legitimacy, Philip stabs the Moor in front of the "brave spirits of Spain" (5.6.3773–74), "thrust[ing] him down to act amongst the devils," in a gesture that recalls Eleazar's stabbing of

Fernando (5.6.3774–75). But while the Spaniard now separates blood from blood, ordering his men to remove the Moor's body "while his blood streams forth" and claiming the "Hereditary right, to the Royall Spanish throne usurp'd by him" (5.6.3795–99), he does so in the dress, makeup, and footsteps of a Moor. And not only does he, like Eleazar, accept and rely on the support of the Queen Mother, whose name, but not past, Philip clears with a potentially compromising pardon. In order to "end a Tragedie" "with Comick joy," he "contract[s] [his] sister unto" the still disguised Hortenso, recreating visually the marriage of Spaniard and Moor that has given Eleazar a legitimating edge in the Spanish court (5.6.3810–11). It is after these performances that Philip's restorative order to banish "all the *Moors*" may come. But with or without it, the tragedy ends with an unsettling irony of the Spanish prince reclaiming Spain in the indelible image of the Moor. If part of the effect is to suggest the "theatricality of blackness," it is also to underscore the revealing mimicry that defines and destabilizes Spain.[25]

No wonder, then, that this is world that would banish all its Moors, writing them into an absolutely expendable and alienable race. For this one Barbarian's inimitable rise to power exposes the permeability not simply of Spain's borders and bodies but also of its defining identities and ideologies. As arbiter of the royal bloodline, Eleazar, the king of Spain, is also symbolically, if temporarily, the *Spanish* king. In thinking of this tragic end, we might think back to the play's beginning, to the fantasy of banishment that catalyzed the crisis of state in the first place. In the face of Mendoza's order, Eleazar insists that he can insinuate himself anywhere. "Hah! Banish me, s'foot, why say they do," he argues, in the vein of Thomas Stukeley:

Ther's Portugal a good air, & France a fine Country;
Or Barbary rich, and has Moors; the Turke
Pure Divell, and allowes enough to fat
The sides of villainy; good living there:
I can live there, and there, and there,
Troth 'tis, a villain can live any where. (1.4.553–61)

Underlying his global fantasy is the assumption that his role as villain gives him a sure way in to any culture (including his native Barbary, which, notably, he does not acknowledge as such). Yet if his villainy is never in question, as it clearly is not, neither is it the point. For what secures and defines Eleazar's place in Spain is not simply his own crafty malevolence but the inherent permeability and malleability of Spain. Whether or not *Lust's Dominion* ends in comedy, the "Spanish Moor's tragedy" is essentially Spain's. And if, at the end of the play, the banishment of all Moors promises a longed for relief, this imaginative or actual culmination emerges not *despite* the Moor's legitimacy as a Spanish subject but necessarily *through* it.

CHAPTER SIX

Cultural Traffic

The History and Description of Africa and the Unmooring of the Moor

AT THE END of the sixteenth century, Queen Elizabeth was ordering select blackamoors out of England; King Philip III was moving toward the official banishment of all Moors from his realm. Within the English theater, Aaron and Eleazar were performing their atrocities, in spectacular excess, in the middle of imagined ancient Roman and contemporary Spanish courts. And everything was in place for the codification and segregation of Moors as an unwelcome and unworthy presence within Europe. Yet, if what I have been arguing is correct, the possibility, plausibility, and even desirability of securing this kind of physical and ideological boundary—of casting Moors out, turning them into political scapegoats, or reducing the figure to stereotype— were challenged by complications within the very representations that gave such discrimination form. Add to that a remarkable, if not revolutionary, textual event: the emergence of the *Geographical Historie of Africa*, produced initially in 1526 by al-Hasan ibn Mohammed al-Wezâz al-Fâsi, whom England would know as "John Leo" and "Leo Africanus." Remarkable because here was an early sixteenth-century account of Africa created by a "real" Moor, who had traveled extensively through northern Africa, lived in Rome, converted to Christianity, and produced Africa's story in both Arabic and Italian. While other texts were writing the Moor tentatively out of European society, this history was writing the Moor persuasively in.

The emergence of the *Historie* was clearly an important event. The text appeared in an unprecedented number of languages and editions across Europe in the sixteenth and seventeenth centuries and influenced the construction of maps up through the nineteenth century, when England's imperialist exploration of the "dark continent" was at a height.[1] In 1600, John Pory brought the Moor's story into England and English as *The History and Description of Africa*, probably basing his edition on a Latin translation of Gian Battista Ramusio's Italian text, itself (we now know from the discovery of an unpublished manuscript) significantly different from the original Italian version.[2] Bolstering his own and John Leo's authority, Pory included within his translation Richard Hakluyt's endorsement that it was "the verie best, the most particular, and methodicall" description of "the countries, peoples, and affairs of Africa" "that ever was written, or at least that hath come to light."[3] And the accolades go on.[4] More recently, Natalie Zemon Davis has tagged it a "bestseller," while Kim Hall has declared it "the single most authoritative travel guide on Africa . . . for three centuries."[5]

Other, largely classical, descriptions of Africa had, of course, already come to light, usually within more expansive cosmographies that mapped Africa as the "third part of the world." But what has made *The History* uniquely interesting, authoritative, even spectacular, then and now, is the fact that its embedded author was, in fact, a Moor. And not just any Moor, but an extraordinary Moor who had a significant foothold both in Islamic Africa and in Western Christendom. From at least Pory onward, *The History and Description of Africa* has been touted as the provocative evidence of its author's unusual negotiation of two religiously and culturally distinct worlds. Using images Shakespeare will hand, now famously, to Othello, Pory, for one, speculates in his introduction that had John Leo

> not at the first beene a More *and a* Mahumetan *in religion, and most skilfull in the languages and customes of the* Arabians *and* Africans, *and for the most part trauelled in* Carouans, *or under the authoritie, safe conduct, and commendation of great princes: I maruell much how euer he should haue escaped so manie thousands of imminent dangers . . . For how many desolate cold mountaines, and huge, drie, and barren deserts passed he? How often was he in hazard to haue beene captiued, or to haue had his throte cut by the prouling* Arabians, *and wilde* Mores? *And how hardly manie times escaped he the Lyons greedie mouth, and the deuouring iaws of the Crocodile?"* (Pory, 6)

Pory apologizes for John Leo's Muslim past and assures English readers that, although the author is "*by birth a* More, *and by religion for many yeeres a* Mahumetan," his "Parentage, Witte, Education, Learning, Emploiments, Trauels, and his conuersion to Christianitie" make him nonetheless "*not altogither unfit to undertake such an enterprize; nor unwoorthy to be regarded*" (Pory, 4). It is Christianity that saves him. "*It pleased the divine prouidence*," Pory claims, "*for the discouery and manifestation of Gods woonderfull works, and of his dreadfull and iust iudgements performed in* Africa . . . *to deliuer this author*" from his "*dangerous trauels*" into the hands ultimately of Pope Leo X (Pory, 7). Neither the Moor's own ethnogeography nor the extra material Pory adds to the text is centered on these providential designs to the degree that this introduction leads us to expect. But the conversion narrative allows the promotion of both author and text as the extraordinary product of two cultures, one dangerous, the other divine.

This emphasis on the double-edged author has become particularly useful in critical and political attempts to complicate conceptions of cultural identity, to understand its inherent hybridity. Struggling with his own vexed national affiliations, W. B. Yeats resurrects Africanus and, in response to an unusual seance, writes letters to and from Africanus's ghost for six years (!).[6] By the time that Yeats is through with this complex projection, Africanus is "a distinguished poet among the Moors."[7] But according to Oliver Hennessey, he is also for Yeats a "liminal" figure symbolically aligned with both the oppressor and the oppressed, with an imperialist Europe and England as with the colonial spaces of Africa and Ireland, all which therefore cross in the mix and mix in the cross.[8] Recent critics have turned as well to Africanus, the "wily bird," using his dual subject position to address the inevitable clash of the West and non-West, Islam and Christianity, Africa and Europe.[9] Thinking through the lens of postcolonialism, Jonathan Burton represents author and text as an "important example of how Eurocentric principles such as European Christian superiority and entitlement were challenged and even reshaped by their non-Western counterparts," Africanus's own strategic production of his "hybridity" being pivotal to that process.[10] Natalie Davis titles her history of al-Hasan al-Wazzan (whose name, she notes, means "the weigher") *Trickster Travels: A Sixteenth-Century Muslim Between Worlds*, and her introduction begins with the idea of "crossing"—she herself crossing, as few scholars have done, into the Arabic language and cultures that surround al-Wazzan's life and writings.[11] Culturally and spiritually, her Moor "moves back and forth between Europe and Africa," "back and forth between his identity as a Muslim and his identity as a Christian convert."[12] He is a "trickster" invested in Africa and Islam and "the unity of Africa through Islam," "painful[ly]" though productively "unmoor[ed]" in Italy, diverging from European and North African models to comment "on the world at a time of new and mixed identity," and "think[ing] carefully about what he should say and especially what he should *not* say" before his European audiences.[13]

But suppose we take that "time of new and mixed identity" one step further. Suppose we consider al-Wazzan's geographical history apart from his biography and look at the description of Africa apart from the Moor. The text, after all, contains very little of al-Wazzan's own story and, with the exception of a few passages, is told from a third- rather than first-person point of view. Davis herself notes how few traces we have of this "shadowy figure" beyond his writings, and she must reach outside those texts to speculate on his marital status, for example, or to resolve the tension between his apparent commitment to Islam and his conflicting use of "words inexcusable from an Islamic point of view."[14] Moreover, while Yeats may imagine that he can write to Africanus "as if to Africa," not only is Africa's story not the Moor's, the Moor's story is not Africa's.[15] Al-Wazzan's position between the worlds of Europe and North Africa no doubt gives his history a unique perspective. But the vision of Africa that results is not itself so neatly—or tensely—divided between those worlds, even when that vision is augmented and translated by a man, Pory, who promoted and participated in the colonial project of Virginia and whose evangelical Christian agenda, with respect to John Leo, is clear. *The History and Description of Africa* that becomes such a highly lauded, authorized, and sensational resource in early modern England depicts Africa, especially northern Africa, as a place whose longstanding external and internal traffic has left its mark—a place where "strangers" from inside and outside the continent's borders intermingle and intermix, where colors and categories of identity are invariably in flux, and where histories of linguistic, religious, and cultural change complicate the differentiation of peoples. Its "nations" house a plethora of local communities, absorbing and reflecting ongoing cultural and material exchange. Never simply the Islamic alternative or antithesis to Christian Europe, the Africa of *The History*, in short, takes definition from an extensive nexus of diverse and evolving cultures, historically and currently open to the world.

* * *

The History and Description of Africa may well be an "unreliable translation of the faulty Latin translation of the already problematic Italian version," and I take seriously Oumelbanine Zhiri's worry about our scholarly dependence on its authority.[16] To look at the English *History* is not to hear the voice of al-Wazzan but the voice of John Pory, both as he translates a translation which he takes as the Moor's text and as he adds to it his own materials—a "generall description of all Africa," a substantial, "particular description of all the knowne borders, coastes and inlands of Africa, which Iohn Leo hath left vndescribed," and concluding summaries of Africa's princes and religions.[17] (In what follows, I speak of the translated text, the voice constructed and transmitted by Pory, as belonging to "Africanus" in order to differentiate it from the materials which Pory authored independently.) It is the English text, however, that provides seventeenth-century England a new and improved source on Africa.

As critics have long noted, Pory's translation of *The History* stands suggestively behind as well as within *Othello*, paving the imaginative way for Shakespeare's stunning and innovative choice to fill the role of tragic hero with a Moor who is also "of Venice." Jonathan Burton, in arguing for "the subversive nature of Africanus," has urged us, wisely, to "disentangle Africanus and Othello."[18] Indeed, the one moment Shakespeare invokes *The History* most blatantly and crucially—in Othello's testimony before the court, associating him with a dangerous landscape where the wild things (cannibals, Anthropophagi, and men with heads in their chests) are—actually echoes John Pory, not John Leo. But while Othello is not Africanus, or Pory, or even a hybrid combination of the two, after *The History* the dramatic representation of the Moor takes a striking turn. Where before the leading Moors figured on the stage were notoriously "bad" or, in the case of the triumphant Moroccans in *Alcazar*, countered by an evil antitype, *Othello* puts a noble Moor with invaluable military credentials at the center of its action and its Venetian court. Instead of pivoting on an illicit sexual liaison with a duplicitous Gothic queen or a lascivious queen mother, in *Othello* the Moor's integration into Europe is evidenced and fostered—if also, in the wrong hands, troubled—by his sanctioned marriage to a Venetian senator's daughter. It is tempting, then, to credit *The History* with altering the early modern staging of the Moor, though that kind of claim can only be a teasing speculation. Still, the bound-breaking *History and Description of Africa* directly and indirectly sets the stage for *Othello*'s tragically heroic Moor of Venice, providing, in its moment, the historical flip side of Hakluyt's imperialist narratives and Queen Elizabeth's discriminatory letters and helping us understand, in ours, how an "extravagant and wheeling" Moorish "stranger" could be "of here and everywhere" (*Oth.* 1.1.135–36). For within this newly circulated depiction of Africa, Moors, Jews, Negroes, Romans, Goths, Turks, Arabians, Persians, Muslims, Christians, and Europeans intersect and interact as the forces of economics, conquest, chance, and convenience dictate. More than the historical representations it stands beside, *The History* unsettles Africa's boundaries and "unmoors" the Moor from constructs of color, religious or ethnic purity, and place, giving precedence and prominence to the unpredictable dynamics of cultural change and exchange.

For starters, Africanus (the voice translated by Pory) makes clear that the first Africans were not, in fact, "Africans," in any ethnically pure sense; they likely immigrated from Asia or what is now the Middle East. Africanus is nonplussed by the uncertainties and impurities of their origins. Acknowledging that "historiographers doe much disagree" over the matter, he asserts that "the originall of the people of Africa" (by which he means northern Africa) were either Palestinians, "expelled out of their owne countrie by the Assyrians," "Sabeans a people of Arabia foelix," "put to flight by the Assyrians or Aethiopians," or descendants of "certaine people of Asia," chased by wars to Greece and then to Africa (Africanus, 129, 130). "The first that euer inhabited these partes" and for whom the continent itself may have been named, Africanus reports, was probably an outsider, "*Ifricus* the king of Arabia Foelix," who was forced from his Middle Eastern homeland into Carthage (Africanus, 122).[19] Within *The History* Negroes stand distinct from these, "the tawnie people" or "Moores," having a decidedly different African homeland and history (Africanus, 130). Long after Barbary had been settled, according to Africanus, they were "found out" in "great numbers" in the "land of Negros," as if they had always been there, living "a brutish and sauage life, without any king, gouernour, common wealth, or knowledge of husbandrie," outside the realms and reach of civilization (Africanus, 819).[20] Yet as offspring of one of the sons of Chus (the North Africans of the other), they shared not only the biblical lineage but also the geographical dislocation of the northern Africans, descending, Africanus posits, from the Philistines ("Philistims") whose country of origin bordered on Israel (Africanus, 130).

If the "originall" Africans were from elsewhere, so were defining parts of their culture, as *The History* makes clear, their customs, place-names, languages, and religions evolving over time, through a series of conquests and changes in rule. The new Africans in the north were conquered in succession by the Romans, Goths, and, in places, by the Arabians as well as by "some other forren people" who founded and named innumerable cities and towns

(Africanus, 400), and the material and ideological imprint of these "forren" influences appears across the text. Africanus asserts, for example, that the Romans named the marketplace of Fez, "the principall citie of all Barbarie," "Caesaria," after "that renowned conqueror *Iulius Caesar*" (Africanus, 416, 438).[21] More importantly, he explains in some detail how the Christianity brought in by the Romans and Goths and the Mohammedanism introduced later by the Arabians displaced and replaced "the African religion," initially "idolatrie" (Africanus, 162–63).[22] With these changes in religion, "original" customs disappeared. Though at one time "euery African towne had their peculiar feast," Africanus reports, "when the Christians once enioied Africa" those feasts "were vtterly abolished and done away" (Africanus, 428). So too in the case of the presumably more isolated Negroes. Africanus at first underscores their religious autonomy (albeit through a quasi-Christian vocabulary): in the beginning, the Negroes worshiped *"Guighimo," "The Lord of Heaven,"* inspired not "by any Prophet or teacher" but by "God himselfe" (Africanus, 163). Yet under the influence of outsiders, they turned to Jewish, to Christian, then to "Mahumetan lawe" (Africanus, 820). It is the latter that comes to define them, as they become colonized by the Africans to the north. "First subiect vnto king *Ioseph* the founder of Maroco, and afterward vnto the fiue nations of Libya," Africanus explains, "they learned the Mahumetan lawe, and diuers needfull handycrafts: a while after when the merchants of Barbarie began to resort vnto them with merchandize, they learned the Barbarian language" (Africanus, 820). And learned it so well, in fact, that they themselves destroyed all the Christians, Jews, and practitioners of "the African religion" in their midst, "certaine of *Mahomets* disciples" having "so bewitched them with eloquent and deceiueable speeches, that they allured their weake minds to consent vnto their opinion" (Africanus, 163). Cultural identity appears here not given but made—and made from the materials of other peoples. Even as Africanus describes the "African religion" in the north, he reaches forward into other cultures, comparing the "ancient Africans" to contemporary Persians who make gods of fire and the sun, and to the "Romane Vestall virgines" who kept the fires burning, and directing readers wanting more information to "the Persian and African Chronicles," as if these are all of a piece (Africanus, 163).

These histories raise the complex question of what actually is "African." Africanus wrestles with the issue explicitly, wondering whether the northern peoples ever "had a kinde of letters peculiar vnto themselues," before they embraced the Latin language of the Romans and "vsed the letters of the Arabians" (Africanus, 166, 167). His answer is "yes," but to derive it, he speculates backward, from the residue of conquest. "It is likely that a people vanquished shoulde follow the customes and letters also of their conquerors," he argues, "likely that the Romans, when they first subdued those prouinces (as conquerours vsually doe) vtterly spoiled and tooke away all their letters and memorie, and established their owne letters in the stead thereof, to the end that the fame and honour of the Roman people might there onely be continued," and likely therefore that "Africans in times past had their owne proper and peculiar letters" (Africanus, 166). For Africanus, this is the way of conquest, one culture displacing the other, even to the present day. "And who knoweth not," he adds, "that the very same attempt was practised by the Goths vpon the stately buildings of the Romans, and by the Arabians against the monuments of the Persians. The very same thing likewise we daily see put in practice by the Turks" (Africanus, 166–67). From its start, the history of Africa, as Africanus tells it, is a continuum of cultural transformation, the "originall" of the Africans, north and south, impossible to isolate from the influence of "outsiders."

True too even for those "outsiders" whose insinuation has, it seems (perhaps like Aaron's or Eleazar's), gone too far. Africanus is particularly attentive to, if not suspicious of, the legacy of the Arabians, whom he distinguishes carefully from other Africans but who seem nonetheless to be everywhere in Africa's past and present, conquering, trading, coercing, collecting tribute, spreading Islam, and chronicling Africa's history.[23] Ironically, despite this subtle bias, one of the few anecdotes that he offers of himself involves a complicated encounter with Arabians who both con and defend him: stealing his horse and clothes, and leaving him to face unpleasantly cold weather "starke naked," they ultimately turn him loose "vnto the wide world and to fortune," while taking a Jew in his company captive in his stead (Africanus, 171–72).[24] In framing Africanus's history, Pory lists Arabians among Africa's historical peoples, and Africanus himself, do what he might to disentangle the Arab presence from Africa, necessarily acknowledges the long-standing connection. Arabians and Africans were so intermixed in Barbary early on, he explains, that "these two nations at length conioined themselues in one" (Africanus, 135). The result is that even in the present era these populations must "blaze their petigree" to make it clear: "For no man there is [in Barbary], be he neuer so base, which will not to his owne name, adde the name of his nation; as for example, Arabian, Barbarian, or such like" (Africanus, 135). The "name" of "nation" apparently cannot speak for itself, even in the current moment where the legacies of the past prevail.

While conquest thus defines Africa's past, traffic defines its present, complicating "African" identity to a similar, if not even more extensive, extent. As the example of the Arabians suggests, the contemporary Africa that *The History* displays is a place of transformation, where diverse populations not only move freely into territories outside their own but also settle there and intermix, physically as well as culturally. Barbary, of course, borders on the Mediterranean Sea; and the evidence of its exchange is everywhere. The Portuguese appear frequently in descriptions of Morocco and Fez; a Spanish fort marks the landscape of Fez and "ten shops of Spanish Moores," its renowned marketplace (Africanus, 440).[25] On an island off the Tunisian coast, Africanus writes, "Christian, Mauritanian, and Turkish merchants haue their place of residence" and carry on "great concourse," the Moors there having fended off the Spanish early in the sixteenth century with military force and tribute (Africanus, 735). Jews too, he explains, who had been in Africa since earliest times but whose "number is maruellously encreased euer since they were driuen out of Spaine," enter the commercial picture, making and marketing "handy-craftes," setting up "shops and synagogues" (Africanus, 278, 477).[26] Reciprocally, the inhabitants of Barbary "trauell in a manner ouer the whole world to exercise traffique," "for they are continually to bee seene in AEgypt, in AEthiopia, in Arabia, Persia, India, and Turkie" (Africanus, 183).

The signs of traffic are evident even in the descriptions of the "darker," ostensibly more isolated southern territories inhabited by the Negro peoples. These lands are detailed most fully in Pory's "description of all the knowne borders, coastes and inlands of Africa, which Iohn Leo hath left vndescribed."[27] There we see, for example, that the coastal kingdom of "Zanzibar" takes its name from "the Arabians and Persians" (Pory, 54). Not only is it inhabited by "Moores and Mahumetans," who, Pory notes, "have alwaies beene in league with the Portugals" and who "build their houses very sumptuously after the manner of Europe"; its corn comes out of "Cambaya," and its woman "are white, and sumptuously attired after the Arabian fashion with cloth of silke" (Pory, 55–56).[28] We learn from Africanus that, reciprocally here too, "many merchants" "come out of the lande of Negros for trafiques sake" (Africanus, 254).[29] Within this context, it is not surprising that Barbary merchants have spread their language in the land of Negros, not surprising that they appear there marketing European cloth.[30] Nor is it surprising that they "resort" to other "forren regions" with "sundry merchants" including Arabians and Jews, bringing goods from Barbary to trade for gold and slaves, whom they, in turn, take "home" (Africanus, 783, 303). From its Mediterranean territories to its more remote southwestern coasts, the Africa of *The History* takes definition from ongoing cross-cultural commercial exchange.

One significant side effect, crucial to the marking of Africa's cultural identities, is that "strangers" (whom neither Africanus nor Pory distinguish as African or European) do not appear strange here; nor do they seem unwelcome within the territories they have come to inhabit temporarily or, in many cases, permanently. Africanus mentions a number of places in Barbary where "all strangers trauailing that way" tend to be "sumptuously and freely entertained" (Africanus, 291), while Pory draws attention to Moors residing in Negro country who are especially "courteous to strangers" (Pory, 55).[31] Importantly, that "courtesy" includes sexual and marital relations. *The Tempest's* Claribel is neither the last European nor, as the play's reference to Dido underscores, the first to engage herself to "an African" (*Temp.* 2.1.123). Indeed, how interesting that what cues a tempest on Shakespeare's stage in the early seventeenth century is the union of a Milanese daughter and a Neapolitan prince, *not* of a Neapolitan daughter and a Tunisian king (even though Naples was under Spanish rule when the play came out, roughly two years after Moors were officially banned from Spain). Africanus cites a number of instances where "faire and beautifull women are so fonde of strangers that if secret occasion be offered they will not refuse their dishonest company" (Africanus, 299). He also stresses that syphilis, the "French" or "Spanish poxe," is one of Barbary's most prevalent diseases (Africanus, 181), its name and history testifying to widespread cultural and sexual intercourse, what Natalie Davis calls "sexual disorder."[32] Africanus explains: "Not so much as the name of this maladie was euer knowen vnto the Africans, before *Ferdinand* the king of Castile expelled all Iewes out of Spaine; after the return of which Iewes into Africa, certaine vnhappie and lewd people lay with their wiues; and so at length the disease spread from one to another, ouer the whole region: insomuch that scare any one familie was free from the same" (Africanus, 181).[33]

Though here the sexual crossings are associated with Jewish wives, "vnhappie and lewd" Africans, and disease, in other places all sorts of intercourse with "strangers" appear to be a more common and acceptable practice. Coming at the issue from a religious angle, Davis has explained that, although "Islamic law" condemned sex outside marriage or "rightful slave dominion" as sinful, Muslim men could marry free Jewish and Christian women and could have sex with their own Jewish and Christian slaves, while for Muslim women—and Jews and Christians—the "sexual border was firmly closed."[34] Hence, in Fez, a city which Africanus declares "the metropolitan not onely of

Barbary, but of all Africa," it may be in accordance with Islamic law that the "Queene is alwaies of a white skin," perhaps originally one of the "Christian captiues, being partly Spanish, and partly Portugale women" who populate the city (Africanus, 482).[35] In most cases, however, Africanus does not mention religious identities, taboos, or laws: economics drive and legitimize intercourse and intermarriage. Witness, for example, the Numidian city of Techort, whose residents "fauour" strangers "exceedingly," to the point that "they had rather match their daughter vnto strangers, then to their own citizens" (Africanus, 790). There, "for a dowry," the natives "give some certaine portion of lande, as it is accustomed in some places of Europe," the reference to European custom suggesting the possibility that the embedded strangers are Europeans (Africanus, 790). Or witness Tombuto, a kingdom in Guinea, whose "inhabitants, & especially strangers there residing" are "exceeding rich" and whose king "married both his daughters vnto two rich merchants" (Africanus, 824).

If the religious implications of these exchanges are largely submerged within the text, the racial implications emerge more clearly, if sometimes implicitly, especially as they are signposted by color. Both Pory and Africanus understand skin color as an hereditary feature. Pory asserts at one point that it is "transfused from the parents" and explains, at another, that "people of sundry colours" appear within "nations extremely blacke" "by reason of the varietie of women" (Pory, 68, 83). Africanus, too, in describing a Moroccan market town, underscores that the "men are of a tawnie and swart colour, by reason they are descended of blacke fathers and white mothers" (Africanus, 255). Throughout the accounts, especially of the markets, both narrators cite important instances where intermixing has made a color difference. Africanus declares, for example, that "all the inhabitants" of a "*famous mart-towne*" on the Moroccan coast "are of a most white colour, being so addicted vnto friendship and hospitalitie, that they fauour strangers more than their owne citizens" (Africanus, 243, 244). "Fauour" here seems to carry the sexual implications it does elsewhere and to explain the implicit link between the color of the natives and their addition to "friendship": these inhabitants are "most white" not simply in addition to their "intercourse" with (implicitly white, European) "strangers" but indeed because of it. So too, Africanus notices that in Egypt, the "countrey people are of a swart and browne colour" while the "citizens" who inhabit the cities, the centers of trade, and who dress in in European cloth are "white" (Africanus, 856). Pory is more explicit. Speaking of islands off Africa's western coast where the foreign traffic has been extensive, he postulates that "the coniunction betweene the men of Europe and the Negro women" has "bred a generation of browne or tawnie people" (Pory, 96). To find color-coded Africans here is, in more than a few instances, to find the traces of outsiders, emblazoned in natives who may be not only "blacke" and "extremely blacke" but also "tawnie" or "most white."

As critics we have attempted to come to terms with the complications of the African landscape and the African people by using the overarching categories of religion, race, and nation to sort out the natives and finding here a politics of prejudice. In notable places, *The History* does construct difference categorically and outline an early racism. Pory, in particular, uses the story of Africa and Africanus to propel a Christian, evangelical mission—one which he will pursue more vigorously as secretary of the Virginia assembly, embracing the Indians (whose history is, at that moment, ostensibly less mixed) as a more amenable target of his zeal and writing his politics home in letters from the New World.[36] In his efforts to turn John Leo's history into the readable manifestation of "divine prouidence," he invokes established dichotomies of light and dark, drawing a steady ideological line between the "miseries and darknes" [*sic*] of Africa and the "little light" of Christianity, the "true religion" that can transform them (Pory, 1021). This imagery at once overlays and underscores the association of blackness of skin with blackness of soul. It is not surprising to find in his reports "inhabitants" who "are for the most part black" "being Idolaters, and much addicted to sorcery and witchcraft," or, despite his anti-Muslim bias, to find a contrast between "blacke people," "which are for the greatest part Idolaters" and can only "pretend a kinde of ciuilitie both in their apparell, and in the decencie and furniture of their houses," and "Moores and Mahumetans," "a kind, true-harted, & trustie people" "of a colour inclining to white" (Pory, 55).

Further, Pory revises Africanus's general layout of Africa's populations in a way that effectively darkens the landscape, implicitly producing more "deadly enemies to the Christians" than the parent text suggests (Pory, 41). In an introductory outline of the continent, Africanus divides the natives into four groups, the "Africans or Moores," the Numidians, the Libyans, and the "Negros," and he emphasizes especially the distinction between the Moors, the "tawnie" natives who inhabit Barbary, and the "Negros" or "blacke Moores," whose domain is "the lande of Negros" to the south (Africanus, 130, 123). Pory, however, assigns Africa "five principall nations"—the Cafri or Cafates of lower Ethiopia, the Abassins of upper Ethiopia, the Egyptians, the Arabians, and "the Africans or Moores" of Barbary—and he includes within this latter group not only the "white or tawnie Moores" whom Africanus associates with Barbary but also the "Negros or blacke Moores" who, in Africanus, stand distinct in "the lande of Negros" (Pory, 20). The result is that Pory's Africa contains two populations of Negros: the Cafri, the idolatrous and "lawlesse wilde Negros" of lower Ethiopia, whose skin is "blacke as pitch," and the "Negros or blacke Moores" who appear as a subgroup of Barbarians (Pory, 53, 41). All the more blackness, all the more need for Christian light. And all the more evidence, then, in a circular twist, that blackness (along with the "Idolators," "Mahumetans," Negroes, and Moors that it colors) means evil from a Christian moral point of view.

Yet if Pory's religiously and racially coded taxonomy tempts us to distill either his or Africanus's depiction of Africa's people into general population groups or to extract from *The History*'s pages a single, characterizing impression of, say, the Moor or the Negro, then we miss what is crucial to this text and its early modern ethnogeographic vision and what constantly complicates, even challenges, the racial and religious prejudices it also encodes: its insistence on the primacy and contingency of Africa's discrete communities.[37] For, in fact, what makes *The History*'s over nine volumes of material almost maddening to read is that they are filled with a profusion of qualifying particulars, anchored insistently to the local. Notably, Africanus rarely speaks of "Moors" and uses "Africans" mostly to refer to Africa's ancient inhabitants.[38] Instead, when he gives an introductory overview of the continent, he divides each of Africa's four main domains (Barbary, Numidia, Libya, and the land of Negroes) into separate "kingdomes" and those kingdoms into distinct "prouinces," while also breaking the four key population groups into "tribes" (Africanus, 125, 130). Barbary, for example, contains four kingdoms, and its "tawnie Moores" include fiue seuerall people" spread out across a number of provinces (Africanus, 130). Moreover, within the detailed descriptions which appear in the body of the text and which follow a geographic trajectory from Barbary to the land of Negroes, Africanus fractures the provinces further into cities, towns, and naturally bounded communities. Significantly, it is within this last and local level that he details the languages, customs, clothing, appearance, or other characterizing features of the place or people, providing there an emergent if formulaic ethnography. Hence, a given kingdom or province appears as a place not of *one* culture or people but of *many*, often strikingly dissimilar. Appearing side by side within the Moroccan province of Hea, for example, are the "most barbarous and sauage" people of the mountain of Atlas and the "most deuout and religious" people of the "mountain of Iron" (Africanus, 246, 247). In the province of Duccala, one town (Bulahuan) is known for its "famous hospitall," "wherein all strangers trauailing that way, were sumptuously and freely entertained at the common charge of the towne," while a nearby city (Azamur) is renowned for hospitality of quite another sort—"for the horrible vice of Sodomie, whereunto the greatest part of the citizens were so notoriously addicted, that they could scarce see any young stripling, who escaped their lust" (Africanus, 291, 294). Although Africanus does treat the Arabians—more than any other people—categorically, sometimes prejudicially, their characteristics vary too: they can be learned, "wittie," and poetic, constitutionally "vile and barbarous," or "verie rude, forlorne, beggerly, leane, and hunger-starued," depending on where and how they live (Africanus, 156, 157, 161).

Even Pory, despite his evangelical investment in skin color, works at the level of the local. His supplements to John Leo's text begin with a "general description of all Africa" and end with summary documents on the princes and religions of Africa, as I have noted. But the mainstay of what in a modern edition comes to over one hundred pages is his extensive description of the places "John Leo hath left vndescribed." Within those pages, Pory not only breaks the larger areas he surveys into kingdoms, provinces, and sometimes towns, albeit with less regularity and specificity than does Africanus; he also draws attention to the local exceptions that break the general rules, especially of religion and race, exposing the diversity as well as the historical contingency and change that necessarily define Africa's peoples. On the one hand, he offers Mohammedanism as the provenance of the Moors, idolatry as a defining feature of the Cafri, and upper Ethiopia as the hotbed of Christianity (thanks to the assumed presence of *Prete Ianni*, " who seems to have survived as long and as spectacularly in the myths of Africa as Elvis has in the myths of America) (Pory, 54). On the other, he acknowledges that in each of Africa's nations, "some are Gentiles which worship Idols; others of the sect of Mahumet; some others Christians; and some Iewish in religion" (Pory, 20). As well, even while he claims that "all the kingdomes and countries" of southwest Africa, from the Cape of Good Hope up to Capo Verde, are "inhabited by blacke people," he admits that people of "sundry colours" live near "extremely black" "Negros" to the north (Pory, 83). Detailing one area of lower Ethiopia (where the "wilde" and pitch black Cafri are), Pory also exposes inhabitants who are "Moores by religion," Arabians by descent, and tributaries of the Abassins (Pory, 53). There too he locates a city that was "in times past head of all the townes and cities of the Moores" but that now houses residents of both an "oliue-colour" and "blacke" (Pory, 54).

To be sure, in one almost apocryphal response to these kinds of differences, Pory declares it "strange to consider" that on one side of the Senegal River "the people are blacke and well proportioned, and the soile pleasant and fertile" whereas on the other side "they are browne and of a small stature, and do inhabite a barren and miserable countrie" (Pory, 82). His observation (which is, of course, textual, not actual), along with his surprise, had already been prescribed long before in classical texts, and more recently in Hakluyt, where one narrator finds "marveilous and very strange" the fact that on one side of the Senegal "the inhabitants are of high stature and black, and on the other side, of browne or tawnie colour, and low stature" (Hakluyt 6:167–68). If Pory's expression exoticizes the difference similarly, taking the sign as a wonder almost de rigeur, the image here—of natives, black and brown, short and tall, living side by side with barely a river between them—actually underscores what sets *The History* apart from earlier visions: its insistence on the diversity of Africa's peoples and the permeability and mutability of their cultures. Given the complicating particulars which Africanus and Pory necessarily display from point to point throughout (despite a politics, in Pory's case, that would have it otherwise) perhaps the wonder is not that these natives are not separated further, but that they are separated at all.

The structural conjunction of Pory's and Africanus's texts actually clinches the point, amplifying the fluidity of Africa's geographic borders and the variability of the Africans' cultural identities across time as well as space. For Pory's additions—especially his general and particular descriptions of the continent—are not simply an extension of Africanus's vision but also, explicitly, a revision. Layering his own classification of Africa's nations on top of Africanus's, Pory announces that what he presents is the "best moderne diuision of Africa, for these our times" (Pory, 23). "For these our times": the message is that the Africa of 1526 needs to be updated now in 1600. And updated it is, in ways that, I think, pave the way for the New World projects which eventually depend on western Africa and its Negroes. For al-Wazzan in the early decades of the sixteenth century and England in the decades that immediately follow, it is Barbary that really matters, that provides the pivotal ground for evolving global economies. For the Christianizing Pory, on the brink of a new century and an emerging westwardly oriented world, the consuming focus is Africa's dark side, its idolatrous Negro peoples and its lower domains, which best evidence the need for providential intervention. The differences between Africanus's and Pory's visions suggest both the subject of Africa and the writing of Africa's history as works in progress: within the

English *History*, the outlines of the African nations, like the cultures of the inhabitants themselves, change with the times, requiring additions and revisions that are at once extra and essential.

Ultimately, then, there is no Moor within this text. *The History* tells the story neither of the historical al-Wazzan nor of "the Moor," if we mean by that a singular, essentialized ethnic subject who can stand for all Moors. Criticism now routinely cites Africanus's disclaimer that "for mine owne part, when I heare the Africans euill spoken of, I wil affirme my selfe to be one of Granada: and when I perceiue the nation of Granada to be discommended, then will I professe my selfe to be an African" as the crux of his—and/or al-Wazzan's— biography (Africanus, 190).[39] Here, in a nutshell, is the self-authorizing Moor, uniquely "moored" in Africa, using a hybrid self-construction to cross—or cross in and out of—Europe. Yet if we consider what it means to be an "African" or a "stranger" across this text that, tellingly, never uses the word "European," these poles of identity do not simply merge into a sincerely or strategically constructed hybrid self. Rather, each unravels into myriad particulars, exposing the variety within, not just between, these otherwise general terms. Even in the rare glimpses Africanus does provide of himself, there is no clear line between what marks him as "African," and what as a "meere stranger" (Africanus, 303). We see him engaging with Africa's peoples and they with him in a number of different ways, each contingent on the moment. He is "louingly entertained," fed, schooled, enlisted to arbitrate civil disputes, willing to give money and aid to the natives, as circumstance allows or demands (Africanus, 234).[40] And when he speaks of Africa through the images of Europe—comparing the "cloath-garment" made and worn by the people of Hea to "those couerlets or blankets which the Italians lay vpon their beds" (Africanus 227), or the "certaine garment with wide sleeues" worn by the "doctores and ancient gentleman" of Fez to the dress of "the gentlemen of Venice" (Africanus, 446), or the "little round spot" Barbary's women paint "on the bals of their cheecks" to a "French crowne" (Africanus, 159)—he gives us Hea, ancient Fez, and Barbary instead of Africa, and Italy, Venice, and France instead of Europe.

In four years Shakespeare will create a Moor who connects himself to the ancient and modern cultures of Egypt, Judea, Arabia, and Turkey as well as to an exoticized Africanesque terrain, and who is at home, at least at the start, in both Venice and Cyprus. Shakespeare will create a Moor, that is, who is decidedly not "of" any one place inside or outside Africa, who is surrounded but not confined by a constricting discourse of "blackness," endorsed by some, but not all, in Venice, and whose presence within Venice revises rather than fulfills the axis of difference through which all (not just his) cultural identities are read. We cannot say that the publication of *The History* in 1600 or the popularization of its embedded Moor made all of this difference. What we can say, however, is that at the turn of the century, when the English (as well as the Spanish) state was officially endorsing discrimination against Moors and "blackamoors," the account of Africa that is most widely and enthusiastically acclaimed is one that exposes both the diversity of Africa's histories and peoples and the contingency of its terms. After the emergence of *The History*, it may not have been inevitable that Shakespeare would imagine a Moor, complexly, as "an extravagant and wheeling stranger / Of here and everywhere"—a phrase that unmoors the Moor provocatively, at precisely the moment that its speaker (Roderigo) works to amplify and decry his "strangeness." But given *The History*'s preeminence among the available texts on Africa, neither would it have been surprising. For despite his own Christian biases, Pory produces "the best moderne" vision of Africa for his own time— one where Moors come in "sundry colours," religions, "nations," and places, where "Africans" and "strangers" continually interact and intersect, and where cross-cultural traffic and transformation make all the difference.

CHAPTER SEVEN

The "stranger of here and everywhere"

Othello and the Moor of Venice

IN THE OPENING scene of *Othello*, Iago enlists Roderigo in a scheme against an unnamed "Moor," and together they convince the mostly unsuspecting Brabantio that he has been robbed, that his "fair daughter" has fallen into "the gross clasps of a lascivious Moor" (1.1.121, 125). At first Brabantio resists their plot, protesting that "this is Venice" and his house, "not a grange" (1.1.105–6). To amplify the urgency of their claims, Roderigo insists:

> Do not believe
> That from the sense of all civility
> I thus would play and trifle with your reverence.
> Your daughter—if you have not given her leave—
> I say again hath made a gross revolt,
> Tying her duty, beauty, wit, and fortunes
> In an extravagant and wheeling stranger,
> Of here and everywhere. (1.1.129–36)

Where Brabantio associates the urban setting of Venice with a distinctive security, Roderigo emphasizes rather the dangerous penetration of the "here" by the "stranger" of "everywhere." In a gesture of "gross revolt" whose very discovery disturbs the "sense of all civility," the daughter has "tied" her home-grown, patriarchally valued "duty, beauty, wit, and fortunes" to the "extravagant"—that is, wandering or vagrant—stranger.[1] Yet if his presence betrays the disruptive influx of the "everywhere," Roderigo's depiction associates him also with the "here." This—a society that includes an extravagant and wheeling stranger—is, it seems, Venice too.

These lines appear in the First Folio, not in the 1622 quarto, the earliest extant script, and critics are unsure whether the passage, including lines 120 to 136, is an addition or revision, or, what may be more likely, a remnant from an earlier original, from which both quarto and Folio might have been separately drawn.[2] Yet Roderigo's depiction of the Venetian stranger brings up an issue underscored by the play's title, which in its first and then preeminent incarnation was simply "the Moor of Venice."[3] Barbara Everett has postulated that Shakespeare was "compelled" to build a play from its source, Giovanni Battista Giraldi Cinthio's *Gli Hecatommithi* (1566), by the very idea behind this "race-title," compelled, that is, "by the random premise of Cinthio's opening phrase, 'Fu già in Venezia un Moro', 'There was in Venice a Moor.' "[4] For critics, by and large, the presence of a Moor *in* Venice, not to mention the concept of a Moor *of* Venice, has seemed a curious anomaly which provokes the dramatic crisis. From A. C. Bradley on, the Moor's position as an outsider within Venetian society has provided an obvious answer to what is arguably *Othello*'s central question: why is the Moor vulnerable to Iago's lies?[5] Our understandings of what it means to be an "outsider" have become increasingly attuned to historical, political, and racial nuances and to the double-edged complications of hybridity, mimicry, and representational indeterminacy, as I have suggested in my Introduction. Still, critics tend to follow Iago's cues, endorsing the assumption that because Othello is a Moor, he inhabits a uniquely "precarious" position within Venice: a "cultural stranger," who has lost "his own origins," he appears in these readings as literally and figuratively out of place, catastrophically "unable to grasp" "Venetian codes of social and sexual conduct."[6]

But is the Moor necessarily out of place in Venice? Cinthio's opening premise does seem somewhat "random," since the cultural identity of the Moor has little impact on the crisis. The Moor and his new wife Disdemona live in uninterrupted "*tranquillità*" in Venice until a routine changing of the guard dictates that he head to Cyprus to become the "*Capitano de soldati*" there.[7] In Cinthio's story there are no Turks and no imminent Turkish threat to propel Venice's embrace of the Moor. An experienced military commander, he is held very dear ("*molto caro*") by the Signoria under ordinary, not extraordinary, circumstances (377). Trouble begins only when the scene shifts to

Cyprus, where an ensign (*"l'Alfiero"*), "a man of the most depraved nature in the world" (*"della più scelerata natura, che mai fosse huomo del mondo"*), has been stationed (378). Unfortunately for all involved, the ensign falls in love with Disdemona. But because she repeatedly rebuffs his advances (he thinks because she desires the captain, the Cassio figure, instead), his love turns to "bitterest hate" (*"acerbissimo odio"*) (379). Intent, above all else, on ruining her (*"intento al danno di questa misera Donna"*), the ensign therefore plots to obliterate the two obstacles in his way: the captain and the marriage (379–80). Along the way (actually very late in the tale), the ensign must destroy the Moor as well; but it is Disdemona's unyielding passion that is the ensign's prompt, her ruin that is his goal. Tellingly, after undoing the Moor, the ensign goes on to defame and accost another of his countrymen, who is decidedly not a Moor.

In Cinthio, Venice does register the Moor's alterity. Although the opening lines introduce the Moor as *"molto valoroso,"* Disdemona's love grounded on his *"virtù,"* the narrator subsequently notes that her parents "strove all they could to induce her to take another husband" (*"facessero ciò, che poterono, perche, ella altro marito si prendesse, che lui"*) (377). In the absence of any other reason, we have only his Moorish identity to suspect. In addition, when the horrible consequences of the ensign's deceptions are discovered (the captain loses a leg, Disdemona, her life), the Signoria's first response is to torture the Moor for "the cruelty inflicted by a [B]arbarian upon a lady of their city" (*"intesa la crudeltà, usata dal Barbaro, in una lor cittadina"*) (388). In the Italian text "Barbarian" is a proper noun, not the incriminating common noun, "barbarian," which appears in most of the English translations currently appended to *Othello*.[8] The reference works nonetheless to up the ante on the offense; that a foreigner (whose Barbarian identity comes into the narrative only when his crimes come out) inflicted "cruelty" on one of "their" city seems to make matters worse. The Moor is never exonerated; he is tortured, imprisoned, banished, and then killed by Disdemona's kin, as, the narrator adds, "he merited" (*"com' egli meritava"*) (388). Still, it is the ensign, and not the Moor, whom the story condemns as "the wickedest of all bad men" (*"peggiore di tutti gli scelerati"*), the ensign, and not the Moor, whose designs produce social trauma and moral disdain within the fiction and whose destiny provides its didactic vehicle (387). Cinthio's ensign is actually the one to strike the fatal blows against Disdemona, with a loaded sock, before he and the Moor bring the house (literally, the ceiling) down on her. If cultural dislocation helps catalyze the catastrophe, it is the ensign's displacement from, not the Moor's displacement within, Venice that is at fault. The

"tradition" that emerges in the last quarter of the century and extends through *Othello*—that is, if we consider the insistence, say, in *Titus Andronicus* and *Lust's Dominion* that cultural boundaries are fluid, cross-cultural relations improvised, and the Moor's place in Europe neither predetermined nor precluded—not only does the presence of the Moor *in* Venice seem less perplexing as an abstract idea; the possibility of a Moor *of* Venice seems more viable and variable as a starting point of definition.[13] To be sure, in *Othello*, Iago does everything in his power to turn Othello into a disenfranchised "stranger," to alienate him not only from himself, but also from the military and domestic anchors that give him, and Venice, definition. In the process, as critics have adeptly shown, Iago repeatedly reconfigures the meaning of "race" and emphasizes the incriminating transparency of blackness to negatively color what the Moor perceives and how he is perceived.[14] Yet what gives Iago's corrosive—we would say "racist"—discourse both its challenge and its edge, and what contributes crucially to the drama's defining tension, is the all too likely prospect that a Moor *in* Venice could be as well a Moor *of* Venice.

* * *

Historically, *Othello* has been at the center of controversy in a way that the other plays I have been considering have not, not simply because it has long been the most popular (dare I say, the best?) play of the lot and so the most discussed, but also because its Moor is the tragic hero. Within the Shakespearean canon, *Othello* stands beside such plays as *Hamlet*, *Measure for Measure*, *Macbeth*, and *King Lear* as part of Shakespeare's sustained attempt to scrutinize, even revolutionize, the notion of the subject, to explore and expose the uncertain, unnerving parameters of an individuated interior, in Iago's words, the "native act and figure of [the] heart" (1.1.62), and, if Stephen Greenblatt is right, to pave the way for Freud.[15] The original Othello, Richard Burbage, helped bring down to earth the "hyperbolic" acting style popularized by Marlowe's superstar, Edward Alleyn (who also played the histrionic Muly Mahamet), ushering in a kind of "personation" that allowed for a closer identification between the audience and the actors.[16] Yet even before Thomas Rymer declared Shakespeare's dramatics "barbarous," his ennobling of a "Black-a-moor" outrageous, or John Quincy Adams puzzled over "what induced the Poet to take a negro for an example of jealousy," the Moor's appearance presented a unique complication.[17] For however Burbage was made up or costumed (possibly in a "wiry wig") and however his skin color was manifest (probably darkened via the "oil of hell"), the script codes Othello unmistakably as "black."[18] The term has always been a misnomer, a category of coloredness rather than an actual skin color. Still, as a feature more visible than, say, the Jewishness of Marlowe's Jew of Malta, or the Scythian heritage of Marlowe's Tamburlaine, or even the morally incriminating deformity of Shakespeare's Richard III, Othello's blackness announced a unique and ineluctable difference between English audiences and the hero with whom they were being newly encouraged to identify.

Long since, that blackness has proven a particular sticking point in mainstream theater and film, both dominated, as we well know, by white, Anglo-American casts.[19] Witness how long it would be before "a black American," Paul Robeson, would breech the color barrier and would "play Othello to a London audience in a major theater" (in 1930) or to an American audience on Broadway (in 1943).[20] Witness, too, more recent, schizophrenic productions which play up Othello's ethnicity at the same time as they play down or stereotype his "blackness"—recalling the color anxiety embedded in the once vexing question of whether to stage the Moor as African (black) or Arabian (nonblack). In Orson Welles's 1952 film, for instance, Othello is Moroccan; but the experimental lighting universalizes and neutralizes the color of his (and everyone's) skin by correlating changes in passions and perspectives to changes in hue.[21] In Laurence Olivier's stage and screen performances of 1964 and 1965, Othello is presumably West Indian, though reviewers saw him also as West African; yet Olivier's makeup ("Max Factor 2880" and "Negro No. 2") mimicked "white stereotypes of blackness," as Barbara Hodgdon has suggested, and provoked an apocryphal anxiety that his skin color could wipe off onto "white" characters, as it apparently did.[22]

The plays which preceded *Othello* created no such problem, no such split in ideology or performance, precisely because their Moors did not double as heros. Even if *Titus* brings the Moor uncomfortably close to home, Aaron is an unrelenting and unredeemable villain, his soul and his role "black like his face." Although in *Lust's Dominion* Eleazar has one legitimate foot on Spanish soil through a noble marriage, another of his body parts is condemnably "injointed" with the "lascivious" Queen Mother of Spain.[23] And while *Alcazar* insists, in its historical frame, on the majesty of the legitimate Moroccan line, the revenge plot proffers the tragic antagonist Muly Mahamet, whose atavistic histrionics confirm and entrench his villainy. If these plays play conservatively into biases against blackness at the same time as they attempt to come to more complicated terms with the Moors' relation to

Europe, *Othello* starts with a more radical tactic. The play will end, like *Titus* and *Lust's Dominion*, with the Moor's alienation. But the tragedy begins with the assumption that Othello is a "most worthy," "noble" (1.2.91–92), and "valiant" general (1.3.48), who has "done the state some service" and whose tragic self-destruction will be a tragedy for that state (5.2.338).[24]

Begins—or almost begins. Before we ever meet "the Moor of Venice," we are thrust into the calamity that surrounds and, we gradually learn, involves him on the shadowy and sinister Venetian streets, giving his blackness pertinence and putting his heroism on pause. It is through Venice that we must first read its Moor. Yet reading Venice is not, and was not, a simple process, its identity not easy to distill. Across early modern English texts and translations, Venice appears as a multivalent, sometimes contradictory, even mystified cultural space, its representations constituting what some scholars have catalogued as "myth."[25] During the decades immediately preceding *Othello*, debates over legislation restricting foreigners in London gave Venice's reputation as a place hospitable to "strangers" particular currency. In 1593, for example, John Wolley, a member of Elizabeth's Privy Council, opposed such legislation by arguing that "Venice could never have been so rich and famous but by entertaining of strangers, and by that means have gained all the intercourse of the world."[26] Moreover, the sources Shakespeare is most likely to have consulted—Thomas's *History of Italy* and Lewkenor's *Commonwealth and Government of Venice*—do emphasize Venice's lucrative openness.[27] In calling up the conflict between the Venetians and the Turks, the play also points to (even if it simultaneously eclipses) a history which had come to a head in 1571, with the Christian defeat of the Turks at Lepanto.[28] That event, the famed battle of Lepanto, in some ways marked the beginning of the end of Venetian glory, followed as it was by the loss of Cyprus to the Turks and the decline of multinational support for Venice. The Christian victory was nonetheless touted as a high-water mark in Venetian history. In *His Majesties Lepanto, or Heroicall Song* (1603), James I himself exalts Venice as a last Christian refuge, ordained by God, and heroically saved from the "faithlesse" "Mahometists" (and their patron, Satan) by a multinational "Christian Nauie" of Greeks, Spaniards, Germans, and Italians.[29]

Yet while these histories do lie behind and within *Othello*, producing a Venice favorably inclined toward its Moorish general, the opening scene prefaces that heroic political vision with the much darker social landscape of, ironically, comedy—and in particular, one of Shakespeare's darkest, "problem" comedies, *The Merchant of Venice* (1596–97), as Michael Neill has suggested.[30] However much the earlier play raises to question "which is the merchant here? and which the Jew?", however much it understands the almost inevitable fungibility of identity in a world driven by mercantilic credit and exchange, the Venice of *The Merchant* holds and upholds "laws" against the "alien" and puts them inflexibly into action against the Jew (*MV* 4.1.348–49). In Belmont, a Moroccan prince can stand beside an assortment of European lords (Neapolitan, Spanish, French, German, Scottish, English) as a possible suitor for its globally acclaimed bride. But in Venice, not only is the mixed marriage between a Christian and a Jew cause for secrecy, anxiety, and exile; a Jew's attempt to lay claim to law renders him a disenfranchised outlaw. It is not clear whether or not Shakespeare knew in 1596 that early in that same century (1516) Venice had become the site of the first official Jewish ghetto; the available source, Thomas's *History*, which emphasizes the liberty of Venice's strangers, makes no mention of this past.[31] Still, *The Merchant*'s Venice is clearly a place where unprecedented extremes of segregation and discrimination could happen, and do—at least around the Jew.

The Moor, of course, is not the Jew, even though that figure (in the form of Marlowe's Jew of Malta) provides an important model for characterizations of Moors. Set Barabas next to Aaron, the Jew who works behind the scenes next to the Moor who acts in the proximity of the court, for example, and the Moor stands out as having significantly more leverage and legitimacy (though not necessarily more success). So too if we set *The Merchant of Venice*, whose Jew is legally outlawed, next to *Othello*, whose Moor is not. In *Othello* there are no laws against the alien. The Venetian duke actually stops the irate senator, Brabantio, from throwing the "bitter letter" of the "bloody book of law" at the Moor (1.3.68–69). Still, *Othello*'s opening scene displays "a society capable of treating any stranger, any ethnic outsider with the same calculating cruelty it meted out to Shylock," as Neill has argued.[32] The initial exchange between Iago, Roderigo, and Brabantio is, after all, a veritable orgy of outrage, stereotype, and defamation. When the play begins Iago is working to convince a skeptical Roderigo that he, Iago, really does "hold [the Moor] in [his] hate" (1.1.6). Roderigo is angry at Iago for withholding crucial knowledge (that Desdemona and Othello have eloped, we later learn) and for serving the Moor, and he is none too fond of "gondolier[s]," "knave[s] of common hire" (1.1.124). Brabantio has "charged" Roderigo "not to haunt about my doors," declares Iago a "villain," and laments a daughter who "deceives me / Past thought" (1.1.97, 117, 164–65). And Iago not only hates the Moor; he derogates the "Florentine" Cassio and despises "duteous and knee-crooking knave[s]" who serve, without serving their turns upon, their masters (1.1.19, 45). In order to insure his own good faith (which is, of course, highly questionable), Iago even dangles the act of hating—"if ever I did dream . . . , abhor me," "despise me if I do not"—before Roderigo, like a rotten carrot on a stick, as possible retribution (1.1.4–5, 7).

Although the Moor is not the only target here, he soon becomes the focus of these tirades. By the time the three are through, they have figured the Moor as a "thick-lips" (1.1.66), "an old black ram," "a Barbary horse," and "the devil" (1.1.88, 111, 91) and have accused him of "tupping" Brabantio's "white ewe" and making that by now well-known "beast with two backs" (1.1.89, 116).[33] Brabantio will clean up the language before he gets to court; he will decide that there are (more speakable) "charms / By which the property of youth and maidhood / May be abused" (1.1.170–72), and he will insist that the Moor, whom Desdemona otherwise "feared to look on," must therefore have enchanted her (1.3.99).[34] Even so, the idea of blackness perforates the edges of the "black" arts. And not only does the senator protest the elopement officially; Othello is consequently called to account. Before the act ends, the Moor stands in front of the full senate, defending himself by delivering "a round, unvarnished tale" of his "whole course of love" (1.3.91–92). Even if the state's need to "straight employ [him] / Against the general enemy Ottoman" dictates an easy exoneration, he nonetheless faces a "formal legal hearing" that more than one scholar has declared a bizarre, somewhat counterintuitive starting point for a Shakespearean tragedy (1.3.49–50).[35] No wonder Giuseppe Verdi omitted Shakespeare's initial act entirely in order to open his *Otello* (1887) on a note of untarnished heroism: Otello first takes the stage as an anxiously awaited war hero in Cyprus, where he can be greeted unequivocally with a resounding chorus of "*Evviva Otello!*" and "*Vittoria!*".[36] No wonder either that critics tend to read Othello's position in Venice as uniquely circumscribed, compromised, and uncertain, his place a place of difference, dislocation, and dispute. It is not they (any longer) who cannot tolerate a black and Moorish hero, but, it seems, Venice itself.

And yet, hating the Moor is neither as credible nor as contagious a condition in *Othello* as is hating the Jew in *The Merchant*. Even on the dark, comedic streets of *Othello*'s Venice, terms of prejudice and alienation appear hard to stand by, if not hard to come by.[37] At the same time that the opening scene gives disturbing voice to what will become reiterated staples of racism, it also emphasizes the unsteadiness of that voice, the improvised edges of its articulations, and the uncertainty of its hold. At every turn, Iago's project of turning the Moor's "joy" to "vexation" meets substantial resistance, realizing his worst fears that the Moor "in a fertile climate dwell[s]" (1.1.70–72). For starters, Iago must actively convince Roderigo that he really does "hold" the Moor in "hate," that he is not "in any just term" "assigned / To love the Moor" (1.1.38–39). While Roderigo does dismiss Othello as the "thick-lips," he does not dismiss the possibility that Iago's loyalty lies with the Moor, as, in "terms" of service, of servant to master, it should.[38] Iago must go to great lengths—must even insist that he is not who he is—to prove that his "outward action" is not what it seems and that his apparent, obsequious service to the Moor is instead a calculated subversion (1.1.61). Even then, Roderigo has reason to doubt: one of the great ironies of the play is that Iago's destruction of the Moor is at least partly driven by a desire to serve as his lieutenant in Cassio's stead.[39]

Notably too, although Iago's attacks against the Moor end in stereotype, they do not start there. Neither an automatic nor an assured recourse, the language of what we might call high racism emerges within a cacophony of impromptu activity, improvised in the face of uncertain success and having only questionable effect. At first Iago targets only Othello's military demeanor, not his Moorish features: he faults the Moor for "loving his own pride and purposes," being "horribly stuffed with epithets of war," and using "a bombast circumstance" to evade and "non-suit" the mediators speaking for Iago's promotion to lieutenant (1.1.11–13, 15). These slights do little to satisfy, incite, or even interest Roderigo, who barely engages with Iago's claims and who remains skeptical of Iago's intentions.[40] Taking his cue from Brabantio's house (which the two seem to approach as much by chance as by design), Iago abandons his political argument entirely and locates transgression in the domestic space, which is more pertinent to Roderigo's libidinous cause. At this point, he involves a new player, the betrayed father Brabantio, who is more influential and more legitimately aggrieved than either Iago or Roderigo can claim to be and who can both absorb and promote Roderigo's animosities better than Iago can or, it seems, would. Appropriating the new setting, Iago directs Roderigo to

> Call up her father:
> Rouse *him*, make after *him*, poison *his* delight,
> Proclaim *him* in the street. Incense her kinsmen,
> And, though *he* in a fertile climate dwell,
> Plague *him* with flies: though that *his* joy be joy,
> Yet throw such chances of vexation on't
> As it may lose some colour. (1.1.67–73; emphasis added)

At points here the slippery pronouns render the distinction between Brabantio and Othello—both whose "delight" must be "poisoned," whose "joy"
must "lose some colour"—almost indecipherable.[41] Color itself, which enters
the play's vocabulary now for the first time, does not make a difference or clarify the confusion. It is as if coloring in the subject of vexation matters less than
rousing Roderigo against some "him," who is not Iago and who can be mali-
ciously "made after" in lieu of Iago, the prospect of "his" ruin distracting
Roderigo from the question of Iago's dubious loyalty.

This impromptu change in venue works: Roderigo turns his attention
from castigating Iago to enraging the father, enabling Iago to move from the
defensive to the offensive. With Brabantio the new linchpin for the undoing of Othello, Iago recasts the Moor through the incendiary metaphors,
"black ram," "devil," and so on, that critics have emphasized as an essential
trademark of Iago's patently racist discourse. Yet it is neither he nor his
stereotyping that fully or finally catalyzes Brabantio's crucial turn against
Othello. Brabantio's first response is to reject the "profane wretch" Iago, to
assume that the "villain" has surely "lost [his] wits" (1.1.114, 92). His second
is to accuse the colluding Roderigo of coming forth "in madness, / Being
full of supper, and distempering draughts" and to dismiss the allegations
that Desdemona might have run into the Moor's lascivious hands as "malicious bravery" (1.1.99–101).

It is, in fact, Roderigo, rather than Iago, who finally gets Brabantio's goat,
and does so less by incriminating the Moor than by challenging the senator's
credibility. Like Iago before him, Roderigo is immediately on the defensive, his
assaults against Othello inextricably tangled in his efforts to "answer" Brabantio's charges. Boasting that he can "answer anything" (1.1.119), Roderigo turns
the tables on the father and makes the possibility that he and Iago deserve the
given rebuke contingent exclusively on the possibility (which Roderigo raises
four times in the Folio text) that Brabantio allowed, even approved of, Desdemona's escape. In the Folio version, in fact, Roderigo's whole "dilation" of the
escapade (which includes his only mention of the Moor) is framed by that incriminating conditional.[42] Roderigo "beseech[es]" Brabantio:

If't be your pleasure and most wise consent—
As partly I find it is—that your fair daughter,
At this odd-even and dull watch o' th' night,
Transported with no worse nor better guard
But with a knave of common hire, a gondolier,

To the gross clasps of a lascivious Moor—
If this be known to you, and your allowance,
We then have done you bold and saucy wrongs.
But *if you know not this,* my manners tell me
We have your wrong rebuke. (1.1.119–29; emphasis added)

In the 1622 quarto (which, as I have noted, does not include these lines), Roderigo does not even mention the Moor. Rather, he simply dares the father to see if his daughter "be in her chamber or your house," and taunts him, if he finds her there, to "let loose on me the justice of the state / For thus deluding you" (1.1.136–39). Either way, in either version, it is a lose/lose situation for Brabantio: if he is not culpable for supporting his daughter's transgression, he is guilty of falsely accusing the interlopers of "bold and saucy wrongs." It is in the face of this assault on his own integrity, and not (simply) an assault against the Moor, that Brabantio takes action, calls up "all [his] people," and declares "this accident" "not unlike my dream" (1.1.140–41). Even if we do not read his subsequent vilification of Othello partly as self-defensive displacement activity, it is no small point that Brabantio chooses to marshal (that is, fabricate) his own evidence against the Moor for the court, as if to compensate for the otherwise unsupportable stereotypes within Iago's and Roderigo's scripts. Nor is it a small point that as he does so, Iago sneaks off, acknowledging that it is neither "meet, nor wholesome to [his] place / To be produced . . . / Against the Moor" (1.1.144–46).

Othello's initial appearance is thus framed by and within a social world distinguished by its nasty penchant for prejudice. Yet the effect is neither to stabilize nor to privilege the resulting discriminations as terms that automatically determine and delimit the Moor's place in Venice. To the contrary, it is to contextualize those discriminations within a volatile social exchange which determines *their* place in Venice. For while prejudice circulates in *Othello* as freely as it does in *The Merchant,* in the opening scene of *Othello* (and in what follows), its discursive terms neither fully nor finally circumscribe, prescribe, or prevail. Even in this world of "calculating cruelty," accident trumps ideology, variables trump values, contingencies trump codes. Almost anyone can be a target of derision on Venice's streets—a Florentine, an "ensign," an unwelcome suitor, a gondolier, a betrayed father, a senator, a revolting daughter, as well as a Moor (1.1.32). And while categorical features of culture, class, and color provide the terms for derogation, those terms may not necessarily define the cause. Indeed, what motivates the attacks against Othello is not an abstract, unconditional hate but a certain set of conditions that have preempted his accusers' ambitions and desires: not simply a scapegoat, the Moor has eloped with a prized bride and daughter, and he has chosen Cassio as his lieutenant. In fact, erase Othello's identity as a Moor, and the play might go on: Iago might be no happier being bypassed for military preferment by a Venetian general, Roderigo, no happier being displaced in Desdemona's affections by a Venetian suitor, and Brabantio, no happier being betrayed by his daughter's elopement with a Venetian husband. Brabantio admittedly has warned Roderigo that "my daughter is not for thee" (1.1.99). He has also made clear that if there are "charms / By which the property of youth and maidhood / May be abused," they need not come from a Moor: Brabantio insists that the "spells and medicines" which have "corrupted" Desdemona have been "bought of mountebanks," an occupation in which Venetians reputedly excelled (1.3.61–62).[43]

The play, of course, would not go on; Othello's identity as a Moor is crucial. But as that identity is carried through the prescriptions and presumptions of prejudice, it evades and unsettles their score. We are not watching a discriminatory discourse guaranteed to be effective prove, anticlimatically, effective; rather, we are watching its obstruction—and not just in the case of any Moor, but in the case of a Moor who has, in eloping, violated social custom. Iago will be the first, though not the last, to argue that Othello's safeguard is the Venetian state, which "cannot with safety cast" out the Moor, "for he's embarked / With such loud reason to the Cyprus wars" and "another of his fathom they have none" (1.1.148–49, 151). That the argument is initially Iago's should probably give critics who echo it a bit more pause. Be that as may be, what prevents the immediate alienation of Moor here is not the state but a set of players with conflicting biases and suspicions, who are significantly more preoccupied with defending and securing their own positions than they are with undoing his. Hence, to encounter the Moor constructed in Venice's margins is to confront the contingency of the discourse designed to do him in. It is to recognize that even within a world where prejudice circulates freely, to be produced against the Moor is to produce and expose the self.

* * *

If it is therefore not entirely "meet" to be produced against the Moor, as the opening exchange suggests, against what then is "the Moor of Venice" produced? If at the outset the inflammatory language of stereotype seems only partially, questionably tenable on Venice's streets, how do we enter and read the relation between the Venetians and the Moor? How do we come to terms with identity amid difference, improvisation amid prejudice, culture and crossed cultures amid social chaos, contradiction, and crisis? How, given the complex, constantly compromising world of Venice, can we speak of "the Moor" Othello as he is?

Suppose we return to the issue of origins, to the question of how "the Moor of Venice" has come to be the Moor "of Venice." In 1533, a population of Moors came to Venice as refugees from Tunis, when that city was besieged and overrun by the Turks, though Shakespeare may or may not have been aware of this history or its residual effects on Venice's population.[44] Notably too, Venetian merchants routinely made voyages to North African ports such as Tripoli, Tunis, and Algiers, though it is not clear that these ventures resulted in any kind of permanent immigration.[45] In any case, nine critics out of ten would readily endorse the assumption that the Venetian court has hired Othello from the outside (most likely, North Africa) to be a mercenary soldier.[46] Given what we know, and suspect Shakespeare knew, about Venice's long-standing policy of staffing its ground forces and its highest military offices with "strangers," that is probably the most cogent explanation we can posit. Othello himself declares to his "very noble and approved good masters" of the Venetian court that from the time his "arms" "had seven years' pith" until some nine months ago, "they have used / Their dearest action in the tented field" across "this great world" (1.3.78, 84–87).

But in even the most persuasive arguments, which admit their speculative edges, any such conclusion relies, must rely, on inference. Elizabeth Hanson, for one, acknowledges that "the mercenary foundation of Othello's position" is "*largely subtextual,* hinted at only in Iago's and Roderigo's outbursts of nativist resentment" and that Othello's mercenary status has been "mystified through transactions occurring before the play begins" and "merge[d] into assimilation."[47] There are other models, as we have seen. *Titus* actually stages the transaction that brings Aaron, a prisoner of war, to Rome, presenting the Moor's "incorporation" there as an inevitable aftereffect of the conquest of the Goths, however blurry and open-ended both conquest and its consequences prove to be. In *Lust's Dominion,* Eleazar claims a Barbarian heritage and a conquered past, pointing to a specific moment when his father's empire was destroyed and he himself absorbed by Spain. In *Othello,* by contrast, there is neither a term (such as "incorporation") nor an historical event (such as conquest) to explain the Moor's presence in Venice. Nor is there a geographic antecedent that surfaces as a contrasting home. Iago declares the Moor a "Barbary horse" as a means of proving him an unnatural husband for the Venetian Desdemona. In Act Four, he catalyzes in Roderigo an anxiety that, unless Cassio is killed and his assumption of Othello's post halted, Othello will naturally return—with his prized wife—"into Mauretania," where the Moorish stranger belongs (4.2.224). Yet these associations are Iago's. Roderigo otherwise expects the Moor to "return again to Venice" (4.2.223). Though Shakespeare's Moor is not, like Cinthio's, a Barbarian, Shakespeare starts with Cinthio's premise that there lives in Venice a Moor.

That premise in and of itself is not the source of crisis or controversy, though in filling in the gaps of Othello's history we risk making it so. To start with the question of how Othello has come to be in Venice is already to start with a conclusion, to produce his presence as an unstated but implicit problem. It is to single out the Moor as a subject whose position in Venice *needs* to be explained as, say, the Florentine Cassio's does not. It is to decide in advance that the "stranger" "of everywhere" could not also be at home "here," even though characters such as Iago and Roderigo, whose names are haunted by Spanish "spirits," are.[48] Within this framework, the drama would seem to operate counterintuitively, through an inverted teleology, a predetermined and overdetermined outcome taking precedence over improvisation and suspense. For if the driving problem is the Moor's already installed but inevitably unwelcome presence, then Iago's assaults against him function as the predictable *end*, the capstone, of hostilities and anxieties arising within an unstaged backstory, rather than as the disruptive *beginning* of an unpredictable and evolving sequence of events. Any evidence that the Moor fits in, that he knows Venice sometimes better than Venice knows itself, therefore presents as a symptom of assimilation, compromise, or co-optation, "an embrace and perpetual reiteration of the norms of another culture."[49] When he then falls for and from Iago's fictions, the wheel comes full circle: Othello's alienation, in effect, proves his alienation, an inability to read Venice's "country disposition" that we have assigned him from the outset (3.3.204). It is as if long before Iago attempts to punish his audiences with their knowledge ("what you know, you know"), we are caught in the terms of our own interrogations, and we risk turning what we presume to know—that the Moor is out of place "here"—into all we need to know (5.2.301).

Importantly, within Shakespeare's dramatic fiction, no one questions how Othello came to be in Venice, where his "acceptance" "goes without explanation," as Emma Smith has noted.[50] Nor does Othello seem inclined at any point to explain his presence. To the contrary, under pressure from Iago, he admits only that he "fetch[es]" his "life and being" from culturally unidentified "men of royal siege" and that that information, by his own volition, is "yet to know" (1.2.21–22, 19). Under pressure from the senate, he describes his telling of "the story of [his] life" (1.3.129) before Brabantio and Desdemona (and I will return to this crucial exchange). But the story, set in an exotic elsewhere, filled with cannibals, Anthropophagi, and men with heads in their chests, predates Othello's life in Venice, while the narrated moment of telling happens once he is already established there, already "oft invited" into Brabantio's house (1.3.128). The transition that we might otherwise suppose to be a crucial touchstone, the Moor's inauguration as a subject of Venice, does not emerge between these seamlessly conjoined pasts and appears therefore significantly insignificant to his self-defense and definition. In fact, the cultural crossing that structures the action is Othello's move out of, not into, Venice. As Neill has emphasized, the play's momentum is "remorselessly one-way," involving only a "single significant change of place—the voyage from Venice to Cyprus at the end of the act 1."[51] It is explicitly against that unfolding geographic trajectory, and not an implicit prior dislocation, that the play maps Othello's unraveling stability.

In not explaining, not making an issue of, Othello's entry into Venetian society, *Othello* creates a significant gap in just the place we, and English spectators, might be predisposed to look for signs of crisis. But instead of mystifying Othello's history or coding his origins as lost, the resulting effect is to wrest the Moor's tragedy from just these kinds of master narratives, defined before the fact by cultural boundaries and biases. If there is no definitive origin for Othello's stationing as "Moor of Venice," for the incursion of the "stranger" into the "here," neither is there an historically prior or culturally fixed rationale that can explain or predict the hostility that erupts around him. Even in this environment where heated terms of prejudice circulate, the assault against the Moorish "stranger" is not a foregone conclusion, neither his position nor Venice's settled or unsettled by his coming, whenever or however that has occurred. Granted, the play does start in medias res. But its retroactive point of departure is Othello's elopement with Desdemona and appointment of Cassio at lieutenant. These events are neither poised nor posited as boundaries, the limit case of culture, to define the crux of "plausibility" of what would or would not be believed about the Moor in Venice, what behaviors would or would not be tolerated from him there.[52] Rather, they are local conditions, the precise and particular obstacles that obstruct Iago's and Roderigo's frustrated ambitions, that coincide just before the drama begins (when those frustrations peak) and that inspire Iago, who has been serving the Moor, to initiate a plot against him now and only now. By reaching backward only this far, into the almost present past, the play emphasizes the contingency of, and the contingencies that are, the passion and the cue for what follows, even when what follows feeds on prejudice. What is at stake and on display throughout the play, after all, is not how Othello has come to be "the Moor of Venice" but how that established identity comes *not* to be. And that is a matter that emerges within the radically uncoded present, not an implicit and coded past.

To pick up Othello's story, then, in the volatile environment where the play insists we must, to view Venice's relation to the Moorish stranger in the here and now of Venice, is to recognize that the terms of that relation derive not only from the Venetians but also, as significantly, from the Moor.[53] If the opening scene prompts us to read the Moor through Venice, once Othello appears the play prompts us, reciprocally, to read Venice through the Moor, proposing and endorsing him as representative of the Venetian state. Othello, by his own admission, has lived in Venice for the past nine months. The play does not label his social status—does not indicate whether he is a citizen, say, a denizen, or a resident alien—any more than it delineates the original rationale or foundation for that status. It does, however, suggestively assign Othello a notable degree of domestic leverage that emerges apart from (and is almost at odds with) his military service. We are used to understanding Othello's move from Venice, where he is anchored by his "occupation," to Cyprus, where he is undone by the disturbing erotics of marriage and the irrepressible (though interruptible) pressure of the marriage bed, as a shift from the political to the domestic (3.3.359).[54] Yet in Venice Othello's first actions happen in the proximity of a residence, a "lodging" and, what seems the same place, a "house" (1.2.45, 48), that gives him a domestic bearing. Throughout, the play grounds its tacitly "Venetian" characters through just these kinds of sites. Brabantio's "house" is obviously pivotal to the opening scene. But the play is also filled with an unusual number of unseen abodes. Iago arranges to meet Roderigo "at my lodging" in Venice (1.3.366) and to plant Desdemona's handkerchief "in Cassio's lodging" in Cyprus (3.3.323), while Bianca intercepts Cassio in Cyprus while she is going to his "lodging" and he, coming to her "house" (3.4.166–67). It may well be true, as Emma Smith suggests, that Shakespeare distinguishes "lodgings" as less permanent than the "houses" here, though in Othello's case the two seem to merge.[55] But whatever the precise configurations of these spaces, it is important that in a world where everyone seems to have a place to be, the Moor is no exception, appearing no less (if also no more) embedded on the home front than his Venetian, Florentine, or Cypriot peers.

In fact, by aligning Othello with a residence, as a site and subject, the play signposts the surety and autonomy of his footing within Venice—even and especially amid circumstances that would otherwise constrain his actions. From the very moment he appears, the ever-prodding Iago prods him to "go in" to the lodging they stand before, to retreat from the advancing threat of an unnamed but powerful "him"—a "*magnifico*" who turns out to be Brabantio (1.2.30, 10, 12).[56] In response, Othello takes his own discovery into his own hands and declares emphatically that he "must be found" (1.2.30). In part, what he exhibits is an abiding confidence both that the "services" he has "done the Signory" will "out-tongue" any "complaints" (1.2.18–19) and that his "parts," "title," and "perfect soul," which exceed those "services," will "manifest [him] rightly" (1.2.30–32). Yet his imperative self-positioning emerges in response and challenge to Iago's directives and control. In a telling but unnecessary explication, Othello commands Iago to "know": "But that I love the gentle Desdemona, / I would not my unhousèd free condition / Put into circumscription and confine / For the seas' worth" (1.2.24–28). In so doing, he places his own authority to "know" over and against that of the informing Iago, prescribing what is the crucial knowledge here: that he, and he alone, sets the terms of his "unhousèd free condition" and, reciprocally, of his "housing." Within the symbolic economy of the play, these words anticipate the tragic limits of Othello's love, his ominous association of marriage with confinement. Yet in and at this moment within the dramatic fiction, the speech act functions to confirm and secure Othello's "free condition" on the streets of Venice and in the face of the overbearing Iago, who would otherwise hem him in.

Even when Othello comes under pressure from the state, he insists on standing his ground, literally and figuratively. When Cassio and his faction enter the scene with urgent political business, Othello continues to direct his own discovery. The fact that the "business" is "of some heat" is obvious (1.2.40). Cassio emphasizes that the duke "requires" Othello's "haste-post-haste appearance / Even on the instant" (1.1.37–38), explaining that "many of the consuls" have already gathered at court, that Othello has already "been hotly called for" at his "lodging," and that, when he was not found there, "the Senate" "sent about three several quests / To search [him] out" (1.2.43–47).

These requests suggest the Moor as someone who is "to be found" when the state comes calling.[57] But rhetorically Othello turns that "finding" into a self-generated event. Echoing the very words, "I must be found," he has used to counter Iago's attempted incursions on his agency, he proclaims " 'tis well I am found by you," as if the "I" is the acting subject, being found an action verb (1.2.47). In effect, he is not wrong; "search him out" as they will, the court's envoys can only discover him when he puts himself forward.

While surrounded by those who would "find him out" in every sense of the word, Othello manages to step outside the public gaze, into a figurative if not literal room of his own. In an ostensibly eccentric dramatic gesture, he interrupts the progress to court in order to "but spend a word here in the house" (1.2.48)—probably, still, his "lodging"—and then disappears off stage, into that interior. Although we assume that the "word" is with Desdemona, neither we nor the characters are privy to it, and Shakespeare seems to go out of his way to emphasize that we cannot see within. Here as not in other cases, the loaded "house" appears invulnerable to penetration, especially to the kind of voyeuristic pleasure and incrimination that Iago has used to transform Brabantio's "guardage" into a "grange" and will use to transform Othello's and Desdemona's conjugal bed in Cyprus into a site and cipher of a dangerously unbounded eroticism (1.2.70).[58] Left out on Venice's streets with nothing to do but wait, Cassio (perhaps like us) wonders "what makes [Othello] here" (1.2.49). Iago tries to supplement the scene with a lurid fantasy, declaring that Othello "hath boarded a land-carrack" and will be "made for ever" "if it prove a lawful prize," but these insinuations fall flat (1.2.50–51). Faced with Cassio's apparent confusion, Iago resorts to an untainted matter of fact: "he's married" (1.2.52). And although he is poised to explain to whom ("Marry, to—"), Othello emerges and interrupts his discourse before Desdemona's name can be spoken or marred, as it will be so readily in Cyprus (1.2.53). This, indeed, is not Cyprus, where it takes some time for Othello's ships for find their "footing" and where, in the meantime, Othello and Desdemona become the subjects of a polymorphically perverse erotic banter that may well seed the catastrophe to come (2.1.76). This, rather, is Venice and Othello's house, not a grange.

If these details seem incidental to the action, superfluous to the plot, they are crucial in establishing Othello's embeddedness in Venice on more than just military grounds. For whether his "lodging" is permanent or transient, whether or not his "house" is in any sense a home, his movement in and around the site(s) translates as a domestic "footing" that, though it comes with no explicit mark or measure of citizenship, seems remarkably secure. We do need to make a distinction between Othello's social standing and his marital relationship, the one defined through stabilizing exteriors, the other through uncertain interiors (and I will return to these). For what I am talking about is Othello's status as a domestic subject within Venice, and not his role as husband within a marriage, although the two will intersect. What I am talking about, that is, is the play's insistence that Othello has a place "here," as much as has Iago, if not also Brabantio. And while that place does not register the specific terms of Othello's residency, it nonetheless exposes his resiliency as a Venetian subject.

This positioning provides an important preface and supplement to the scenes at court where Brabantio challenges Othello and where the Venetian court's acceptance of the Moor and the marriage could be—and has been—taken as political expediency.[59] Yet even there Othello has notable leverage in defending and defining his (and Desdemona's) domestic position. In response to Brabantio's incrimination of the courtship, Othello sets the bounds of what he will or will not show, exposing the inside of Brabantio's house, not his own, stopping well short of the site and circumstances of the elopement, and confirming only that "I have married her" (1.3.80). Moreover, the duke lets Othello determine the terms of the proceedings, calling for Desdemona at the Moor's request, and hearing his testimony in the meantime. These responses may well be contingent on other pressures. There is, after all, no action or reaction here that is not: because drama hinges on the illusion that what we are watching is being improvised in the moment, from always unfolding contingencies, we are always in a sense in medias res, as the opening scene underlines.[60] But if the court's endorsement of Othello's social choice is conditioned on the Turkish threat, it is conditioned as well on his credibility as a domestic subject. Not only is the senate at least as ready to hear that Othello won Desdemona "by request and such fair question / As soul to soul affordeth" as that he "by indirect and forcèd courses" "subdue[d] and poison[ed]" her (1.3.112–15). Despite Othello's protestations that he is "rude" in "speech" and unlikely to "grace [his] cause / In speaking for [him]self," the senate and duke, in fact, count on him to represent his own domestic affairs in a way that defies further dispute (1.3.82, 89–90)—that is, to provide a "wider and more overt test" of truth than the "thin habits and poor likelihoods of modern seeming" which Brabantio voices (1.3.108–9). Whether or not Othello's exoneration is a foregone conclusion, at this absolutely critical moment the court relies on him to speak persuasively over and against the aggrieved Venetian senator as Moor "of Venice" and to have the last word on a marriage.

To understand Othello as a representative "of Venice," grounded by more than politically indispensable military or mercenary parts, is not however to deny or eclipse the importance and impact of his difference, his unique and, for a hero, dramatically unprecedented identity as "stranger" and Moor. It is rather to rethink what it means to be a "stranger," to review where and how we draw the lines around his and Venice's cultural position, and to reconsider from whom and what we take our cues. It is to recognize that the exchange between Venice and the Moor is a mutual exchange, as central to Venice's identity as it is to the Moor's, its shaping influences reciprocal, continual, and continuous. For at least as much as Venice defines the Moor, *Othello* insists, the Moor defines Venice—and defines Venice through (not despite) his "strangeness."

The signal moment in Othello's career in—and rewriting of—Venice comes when he testifies before the court and recounts a "course of love" that pivots on his telling of his "travailous history" (1.3.139).[61] In that history, as by now may go without saying, Othello associates himself with a series of "disastrous chances," with "moving accidents by flood and field" and "hair-breadth scapes in th' imminent deadly breach," with capture by "the insolent foe" and a consequent enslavement and "redemption" (1.3.134–38). He sets those "dangers" in an exotic landscape, marked by "antres vast and deserts idle," "rough quarries, rocks, and hills whose heads touch heaven," and peopled with "the Cannibals that each other eat / The Anthropophagi, and men whose heads / Do grow beneath their shoulders" (1.3.167, 140–41, 143–45). Othello's words here directly echo Pory's sensationalized introduction to Africanus's *History* as it promises a story of the "*imminent dangers*" the Moor confronted and the "*marvels*" he survived—including "*how many desolate cold mountaines, and huge, drie, and barren deserts passed he,*" "*how often was he in hazard to haue beene captiued, or to haue had his throte cut by the prouling* Arabians, *and wilde Mores,*" "*how hardly manie times escaped he the Lyons greedie mouth, and the deuouring iawes of the Crocodile.*" This kind of display is apparently how to make a travel story sell—one that recurs, for example, in the Hakluyt accounts and in Walter Ralegh's *Discovery of Guiana* (1595) (though not as prominently as the emphasis on it in our criticism might lead us to believe).[62]

Within *Othello*, however, this intertextual transaction has created interpretive problems. For it not only begs the question of where the Moor stands within the dramatic fiction—whether he speaks through Europe wittingly or unwittingly, by choice or force, having or knowing no other way in; it also raises the issue of where Shakespeare stands as his author—whether he writes Europe's voice into the Moor's wittingly or unwittingly, strategically exposing or endorsing Othello's cultural co-optation or naively exhibiting his own.[63] Within recent scholarship, the speech has become one of the most controversial in the play, precisely because it invokes the exoticism that appears in Europe's colonialist discourse and can work there to prime the colonial subject for ideological, if not actual, alienation: here at a critical moment when Othello speaks most directly of and for himself, scholars have stressed, he seems to "submit" to a narrative that is Europe's, and not his own.[64]

And yet, I would argue, the play gives no indication that these *are* Europe's terms. That is, while Shakespeare clearly—and, it seems, self-consciously—borrows his exotic images from European texts, he does not situate those images as either his or Venice's prescription for what the Moor should be. Tell what extravagant and wheeling stories he may, the Othello who appears before us is *not* an exotic adventurer, fending off cannibals and Anthropophagi and insolent foe. He is a general for the Venetian army, who has just married a Venetian noblewoman and established a decidedly domestic and potentially permanent tie to Venice. While the method he has chosen (elopement) is unorthodox, the social structure into which he has written himself (marriage) inherently is not. If spectators and scholars looking just to the "cruel hands" of Moors in Hakluyt, the *"manie thousands of imminent dangers"* in Pory's trailer, or, for that matter, Muly Mahamet or Aaron are surprised by Othello's unstinting professionalism and conventionality, Venice's leading political operatives are unanimously not. To the contrary, the duke expects the Moor to be a "valiant" general, better versed than anyone on the "fortitude" of Cyprus (1.3.221) and insists that, to defend Cyprus, "opinion," the "sovereign mistress of effects," prefers Othello as the "safer" choice over the "substitute" (Montano) already stationed there (1.3.222–24). Montano himself anticipates that the Moor will prove a "brave" and "worthy governor" (2.1.39, 31). Cassio waits for Othello to "give renewed fire to our extincted spirits, / And bring all Cyprus comfort" (2.1.81–82). Even Brabantio, after dreaming of the "accident" with Desdemona, has done nothing to prevent it until Roderigo, as it were, lights his fire (1.1.141). In fact, the duke expects Othello ultimately to gain the senator's "favour" as Desdemona's "lover" as well as to "privately determine" the disposition of his new wife to everyone's satisfaction (1.3.199–200, 273).

Othello's life story thus stands at an exotic remove from who he is as well

as from (what is almost the same) who Venice expects him to be in the present of the play. Here is a moment within the dramatic fiction, then, that Othello sets the script, introducing into the play, as part of his own repertoire,
subjects and images that no one else has used, and altering Venice's cultural
imaginary. Though literally these *are* Europe's terms, the play neither situates
nor registers them as such, choosing rather to represent the Moor's voice as
the Moor's. Venice, of course, has heard the stories before (which we get only
in outline): Othello embeds his exotics in the recent past as the centerpiece of
his "whole course of love," as the "mighty magic" which he used to seduce
Desdemona and entertain her father (1.3.93). But instead of appearing as a
completed cross-cultural encounter of Venice *with* the Moor, the scene of
telling that Othello recounts exhibits and enacts an ongoing cultural exchange
between Venice *and* the Moor—or better put, between the Moor and Venice.
Within it, Othello presents himself and his life story not simply as the mediated object of discourse and desire but also, as essentially, as the mediating
subject. Though Othello does admit responding to Brabantio's and Desdemona's cues, he simultaneously makes clear that it was not *their* desires that
determined *his* terms, but *his* terms that determined *their* desires. As Othello
tells it, Brabantio requested an accounting of "battles, sieges, fortunes"
(1.3.130)—the very kind of martial "feats" that already suit the preoccupations
of the Venetian senate and propel their political investment in the Moor
(1.3.88). Yet what Othello narrated instead, he attests, were dangers and disasters, giving his history and himself an adventurous edge and prompting Brabantio to question him "still" (1.3.129). As Othello tells it too, initially "the
house affairs" drew Desdemona's attention (1.3.147), she hearing his stories
"by parcels," "not intentively," until he "took once a pliant hour, and found
good means / To draw from her a prayer of earnest heart / That I would all my
pilgrimage dilate" (1.3.151–55). Instead of giving her that "all," however, he admits that he often focused rather on "some distressful stroke" and so "beguile[d] her of her tears" (1.3.156–57). That she "loved [him] for the dangers
[he] had passed" is the end, not the beginning, of the exchange, the effect, not
the origin, of his "witchcraft" (1.3.167, 169).

In bringing the scene of telling into the Venetian court, then, Othello not
only does *not* tell his full life story, from his "boyish days / To th' very moment
that [Brabantio] bade [him] tell it" (1.3.132–33); he also makes clear that he has
not told that story before—not, at least, with equal emphasis on all its parts.
The "witchcraft" he confesses and exposes, the "process," lies rather in self-
consciously shaping a "tale" of dangers and disasters that would and does win

at least one daughter, maybe two (1.3.142, 171). Hence, to clear his name, he exoticizes neither himself nor his past; he shows how he has effectively, seductively, exoticized his "travailous history," how he has stressed his distresses and singled out the "disastrous chances" from its "all." The intertextual transaction between *Othello* and its exotic referents works thus against the grain of "truth." For exoticism appears here as the linchpin of Othello's *strategy*, not just of his story. What we see then is an important narrative "process," the Moor engaging in a cross-cultural exchange that works to transform, rather than merely play to, Venetian culture.

While Othello's testimony seduces his Venetian spectators, teasing out their desires to hear of his exotic experiences in "this great world," instead of creating or confirming a boundary between the two, between the traveler's exotic "everywhere," and the domesticated "here" of Venice, he suggestively bridges the gap.[65] That is, he embeds the "great world" within Venice as part of its own symbolic economy, producing his extraordinary experiences as a source of imagery and meaning for Venice itself. Just before Othello makes a narrative transition between his past elsewhere and his courtship here, between his history and Desdemona's, he emphasizes what is perhaps his most exotic figure, the Cannibals, first describing them as subjects who "each other eat" and then renaming them as or listing them beside "the Anthropophagi." If these two figures are technically different, the one group eating only its own, the other happy to eat others, they reinforce each other almost to a point of redundancy.[66] With this emphasis set, Othello then inserts the image as metaphor into his depiction of Desdemona, explaining that she "devour[ed] up my discourse" with "a greedy ear" (1.3.149–50).

Critics have explored at length the implications of this translation for the representation of the desiring female and female desire, which are thus rendered exotic, if not monstrous.[67] Equally important, though, are the implications for the exotic figure itself, which here serves as the rhetorical vehicle for representing Venice. According to Quintilian, metaphor ("*translatio*") relies on the transfer of one term "from the place to which it properly belongs" to another term, which is somehow insufficient and needs clarification or ornamentation.[68] And in *Othello*, it is the image of cannibalism that is transferred out of its proper context to supplement the depiction of the implicitly insufficient Venetian subject, holding a meaning that the subject herself does not. One effect of its deployment may be to defamiliarize the familiar, to turn the desiring female into an exotic. Yet the inherent "doublenesse" of metaphor—which fascinated, if not troubled, rhetoricians such as

Puttenham, as Madhavi Menon has suggested—allows the converse possibility of familiarizing the unfamiliar, the image of "devouring" making the attentive female audience, Desdemona, more comprehensible than she otherwise might be.[69] In either case, the image of the cannibal that Othello brings out of the proper context of his past becomes crucial here to the depiction and deciphering of the Venetian present, as both the bridge and the crux of meaning.

It is perhaps not such a big leap, then, for Othello to set his exotic imagery alongside the vocabulary of Christianity which has already emerged as Venice's own (in the notable references to hell, damnation, pagans, prayer, godliness, souls, and such that pervade the opening scenes)—not such a big leap, that is, for him to figure Desdemona as a discourse cannibal at one moment and to speak of the "prayers" he drew from her and the stories of "pilgrimage" she asked from him at another. Nor does it seem such a big leap for him to put terms of strangeness and wonder in her mouth, when he describes her as swearing that his story " 'twas strange, 'twas passing strange / 'Twas pitiful, 'twas wondrous pitiful"—or to put those terms next to her alleged wish that "heaven had made her such a man" (1.3.160–62). Othello's narrative "process" works to make the strange contiguous with the familiar, the exotic world of wonders with the Christian "world" of a Venetian woman's "sighs" (or, in the quarto, "kisses") (1.3.159). It is, it seems, plausible to imagine—as Othello suggests that Desdemona has imagined—the Moor teaching "a friend that loved her" "how to tell my story," and that friend using it to woo and win her (1.3.164–65). The story, after all, has no explicit geographic or ethnographic markers to tag it as the Moor's: while the outlandish catalogue points most directly to Pory's Africa, its terms are generic, echoing representations of such places as Montaigne's cannibal-laden Brazil.[70] If the exotic images that Othello calls up first appear remote to Venice, within his testimony they become a fungible part of the Venetian social landscape, their seductiveness figured not only as translatable to the "here" but also transferable within it.

In positioning Othello as the "stranger of here and everywhere," of everywhere *and* here, the play then presents the Moor as the mediator, not the sign, of difference. If in Cinthio's narrative the condition that "there once lived in Venice a Moor" is a fait accompli that can only be undone, in Shakespeare's play it is an active site of improvisation and transformation. For whenever or however Othello has come to Venice in the first place, under whose auspices and for what cause, it is not simply the Venetians who dictate the terms of tolerance, cross-cultural intersection and embrace, but also the Moor. In bringing the world to Venice and Venice to the world, he propels an interactive process that knows no cultural bounds. Othello, of course, will fall; his life as "Moor of Venice" will unravel. But what makes his transformation so tragic to the dramatic fiction and so crucial to his nemesis within it is the fact that, as a subject of Venice, the Moor must be followed, he as much as anyone setting the stage and story—ultimately making it impossible for a figure such as Iago, who would draw an indelible line between "an erring barbarian and a super-subtle Venetian," to be who he is (1.3.348–49).

* * *

If Othello actively shapes the society that he inhabits, how is it that he falls so easily into Iago's fictions, readily imagining and ingesting the "green-eyed monster" in Iago's thought (3.3.169), deciding that he himself is "abused" and his wife "false" before even calling for (not to mention, seeing) "ocular proof" of her unfaith (3.3.270, 281, 362)? What does it mean that, with relatively little prodding, "the Moor of Venice" will take it upon himself to kill his Venetian wife for a "cause" that is as specious as it is unspeakable (5.2.1)? How are we to understand the Moor's tragic undoing, the "heavy act[s]" that Lodovico must take home and "relate" to Venice (5.2.371)? At the end of the play, the Othello standing before his Venetian peers is a "rash and most unfortunate man," outed by the dead body of his murdered wife (5.2.281). As the spectators on stage confront the "strange truth" of how this "monstrous act" came to be, even Othello admits that "this act shows horrible and grim" (5.2.187, 201). Despite his eloquent attempts to explain himself nonetheless as an "honourable murderer" who did "naught" "in hate, but all in honour," who "loved not wisely, but too well," the oxymorons ultimately give way, leaving him no recourse but to kill himself as if he were a Turk (5.2.292–93). To speak of Othello as he is at the end of the play is to speak of things that, it seems, would not be believed in Venice—that would, according to Lodovico and Gratiano, "poison sight" and lead a Venetian senator such as Brabantio to "do a desperate turn," were he not already dead (5.2.363, 205).

As we ourselves try to make sense of Othello's "desperate turn," it might be tempting to read his deterioration as the defeat of the cultural exchange that the Moor initiates in Venice and the triumph of the racial and cultural discriminations that Iago would install there instead. We could read Othello's tragedy, as critics have, as an unfortunate but inevitable fall into type or stereotype and to interpret the accidents that determine the fate of this particular "Moor of Venice" as the ineluctable destiny of *the* Moor, any Moor, in Venice. We could imagine, that is, that Shakespeare attributes to Othello behaviors, desires, or humors that are essentially, categorically "Moorish" and that, though they may have been repressed or suppressed for a while within Venice, inevitably return to prove him vulnerable and his presence untenable there.[71] Even if we grant that the Moor's difference initially gives him leverage within Venice, we could argue that, under the pressure of Iago's racist discourse, Othello learns rather to understand that difference as a liability and to read himself categorically and derogatorily as Moor.[72] Either way, whether the ending produces an Othello who finally is, or merely believes himself to be, an unaccommodated black stranger, his Moorishness nonetheless would explain his tragic transformation, now "graz[ing]" and "pierc[ing]" his "solid virtue" where before, Lodovico asserts, "shot of accident" and "dart of chance" could not (4.1.258–60).

Iago, after all, picks up in Cyprus where Brabantio left off in Venice and encourages Othello to view Desdemona's miscegenous desire as "rank," "foul," and "unnatural" (3.3.236–37). Iago first suggests, by not suggesting, that beneath her love she "seemed" to "fear [Othello's] looks" (3.3.210). He then seizes on Othello's ambiguous hypothesis that, though he "do[es] not think but Desdemona's honest," "nature" has somehow "err[ed] from itself" (3.3.229, 231), and craftily pins that erring on her choice of a spouse *not* "of her own clime, complexion, and degree" (3.3.234). He further cautions Othello to anticipate that Desdemona's "will" ultimately "may fall to match you with her country forms, / And happily repent" (3.3.240–42). Miscegenation is, of course, our term, not Shakespeare's, and here the articulation of a cross-race union is blurred into the vaguer denotation of "country forms" and difference of "degree." Still, these insinuations prompt Othello toward a self-consciousness about his distinctive skin color and, in that sense, his race. When he first tries to understand Desdemona's alleged betrayal, he reasons: "Haply, . . . I am black / And have not those soft parts of conversation / That chamberers have" (3.3.266–68)—a marked turn from his earlier more positive, even prideful association of his "rude" "speech" with his all-consuming military career (1.3.82). He does speculate on an alternative reason (his age) only to dismiss that, and maybe everything, as "not much," and he may initially be grasping at straws here to make credible what otherwise seems incredible (3.3.269). Nonetheless, he later uses the blackness of his "own face" to declare Desdemona's "name," once "as fresh / As Dian's visage," morally "begrimed and black" (3.3.388–89), and he calls on "black Vengeance" to replace his "fond love" (3.3.447, 446). In the end, the more Iago talks, the more Othello's darkness seems to become a sign and source of trouble. No wonder, then, that his blackness would become the persistent centerpiece of an *Othello* myth.

Yet while issues of culture and color do filter into the crisis that Iago constructs and Othello begins to live, those issues are decidedly, perhaps surprisingly, *not* the centerpiece either of Iago's accusations or Othello's anxieties. For notably, Iago does not ground his fictions on the racist discrimination he has tested within Venice, turning the Moor directly into the subject of suspicion and "intermingling everything [Othello] does" with a reminder that he is, alas, a Moor, alien and black (3.3.25). Rather, Iago selects Desdemona as the more pliable and plausible target, drawing on the arguably more conventional misogynous discourses which, as critics have shown, circulate across the play and provide a set of discriminations that are more inclusive and precise, if not also more persuasive, than the more amorphous terms of race or culture.[73] It is Desdemona's potential for deception, which in turn impugns and becomes her sexual behavior, that is the easy mark. Brabantio has already alerted Othello to the ominous fact that "she has deceived her father, and may thee," has already rendered elopement and adultery suggestively contiguous (1.3.291). Iago uses that deception and those words to play the race and culture card, to remind Othello that Desdemona "did deceive her father, marrying you," seeming to fear what she loved (3.3.209). But Iago moves well beyond this "unnatural" choice of spouse to turn Desdemona's dishonesty into an essential feature of her character and gender, setting her up not just to represent "maidens of quality" who, "without their parents' consent, . . . run away with blackamoors," but to represent wives "in Venice" who "let God see the pranks / They dare not show their husbands" and whose "best conscience / Is not to leave't undone, but keep't unknown" (3.3.205–7).[74] This is her "country disposition," which is "Venetian," though Venice qualifies what wives show, not necessarily who they are (3.3.204). But that "country" points more directly (with the obvious pun on "cunt") to the wife's unchaste sexual body. It is that body that Iago will prop up with prurient "proofs" (3.3.326): the handkerchief, which substitutes for her body as a "common thing" (3.3.305), and Cassio's erotic dream of " 'Sweet Desdemona,' " which Iago invents and embodies to "thicken other proofs, / That do demonstrate thinly" (3.3.420, 431–32).[75] The all too believable fiction here is not merely that Desdemona may "recoil" to "her better judgement" when she cannot "match" the Moor with her "country" (or countrymen's) "forms" (3.3.240), but that she is a wife, acting dishonestly on her desires, as wives will to do in Venice, and driven at least as much by attraction to a sexually fluent Florentine as by repulsion from the Moor.

In separating Iago's manipulation of gender from his racial and cultural discriminations, I do not mean to undo important work that has unveiled the imbrication of constructions of gender with constructions of race or, for that matter, other registers of identity, such as class or religion.[76] No discourse exists in a vacuum, as the play on "country" here attests. My point is rather that in *Othello*, at the least, these intersections are volatile and dynamic, their terms variable, unbalanced, and unequal, not all applied with equal fervor or equal effect at any given moment. Although different registers of identity do coexist within Venice's discursive field, even as they complement each other they may simultaneously conflict. Indeed, Iago's primary choice of venue is traumatically torn, his manipulation of gender stereotypes emerging at once in conjunction *and* in conflict with his racial indictments. In resorting to terms that can include but are not exclusive to a "mixed" marriage, Iago underplays the importance of that factor, as if tailoring his discourse to a Moor who is not, and does not expect to be, alienated or estranged. Where Iago's references to Othello's complexion and clime, on the one hand, separate the Moor from Venetian society, his obsession with Desdemona's dishonesty, on the other, writes Othello in among Venetian "cuckolds" who unwittingly "liv[e] in bliss" and who need to know what women do with their "country forms" in Venice (3.3.170).

No wonder, then, that even as Othello acknowledges his own blackness, he identifies the problem as the "curse of marriage, / That we can call these delicate creatures ours, / And not their appetites!" (3.3.271–73)—including himself among the "we" of husbands and imagining his situation as "the plague to great ones" and a "destiny unshunnable" (3.3.276, 278).[77] No wonder either that, at the crucial moment of truth, he premises the murder of his wife on the idea that "she must die, else she'll betray more men"—not, it must be said, more Moors (5.2.6). As Othello positions himself as the arbiter of "Justice," he extracts himself, an abstract "I," from clime, complexion, and degree, and locates the "cause" (which goes without saying) in her signifying body, not his (5.2.17). And what he invokes and repels as he looks at that body, refusing to "shed her blood" or "scar that whiter skin of hers than snow," is not the racially loaded spectacle of black against white that we may see, but the sexually loaded spectacle of red (sexual blood) against white (virginal sheets) that he would erase or hide (5.2.3–4).[78]

In emphasizing the domestic edges of Iago's fictions and Othello's fall, the play insists that we look beyond the cultural narratives and stereotypes that could ideologically subdue and categorically undo the Moor. It prompts us to view Othello's tragedy (as we would the tragedies of Hamlet, Macbeth, and Lear) not only from the outside in but also from the inside out. Iago clearly exploits the marital relation to alter Othello's vision, doing in Cyprus what he could not do in Venice. But in Cyprus as well that relation becomes an unprescribed site of improvisation and negotiation between Othello and Desdemona, requiring that we take Othello on his own terms, as a tragic hero whose fate is as contingent on his interactions with his wife as on the manipulations of his nefarious ensign. Indeed, what makes the tragedy intriguing and cathartic, rather than, in Aristotelean terms, pathetic, is that instead of simply falling into another's narrative, into the trap of stereotype, Othello participates in a story of his—and Desdemona's—own making. Signally, before Iago's sustained invasion of Othello's thoughts can even begin to take hold, it is interrupted by Desdemona's intervention on Cassio's behalf. However much that suit catalyzes Othello's jealousy of Cassio and so plays into Iago's hand, it exposes and engenders or inflames a potentially disturbing tension within the marriage that puts at stake and at risk the fundamentals of power, voice, authority, desire, and gender. For, as I have argued elsewhere, in speaking for Cassio, Desdemona speaks boldly, transgressively, even combatively for herself, making clear that while she is not now requesting a "boon" "touching [Othello's] love indeed," someday she will, and that "it shall be full of poise and difficult weight, / And fearful to be granted" (3.3.77, 82–84).[79] In addressing Cassio's unruly behavior, Othello must therefore come to terms with hers, and as he does so, the political becomes deeply, perplexingly personal. Othello twice asserts "I will deny thee nothing," to shut the matter down, as if to deny Cassio is to deny Desdemona, and he then asks to be left "but a little to myself," as if to give in to her is to deny and negate himself (3.3.77, 84, 86). However we choose to read the marital dynamic and the positions (aggressive, submissive, erotic, and such) husband and wife take within it, at its center—and at the center, therefore, of Othello's tragic decline—is a volatile tension that exceeds, even if it feeds, Iago's "uncleanly apprehensions" (3.3.143). To view Othello through that tension, as the play insists we must, is to understand his character as not only deeply embedded in a domestic relationship but also inextricably improvised from it.

Even as that relationship begins to unravel to a breaking point of no return, the Moor's ability to reshape Venice does not. That is, even as Othello becomes estranged from his wife, from himself, and from behaviors that

would be believed in Venice, his "occupation" "gone," the play does not collapse his identity as a stranger into the idea of estrangement or halt the play
of cultural exchange that has been so crucial to his story (3.3.359). To the contrary, as Othello attempts to negotiate the treacheries of a spoiled wife and
marriage, he continues to bring the "everywhere" into the "here" as a potent
touchstone of meaning. Iago will attempt to turn the "world" against the
Moor, exclaiming "O monstrous world! Take note, take note, O world"
when Othello challenges his honesty (3.3.379). Yet the world remains
Othello's oyster: he himself swears "by the world" to verify and validate his
questionable ambivalence, his concurrent but incompatible beliefs that Desdemona is "honest" and that she is not, that Iago is "just" and that he is not
(3.3.385–87). To justify the otherwise unfathomable desire for revenge that
newly consumes and transforms him, Othello maps it onto a Mediterranean
geography as the "icy current and compulsive course" of "the Pontic Sea,"
which "ne'er feels retiring ebb, but keeps due on / To the Propontic and the
Hellespont" (3.3.453–56).

These passing references may do little more than expose "the world" as a
clarifying vehicle of the Moor's self-reflection at a moment when Iago would
make it, and Othello, "monstrous." But Othello's re-presentation of the fate-
ful handkerchief instances his ability to transform the society he inhabits.
Adding a newly exotic edge to the already overdetermined meanings of that
prop, he brings its "magic" home in a way that not only authorizes his position but shapes Desdemona's as well, naturalizing the present even as he exoticizes the past. In a speech that has become a well-known signpost of his
"prehistory," contiguous with the life story he invokes at court, Othello depicts the handkerchief as a gift given to his mother by an Egyptian "charmer,"
woven by a sibyl, and containing "magic" in its "web" (3.4.56, 68).[80] Embedded within this exotic history is a heavy legacy of marital faith, loading the
token with the power, in its presence, to sign the husband's love and, in its absence, to lay in the wife's lap a marriage-breaking "perdition" (3.4.66).[81]
Though Iago first turns the prop into crucial proof, Othello reappropriates
the token for himself to mediate a battle of marital wills—to arbitrate, within
a vexed exchange with Desdemona, what is most relevant, "most veritable,"
"possible," and "true" (3.4.67, 74–75). While he means to call his wife to task
for losing the handkerchief by asking her to produce it, she enters the exchange with a potentially explosive agenda of her own. Having just ordered a
clown to "enquire" Cassio "out" and "bid him come hither," she has presumptively arranged the reconciliation with Othello (3.4.13, 17). Hence, while Oth-

ello gears up to press his cause, bantering about the "heraldry of hands" and finding her hand too "liberal," "hot, hot and moist!" she interrupts him (3.4.36–37, 45). Insisting that she "cannot speak of this," she reminds him of his "promise" and announces that she has "bid Cassio to come speak with [him]" (3.4.46, 48). What follows is an almost comic back-and-forth between the two speakers and causes, with Othello insistently demanding "the hand-kerchief!" "the handkerchief!" while his wife as insistently talks of Cassio (3.4.91, 94). But what makes matters seriously worse is that Desdemona does not simply counter Othello's issue with an issue of her own; she treats his request with a dismissive insouciance. If on the side she is covering for the handkerchief's loss (which she has noticed), her reactions nonetheless belittle his demand as "a trick to put me from my suit" (3.4.86). It is in the face of this emergent disregard that Othello produces the token's past, weaving "magic" into its "web" in order to make her "look to't well," as to him and to his demand (3.4.75). His exotic story provides an explanatory context for his interest, substituting for the "truth" he does not yet want to disclose and giving needed credence to an obsession which otherwise appears "startling" and "rash."

The exchange will reach no resolution; Desdemona holds her ground until Othello exits in frustration, on an impassioned "'swounds!" (3.4.95). Yet his representation of the handkerchief's "magic" subtly cues a transformation in Desdemona at this moment, from a position of unstinting skepticism to a loosened embrace of "wonder." Before the exchange, she registers the hand-kerchief's loss only to deny its import, imagining that if her "noble Moor" were *not* "true of mind, and made of no such baseness / As jealous creatures are," that loss might put him to "ill thinking" (3.4.24–27). Whatever hints of insecurity her hypothesis holds, her articulated resolve is to believe that Othello is inherently, even racially, incapable of jealousy and change, that "the sun where he was born / Drew all such humours from him" (3.4.28–29). But after Othello weaves his exotic explanation, she not only begins to question the pertinence of his terms, whether they are "possible" and "true"; once he exits she admits seeing what she "ne'er saw . . . before" and acknowledges newly that there is "sure" "some wonder in this handkerchief" (3.4.96–97). Regardless of whether she actually buys into the literal magic that Othello imposes on the prop, she projects his "wonder" there, according it properties that, for whatever reason, are worth "some" note. The magic Othello produces, then, not only provides her terms for understanding and validating his reactions; it also incites her to wonder herself, her naïve surety giving way to the possibility that things—and husbands—change, that there are more things in heaven and earth than have been dreamt of in her philosophy.

Like Othello, Desdemona will see the insidious truth behind the tragedy too late to alter the outcome, to contain, curtail, or even counteract the alienation between them. Such is the process of tragedy. But to the end, Othello insists on the compatibility of his domain and hers, the far-reaching world of "wonder" and the domestic space of marriage, using the intersection to construct meaning in Venice. When he makes a final account of himself and his "unlucky deeds," he puts his own voice into the mouth of Venice, dictating the terms that Lodovico should relate, and not "extenuate." Improvising a self-image, as I have discussed in the Introduction, Othello moves through a progressive series of possibilities, starting with an unfathomable self "that loved not wisely, but too well," "not easily jealous, but being wrought, / Perplexed in the extreme." What is especially remarkable here is that he uses exotic figures as the means to clarify this confused domestic impression. "The base Indian" (or Judean) who "threw a pearl away / Richer than all his tribe" and the one "whose subdued eyes, / Albeit unusèd to the melting mood, / Drops tears as fast as the Arabian trees / Their medicinable gum" become the naturalizing precedents for the lover's consternation, his conflicted position as one who loved "not wisely" and "too well," who was "not easily jealous" but apparently easily perplexed. Within the familiar form of the blazon, the exotic displaces and replaces the domestic as the vehicle of sense, ameliorating the perplexities of a love that can be "wrought."

What results is an inclusive, unbounded cultural vision, in which the images and icons of everywhere fill in the symbolic economy of the here. To be sure, at the very end Othello resorts to the established opposition between the Venetians and the Turks, raising the specter of stereotype—of "a malignant and a turbaned Turk" who "beat a Venetian and traduced the state." Yet significantly, he sets that drama in "Aleppo"—a "gateway" city in Turkey that was to the desert trades what Venice was to the sea—reminding his audience that what happens there also happens here.[82] What he produces, ultimately, is a sort of cultural amalgam of a Moor who gestures with an Indian/Judean hand, cries Arabian tears, impersonates a Turk, and kills himself—with a "sword of Spain"—as that Turk, just as the Turk killed a Venetian (5.2.252), making it hard to know where the Moor begins and these other subjects end.[83] Appropriately, layered on top is a cross-cultural and intracultural kiss between not merely a Moor and a Venetian, but also a Venetian husband and wife.

Othello, the Moor of Venice, dies. Venice will literally inherit from him:

at his death Gratiano will "keep the house / And seize upon the fortunes of the Moor," since as Brabantio's brother, he is also Othello's uncle-in-law and heir.[84] Yet the legacy Othello leaves—the open-ended cultural exchange he embodies and propels—extends tellingly beyond his own particular "fortunes." Though we cannot, and need not, credit Othello specifically with making all the difference, by the end of the play the world seems to be everywhere in Venice. Emilia imagines, at one point, "a lady in Venice" walking "barefoot to Palestine" for "a touch of [Lodovico's] nether lip" (4.3.34–35), and, at another, "every honest hand" whipping "rascals naked through the world, / Even from the east to th' west" (4.2.142–44), the exotic landscape carrying in each case the currency and transparency of cliché. Yet if these references map the world out there, Shakespeare also brings the outlandish tropes and props of "all the world" into the everyday. Emilia, for example, objects to husbands who "pour our treasures into foreign laps," which could themselves be Venetian (4.3.83), while, in passing, Desdemona weighs her "purse full of" Portuguese "crusadoes" against the handkerchief as the object she would rather have lost (3.4.23–24), as if the two are comparable as signs and safeguards of love. Moreover, within a conversation that seems a curious detour from the plot, Desdemona asks Emilia whether she would "abuse" her husband "for all the world" (4.3.59). In response, Emilia fills in the seemingly vacant figure of speech, objecting that the world is a "huge thing" and "a great price / For a small vice" (4.3.64–65). Augmenting her point, she sets that "world" (for which she would trade her body) against trivial items (for which she would not trade)—"a joint-ring," "measures of lawn," "gowns, petticoats," "caps," or "any petty exhibition"—using "all the whole world" as synecdoche to suggest a contrasting, though unspecified, materiality (4.3.68–70). To have "the world"—which *is* to be had—is to have something that could make a husband a "monarch" and could change the moral landscape: if you had "the world for your labour," she insists, "you might quickly make . . . right" any "wrong" you had done within it, within "your own world" (4.3.71, 75–77). If her intent is to unsettle Desdemona's sexual naïveté, the effect is to establish "the world" as a plausible measure of what women could—and should—"play for" (4.3.80).

Desdemona may not herself play "for the world," though she seems to have married into it. But she too claims that world—and with it, the Moor—as a part of her own heritage and identity. Her speculations about the worldly limits of female fidelity are preceded and prompted by her contemplation of her own strangely deteriorating marriage. To comprehend that crisis, she re-

members that her "mother had a maid called Barbary" and that Barbary sang
a " 'Song of Willow' " that "expressed her fortune" (4.3.24, 26–27). Desdemona takes on Barbary's voice and story as her own, the class differences
notwithstanding, presenting—and becoming—a woman who "was in love"
with one who "proved mad, / And did forsake her" (4.3.25–26). Barbary's identity as lover overshadows her cultural or racial features to the point that her
unspecified identity, as or as not Moorish, matters less to Desdemona than the
maid's resemblance to herself. At this moment, the signs of the Moor—along
with the "process" propelled by the particular Moor, Othello—appear so
deeply embedded in the Venetian domestic terrain that they cannot be separated out, "Barbary" naming a figure who may or may not be a Moor. Desdemona's history, thus, takes the idea of cultural exchange to another level,
pressing it beyond the bounds of character, geography, and history, raising the
possibility that before there was in Venice a Moor, there was a maid called
Barbary, "the name of the Moor" written indelibly and indistinguishably onto
the body of Venice.

To look to "the Moor of Venice," then, is to see a "world" in progress, a
process of cross-cultural exchange that not only opens out but also opens in,
to the improvised interiors of domestic life. That world extends, significantly,
beyond character and culture and even beyond the play. For indeed, the Florentine Claudio has already lived a comic version of the Moor's tragedy in
Much Ado, vying for Hero of Messina against the malicious plots of the bastard of Aragon, Don John. In addition, King Leontes of Sicilia will replay
Othello's trauma of doubt in double time in *The Winter's Tale*, directing his
outrageous suspicions against his Bohemian rival and his Moscovite queen. In
these plays too, the cultural will compete with the domestic as the crux of social disaster: the prolix gender-bashing of Beatrice and Benedick in *Much Ado*
outvoices the understated but residual culture wars between Aragon, Messina,
and Florence, setting the tone (and volume) for that unfortunate story; likewise, the queen Hermione's pregnancy in *The Winter's Tale* overshadows her
foreign heritage as the starting point of both identity and crisis. To set these
plays against *Othello* is to see that the Moor's story is never exclusively his
own—or, rather, is his own, if we understand that story as insistent on the extravagant interplay of cultures here and everywhere, within the domestic as
across the strange. Even though these plays include characters and discourses
that would close such cultural crossings down, that interplay provides the
modus operandi of their own dramatic inventions. There can be no greater
irony in *Othello* than that the figure of Iago is himself fashioned on a Moor

(Aaron), who is fashioned on a Jew (Barabas) who resembles a Turk (Ithamore). Do what he can to hate one Moor, Iago necessarily "follows" another, his self-defining, self-abnegating hypothesis "were I the Moor" appearing truer than he knows (1.1.58, 57).

Ultimately, at its core *Othello* is a domestic tragedy, and in the end, we cannot really tell where Venice's story stops and the Moor's story begins, so seamless and boundless is the cross-cultural exchange that Shakespeare stages. Though Iago would have us know what we know and read the world through stereotypes, "the great world" itself, even in its most exotic expressions, provides the vehicle for breaking such fictions down, for reimagining as a dynamic and unscripted interaction the relation between Venice and the Moor, the domestic and the strange, the here and the everywhere. Try as Iago might to teach us otherwise, to speak of Othello as he is at any point in the play is not to speak categorically of "the Moor," invoking a modern politics of identity that does not quite apply. Nor is it to speak simply through a Venice which would or would not believe—or believe in—him. It is rather, crucially, to speak of a "Moor of Venice" who, even as and when he falls, shapes the society he inhabits from the histories of the world. To tell his story is to acknowledge his part in the telling—to recognize that what we know and how we know come, in part, from him.

CONCLUSION

A Brave New World

IN 1611, SOME seven years after the emergence of *Othello*, *The Tempest* would turn to a new dramatic space and subject, pointing suggestively to the New World that was fast becoming the preoccupying centerpiece of England's reach outward. The full text of William Strachey's "true reportory" of "the wrack on Bermuda" (1610), a key source, ultimately charts a voyage to Jamestown, a colony that has been long considered a crucial landmark of "the birth of America."[1] Yet the colonial geography of *The Tempest* is notably vague, its "brave new world" poised somewhere, but not definitively anywhere, between Europe and the west (5.1.183).[2] In fact, what the play maps more precisely is the geographic and ideological transition to this new world from the "old" world of "Afric," Shakespeare's one explicit reference to the proper name (2.1.69). Having just celebrated the "sweet marriage" of his "fair daughter Claribel to the King of Tunis" (2.1.70–71), the Neapolitan king and his party find themselves shipwrecked on what seems an "uninhabitable, and almost inaccessible" island (2.1.39). As they try to make sense of where they are, Africa becomes their familiarizing touchstone: imagining that their "garments are now as fresh as when [they] put them on first in Afric" (2.1.68–69), they squabble knowingly over the precedent of Africa's legendary past (over the difference between Tunis and Carthage) to praise Claribel as "that rarest that e'er came there" since "widow Dido's time" (2.1.97, 75). Sebastian chastises his brother, the king, for choosing not to "bless our Europe with your daughter, / But rather lose her to an African" (2.1.123–24), but only in the face of the "great loss" of the Neapolitan prince, Ferdinand, who seems to have drowned in the tempest. Otherwise, the union of Europe and Africa, Claribel and the Tunisian king, has promised a "prosperous "return" (2.1.72).

But if Africa is here a touchstone of meaning and comfort, it is also one that is being newly, if accidentally, bypassed. The sequence of events that Prospero crafts in order to enable his return to Europe and his daughter's marriage to Ferdinand upstages Claribel's unstaged marriage to the king of Tunis. The future of Italy comes to lie, therefore, not in the prosperous bond that has taken shape in the established space of Africa but in the unpredictable relations that are taking shape before our eyes in the uncharted terrains of the island. If there is one thing that the play underscores, it is that this "new world" requires different terms of approach and accommodation, different kinds of improvisation, different interpretations of the familiar and the "strange," of the "thing[s] of darkness" one must "acknowledge," even own (5.1.289, 275–76). The "English diaspora" began to mark and hold its ground, in fact, with narratives such as Strachey's.[3] And *The Tempest* itself represents (that is, both is and figures) a certain turning point in the history and literature of England's move into "the world," dramatizing an evolving shift of interest from the multilayered, culturally mixed exchanges in the Mediterranean to a hugely promising, if uncertain, future in the west.

This is not the end of the story of complex racial and cultural inscription, of course, but in a way another beginning. For although the evolution of chattel slavery in the New World would catalyze the stabilization of a recognizable racism against "black" subjects, early encounters with the Indians there brought a new kind of "darkness" into the picture, unsettling the still unsettled terms of difference that circulated around African subjects. *The Tempest's* Caliban has proven over time to be unusually unreadable—perhaps as much, though not in the same way, as the Moor—his image occupying a range of places on a spectrum of civility and savagery which it also simultaneously defined.[4] Within the play, while Caliban is to some a "hag-born" and "poisonous slave" (1.2.283, 319), a "misshapen knave," a "demi-devil" (5.1.268, 272), to others, a "fish" (2.2.25), it is nonetheless hard to tell where his language stops and Prospero's (and Miranda's) begins. Set him next to Miranda, the circumscribed daughter, or Ferdinand, the temporarily enslaved prince, as the play demands that we do, and Caliban's position as a cultural subject seems all the more unpredictable, uncodified, open-ended. Prospero may claim "this thing of darkness" as his own, but what is to happen then? As the Europeans prepare to return to Europe, Caliban stands before them (and us) as an incomprehensibly "strange thing" (5.1.289)—a sign of how indeterminate discriminatory vocabularies still were.

Activity in the Mediterranean, of course, had not ceased by 1611. Nor did Moorish characters disappear altogether from the English stage after *Othello*. But once activity in the New World began to reconfigure England's economic priorities, where and how it looked for its own prosperous returns, the Moor was no longer a featured dramatic subject, no longer figured as the motivating agent of cultural change and exchange. To the contrary, in Jacobean plays, Moors appear most frequently in secondary roles, defined and delimited by the subordinating axes of gender and class. Witness, for example, Zanthia in John Marston's *Wonder of Women; or, the Tragedy of Sophonisba* (1606), Zanche in John Webster's *White Devil* (1611–12), and Zanthia in Beaumont and Fletcher's *Knight of Malta* (1616)—all female servants of questionable integrity and unquestionably limited agency. As well, at the end of that era, when William Rowley remakes *Lust's Dominion* as *All's Lost by Lust* (ca. 1619–20), the Moor's potential to remake the history of Spain in his own image is substantially reduced.[5] While the leading Moor Mulymumen eventually usurps the Spanish crown, he is not the first to challenge or overthrow the lecherous Spanish king (Rodorique), is not able to marry the Spanish woman (Jacinta) of his sexual and political dreams, and is not installed as "the first of Moors ere was King of Spain" until the very end of the play (5.1.204). When he is installed, his reign appears therefore as the unstageable outcome of an inherently troubled regime, his impact and import unclear. Tellingly, too, in 1630, when Heywood creates a sequel to his *Fair Maid of the West*, although the king of Fez, Mullisheg, has a larger role than he has in Part One, he has a smaller part in the construction of culture. For in Part Two, it is not he who shapes the fortunes of the English Bess (as he does, at the end of Part One), but the English Bess and her cohorts who reshape the fortunes of the Moorish kingdom and Moorish king, as mediators of both literal and figurative conversion. In fact, the issue of conversion—in such plays as Robert Daborne's *A Christian Turned Turk* (1612) and Philip Massinger's *The Renegado* (1630)—gives a particular prominence rather to the Turk as an icon of cultural change and exchange, albeit via characterizations that border on caricature.

Ultimately, then, the dramatic landscape shifts, with figures such as Caliban puncturing the boundaries of difference on one side, the specter of the Turks proffering the possibility of conversion on the other, and the Moor embedded in the middle as a subject more easily circumscribed than either. But if the interest in the Moor, as a figure central to England's expanding material and ideological investment in "the world," was therefore short-lived, it was not short sighted. From *Alcazar* to *Othello*, the representation of the Moor presses on the boundaries of culture, exposing "all the world" as a work in progress, improvised, for better or for worse, from the unpredictable variables of exchange. Even in the face of blackness, early modern dramatists aligned the Moor with multiple and multiplex identities. And while it would be common to imagine turning Turk, or to washing an Ethiop white, there could be no comparable tag line for the Moor. For ultimately, to speak of the Moor "as he was" at the turn of the sixteenth century, when England was making its own way in the world, was necessarily to acknowledge the complexity and contingency of cultural identity and the provisional meanings of place. In the end, within the dramatic and historical texts that were bringing the Moor's story into prominence in England, the Moor is never simply the representative of a racial or cultural difference, but a figure whose dynamic engagement with Europe makes race and culture continually different.

NOTES

INTRODUCTION

1. Quotations from this play are from William Shakespeare, *Othello, the Moor of Venice*, ed. Michael Neill (Oxford: Oxford University Press, 2006). Except where stated otherwise, references to Shakespeare are from *The Riverside Shakespeare*, ed. G. Blakemore Evans et al. (Boston: Houghton Mifflin, 1974).

2. See Neill's appendix (464–65) on the debate over these well-known textual alternatives.

3. See Neill's note to the line (5.2.338), which suggests the echoes in Venetian histories.

4. The glosses here are from Leslie Brown, ed., *The New Shorter Oxford English Dictionary*, (1973; Oxford: Clarendon Press, 1993).

5. Eldred D. Jones, *Othello's Countrymen: The African in English Renaissance Drama* (London: Oxford University Press, 1965) and *The Elizabethan Image of Africa* (Charlottesville: University Press of Virginia, 1971).

6. Michael Neill, "'Mulattos,' 'Blacks,' and 'Indian Moors': Othello and Early Modern Constructions of Difference," *Shakespeare Quarterly* 49, no. 4 (Winter 1998): 364, reprinted in *Putting History to the Question: Power, Politics, and Society in English Renaissance Drama* (New York: Columbia University Press, 2000), 269–84, which I cite hereafter. See also my essay, "Making More of the Moor: Aaron, Othello, and Renaissance Refashionings of Race," *Shakespeare Quarterly* 41, no. 4 (Winter 1990): 434–35.

7. Neill, "'Mulattos,'" 365.

8. Henry Louis Gates, Jr., ed., *"Race," Writing, and Difference* (Chicago: University of Chicago Press, 1985). See especially the "Editor's Introduction: Writing 'Race' and the Difference It Makes," 1–20.

9. G. K. Hunter, *English Drama, 1586–1642: The Age of Shakespeare* (Oxford: Clarendon Press, 1997), 79.

10. Thomas Dekker, *Lust's Dominion; or, The Lascivious Queen*, ed. J. Le Grey Brereton (1657; Louvain, Belgium: Librarie Universitaire, Uystpruyst, 1931), 154–55.

11. Citations from *The Battle of Alcazar* are from *The Works of George Peele*, ed. A. H. Bullen, vol. 1 (1888; Port Washington, N.Y.: Kennikat Press, 1966).

12. Jonathan Gil Harris, "Rematerializing Shakespeare's Intertheatricality: The Occidental/Oriental Palimpsest," 19, from a forthcoming book project.

13. Thomas Heywood, *The Fair Maid of the West, Parts I and II*, ed. Robert K. Turner, Jr. (Lincoln: University of Nebraska Press, 1967).

14. From *Tamb. I* 3.3.136; *Tamb. II* 1.1.61–64. Quotations from Marlowe are from Christopher Marlowe, *The Complete Plays*, ed. Frank Romany and Robert Lindsey (London: Penguin Books, 2003), except where otherwise stated.

15. For a concise, wide-ranging survey of ostensibly "racist" representations, see especially Virginia Mason Vaughan and Alden T. Vaughan, "Before *Othello*: Elizabethan Representations of Sub-Saharan Africans," *William and Mary Quarterly* 3rd ser. 54, no. 4 (January 1997): 19–44.

16. Richard Hakluyt, *The Principal Navigations, Voyages, Traffiques & Discoveries of the English Nation*, 12 vols. (1589; Glasgow: James Maclehose and Sons, 1903–5). All quotations from Hakluyt are from this edition unless otherwise stated.

17. John Pory, in *The History and Description of Africa* by Al-Hassan Ibn-Mohammed Al Wezâz Al-fâsi, ed. Robert Brown, 3 vols. (London: Hakluyt Society, 1896), 1006, 6.

18. Quotations from this play are from William Shakespeare, *Titus Andronicus*, ed. Jonathan Bate (London: Routledge, 1995).

19. John Ryle, "The Many Voices of Africa," *Granta: The Magazine of New Writing* 92 (Winter 2005), 9; emphasis added.

20. Ryle, 9.

21. Nicholas D. Kristof, "Shrugs for the Dead," *New York Times* (August 8, 2006), A17.

22. Kristof, A17.

23. Celia Daileader, *Racism, Misogyny, and the Othello Myth: Inter-racial Couples from Shakespeare to Spike Lee* (Cambridge: Cambridge University Press, 2005), 6, 10.

24. Gary Taylor, *Buying Whiteness: Race, Culture, and Identity from Columbus to Hip Hop* (New York: Palgrave, 2005), 44. Taking "whiteness" as the trope that has made a transhistorical difference from "Columbus to Hip Hop," Taylor presents skin as the "first sign system" one "learns to read," its color hard to miss, and "the word moor" as having "everything to do with dark flesh" in *Othello* (2).

25. This question comes from Emma Smith.

26. G. K. Hunter, "Othello and Colour Prejudice," in *Dramatic Identities and Cultural Tradition: Studies in Shakespeare and His Contemporaries* (New York: Barnes and Noble Books, 1978), 31–59. As Mary Floyd-Wilson points out in a useful summary of "Moors, Race, and the Study of English Renaissance Literature: A Brief Retrospective," *Literature Compass* 3, no. 5 (September 2006): 1044–52, doi:10.1111/j.1741–4113.2006. 00366x, Hunter's essay was initially published in 1967.

27. Jones, *Othello's Countrymen*, 37, 3.

28. Jones, *Othello's Countrymen*, 109.

29. William Shakespeare, *The Tempest*, ed. Stephen Orgel (1987; Oxford: Oxford University Press, 1998).

30. See the Sierra Leone Writers Series homepage at www.sl-writers-series.org. I am grateful to Emma Smith for bringing this site to my attention.

31. Edward Said, *Orientalism* (New York: Vintage Books, 1978).

32. Elliot H. Tokson, *The Popular Image of the Black Man in English Drama*, 1550–1688 (Boston: G. K. Hall, 1982), ix.

33. Tokson, 2, 19.

34. Anthony Gerard Barthelemy, *Black Face, Maligned Race: The Representation of Blacks in English Drama from Shakespeare to Southerne* (Baton Rouge: Louisiana State University Press, 1987), 202. Barthelemy concludes, "How these assumptions . . . have come to shape our lives and the opinions of our contemporaries about blacks is, I am afraid to say, all too easy to assess. For many, blackness still signifies evil and sin, and black people remain the Other, excluded still" (202).

35. Barthelemy, x; see also 1–17.

36. The one exception is Jack D'Amico, *The Moor in English Renaissance Drama* (Tampa: University of South Florida Press, 1991), which reads "Moorish culture" against the stable backdrop of a "Western perspective" (76, 78). Though D'Amico argues that Renaissance dramatists press spectators to reassess "certain racial, religious, and cultural preconceptions," for him that reassessment happens only along a rigid self/other divide (1). In the end what prompts and defines the revision are Moorish characters who reflect "Western values" (119), exhibiting "a basic human need to protect one's own" (137), a "human capacity for survival and renewal" (145), and a "common human complexion" (177).

37. Gates, 2.

38. See especially Peter Hulme, *Colonial Encounters: Europe and the Native Caribbean, 1492–1797* (London: Methuen, 1986); and Paul Brown, " 'This thing of darkness I acknowledge mine': *The Tempest* and the Discourse of Colonialism," in *Political Shakespeare: New Essays in Cultural Materialism*, ed. Jonathan Dollimore and Alan Sinfield (Ithaca, N.Y.: Cornell University Press, 1985), 48–71. See also Martin Orkin, "Othello and the 'plain face' of Racism," *Shakespeare Quarterly* 38 (1987): 166–88.

39. Key examples include Karen Newman, " 'And wash the Ethiop white': Femininity and the Monstrous in *Othello*," in *Shakespeare Reproduced: The Text in History and Ideology*, ed. Jean E. Howard and Marion F. O'Connor (New York: Methuen, 1987), 143–62; Ania Loomba, *Gender, Race, and Renaissance Drama* (Manchester: Manchester University Press, 1989); Michael Neill, "Unproper Beds: Race, Adultery, and the Hideous in *Othello*," *Shakespeare Quarterly* 40, no. 4 (Winter 1989): 383–412; Margo Hendricks and Patricia Parker, eds., *Women, "Race," and Writing in the Early Modern Period*, (London: Routledge, 1994); Kim F. Hall, *Things of Darkness: Economies of Race and Gender in Early Modern England* (Ithaca, N.Y.: Cornell University Press, 1995). On these contributions, see Peter Erickson, "The Moment of Race in Renaissance Studies," *Shakespeare Studies* 26 (1998): 27–36. Subsequent extensions of this trajectory include: Dympna Callaghan, *Shakespeare Without Women: Representing Gender and Race on the Renaissance Stage* (London: Routledge, 2000); Arthur L. Little, Jr., *Shakespeare Jungle Fever: National-Imperial Re-Visions of Race, Rape, and Sacrifice* (Stanford, Calif.: Stanford University Press, 2002); and Joyce Green MacDonald, *Women and Race in Early Modern Texts* (Cambridge: Cambridge University Press, 2002). See also Catherine M. S. Alexander and Stanley Wells, eds., *Shakespeare and Race*, (Cambridge: Cambridge University Press, 2000); in it, Margo Hendrick's

essay, "Surverying 'race' in Shakespeare," provides a particularly useful overview of early modern race studies.

40. Pivotal to these developments have been Said, *Culture and Imperialism* (New York: Vintage Books, 1993); Homi K. Bhabha, *The Location of Culture* (London: Routledge, 1994); Robert J. C. Young, *Colonial Desire: Hybridity in Theory, Culture and Race* (London: Routledge, 1995). See also Ania Loomba, *Colonialism/Postcolonialism* (London: Routledge, 1998). Loomba, *Shakespeare, Race, and Colonialism* (Oxford: Oxford University Press, 2002) has set the terms for postcolonial studies of the early modern period. See also Jyotsna Singh, "Othello's Identity, Postcolonial Theory, and Contemporary Rewritings of *Othello*," in Parker and Hendricks, eds., 287–99, and *Colonial Narratives/Cultural Dialogues: "Discoveries" of India in the Language of Colonialism* (London: Routledge, 1996); Loomba and Orkin, eds., *Post-Colonial Shakespeares* (London: Routledge, 1998); Thomas Cartelli, *Repositioning Shakespeare: National Formations, Postcolonial Appropriations* (London: Routledge, 1999); Imtiaz H. Habib, *Shakespeare and Race: Postcolonial Praxis in the Early Modern Period* (Lanham, Md.: University Press of America, 2000); and Shankar Raman, *Framing "India": The Colonial Imaginary in Early Modern Culture* (Stanford, Calif.: Stanford University Press, 2002).

41. See my inaugural essay on the topic, "Making More of the Moor," 433–54.

42. In "*Othello* and Africa: Postcolonialism Reconsidered," *William and Mary Quarterly* 3rd ser. 54, no. 1 (January 1997): 45–64. See also Lynda Boose, " 'The Getting of a Lawful Race': Racial Discourse in Early Modern England and the Unrepresentable Black Woman," in Hendricks and Parker, eds., 35–54; and Singh, "Othello's Identity."

43. Hall, 2, 62.

44. Hall, 7.

45. See Loomba, *Shakespeare, Race, and Colonialism*. Influential explorations of these geographies include Daniel J. Vitkus, *Turning Turk: English Theater and the Multicultural Mediterranean, 1570–1630* (New York: Palgrave Macmillan, 2003); Jonathan Burton, *Traffic and Turning: Islam and English Drama, 1579–1624* (Newark: University of Delaware Press, 2005); Singh, *Colonial Narratives*; and Raman, *Framing "India"*. See also Nabil Matar, *Islam in Britain, 1558–1685* (Cambridge: Cambridge University Press, 1998); and *Turks, Moors, and Englishmen in the Age of Discovery* (New York: Columbia University Press, 1999).

46. See especially David J. Armitage and Michael J. Braddick, eds., *The British Atlantic World, 1500–1800* (Houndsmills, U.K.: Palgrave Macmillan, 2002); and Paul Gilroy, *The Black Atlantic: Modernity and Double Consciousness* (Cambridge, Mass.: Harvard University Press, 1993). Compare Christine Daniels and Michael V. Kennedy, eds., *Negotiated Empires: Centers and Peripheries in the Americas, 1500–1820* (New York: Routledge, 2002). On the Mediterranean, see Fernand Braudel, *The Mediterranean and the Mediterranean World in the Age of Philip II*, trans. Sian Reynolds, 2 vols. (New York: Harper & Row, 1972); and, in counterpoint, Peregrine Horden and Nicholas Purcell, *The Corrupting Sea: A Study of Mediterranean History* (Oxford: Blackwell, 2000). I am grateful to Chris Chism for calling my attention to (and lending me her copy of) the latter study. See also Vitkus, *Turning Turk*, 1–44, on "the Mediterranean context."

47. Harris, *Sick Economies: Drama, Mercantilism, and Disease in Shakespeare's England* (Philadelphia: University of Pennsylvania Press, 2004), 66; see also 52–82. Though "tainted" by the differences of usury and Judaism, Harris argues, the Jew represents one layer of a "palimpsest" onto which a number of foreign bodies could be superimposed and the hybridity of cultural identity, especially that of Europe, exposed (62, 78). Compare James Shapiro, *Shakespeare and the Jews* (New York: Columbia University Press, 1996), esp. his discussion of "race, nation, or alien," 167–93. On the historical intersection of Jews and "blacks," see Jonathan Schorsch, *Jews and Blacks in the Early Modern World* (Cambridge: Cambridge University Press, 2004).

48. Mary Floyd-Wilson, *English Ethnicity and Race in Early Modern Drama* (Cambridge: Cambridge University Press, 2003). Related work includes: Sujata Iyengar, *Shades of Difference: Mythologies of Skin Color in Early Modern England* (Philadelphia: University of Pennsylvania Press, 2005); and Jean Feerick, "Spenser, Race, and Ire-land," *English Literary Renaissance* 32, no. 1 (Winter 2002): 85–117.

49. See Vitkus, *Turning Turk*, 24–44 esp.

50. Neill, *Putting History to the Question*, 269–84.

51. In *Turks, Moors, and Englishmen*, Matar presses (and stretches) the connection to create a defining triangulation between "Britons, Muslims, and American Indians"; see 83–107. Neill makes what I think are more viable connections to East and West Indian subjects, in *Putting History to the Question*, 269–84. On the relation between Barbary and the Turks, see Kenneth Parker, "Reading 'Barbary' in Early Modern England, 1550–1685," *Seventeenth Century Journal* 19, no. 1 (Spring 2004): 87–115. For a useful overview of the Ottoman Empire in this period, see Daniel Goffman, *The Ottoman Empire and Early Modern Europe* (Cambridge: Cambridge University Press, 2002).

52. In *Turning Turk*, Vitkus claims that while Moor and Turk "were sometimes used to refer specifically to the people of Morocco or Turkey," "more often they signified a generalized Islamic identity" (91). See also Matar, *Britain and Barbary, 1589–1689* (Gainesville: University Press of Florida, 2005), who treats "the Moor on the Elizabethan stage" as "a direct result of England's diplomatic initiative into Islamic affairs" (13); and Burton, *Traffic and Turning*, who elides Moorish and Turkish ambassadors.

53. In *Turning Turk*, for example, although Vitkus reads Othello as a "hybrid" figure who cannot be "identified with any specific ethnic label" (90), he argues that Othello's suicide "reenact[s] a version of his own circumcision, signifying his return to the 'malignant' sect of the Turks and his reunion with the misbelieving devils" (104). See also Julia Reinhard Lupton, *Citizen-Saints: Shakespeare and Political Theology* (Chicago: University of Chicago Press, 2005); and Jonathan Bate, "Othello and the Other," *Times Literary Supplement* (October. 19, 2001), 14–15.

54. See, for example, Vitkus, *Turning Turk*, who presents the Mediterranean as an unsettling "alien" space (22); and Harris, *Sick Economies*, who argues that the Jew's hybridity provokes an "economic anxiety" about the indeterminacy of material value (82).

55. See, for example, James A. Williamson, *A Short History of British Expansion*, 2nd ed., 2 vols. (New York: Macmillan, 1931), which covers the "external aspects" of the "history of the British people" from 1066 through the 1920s, but which omits the "purely con-

tinental phases of British relations with the peoples of Europe" on the grounds that those negotiations comprise a separate and separable "political history" (v). See also J. H. Elliot, *The Old World and the New, 1492–1650* (Cambridge: Cambridge University Press, 1970), which treats westward expansion largely in isolation from England's.

56. Barbara Fuchs, *Mimesis and Empire: The New World, Islam, and European Identities* (Cambridge: Cambridge University Press, 2001).

57. See Deborah Root, "Speaking Christian: Orthodoxy and Difference in Sixteenth-Century Spain," *Representations* 23 (Summer 1998): 118–34.

58. Thomas Preston, *Cambyses, King of Persia*, in *Drama of the English Renaissance, I: The Tudor Period*, ed. Russell A. Fraser and Norman Rabkin (New York: Macmillan Publishing, 1976), 61–80.

59. Robert Greene, *Selimus, Emperor of the Turks*, in *Three Turk Plays from Early Modern England*, ed. Daniel J. Vitkus (New York: Columbia University Press, 2000), 55–147.

60. An odd shepherd, Bullithrumble, appears in the midst of the political turmoil, having all the markings of a "homespun English fool" and reanimating "an old tale well known in the native English tradition" of pastoral impersonation, the ubiquitous prince in sheep's clothing, but it is the bound of sovereignty, not state, that is crossed and crucial here (Vitkus, "Introduction," in *Three Turk Plays*, 20).

61. *The Tragedie of Solimon and Perseda* (London: Edward Allde); William Shakespeare, *The Merchant of Venice*, ed. M. M. Mahood (1987; Cambridge: Cambridge University Press, 2003).

62. For a concise overview of England's overseas activity, see Williamson, *Short History*, esp. 92–97; see also my critique in note 52 above.

63. Richard Hakluyt, "Epistle Dedicatory in the first edition of 1589," in *Principal Navigations*. The classical cosmographies include *The excellent and pleasant worke of Julius Solinus Polyhistor*, trans. Arthur Golding (London, 1587); *The Rare and Singular worke of Pomponius Mela*, trans. Golding (London, 1590); and Stephen Batman, *Batman uppon Bartholome, his Booke: De Proprietatibus Rerum* (London, 1582). See also Johannes Boemus, *The Fardle of Façions*, trans. William Waterman (London, 1555; New York: Da Capo Press, 1970), which appeared earlier.

64. On the move toward a coherent mercantilism, see Harris, *Sick Economies*, esp. 3–13. On privateering, see Kenneth Andrews, *Elizabethan Privateering: English Privateering During the Spanish War, 1585–1603* (Cambridge: Cambridge University Press, 1964). See also Robert Brenner, *Merchants and Revolution: Commercial Change, Political Conflict, and London's Overseas Traders, 1550–1653* (Cambridge: Cambridge University Press, 1993).

65. For extensive views of activity in Barbary, see Matar, *Britain and Barbary*; E. W. Bovill, *The Battle of Alcazar: An Account of the Defeat of Don Sebastian of Portugal at El-Ksar el-Kebir* (London: Batchworth Press, 1952); and D'Amico, 7–40. Especially pertinent is the account of "The Ambassage of M. Edmund Hogan . . . from her Highnesse to Mully Abdelmelech Emperour of Morocco" in 1577, in Hakluyt, 6:285–93.

66. Matar, *Britain and Barbary*, 13; see also Matar, *Turks, Moors, and Englishmen*, 32–34; and Burton, *Traffic and Turning*, 53–91.

67. Matar, *Britain and Barbary*, 13.

68. See especially Karen Ordahl Kupperman, *Indians and English: Facing Off in Early America* (Ithaca, N.Y.: Cornell University Press, 2000). See also Mary C. Fuller, *Voyages in Print: English Travel to America, 1576–1624* (Cambridge: Cambridge University Press, 1995).

69. See especially David Armitage, *The Ideological Origins of the British Empire* (Cambridge: Cambridge University Press, 2000); and Anthony Pagden, *Lords of All the World: Ideologies of Empire in Spain, Britain and France, c. 1500–c. 1800* (New Haven, Conn.: Yale University Press, 1995).

70. For a particularly pertinent discussion of "culture" in this period, see David Lee Miller, Sharon O'Dair, and Harold Weber, "Introduction," in *The Production of English Renaissance Culture*, ed. Miller et al. (Ithaca, N.Y.: Cornell University Press, 1994), 1–12.

71. Early modern scholars tend to think blackness was already a preeminent sign of race by the seventeenth century; compare Roxann Wheeler, *The Complexion of Race: Categories of Difference in Eighteenth-Century British Culture* (Philadelphia: University of Pennsylvania Press, 2000), who argues that color-based conceptions of race did not stabilize until the end of the eighteenth century. See also Winthrop Jordan, *White over Black: American Attitudes Toward the Negro, 1550–1812* (Chapel Hill: University of North Carolina Press, 1968).

72. I am drawing here on Elin Diamond's provocative conception of performance as a "doing and a thing done"; from her introduction to *Performance and Cultural Politics*, ed. Elin Diamond (New York: Routledge, 1996), 4–5.

73. Barthelemy, *Black Face*, 72, 147. See also Tokson and D'Amico.

74. Tokson, 141; see his chronological list of these plays.

75. The most influential examples include Tokson, who covers the period 1550–1688; Barthelemy, *Black Face*, which covers plays from 1589 to 1695.

CHAPTER ONE

1. My summary (and my spelling of proper names), here and below, draw primarily on the detailed account in Bovill, *The Battle of Alcazar*. Also helpful have been Matar, *Britain and Barbary*, 12–20; D'Amico, 7–40; and Leeds Barroll, "Mythologizing the Ottoman: *The Jew of Malta* and *The Battle of Alcazar*," in *Remapping the Mediterranean in Early Modern English Writings*, ed. Goran Stanivukovic (New York: Palgrave Macmillan, 2007), 117–30. An earlier version of this chapter appeared in Stanivukovic, under the title "*The Battle of Alcazar*, the Mediterranean, and the Moor," 97–116.

2. On this spectacle, see Bovill, 159.

3. A useful bibliography of early accounts appears in John Yoklavich, ed., *The Dramatic Works of George Peele*, vol. 2 (New Haven, Conn.: Yale University Press, 1961), 369–73. See also Yoklavich's discussion of these texts, 226–36, and Bovill, 149n2.

4. *Montaigne's Essayes*, 3 vols., trans. John Florio, intro. L. C. Harmer (London: Dent, 1965), 2:405–6.

5. These include the pamphlet *Newe Newes contayning A Shorte rehersall of the late enterprise of certain fugytive Rebelles: fyrst pretended by Captaine Stukeley* (1579), Anthony

Munday's *The English Romayne Lyfe* (1582), the chapbook *The Famous History of Stout Stukley: or, His valiant Life and Death* (1638) and a ballad appended to it but written earlier, "The famous life and death of the renowned *English* gallant, *Thomas Stukley*" (1612?). On these and other accounts, see Yoklavich, 247–73.

6. On the "enormous literature of 'Sebastianism,'" see Yoklavich, 257, and Bovill, 155–56. A contemporary text, "Strange Newes of the Retourne of Don Sebastian" (1598), survives only in the Stationer's Register.

7. Referenced in Matar, *Islam in Britain*, 36.

8. In *Othello's Countrymen*, Jones aptly identifies the play as the "first full-length treatment of a Moorish character in English dramatic literature" (42). "The presentation of Africans as individualized characters worthy of detailed treatment began," he writes, "when George Peele seized upon an historical occurrence which projected a Moor into great prominence in European eyes, and brought Europe and Africa spectacularly together" (40). On the dating of the play, see A. R. Braunmuller, *George Peele* (Boston: Twayne Publishers, 1983), 69.

9. *On Muly Molocco*, see Yoklavich, 221–23.

10. *The Famous History of Captain Thomas Stukeley* (Malone Society Reprints, 1970; Oxford: Oxford University Press, 1975). Quotations (referenced by line numbers only) are from this edition.

11. Thomas Heywood, *If You Know Not Me, You Know Nobody*, in *The Dramatic Works of Thomas Heywood*, 6 vols. (1874; New York: Russell and Russell, 1964), vol. 1, cited by page numbers. On Heywood's nationalism and its expression in his *Apology for Actors*, see Crystal Bartolovich, "Shakespeare's Globe?" in *Marxist Shakespeares*, ed. Jean E. Howard and Scott Cutler Shershow (London: Routledge, 2001), 178–205, esp. 182–83.

12. Matar, *Britain and Barbary*, 17.

13. The histories of these negotiations, which I outline below, are detailed in Bovill, 43–52, and D'Amico, 15–32. Though Bovill's argument is dated by its belief in "the Moorish mind and its profound ignorance of the western world" (182), and D'Amico's by its insistent humanism (see note 35 to my Introduction), both sources uncover important archival evidence.

14. See D'Amico, 15. Several of these factors are mentioned in Hakluyt, 6:285.

15. See D'Amico, 17; and Bovill.

16. Matar, *Britain and Barbary*, 15.

17. Matar, *Britain and Barbary*, 2.

18. Matar, *Britain and Barbary*, 3.

19. Bovill's argument centers on this triangulation, and the following summary relies largely on his account.

20. From *Calendar of State Papers, Spanish, 1568–79*, 481; quoted in Bovill, 44.

21. Bovill, 46. There is no record of the outcome, but Bovill speculates that Hogan was acquitted since he soon begins to advocate for the lifting of the ban.

22. See D'Amico's critique of Bovill, 17–19.

23. Bovill (179) points to the example of Henry Roberts, who, when he writes to Ahmed el-Mansur, admits that he "forbeare[s] here to put down in writing" "the particulers of my service, for divers and reasonable causes" (Hakluyt, 6:427).

24. Myra Jehlen, "History Before the Fact; or, Captain John Smith's Unfinished Symphony," *Critical Inquiry* 19, no. 4 (Summer 1993), 681. See my discussion in "Making More of the Moor," 438–42.

25. Matar, *Britain and Barbary*, 15; see also Bovill, 181–82.

26. Matar, *Britain and Barbary*, 13–15.

27. Bovill, 22.

28. On Sebastian's defeat and death, see Braunmuller, 67; Bovill, 148–57; and Yoklavich, 226.

29. *Montaigne's Essayes*, 2:403. Compare Thorlief Larsen, "The Historical and Legendary Background of Peele's 'Battle of Alcazar,' " *Proceedings of the Royal Society of Canada* (1939): 185–97. Larsen argues that the "political consequences" of Portugal's fall were not yet "realized or understood" in Europe, and that, rather, "what had impressed the popular imagination apparently was the ghastly slaughter which took place at the battle, and the fact that no fewer than three kings had there lost their lives" (185–86).

30. Braunmuller, 67.

31. D'Amico, 20–21.

32. See Braunmuller, 69–70; and Walter W. Greg, *Two Elizabethan Stage Abridgements* (Oxford: Clarendon Press, 1923), 85–93.

33. Hunter writes: "Peele makes strenuous efforts to explain the genealogical intricacies of the Barbary kingship and to clear up the tangle of political aims that link King Sebastian of Portugal, Philip II of Spain, Tom Stukeley (the Pope's candidate for 'King of Ireland'), the Turkish Emperor, and Queen Elizabeth herself. What his realistic aims achieve is in fact a picture of the tangled web of *Realpolitik* in which all the characters are enmeshed" (*English Drama*, 79).

34. Larsen, 193.

35. Joseph Candido, "Captain Thomas Stukeley: The Man, the Theatrical Record, and the Origins of Tudor 'Biographical' Drama,' " *Zeitschrift für Englische Philologie* 105, nos.1–2 (1987): 54, 50, 51.

36. For a prominent example, see Braunmuller, who suggests that Sebastian's descent "from the English house of Lancaster" makes his story especially pertinent to the promotion of an Elizabethan nationalism, the "politics and war in northern Africa" providing "only an exotic" frame (66). See also Peter Hyland, "Moors, Villainy and the Battle of Alcazar," *Parergon* 16 (1999): 85–99.

37. Barthelemy, *Black Face*, 78; see 72–84. In Tokson too, Muly's "blackness" is what stands out, implicated in and implicating all the denotations ("'the Moor,' 'this Negro moore,' and 'this Negro' ") that describe him and the "good" Abdelmelec, who, though "only referred to as a Moor," was "probably intended to be shaded to some degree" (40).

38. Matar, *Britain and Barbary*, 16–17, 20.

39. See, too, the prologue to Act Two, where the Presenter announces that "Nemesis, with bloody whip in hand, / Thunders for vengeance on this Negro-Moor" (2–3).

40. Barthelemy, *Black Face*, 78.

41. Braunmuller, 73, makes this case.

42. On this ancestry, see Bovill, 36–39; and Yoklavich, 227.

43. Yoklavich, 350; D'Amico, 82.

44. Barroll, "Mythologizing the Ottoman," 128.

45. I am grateful to Linda Woodbridge for calling my attention to Shakespeare's reference. On Amurath (who allegedly killed his brothers to secure the throne), see the notes to 2 Henry IV 5.2.48 in The Riverside Shakespeare.

46. From the Levant Company's charter of 1580; Hakluyt, 5:178–91.

47. See my discussion in Spectacles of Strangeness: Imperialism, Alienation, and Marlowe (Philadelphia: University of Pennsylvania Press, 1993), 82–108.

48. Hunter reads this isolation instead as "a total freedom in villainy that gave Peele's image of Muly Mahamet its contemporary reputation"; English Drama, 80.

49. Compare Jones, Othello's Countrymen, who argues that Alcazar starts as "a typical revenge play" which is then blurred into chronicle (44).

50. Compare John Gillies, Shakespeare and the Geography of Difference (Cambridge: Cambridge University Press, 1994), and his conceptualization of the theatrum mundi, 70–98.

51. On these false promises, see also Barthelemy, Black Face, 82–83.

52. Yoklavich, 218.

53. See David Bevington, Tudor Drama and Politics: A Critical Approach to Topical Meaning (Cambridge, Mass.: Harvard University Press, 1968), 209–11, on the topicality of this representation.

54. I am using The Riverside Shakespeare here.

55. See Yoklavich, 251.

56. See Bovill, 79–81.

57. Thomas Fuller, The History of the Worthies of England (1662), ed. P. Austin Nuttall, 3 vols. (New York: AMS Press, 1965), 1:415. See also Camden, who describes him as "a ruffian, a spendthrift, and a notable vapourer" (i.e., according to the OED, a "boastful, grandiloquent, or vacuous talker"); quoted in Bovill, 80.

58. On Stukeley's history, see Bovill, 80–81; Yoklavich, 247–51; Candido, 52–54; and Larsen, 89–91.

59. Accounts of why Stukeley joined with Sebastian differ. Compare Bovill, 81, and Yoklavich, 251. Fuller's History of Worthies suggests, among other theories, that Stukeley agreed to join with Sebastian "because so mutable his mind, he ever loved the last project (as mothers the youngest child) best" (1:415).

60. Candido, 55. The implicit reference is, of course, to Oliver Goldsmith's Letters from a Citizen of the World (1762); I am grateful to Margreta de Grazia for her comments on the implications of the concept.

61. John Drakakis, "Afterword" in John J. Joughin, ed., Shakespeare and National Culture (Manchester: Manchester University Press, 1997), 336. See also Graham Holderness and Andrew Murphy, "Shakespeare's England: Britain's Shakespeare," in Joughin, ed., 19–41, and Willy Maley, "'This sceptred isle': Shakespeare and the British Problem," 83–108, also in Joughin, ed.

62. Compare Candido, who argues that Tamburlaine provided an "established stage type" onto which Peele, in constructing Stukeley, "grafts popular," individuating details

(56). *Alcazar* makes explicit reference to *Tamburlaine*. Muly Mahamet not only imagines the Turkish bassa as Tamburline, as I have mentioned above; he also echoes Tamburlaine's words ("Tamburlaine . . . must die") to denounce the Turk (1.2.33–36), as *Alcazar*'s editors generally note.

63. See Thomas Fuller, 1:414.

64. Catherine Belsey, *The Subject of Tragedy: Identity and Difference in Renaissance Drama* (London: Methuen, 1985), 41–42.

CHAPTER TWO

1. This chapter is a revision of my essay "*Othello* and Africa: Postcolonialism Reconsidered."

2. Quotations are from William Shakespeare, *Titus Andronicus*, ed. Jonathan Bate, (London: Routledge, 1995).

3. See also Richard Helgerson, *Forms of Nationhood: The Elizabethan Writing of England* (Chicago: University of Chicago Press, 1992), 151–91, whose work makes an excellent case for the economic underpinnings of the project.

4. See my essay, "Imperialist Beginnings: Richard Hakluyt and the Construction of Africa," *Criticism* 34, no. 4 (Fall 1992): 517–38.

5. David Armitage, "The New World and British Historical Thought: From Richard Hakluyt to William Robertson," in *America in European Consciousness, 1493–1750*, ed. Karen Kupperman (Chapel Hill: University of North Carolina Press, 1995), 59; see 52–78. See also Armitage, *Ideological Origins*; and Pagden, *Lords of All the World*.

6. From John Smith's letter "to the Right Honourable, and Worshipfull Company of Virginia" (1622), in *Captain John Smith: A Select Edition of His Writings*, ed. Karen Ordahl Kupperman (Chapel Hill: University of North Carolina Press, 1988), 199; see 198–200. William Strachey's representation of Jamestown appears in "A True Reportory of the Wrack" (1610). See also James Horn, *A Land as God Made It: Jamestown and the Birth of America* (New York: Basic Books, 2005).

7. See my discussion in Chapter 1.

8. On the Barbary Company and trade, see T. S. Willan, *Studies in Elizabethan Foreign Trade* (New York: Barnes and Noble, 1959).

9. The *Oxford English Dictionary* credits Stanley with the phrase. Scholars have suggested but not, to my knowledge, documented an earlier date. See, for example, James A. Rawley, *The Transatlantic Slave Trade: A History* (New York: W. W. Norton, 1981), 11. On the emergence of the idea of the "dark continent," see Patrick Brantlinger, "Victorians and Africans: The Genealogy of the Myth of the Dark Continent," in Gates, ed., 185–222. See also Christopher L. Miller, *Blank Darkness: Africanist Discourse in French* (Chicago: University of Chicago Press, 1985); and Sara Blair, *Henry James and the Writing of Race and Nation* (Cambridge: Cambridge University Press, 1996), 15–59.

10. C. R. Beazley, *Prince Henry the Navigator* (London: Hakluyt Society, 1895), 171.

11. See, for example, the map of Africa from the *Diego Homem Atlas* (1558), part of

which is reprinted in *Europeans in West Africa, 1450–1560*, trans. and ed. John William Blake, vol. 1 (1942; Nendeln/Liechtenstein: Kraus Reprint, 1967), and Abraham Ortelius's world map from the *Theatrum Orbis Terrarum* . . . (Antwerp, 1570), included in Hakluyt (1589). See also, for a very early example, the Catalan map of Northwest Africa (1375), included in Gomes Eannes de Azurara, *The Chronicle of the Discovery and Conquest of Guinea*, trans. Charles Raymond Beazley et al., vol 1 (London: Hakluyt Society, 1896). On traditions of mapmaking, which come into play as well, see Helgerson, 107–47.

12. See J. D. Fage, *A History of Africa*, 3rd ed. (London: Routledge, 1995), 215–43; and Philip Curtin et al., *African History: From Earliest Times to Independence*, 2nd ed. (London: Longman, 1995), 157–60.

13. On Prince Henry's motivations, see Williamson, *Short History*, 57–58; compare Fage, 222. On the myth of Prester John, see Christopher Miller, 32–39.

14. See Curtin et al., *African History*, 157.

15. On the sugar plantations, see Curtin et al., *African History*, 184.

16. See Fage, 231–34. For an example of the reliance of the Portuguese on the local inhabitants, see the description of the building of the fort at Elmina, in Ruy de Pina's *Chronicle of John II* (1500), included in Blake, *Europeans in West Africa*, 70–78. In that case and commonly in others, the Portuguese apparently chose to settle in a place inhabited by two local peoples so that they could, if need be, play one group against the other to secure support for themselves (Blake, 72).

17. See especially Fage, who argues for the overriding appeal of the East, 216–43. Fage makes the case that Africa, in fact, "was not known to produce many of the commodities which Europeans desired" (217) and that the Portuguese acquired African goods for trade in the East, where the demand for European goods was minimal; see 223.

18. Williamson, *Short History*, 82; and Kenneth Andrews, *Trade, Plunder and Settlement: Maritime Enterprise and the Genesis of the British Empire, 1480–1630* (Cambridge: Cambridge University Press, 1984), 101–15.

19. Williamson, *Short History*, 57–60; and Robert Ralston Cawley, *The Voyagers and Elizabethan Drama* (Boston: D. C. Heath, 1938), 83–103.

20. See Curtin, "The External Trade of West Africa to 1800," in *History of West Africa*, ed. J. F. A. Ajayi and Michael Crowder, vol. 1, 3rd ed. (1971; New York: Longman, 1985), 628–29; Curtin, *African History*, 155–56; and Michel Craton, *Sinews of Empire: A Short History of British Slavery* (London: Temple Smith, 1974), 5.

21. Andrews, *Trade, Plunder and Settlement*, 106.

22. For the full account, see Hakuyt, 6:141–53.

23. My thanks to Karen Kupperman for suggesting that the English likely perceived Africa as already taken. On England's actual and textual relation to the East, see Raman; Singh, *Colonial Narratives*; and Said, *Orientalism*. See also Samuel Chew, *The Crescent and the Rose: Islam and England during the Renaissance* (Oxford: Oxford University Press, 1937); and Raymond Schwab, *The Oriental Renaissance: Europe's Rediscovery of India and the East, 1680–1880*, trans. Gene Patterson-Black and Victor Reinking (New York: Columbia University Press, 1984).

24. Williamson, *Short History*, 86.

25. Andrews, *Trade, Plunder and Settlement*, 104; and Williamson, *Sir John Hawkins: The Time and the Man* (Oxford: Clarendon Press, 1927), 32–62, esp. 40.

26. Andrews, *Trade, Plunder and Settlement*, 113. On the economic transformations linked to the East India Company, see Valerie Forman, "Transformations of Value and the Productionn of 'Investment' in the Early History of the East India Company," *Journal of Medieval and Early Modern Studies* 34, no. 3 (2004): 611–41.

27. Craton, 56.

28. Williamson, *Short History*, 162–63; and Craton, 56.

29. For an historical overview of England's Atlantic history, see especially Armitage, ed., *The British Atlantic World*. Additional studies of the evolution of the slave trade include Craton; Rawley; Gary B. Nash, *Red, White, and Black: The Peoples of Early America* (1974; Englewood Cliffs, N.J.: Prentice-Hall, 1982); Paul E. Lovejoy, *Transformations in Slavery: A History of Slavery in Africa* (1983; Cambridge: Cambridge University Press, 1995); and Robin Blackburn, "The Old World Background to European Colonial Slavery," *William and Mary Quarterly*, 3rd ser., 54, no. 1 (Janurary 1997): 65–102. See also Philip D. Beidler and Gary Taylor, eds., *Writing Race Across the Atlantic World: Medieval to Modern* (New York: Palgrave, 2005).

30. Rawley, 24.

31. Curtin et al., African History, 184; and Rawley, 24–28.

32. Williamson, *Sir John Hawkins*, 3–31, esp. 19; and Craton, 30.

33. On Hawkins's failure, see Andrews, "The English in the Caribbean 1560–1620," in *The Westward Enterprise*, ed. K. R. Andrews et al. (Detroit: Wayne State University Press, 1979), 103–23; see also Walter Cohen, "The Undiscovered Country: Shakespeare and Mercantile Geography," in Howard and Shershow, eds., 129–31, on England's faltering "American initiatives" (131).

34. Karen Ordahl Kupperman, "The Beehive as a Model for Colonial Design," in Kupperman, ed., *America in European Consciousness*, 272–92; see also Andrews, *Trade, Plunder and Settlement*, 101–15.

35. Carole Shammas, "English Commercial Development and American Colonization, 1560–1620" in Andrews et al., eds., 173.

36. See C. F. Beckingham, "The Near East: North and North-east Africa" (176–89); P. E. Hair, "Morocco, the Saharan Coast, and the Neighbouring Atlantic islands" (190–96); and "Guinea" (197–207) in *The Hakluyt Handbook*, vol. 1, ed. D. B. Quinn (London: Hakluyt Society, 1974); and also Williamson, "Richard Hakluyt," in *Richard Hakluyt & His Successors*, ed. Edward Lynam (London: Hakluyt Society, 1946), 9–46.

37. Some of the narratives also give attention to the French, whose presence was not as pervasive or imposing as that of these other competitors.

38. From the table of contents of a facsimile of the first edition: Richard Hakluyt, *The Principall Navigations, Voiages and Discoveries of the English Nation*, vol. 1, ed. David Beers Quinn (Cambridge: Cambridge University Press, 1965).

39. Compare Armitage, "The New World," 52–75, and Peter Burke, "America and the Rewriting of World History," in Kupperman, ed., *America in European Consciousness*, 33–51, who sees America having only a "minor place in European historical consciousness" (37).

40. Williamson, *Short History*, 53; and Andrews, 87–100.

41. See Hakluyt, 6:23–27; 6:31–34; and 6:295–348.

42. See Hakluyt, 6:123–24.

43. See also Hogan's account of his negotiations with Abdelmelech (which I discuss in Chapter 1): Hogan mentions being greeted initially by "all the Christians of the Spaniards and Portugals," whom he assumes received him "by the kings commandment" (6:287).

44. In addition to the examples below, see also Hakluyt 7:90–99, where an exchange with Negroes is defined by the English venturers' negotiation of a Spanish and Portuguese presence.

45. According to the *Oxford English Dictionary*, a sucket is a "fruit preserved in sugar."

46. Kupperman, *Indians and English*, 2; see also *Settling with the Indians: The Meeting of English and Indian Cultures in America, 1580–1640* (Totowa, N.J.: Rowman and Littlefield, 1980).

47. See, for example, the account of Hawkins's second slaving venture (Hakluyt, 10:27–29).

48. Compare the description of Indians in, for example, the account of Hawkins's second slaving voyage (10:27–29), where there is less of a gap between the report of the venture and the "ethnographic" detailing.

49. The included accounts of Hawkins's third voyage are "A discourse written by one Miles Philips Englishman, one of the company put on shoare Northward of Panuco, in the West Indies by M. John Hakwins 1568" (9:398–445); "The travailes of Job Hortop, which Sir John Hawkins set on land within the Bay of Mexico . . . 1568" (9:445–65); and "The third troublesome voyage made with the Jesus of Lubeck, the Minion, and foure other ships, to the parts of Guinea, and the West Indies, in the yeeres 1567 and 1568 by M. John Hawkins" (10: 64–74). See also "The voyage of M. Jon Winter, into the South sea by the Streight of Magellan, in consort with M. Francis Drake, begun in the yeere 1577" (11:148–62).

50. Williamson, *Sir John Hawkins*, 143. In addition to the example below, see the account of Hawkins's second slaving venture, 10:9–74.

51. Williamson, *Sir John Hawkins*, 142–44, and Hair, 202–3.

52. The manuscript (British Museum, Cotton MSS., Otho E. VIII, ff. 17–41b) is reprinted in Williamson, *Sir John Hawkins*, 491–534; the quoted passage appears on 509. The bracketed replacements for missing words are Williamson's, the roman type indicating what he offers as fairly certain and the italic, more conjectural. Williamson concludes that the manuscript shows "the unspoiled negro of Tudor days wallowing in every horror known to savage man" (157).

53. Williamson, *Sir John Hawkins*, 143–44, 147–48.

54. Hence the explanation, now suspect, that Africans had better immunity to these diseases and so were the most viable labor source. See Curtin, "Epidemiology and the Slave Trade," *Political Science Quarterly* 83 (1968): 190–216; Curtin et al., *African History*, 182–83, 188–89; and Rawley, 12, 14–15.

55. In addition to the example below, see the account of Robert Dudley's voyage to the West Indies in 1594 (10:204–12).

56. See especially Mary Floyd-Wilson's discussion of Best, *English Ethnicity*, 8–11, which also takes account of context. Compare Neill, *Putting History to the Question*, 272, 276; Boose, "'The Getting of a Lawful Race,'" 43–44; Hall, *Things of Darkness*, 11–12, and Karen Newman, *Fashioning Femininity and English Renaissance Drama* (Chicago: University of Chicago Press, 1991), 78–82.

57. On other versions of this story, see Benjamin Braude, "The Sons of Noah and the Construction of Ethnic and Geographical Identities in the Medieval and Early Modern Periods," *William and Mary Quarterly*, 3rd ser., 54, no. 1 (January 1997): 103–42.

58. See especially Boose, "'The Getting of a Lawful Race,'" 44.

59. Armitage, "The New World and British Historical Thought," 58. I am grateful to Benjamin Braude for his remarks on the Northwest Passage.

60. Greenblatt, *Marvelous Possessions: The Wonder of the New World* (Chicago: University of Chicago Press, 1991), who links this motif of possession to the trope of wonder.

CHAPTER THREE

1. On the place and parody here of due burial, see Francis Barker, "Treasures of Culture: *Titus Andronicus* and Death by Hanging," in David Lee Miller et al., eds., 226–61, esp. 231.

2. Loomba declares Aaron "a textbook illustration for early modern stereotypes of blackness," though she admits that it is hard "to agree on what these stereotypes meant to Renaissance audiences"; *Shakespeare, Race, and Colonialism*, 75–76. See also James L. Calderwood, *Metadrama in Shakespeare's Henriad: Richard II to Henry V* (Berkeley: University of California Press, 1979), esp. 45.

3. I am referring to the well-established parallel with the dialogue in *The Jew of Malta* 2.3.177–215. On Marlowe's manipulation of stereotype in these speeches, see my discussion in *Spectacles of Strangeness*, 82–108, esp. 100–103.

4. For an extensive review and augmentation of this debate, see Brian Vickers, *Shakespeare, Co-Author: A Historical Study of Five Collaborative Plays* (Oxford: Oxford University Press, 2002), 148–243.

5. Compare Jones, *Othello's Countrymen*, who considers "the connexion between Aaron and Muly Hamet" "conjectural" but "the direct descent from Aaron of Eleazar" "undisputed" (60).

6. Ian Smith, "Those 'slippery customers': Rethinking Race in *Titus Andronicus*," *Journal of Theatre and Drama* 3 (1997): 56. For alternative readings of the initial trauma, see Deborah Willis, "'The gnawing vulture': Revenge, Trauma Theory, and *Titus Andronicus*," *Shakespeare Quarterly* 53, no. 1 (Spring 2002): 21–52; and Naomi Conn Liebler, "Getting It All Right: *Titus Andronicus* and Roman History," *Shakespeare Quarterly* 45, no. 3 (Fall 1994): 263–78.

7. Barker, 254. Compare Francesca T. Royster, "White-limed Walls: Whiteness and Gothic Extremism in Shakespeare's *Titus Andronicus*," *Shakespeare Quarterly* 51, no. 4 (Winter 2000): 432–55, who sees Tamora as the more disturbing alien presence within

Rome; and Loomba, *Shakespeare, Race, and Colonialism*, who argues that Aaron and Tamora together are "singled out as pariahs," 77. Related readings include Coppélia Kahn, *Roman Shakespeare: Warriors, Wounds, and Women* (Ithaca, N.Y.: Cornell University Press, 1997); Virginia Mason Vaughan, "The Construction of Barbarism in *Titus Andronicus*," in *Race, Ethnicity, and Power in the Renaissance*, ed. Joyce Green MacDonald (Madison, N.J.: Fairleigh Dickinson University Press, 1997), 165–80; Gillies, 102–12; MacDonald, "Black Race, White Ewe: Shakespeare, Race, and Women," in *A Feminist Companion to Shakespeare*, ed. Dympna Callaghan (Malden, Mass.: Blackwell, 2000), 188–207; and Little, 58–67.

8. Neill, *Putting History to the Question*, 271.

9. Barker, 233. See also my discussion in "Making More of the Moor," 422–47.

10. Neill, *Putting History to the Question*, 275. A pivotal essay on the implications of miscegenation in *Titus* is Boose, "'The Getting of a Lawful Race.'"

11. Underscoring and adding another layer to the cross-cultural connection, Sebastian associates Claribel with the famous Carthaginian "widow Dido," whose legend pivots on her tempestuous erotic engagement with the Roman Aeneas (2.1.98); William Shakespeare, *The Tempest*, ed. Stephen Orgel.

12. On the common association of Jupiter ("Jupiter Capitolinus") with the Capitol, see A. R. Hope Moncrieff, *Classic Myth and Legend* (New York: William Wise, 1934), 31.

13. Mary Floyd-Wilson, *English Ethnicity*, argues that early modern English writers had tried, unsuccessfully, to own that classical inheritance in order to "circumvent[ ] the embarrassments of a northern descent," itself implicitly "barbaric," "dissolute, mingled, and intemperate" (15).

14. Barker argues that in the structural anthropology of this play the only "culture" is Rome's (230–31).

15. See, for instance, Robert S. Miola, *Shakespeare's Rome* (Cambridge: Cambridge University Press, 1983), 42–75, esp. 46; and Barker.

16. For a critique of the claims and politics of representative government, see Sid Ray, "'Rape, I fear was root of thy annoy': The Politics of Consent in *Titus Andronicus*," *Shakespeare Quarterly* 49, no. 1 (Spring 1998): 22–39; and Oliver Arnold, *The Third Citizen: Shakespeare's Theater and the Early Modern House of Commons* (Baltimore: Johns Hopkins University Press, 2007).

17. In trying to explain this apparently puzzling word choice, the editors (Greenblatt et al.) of *The Norton Shakespeare* (New York: Norton, 1997) have interpreted the remark as "ironic, since the Goths were defeated in battle" (see 1.1.85, note 5). Given Titus's almost fatal lack of irony elsewhere, it seems more plausible to assume that this line draws further attention to the questions surrounding that defeat.

18. How we count depends on whether or not we take Marcus's "five" as inclusive of the present moment.

19. On Titus's interest in dismemberment, see Katherine A. Rowe, "Dismembering and Forgetting in *Titus Andronicus*," *Shakespeare Quarterly* 45, no. 3 (Fall 1994): 279–303, who argues that "the severed hands . . . symbolize the horror of the lost fiction of a continuous history" (303).

20. On *The History of Herodian* and its relation to the 1577 chronicle, see Liebler, who is the first to make the case. Other influential source studies include Hunter, "Sources and Meaings in *Titus Andronicus*," in *The Mirror Up to Shakespeare: Essays in Honour of G. R. Hibbard*, ed. J. C. Gray (Toronto: University of Toronto Press, 1984), 171–88; T. J. B. Spencer, "Shakespeare and the Elizabethan Romans," *Shakespeare Survey* 10 (1957): 27–38; and Ralph M. Sargent, "The Sources of *Titus Andronicus*," *Studies in Philology* 46, no. 2 (April 1949): 167–83. See also Nicholas R. Moschovakis, "Persecution as Pagan Anachronism in *Titus Andronicus*," *Shakespeare Quarterly* 53, no. 4 (Winter 2002): 460–86, esp. 477–78; Eugene M. Waith's introduction to his edition of the play (Oxford: Oxford University Press, 1994), esp. 27–38; Vickers, 188–92; and Geoffrey Bullough, *Narrative and Dramatic Sources of Shakespeare*, 8 vols. (London: Methuen, 1957–75), 6:7–10.

21. Liebler, 271, 267. Compare Loomba, *Shakespeare, Race, and Colonialism*, who concludes that *Titus* is "set in the fourth century AD, when the Roman Empire was waning" (76).

22. Compare Habib, 93–95, who argues that the play's "sourcelessness" may derive from a deliberate suppression by the state (93).

23. From "The History of Titus Andronicus," reprinted (with modernized spelling) in *Titus Andronicus*, ed. Waith, 195–203, 198.

24. Waith, 199.

25. Liebler concludes that "Shakespeare's 'Goths' are not the same people who overthrew Rome in the fifth century," but rather represent a sort of generic barbarian, especially of "Eastern origin" (272). See also Vaughan, "The Construction of Barbarism," 168.

26. Compare Barker, 226–35, who argues that these rituals bear markings of the "primitive."

27. Barker, 230–31.

28. Compare Ray, 34, who reads the problem as "political absolutism."

29. These actors may have been made up in black and white cosmetics available in the period; see Callaghan, *Shakespeare Without Women*, 75–96.

30. The classic essay is Greenblatt, "Invisible Bullets: Renaissance Authority and Its Subversion, *Henry IV* and *Henry V*," in Dollimore and Sinfield, eds., 18–47.

31. Having no historical account to turn to, we can only take Titus's already compromised word for it; if we choose not to, his choices seem all the more reactionary.

32. Compare Christopher Crosbie, "Fixing Moderation: *Titus Andronicus* and the Aristotelian Determination of Value," *Shakespeare Quarterly* 58, no. 2 (Summer 2007): 147–73 who argues that Tamora "employs the rhetoric of Rome's civic piety . . . to ensure her own tenuous hold on power" (161).

33. I am grateful to Matthew Cinotti, for provocative conversations about Tamora that have helped me rethink her performance here.

34. See, for example, Habib, 87–120; Ian Smith, "Those 'slippery customers'"; Little, 48–67.

35. Barthelemy, *Black Face*, 93; Gillies, 104. On Taymor's interpretation of the play's politics, see David McCandless, "A Tale of Two *Titus*es: Julie Taymor's Vision on Stage and Screen," *Shakespeare Quarterly* 53, no. 4 (Winter 2002): 487–511.

36. Ray, 33. See also Gillies, 104.

37. Loomba, *Shakespeare, Race, and Colonialism*, 84; emphasis added.

38. Loomba, *Shakespeare, Race, and Colonialism*, 84.

39. Loomba, *Shakespeare, Race, and Colonialism*, 84; emphasis added.

40. Compare Ray, on the interpretation of this conflict and this claim, 33–34.

41. Ray, 33; Gillies, 104.

42. Loomba, *Shakespeare, Race, and Colonialism*, 84; Virginia Vaughan, "The Construction of Barbarism," 175.

43. In efforts to reverse this editorial tendency, Bate argues that, although "the couplet form suggests a self-contained aside," "it would not be out of character for Saturninus to speak these lines publicly"; note to 1.1.265–66.

44. On *Edward II*, see my discussion in *Spectacles of Strangeness*, 143–72. See also Gregory W. Bredbeck, *Sodomy and Interpretation: Marlowe to Milton* (Ithaca, N.Y.: Cornell University Press, 1999), 48–77.

45. See Bate's note to 1.1.321.

46. From Bate's note to 1.1.467–68 and *The Oxford English Dictionary Online* (Oxford: Oxford University Press, 2007).

47. See Bate's note to 1.1.499 on the division of the act, which usually precedes Aaron's first speech.

48. Compare Loomba, *Shakespeare, Race, and Colonialism*, 84, who argues that Tamora's relation with Aaron sets her apart from the Goths and the Romans.

49. Christopher Miller, 6.

50. Loomba, *Shakespeare, Race, and Colonialism*, 81, assigns Aaron a "servile status"; see 79–82. See also Habib, who reads Aaron as a "colonized black subject" (109), limited by "his memory of her past colonization of him as her slave" (110).

51. Greenblatt's contention that Shakespeare anticipates Freud is still, I think, persuasive; "Psychoanalysis and Renaissance Culture," in *Learning to Curse: Essays in Early Modern Culture* (New York: Routledge, 1990), 131–45.

52. On "dull," see Bate's note to 1.1.195.

53. See Bate's note to 2.2.293–94.

54. Barker provocatively uncovers the suppressed violence in the clown scene, though he argues that the violence is "naturalized" by its "occlusion" (255).

55. See Bate's note to 5.1.122.

56. The translation is Bate's; see note to 4.2.20–21.

57. We see signs here of humanist educational practice, whereby students ingested fragments of texts, quite apart from context. See Mary Thoms Crane, *Framing Authority: Sayings, Self, and Society in Sixteenth-Century England* (Princeton, N.J.: Princeton University Press, 1993), esp. 53–76. Lily's *Grammar*, in which the verse appears, depends in part on the practice of reading through idioms and imitating the structure of figures; see Crane, 87–88.

58. Joyce E. Chaplin, "Race," in Armitage and Braddick, eds., 155.

59. According to *The New Shorter Oxford English Dictionary*, "swart" means "wicked, iniquitous; baleful, malignant."

60. The abrupt change in speech is similar to Miranda's in *The Tempest*, when she (depending on how we assign the speech prefixes) suddenly castigates Caliban in 1.2.350.

61. Nor are Iago's lines always speakable in polite scholarly society: I was once asked not to quote them in an essay for a leading Shakespeare journal because of their "vulgarity."

62. See Bate's introduction, 117–21.

63. Titus calls Tamora "a queen attended by a Moor" (5.2.105).

64. Habib reads the relation as part of Aaron's "racial self-reclamation" (106); see esp. 106–10.

65. Compare Marion Wynne-Davies, "'The Swallowing Womb': Consumed and Consuming Women in *Titus Andronicus*," in *The Matter of Difference: Materialist Feminist Criticism of Shakespeare*, ed. Valerie Wayne (Ithaca, N.Y.: Cornell University Press, 1991), 129–51.

66. Compare Royster, who argues that black does erase white; see also Loomba, *Shakespeare, Race, and Colonialism*, 90; and Habib, 106–10.

67. This is not to challenge Boose's excellent piece on what the transmission of black through white means for Renaissance society; see "'The Getting of a Lawful Race'"; it is to emphasize that here that "problem" collides with other concerns.

68. It is, of course, not unusual in this period for women to bear the brunt of accusations when the alleged transgression is sexual.

69. The reference to the "pearl" probably invokes the proverb "a black man is a jewel/pearl in a fair woman's eye," as Bate notes. Compare Othello's representation of himself as someone who "threw a pearl away" (*Oth.* 5.2.343).

70. Editors question the speech prefix here. Although the quarto gives "Romane lord" and the Folio, interestingly, "Goth" (perhaps another sign of the play's effective blurring of cultural boundaries), editors have tended to assign the full speech to Marcus and have thus erased the political tension surrounding Lucius's rise. See the note in Bate to 5.3.72. There is question too about the lines that follow (5.3.87–94), which, in the quarto, are part of the Roman lord's speech. Bate assigns these to Marcus. Either way, crucial and evident here is the public protest.

71. The Riverside assigns both articulations of this refrain to Romans. See Bate's note to 5.3.145.

72. See Arnold.

73. The ballad appeared first in Richard Johnson's *Golden Garland of Princely Pleasure and Delicate Delights*; quotation is from the text provided in the appendix to *Titus Andronicus*, ed. Waith, 207.

CHAPTER FOUR

1. This chapter has appeared in *Studies in English Literature* 46, no. 2 (Spring 2006): 305–22.

2. *Acts of the Privy Council of England* n.s. 26 (1596–97), ed. John Roche Dasent

(London: Mackie & Co., 1902), 16–17. Because the spelling of "blackamoor" varies from text to text, I will use "blackamoor" unless I am quoting a particular text.

3. *Acts of the Privy Council*, 20–21.

4. Quoted in Jones, *The Elizabethan Image of Africa*, 20. See also "Licensing Casper van Senden to Deport Negroes" (1601), in *Tudor Royal Proclamations, 1588–1603*, ed. J. L. Hughes and J. F. Larkin (New Haven, Conn.: Yale University Press,1969), 221.

5. Laura Hunt Yungblut, *Strangers Settled Here Amongst Us: Policies, Perceptions and the Presence of Aliens in Elizabethan England* (London: Routledge, 1996). See also John Michael Archer, *Citizen Shakespeare: Freemen and Aliens in the Language of the Plays* (New York: Palgrave Macmillan, 2005).

6. Harris, *Sick Economies*, 62–71.

7. Yungblut, 89, 91.

8. From the 1601 proclamation.

9. Michael Neill's model of an imbalance between nation- and race-based identities has been helpful; see *Putting History to the Question*, 269–84.

10. Habib, 92. See also Burton, "'A most wily bird': Leo Africanus, *Othello* and the trafficking in difference," in Loomba and Orkin, eds., 56; Hall, 14; Ian Smith, "Barbarian Errors: Performing Race in Early Modern England," *Shakespeare Quarterly* 49, no. 2 (1998): 168–86, esp. 184, and "Those 'slippery customers,'" 45–58; Little, 16, 73–74; Royster, 438–39; Gretchen Gerzina, *Black London: Life Before Emancipation* (New Brunswick, N.J.: Rutgers University Press, 1995), 3–4; Virginia Mason Vaughan, Othello: *A Contextual History* (Cambridge: Cambridge University Press, 1994), 58; and Jones, *Elizabethan Image*, 20.

11. Wheeler, *The Complexion of Race*, 2 (see also 9, 15–17); Neill, *Putting History to the Question*, 275 (see also 268–84). Compare Loomba, "'Local-manufacture made-in-India Othello fellows': Issues of Race, Hybridity and Location in Post-colonial Shakespeares," in Loomba and Orkin, eds., 149, and "'Delicious traffick': Racial and Religious Difference on Early Modern Stages," in Alexander and Wells, eds., 203–34; and Callaghan, *Shakespeare Without Women*, 78.

12. See Andrews's excellent study of the war and the ventures, *Elizabethan Privateering*.

13. *Staying Power: The History of Black People in Britain* (London: Pluto Press, 1984), 12; emphasis added.

14. Gerzina, 5.

15. In discussing the second letter, Fryer notes that only eighty-nine blacks are involved, but he nonetheless evaluates Elizabeth's agenda as more sweeping.

16. For instance, Little, 73; Callaghan, *Shakespeare Without Women*, 75; Hall, 14.

17. Matar, *Turks, Moors, and Englishmen*, 7.

18. Hall, 118.

19. Patricia Parker has explored some of these resonances in a paper, "Sound Government: Morals, Murals, and More," presented at the World Shakespeare Congress, Valencia, Spain, April 19, 2001. See also Neill, *Putting History to the Question*, 365–65.

20. *Acts of the Privy Council*, 16–17; emphasis added.

21. On this voyage and its place in the war, see Wallace T. MacCaffrey, *Elizabeth I: War and Politics, 1588–1603* (Princeton, N.J.: Princeton University Press, 1992), 107–34;

Julian S. Corbett, *Drake and the Tudor Navy: With a History of the Rise of England as a Maritime Power*, 2 vols. (1898; Aldershot, U.K.: Gower, 1988) 2: 375–409; and Andrews, *Drake's Voyages: A Re-assessment of Their Place in Elizabethan Maritime Expansion* (New York: Charles Scribners' Sons, 1967), 158–79, and *Elizabethan Privateering*, 174–75.

22. See *The Last Voyage of Drake & Hawkins*, ed. Andrews (Cambridge: Cambridge University Press, 1972), 16, 45. This collection on the voyage contains documents not included in Hakluyt, from both English and Spanish sources.

23. On these strategies, see *The Last Voyage*, 5.

24. The letter of "Drake and Hawkins to the queen, 16 August 1595," in *The Last Voyage*, 32. An account in Hakluyt gives the amount as "three millions of ducats or five and thirty tunnes of silver" (10:231). On the changing plans, see MacCaffrey, *Elizabeth I*, 108–14.

25. Andrews, *Drake's Voyages*, 172.

26. For the full account, see Hakluyt, 10:226–45.

27. See the "Report by Migual Ruiz Delduayen," in *The Last Voyage*, 218.

28. Andrews, *Drake's Voyages*, 178; see also *Elizabethan Privateering*, 175. For a survey of historians' evaluations of the voyage, see *The Last Voyage*, 7–9.

29. Andrews, *Drake's Voyages*, 178.

30. See Hakluyt, 10:226–45. On Drake's death, see Corbett, 399–400; and Andrews, *Drake's Voyages*, 177.

31. Hakluyt, 10: 264. On the mistranslation, see Corbett, 406–7. Hakluyt notes only one word that was "mistaken" (10: 256).

32. Hakluyt, 10:265.

33. Corbett, 396.

34. *The Last Voyage*, 212. For other references to Negroes fighting for the Spanish, see *The Last Voyage*, 12, 224, and 227.

35. "Antoneli's report on the defences of certain places in the West Indies, 1587," in *The Last Voyage*, 196; in Hakluyt, see 10:135–56.

36. *The Last Voyage*, 192; see also 212. Contreras is the only one to note that the group included women.

37. "Thomas Maynarde's narrative," in *The Last Voyage*, 94; on the publication history of this document, see also 85.

38. Andrews, *Drake's Voyages*, 175.

39. "John Troughton's journal," in *The Last Voyage*, 111. In *Drake's Voyages*, Andrews makes the point that at Rio de la Hache, "some of the Spaniards and about a hundred Negroes helped the raiders to locate hidden valuables" (172); see also Hakluyt, 10:243.

40. *The Last Voyage*, 212. This focus may indeed be why the presence of "Negresses" drops out of most accounts.

41. *The Last Voyage*, 212. This account was published in 1625, in Samuel Purchas, *Hakluytus Post-humus, or Purchas his Pilgrimes*.

42. Maynarde references one settlement thus in passing, *The Last Voyage*, 99.

43. Hakluyt, 10:236.

44. Hakluyt, 10:241. G. B. Harrison describes the scene as a washing and refurbish-

ing of the ships; *A Second Elizabethan Journal: Being a Record of Those Things Most Talked of During the Years 1595–1598* (London: Constable & Co., 1931), 97–99.

45. Troughton, in *The Last Voyage*, 111.

46. "Letter from Francis Drake to Pedro Suarez Coronel, governor of Puerto Rico," in *The Last Voyage*, 174.

47. Drake, in *The Last Voyage*, 174.

48. Harrison, 107–8.

49. Harrison, 108.

50. Harrison, 108.

51. Harrison, 108. Owsley also had been commissioned to negotiate with the Emperor of Morocco in 1589, concerning an English venture to Portugal and Spain. The only record which appears in Hakluyt explains (somewhat obliquely): "At this time also was the Ambassador from the Emperor of Marocco, called Reys Hamet Bencasamp, returned, and with him M. Ciprian, a Gentleman of good place and desert, was sent from Don Antonio, and Captaine Ousley from the Generals to the Emperor" (6:511). Owsley's mission is unclear.

52. Harrison, 108; emphasis added.

53. Contreras, in *The Last Voyage*, 190.

54. Contreras, in *The Last Voyage*, 190.

55. "Report on the return of the English to Porto Belo and subsequent events," in *The Last Voyage*, 230.

56. On this exchange, see also Fryer, 10–12.

57. *Acts of the Privy Council*, 20–21.

58. Gerzina tries to lay out how and how many "blacks" were located in London, but her evidence for the sixteenth and early seventeenth century is necessarily sketchy. See James Walvin, *Black and White: The Negro and English Society 1555–1945* (London: Allen Lane, 1973), esp. 7–10, and Forallin Shyllon, *Black People in Britain 1555–1833* (London: Oxford University Press, 1977), esp. 3–7.

59. See Blackburn, 65–102.

60. Susan Phillips has found provocative references to Negroes in an English-Spanish language manual, *The Spanish Schoole-master* (London, 1591), where a dialogue between a Negro servant and his master appears unremarkable; from her talk, "Multi-lingual Wheeling and Dealing: Dictionaries and the Early Modern Marketplace," Shakespeare Association of America Annual Meeting, San Diego, Calif., April 7, 2007.

61. I am grateful to Maurice Lee, for explaining to me what kind of public documents these "open letters" or "letters patent" were.

62. Quoted in Jones, *The Elizabethan Image of Africa*, 20–21. See also Hughes and Larkin, eds., 221–22.

CHAPTER FIVE

1. Fuchs, esp. 99–117.

2. The trajectory I am tracing here is Root's.

3. On the question of author, see the introduction to Brereton's edition of the play, x–xxxi; Larry S. Champion, *Thomas Dekker and the Traditions of English Drama* (New York: Peter Lang, 1985), 149–51; J. L. Simmons, "*Lust's Dominion*: A Showpiece for the Globe," *Tulane Studies in English* 20 (1972): 11–22, esp. 11–12; and Jones, *Othello's Countrymen*, 60. On the question of the date, see Champion, 150; Brereton, xiii–xvii; and Hunter, *English Drama*, 436.

4. In the Brereton edition, the line numbers correlate with the editor's own line breaks (which I see no reason to preserve). Hence, as here, the number of lines and line numbers in my text will not always add up.

5. Little, 73–74, has posited Venice's commissioning of Othello to fight in Cyprus as a deportation, but this assumption, however provocative, takes some metaphoric license with Shakespeare's text.

6. The idea of a belated revision originated with P. J. Ayres, "The Revision of *Lust's Dominion*," *Notes and Queries*, n.s., 17 (1970): 212–13. See Ayres on the play's possible evocations of the Gunpowder Plot.

7. Root, 119. Ayres too admits that reference to the expulsion may "show nothing more than a familiarity on the part of the dramatists with a well-known and long-established aim of Spanish foreign policy" (213).

8. Brereton, 154–55.

9. Quotations are from Christopher Marlowe, *Edward the Second*, ed. Moelwyn Merchant (1967; New York: Norton, 1992).

10. See Merchant's discussion of the play's date, xi–xiii. The quotation is from the title page of the 1598 text, reprinted in Merchant, xii.

11. For instances of verbal echoes, see the notes in Brereton: 161n126–30, 197n1571–73, 204–5n1870–72, 214n2231–34, 220n2743–45, 224n2872, 227–28n3182–83, 233n3450. Brereton downplays these parallels as "accidental" (197) in order to dispute the possibility that Marlowe was the play's author.

12. Gaveston's fantasies here overlap with Eleazar's: where Eleazar claims that Spain condemns him for spending the "Revenues of the King of Spain" "on smooth boies, on Masks and Revelling" (1.1.128–30), Gaveston anticipates that, once he is back in the king's embrace, he will "have wanton poets, pleasant wits," "Italian masques," "sweet speeches, comedies, and pleasing shows" as well as pages "clad" "like sylvan nymphs," a "lovely boy in Dian's shape," and the like (*Ed. II* 1.1.50, 54–55, 57, 60).

13. The nobles repeatedly condemn Gaveston as "base"; for examples, see *Edward II* 1.1.100 and 1.4.7.

14. See my argument in *Spectacles of Strangeness*, 142–72; and Bredbeck, 48–86. See also Bruce R. Smith, *Homosexual Desire in Shakespeare's England: A Cultural Poetics* (Chicago: University of Chicago Press, 1991), 209–23; and Mario DiGangi, *The Homoerotics of Early Modern Drama* (Cambridge: Cambridge University Press, 1997). On the complexity of the rhetoric of sexuality, see Madhavi Menon, *Wanton Words: Rhetoric and Sexuality in English Renaissance Drama* (Toronto: University of Toronto Press, 2004).

15. On the unseeable nature of sodomy, see especially Alan Bray, "Homosexuality and the Signs of Male Friendship in Elizabethan England," *History Workshop* 29 (1990): 1–19, and *Homosexuality in Renaissance England* (London: Gay Men's Press, 1982).

16. There may also be play with the erotic implications of "country" matters here.

17. On the importance of "purity of blood" to Spanish cultural identity in the early modern period, see Verena Stolcke, "Invaded Women: Gender, Race, and Class in the Formation of Colonial Society," in Hendricks and Parker, eds., 272–86.

18. Compare Barthelemy, *Black Face*, 104, who also attaches Eleazar's "position of legitimacy" to his villainy; and Jones, *Othello's Countrymen*, 60–68, who takes that legitimacy on in order to assess Eleazar's character rather than to address the politics that play out through his characterization.

19. Compare Tokson, who takes the elision of Indian and Moor as a sign of the times, 40–41.

20. Brereton, 154.

21. See Tokson, 63–64.

22. See also *Lust's Dominion* 5.1.2951–52, 3001–2, and 3051–52.

23. Compare Barthelemy, *Black Face*, who reads Eleazar's attraction to Isabella as a sign of his insatiable lust.

24. See my argument in *Spectacles of Strangeness*, 82–108.

25. Little, 98; see also Iyengar, 36–38.

CHAPTER SIX

1. For an overview of the publication history, see Leo Africanus, *Description of Africa*, ed. Robert Brown, lii–lxv.

2. See Oumelbanine Zhiri, "Leo Africanus's *Description of Africa*," in *Travel Knowledge: European "Discoveries" in the Early Modern Period*, ed. Ivo Kamps and Jyotsna G. Singh (New York: Palgrave, 2001), 258–66, 259.

3. Richard Hakluyt, "*An approbation of the historie ensuing, by me* Richard Hakluyt," in *The History and Description of Africa*, 103.

4. Pory also includes endorsements by Ramusio, Abraham Ortelius, John Bodin, and others. See Pory, 103–6.

5. Natalie Zemon Davis, *Trickster Travels: A Sixteenth-Century Muslim Between Worlds* (New York: Hill and Wang, 2006), 4; Hall, 29.

6. See especially Oliver Hennessey, "Talking with the Dead: Leo Africanus, Esoteric Yeats, and Early Modern Imperialism," *English Literary History* 71 (2004): 1019–38.

7. From Yeats's letters, quoted in Hennessey, 1031.

8. Hennessey, 1035.

9. This is the tag Burton popularizes in "'A most wily bird.'" See also Hall, 28–40, who argues that *The History* exposes a colonial "nervousness about where the boundaries of difference lie" (29); and my essay, "Making More of the Moor."

10. Burton, "'A most wily bird,'" 44, 46.

11. Davis, 18. I use her modernization of the Arabic name hereafter. Her opening chapter is entitled simply "Introduction: Crossings" (3).

12. Davis, 109, 153.

13. Davis, 260, 228, 230, 107.

14. Davis, 5, 160; see also 3–10.

15. From Yeats's letters, quoted in Hennessey, 1021.

16. Zhiri, 260; see also "Leo Africanus, Translated and Betrayed," in *The Politics of Translation in the Middle Ages and the Renaissance*, ed. Renate Blumenfeld-Kosinski et al. (Ottawa: University of Ottawa Press, 2001), 161–74.

17. Pory also adds "A relation touching the state of *Christian Religion in the dominions of* Prete Ianni, taken out of an oration of *Matthew Dresserus*, professour of the Greeke and *Latine toongs, and of Histories, in the Vniuersitie of Lipsia*" (1030–47) and an account of an admittedly ineffective "ambassage sent from Pope *Paule* the fourth *to* Claudius *the Emperour of Abassia* . . . for planting of the religion and ceremonies of the *church of Rome in his dominions*" (1048–63).

18. Burton, *Traffic and Turning*, 234.

19. On the naming of the continent, see Davis, 125–26.

20. Robert Brown challenges Africanus's time-line; see 838, n. 1.

21. For other examples of places named by outsiders, see Africanus, 129, 133.

22. See Africanus, 162–65.

23. For example, see Africanus, 156–60, 165, 182, 184, 271, 274, 298, 317, 484.

24. For the full incident, see Africanus, 170–72.

25. For instances of the Portuguese presence, see Africanus, 287, 288, 289, 291, 294, 397, 513; on the Spanish presence, see 518–19, 533–34. See Davis, 20, on the cultural mix of Fez.

26. Other references to Jewish populations include Africanus, 290, 318, 477; see also 181, discussed below.

27. For this section, see Pory, 24–102.

28. For additional instances of outsiders settled in the region, see Pory, 52–54, 59, 65.

29. For other mention of Negro traders, see also Africanus, 283.

30. On the exchange of cloth, see Africanus, 822; on the appearance of Barbary merchants in areas outside Barbary, see also Africanus, 283, 735, 783, 820, 824, 826, 827.

31. See, for example, Africanus, 230, 283, along with the instances below.

32. Davis, 119.

33. On the intersection of trade and syphilis, see Harris, *Sick Economies*, 29–51. See also Greg W. Bentley, *Shakespeare and the New Disease: The Dramatic Function of Syphilis in* Troilus and Cressida, Measure for Measure, *and* Timon of Athens (New York: Peter Lang, 1989).

34. Davis, 135–36.

35. The founder of Fez, one "Idris," was himself the offspring of a prominent Mauritania and his maid, Africanus notes, a slave who "had beene turned from the Gothes religion to the Moores" (Africanus, 417).

36. Karen Kupperman has emphasized the evangelical edge of the Jamestown colony, and brought my attention to Pory's role in it, in her paper "Why Jamestown Matters," delivered at the McNeil Center, University of Pennsylvania, June 29, 2006.

37. See, for example, Loomba, *Shakespeare, Race, and Colonialism*, 107; Matar, *Turks, Moors, and Englishmen*, 127; and Vitkus, *Turning Turk*, 90.

38. See, for example, Africanus, 248, 258, 701, 714, 729, 736.

39. Burton has been especially influential; see *Traffic and Turning*, 243. Davis's argument, as I have noted at the start of the chapter, follows suit.

40. See Africanus, 236–38, 240, 249–50, 301–3.

CHAPTER SEVEN

1. See the note to 1.1.135 in Neill's edition of Othello. Neill suggests "extravagant" as "a characteristic attributed to barbarians generally." See also the note to 1.1.149 in the New Variorium Edition of *Othello*, ed. Horace Howard Furness (1886; New York: Dover, 1963).

2. For a useful survey of the textual issues and arguments, see E. A. J. Honigmann, *The Texts of* Othello *and Shakespearian Revision* (London: Routledge, 1996), and Neill, ed., 405–33. See also William Shakespeare, *Othello*, ed. Norman Sanders (Cambridge: Cambridge University Press, 1984), 193–207.

3. See the Accounts of the Master of the Revels, Edmund Tilney, quoted in Sanders's introduction, 1. Barbara Everett names this the preeminent title in Shakespeare's day; " 'Spanish' Othello: The Making of Shakespeare's Moor," in Alexander and Wells, eds., 65.

4. Everett, 65.

5. A. C. Bradley, *Shakespearean Tragedy: Lectures on "Hamlet," "Othello," King Lear," "Macbeth,"* 2nd ed. (1905; rpt. London: Macmillan, 1929), 175–242.

6. Loomba, "Sexuality and Racial Difference," in Barthelemy, ed., 171; Greenblatt, *Renaissance Self-Fashioning: From More to Shakespeare* (Chicago: University of Chicago Press, 1980), 245; Michael D. Bristol, *Big-Time Shakespeare* (London: Routledge, 1996), 185–86. For other readings in this vein, see Little, esp. 72–78; Habib, esp. 135–46. Compare Neill, *Putting History to the Question*, 207–36.

7. Both the Italian text and the English translations, where quoted, come from an appendix in the New Variorium *Othello*, 377–89, here 377. Hereafter, page numbers appear in my text.

8. It is likely that Shakespeare read the Italian version, or a French translation of 1584. See Sanders, ed., 2–3. In addition to the Variorum translation, the translation in *Othello*, ed. Edward Pechter (New York: Norton, 2004), 160, changes "Barbarian" to "barbarian." Bruno Ferraro's translation in Neill, ed., preserves "Barbarian," 443.

9. William Thomas, *The History of Italy*, ed. George B. Parks (1549; Ithaca: Cornell University Press, 1963), 9; Lewes Lewkenor, trans., *The Commonwealth and Government of Venice*, by Cardinall Gasper Contareno (London, 1599), 1. Lewkenor notes that Contareno's text was written some eighty years before his own translation; see his comments "To the Reader," A4v.

10. From Sebastian Munster, *Cosmographia* (1550), translated by and included as "Sebastian Munster's description of the Citie of Venice" in Lewkenor, 172.

11. Thomas, 78; page numbers hereafter appear in my text. This point also appears in Lewkenor, 15–16.

12. Lewkenor, 16, 18.

13. Compare Emma Smith, *William Shakespeare Othello* (Hordon: Northcote House Publishers, 2004), who argues that "A Moor—literally a black man from North Africa—cannot ever be 'of' Venice" (4); I like her provocative reading of the ambiguities inherent in "of" (4–5). See also Camille Wells Slights, "Slaves and Subjects in *Othello*," *Shakespeare Quarterly* 48, no. 4 (Winter 1997): 377–90, who allows for the possibility that he can be (though in a different way from what I suggest below).

14. On Iago's multiple inscriptions of race, see Floyd-Wilson, *English Ethnicity*, 132–60; and Burton, *Traffic and Turning*, esp.250–54.

15. Greenblatt, "Psychoanalysis and Renaissance Culture." Influential studies on the question of interiority in the early modern period include Elizabeth Hanson, *Discovering the Subject in Renaissance England* (Cambridge: Cambridge University Press, 1998), and Katharine Eisaman Maus, *Inwardness and Theater in the English Renaissance* (Chicago: University of Chicago Press, 1995).

16. Julie Hankey, ed., *Plays in Performance:* Othello (Bristol: Bristol Classical Press, 1987), 10. See also Andrew Gurr, *The Shakespearean Stage, 1574–1642*, 3rd ed. (1992; Cambridge: Cambridge University Press, 1993), 95–103, esp. 99 on "personation," and 90 on Muly Mahamet.

17. Thomas Rymer, *A Short View of Tragedie* (London: Richard Baldwin, 1693), 91; John Quincy Adams, *Diary*, vol. 2, ed. David Grayson Allen et al. (Cambridge: Belknap Press, 1981), 84.

18. Emma Smith, 47. See also Callaghan, 75–96.

19. Emma Smith is especially attentive to performances; see esp. 45–49. See also Virginia Vaughan, *Othello*, 93–232, and *Performing Blackness on English Stages, 1500–1800* (Cambridge: Cambridge University Press, 2005); and Hankey, 1–134. On color casting, see Callaghan, 75–96; Denise Albanese, "Black and White, and Dread All Over: The Shakespeare Theatre's 'Photonegative' *Othello* and the Body of Desdemona," in *New Casebooks* Othello*: Contemporary Critical Essays*, ed. Lena Cowen Orlin (New York: Palgrave Macmillan, 2004), 220–49; and Ayanna Thompson, ed., *Colorblind Shakespeare: New Perspectives on Race and Performance* (New York: Routledge, 2006). On *Othello* in film, see Barbara Hodgdon, "Race-ing *Othello*, Re-engendering White-Out," in *Shakespeare, the Movie: Popularizing the Plays on Film, TV, and Video*, ed. Lynda E. Boose and Richard Burt (London: Routledge, 1997), 23–44, and Anthony Davies, "Filming *Othello*," in *Shakespeare and the Moving Image: The Plays on Film and Television*, ed. Anthony Davies and Stanley Wells (Cambridge: Cambridge University Press, 1994), 196–210. See also Lois Potter, *Shakespeare in Performance:* Othello (Manchester: Manchester University Press, 2002).

20. Vaughan, *Othello*, 181–82. On Robeson, see Peter Erickson, *Citing Shakespeare: The Reinterpretation of Race in Contemporary Literature and Art* (New York: Palgrave Macmillan, 2007, esp. 77–101.

21. On Welles and *Othello*, see Scott L. Newstok, "*Touch* of Shakespeare: Welles Unmoors *Othello*," *Shakespeare Bulletin* 23 (Spring 2005): 29–34. See also Nicholas Jones, "A Bogus Hero: Welles's *Othello* and the Construction of Race," *Shakespeare Bulletin* 23 (Spring 2005): 9–28.

22. Hodgdon, 26; the description of the makeup is from Olivier's autobiography. See also Hankey, 109–13.

23. I take the word "injointed" (i.e., united) from *Othello*, from a messenger's report that the worrisome Ottomites have "injointed with an after fleet" (1.3.36).

24. For a different treatment of Othello's stature as hero, compare Frances Dolan, "Revolutions, Petty Tyranny and the Murderous Husband," in *Shakespeare, Feminism and Gender: Contemporary Critical Essays*, ed. Kate Chedgzoy (Houndsmills: Palgrave, 2001), 202–15.

25. On the myth, see David C. McPherson, *Shakespeare, Jonson, and the Myth of Venice* (Newark: University of Delaware Press, 1990) and Vaughan, *Othello*, 13–34. Compare Neill, *Putting History to the Quesion*, 207–11; Emma Smith, 22–23; and Jacob Burckhardt, *The Civilization of the Renaissance in Italy* (1929; New York: Harper & Row, 1958), 82–95.

26. Quoted in Shapiro, 183; see also 180–89.

27. For an overview of *Othello*'s historical sources, see Neill, ed., 18–20, and Sanders, ed., 10.

28. See McPherson, 75, and Emrys Jones, "*Othello, Lepanto*, and the Cyprus Wars," *Shakespeare Survey* 21 (1968): 47–52. A key source for Shakespeare was, of course, Richard Knolles, *General History of the Turks* (London: Printed by Adam Islip, 1603).

29. (King James I), *His Majesties Lepanto, or, Heroicall Song, being part of his Poeticall exercises at vacant houres* (London: Simon Stafford and Henry Hooke, 1603), C2v, B2r, B4r. James also declares Venice an "artificiall Towne" and a "wondrous sight," because it stands "without a ground," "an Ile" being "all her market-place, / A large and spacious part" (B2v).

30. Neill, *Putting History to the Question*, 208–9. On the generic mix, see Michael D. Bristol, " Charivari and the Comedy of Abjection in *Othello*," in Orlin, ed., 78–102.

31. I am grateful to Jeri Johnson for drawing my attention to this part of Venice's past. "Ghetto" actually "refers to the section of Venice where metal foundaries were located and Jews were confined in 1516"; Roland Sarti, *Italy: A Reference Guide from the Renaissance to the Present* (New York: Facts on File, Inc., 2004), 346. As Sarti notes, "segregation became systematic under Pope Paul IV (1555–59), when all Jews were confined to walled ghettoes" (346). See also McPherson, 63–67.

32. Neill, *Putting History to the Question*, 208–9.

33. One of my favorite reincarnations of the "beast with two backs" occurs in Florence King, *Confessions of a Failed Southern Lady* (New York: St. Martin's, 1990), 80. I am grateful to Jeri Johnson for introducing me to this book.

34. I have discussed Brabantio's changing story in "Making More of the Moor," 449.

35. Robert Heilman, *The Magic in the Web: Action and Language in* Othello (Lexington: University of Kentucky Press, 1956), 129; and Mauss, 104–27.

36. From the libretto of Arrigo Boito, published by RCA Records, New York, 1978, 29.

37. Compare Neill, *Putting History to the Question*, 284, who sees "the sustainability of the racial scapegoating" questioned at the play's end.

38. See the note (to line 1.1.38) on "term" in Neill, ed.

39. For an excellent treatment of the multiple substitutions, and the trope of substi-

tution, that drive the play, see Hanson, "Brothers of the State: *Othello*, Bureaucracy and Epistemological Crisis," in Orlin, ed., 125–47.

40. I am grateful to the students in my *Othello* seminar at Rutgers University, in fall of 2003, whose impromptu performance of this conversation helped me realize how dissociated Roderigo and Iago are from each other here.

41. Compare Sanders, ed., whose suggestion that "all" of these pronouns "refer to Othello," nonetheless registers the notable linguistic confusion; note to 1.1.69.

42. I borrow the concept of dilation from Patricia Parker, "Shakespeare and Rhetoric: 'Dilation' and 'Delation' in *Othello*," in *Shakespeare & the Question of Theory*, ed. Patricia Parker and Geoffrey Hartman (New York: Methuen, 1985), 54–74, 56.

43. Taking his cues from Ben Jonson's *Volpone*, McPherson contends that Venetians were "the most famous of all mountebanks" (75).

44. McPherson, 75. See also Frederick C. Lane, *Venice: A Maritime Republic* (Baltimore: Johns Hopkins University Press, 1973), 350. In 1540, after the Turks had come and gone, the king of Tunis himself took refuge elsewhere in Italy, in Sicily and Naples; Braudel, 772.

45. Braudel, 468.

46. See, for example, Hanson, "Brothers of the State"; Margo Hendricks, "'The Moor of Venice,' or the Italian on the English Renaissance Stage," in *Shakespearean Tragedy and Gender*, ed. Shirley Nelson Garner and Madelon Sprengnether (Bloomington: Indiana University Press, 1996), 193–209, esp. 199–200; and Vaughan, *Othello*, 35–50. On the legibility of military power and place in the play, see Julia Genster, "Lieutenancy, Standing in, and *Othello*," in Barthelemy, ed., 216–37, esp. 216; and Paul A. Jorgensen, *Shakespeare's Military World* (Berkeley: University of California Press, 1956).

47. Hanson, "Brothers of the State," 133; emphasis added.

48. See Eric Griffin, "Un-sainting James: Or, *Othello* and the 'Spanish Spirits' of Shakespeare's Globe," *Representations* 62 (1998): 58–99; see also Everett.

49. Greenblatt, *Renaissance Self-fashioning*, 245.

50. Emma Smith, 41. Smith's deeply informed reading of both the play and its contexts has been particularly useful to my own interrogations.

51. Neill, *Putting History to the Question*, 208.

52. See Alan Sinfield, "Cultural Materialism, *Othello* and the Politics of Plausibility," in Orlin, ed., 49–77, on the ways "plausibility" guides our interpretations.

53. For an early model of taking cues from certain characters, compare Carol Thomas Neely, "Women and Men in Othello: 'What should such a fool / Do with so good a woman?,'" in *The Woman's Part: Feminist Criticism of Shakespeare*, ed. Carolyn Ruth Swift Lenz et al. (Urbana: University of Illinois Press, 1980), 211–39.

54. On the ways that bed is kept before our attention, see Neill, *Putting History to the Question*, 237–68.

55. Emma Smith, 58–61.

56. At first it is not clear whether Iago is pointing to Brabantio or Roderigo, both who speak "scurvy and provoking terms / Against [Othello's] honour" (1.2.7–8).

57. I have emphasized this point, which I mean to complicate here, in "*Othello* and

the Moor," in *Early Modern English Drama: A Critical Companion*, ed. Garrett Sullivan et al. (Oxford: Oxford University Press, 2005), 140–51.

58. The pivotal reading here is Neill's in *Putting History to the Question*, 237–68, cited above (note 54).

59. See, for example, Loomba, *Shakespeare, Race, and Colonialism*, 103, who argues that "because Othello is needed in order to combat the Turks, the Senate"—though not Brabantio—"is willing to regard him as 'more fair than black.'"

60. Though this characteristic is not necessarily unique to drama, it is essential to it.

61. See Neill's note (to 1.3.139) on the choice of "travailous"—which, Neill argues, "is exactly the kind of slightly pompous, recherché phrase that Othello favours"—over the Folio's "trauellours."

62. On the functions of the exotic in these kinds of discourses, see Greenblatt, *Marvelous Possessions*; Mary B. Campbell, *The Witness and the Other World: Exotic European Travel Writing*, 400–1600 (Ithaca, N.Y.: Cornell University Press, 1988); and Peter Mason, *Deconstructing America: Representations of the Other* (London: Routledge, 1990).

63. See also my discussion in "Othello on Trial," in Orlin, ed., 148–70, 152–57 especially.

64. Greenblatt, *Renaissance Self-fashioning*, 237. See Habib's treatment of Othello as a silenced "subaltern," 135–46, and note 6 above, for work which advances a similar argument. The European edge of this passage was apparently amplified in the 1997 "photo-negative" production staged by the Washington Shakespeare Company, with Patrick Stewart voicing the exotic references as "a sardonic challenge to the (black) Venetian Senate" (Neill, ed., 67); see Neill, ed., 66–67.

65. Compare Loomba, *Shakespeare, Race, and Colonialism*, who argues that Othello "consolidates his own position in Venice by establishing his distance from cannibals and monsters whom he has overcome" (107).

66. On European discourse on the Caribbean, in which these figures take shape, see Hulme, *Colonial Encounters*; and Hulme and Neil L.Whitehead, eds., *Wild Majesty: Encounters with Caribs from Columbus to the Present Day: An Anthology* (Oxford: Clarendon Press, 1992). The spectacle of humans eating human flesh may always, in its shock value, trump the particulars of that flesh; do we remember, after all, who ate whom in 1972, when a Uruguayan plane crashed in the Andes, leaving the survivors to eat the dead—or even that it was a Uruguayan plane, in the Andes, in 1972? The story is documented, compellingly, in Piers Paul Read, *Alive: The Story of the Andes Survivors* (1974; New York: Quality Paperback Book Club, 2000).

67. A crucial source is Newman, *Fashioning Femininity*, esp. 71–93.

68. Quintilian, *Institutio Oratio*, as cited in Menon, *Wanton Words*, 13. For fuller discussion of the workings of metaphor, particularly as it impacts on sexuality, see Menon, 5–34.

69. George Puttenham, *The Arte of English Poesie* (1585), cited in Menon, 20.

70. See Michel de Montaigne's essay on "the Caniballes." Other instances can be found in *Mandeville's Travels* (1499), Hakluyt's *Navigations*, English translations of classical cosmographies such as Pliny's *Naturall History* (1587), and Ralegh's *Discovery of Guiana*.

71. See Loomba, *Shakespeare, Race, and Colonialism*, 95, who argues that "Othello ultimately embodies the stereotype of Moorish lust and violence—a jealous, murderous husband of a Christian lady." See also Barthelemy, *Black Face*, 161–62. For a provocative alternative, which sees Othello's characterizing Moorishness coming into play, through humoral psychology, in a "hybrid" form, see Floyd-Wilson, *English Ethnicity*, 150–59. See also Vitkus, "Turning Turk in *Othello*: The Conversion and Damnation of the Moor," *Shakespeare Quarterly* 48, no. 2 (Summer 1997): 145–76, who, acknowledging (and usefully complicating) the hybridity of Othello's type, concludes that Othello ultimately "exhibits the worst features of the stereotypical 'cruel Moor' or Turk" (176).

72. See, for example, Janet Adelman, "Iago's Alter Ego: Race as Projection in *Othello*," *Shakespeare Quarterly* 48, no. 2 (Summer 1997): 125–44.

73. Daileader's emphasis on the gendered part of the *Othello* myth is, I think, particularly apt. On the play's misogynous discourses, see especially Valerie Wayne, "Historical Differences: Misogyny and *Othello*," in Wayne, ed., 153–79; Boose, " 'Let it be Hid': The Pornographic Aesthetic of Shakespeare's *Othello*," in Orlin, ed., 22–48; and Catherine Belsey, "Desire's Excess and the English Renaissance Theatre: *Edward II, Troilus and Cresside, Othello*," in *Erotic Politics: Desire on the Renaissance Stage*, ed. Susan Zimmerman (New York: Routledge, 1992), 84–102. Boose points out that "it isn't just Othello who calls the woman he loves a 'whore'—it is every male in the drama who has any narrative relationship with a woman" (37).

74. From Thomas Rymer, *A Short View of Tragedy* (1693), excerpted in Pechter, 202.

75. See Boose " 'Let it be hid,' " on the pornographic, and Neill, 237–68 on the resulting scopophilia.

76. Defining work on the ways race and gender intersect in *Othello* includes Newman, *Fashioning Feminity*, esp. 71–93; Neil, " 'Unproper Beds' "; and Parker, "Fantasies of 'Race' and 'Gender': Africa, *Othello* and Bringing to Light," in Hendricks and Parker, eds., 84–100. On intersections with class, see especially Peter Stallybrass, "Patriarchal Territories: The Body Enclosed," in *Rewriting the Renaissance: The Discourse of Sexual Difference in Early Modern Europe*, ed. Margaret W. Ferguson et al. (Chicago: University of Chicago Press, 1986), 123–42. On the play of race and religion, see especially, Vitkus, "Turning Turk in *Othello*."

77. On the sexual contexts surrounding these marital tensions, see Robert Matz, "Slander, Renaissance Discourses of Sodomy, and *Othello*," *ELH* 66, no. 2 (1999): 261–76.

78. On the ways the classical and grotesque bodies come into play here, see Stallybrass.

79. See "Strategies of Submission: Desdemona, the Duchess, and the Assertion of Desire," *Studies in English Literature* 36 (Spring 1996): 1–17, and "Improvisation and *Othello*: The play of race and gender," in *Approaches to Teaching Shakespeare's Othello*, ed. James R. Andreas et al. (New York: Modern Language Association, 2005), 72–79. For a provocative reading of female will and constancy, see Kathryn Schwarz, " 'My intents are fix'd: Constant Will in *All's Well That Ends Well*," *Shakespeare Quarterly* 58, no. 2 (Summer 2007): 200–27.

80. Harry Berger, "Impertinent Trifling: Desdemona's Handkerchief," in Orlin, ed., 103–24, 108.

81. See Berger; Boose, "Othello's Handkerchief: The Recognizance and Pledge of Love," in Barthelemy, ed., 55–67; and Newman, *Fashioning Femininity*.

82. Horden and Purcell, 393.

83. Compare Hanson, "Brothers of the State," who argues (provocatively) for a play of substitution whose implication and consequence is finally "a radical absence of identity" (141).

84. The house in question could also be Brabantio's, though at the moment of its transmission, it is part of what "succeeds" on Gratiano at the Moor's, not the senator's, death.

CONCLUSION

1. See, for example, Horn, *A Land As God Made It*. See also Kupperman, The Jamestown Project (Cambridge, Mass.: Harvard University Press, 2007).

2. The critical debate on this issue is extensive. See, for example, Bartolovich, "'Baseless Fabric': London as a 'World City,'" in *"The Tempest" and Its Travels*, ed. Peter Hulme and William H. Sherman (Philadelphia: University of Pennsylvania Press, 2000), 13–26; Richard Wilson, "Voyage to Tunis: New History and the Old World of *The Tempest*," *ELH* 64, no. 2 (Summer 1997): 333–57; and Andrew Hess, "The Mediterranean and Shakespeare's Geopolitical Imagination," in Hulme and Sherman, 121–30.

3. In *The English Literatures of America, 1500–1800* (New York: Routledge, 1997), Myra Jehlen and Michael Warner (eds.) begin their section on "The English Diaspora" with the Strachey narrative; see Warner's discussion, 101–3.

4. For a useful survey of the "incredibly flexible" (ix) image of Caliban, see Alden T. Vaughan and Virginia Mason Vaughan, *Shakespeare's Caliban: A Cultural History* (1991; Cambridge: Cambridge University Press, 1996).

5. William Stork ed., *William Rowley: His* All's Lost by Lust *and* A Shoemaker, A Gentleman (Philadelphia: John C. Winston Co., 1910).

BIBLIOGRAPHY

Adams, John Quincy. *Diary*. Ed. David Grayton Allen et al. Vol. 2. Cambridge: Cambridge University Press, 1981.

Adelman, Janet. "Iago's Alter Ego: Race as Projection in Othello." *Shakespeare Quarterly* 48, no. 2 (Summer 1997): 125–44.

Africanus, John Leo. *The History and Description of Africa and the Notable Things Therein Contained*. Trans. John Pory. Ed. Robert Brown. London: Hakluyt Society, 1896.

Albanese, Denise. "Black and White, and Dread All Over: The Shakespeare Theatre's 'Photonegative' *Othello* and the Body of Desdemona." In Orlin, ed., 220–49.

Alexander, Catherine M. S., and Stanley Wells, eds. *Shakespeare and Race*. Cambridge: Cambridge University Press, 2000.

Andrews, Kenneth. *Drake's Voyages: A Re-assessment of Their Place in Elizabethan Maritime Expansion*. New York: Charles Scribner's Sons, 1967.

———. *Elizabethan Privateering: English Privateering During the Spanish War, 1585–1603*. Cambridge: Cambridge University Press, 1964.

———. "The English in the Caribbean 1560–1620." In Andrews et al., eds., *The Westward Enterprise*, 103–23.

———. *Trade, Plunder and Settlement: Maritime Enterprise and the Genesis of the British Empire, 1480–1630*. Cambridge: Cambridge University Press, 1984.

———, ed. *The Last Voyage of Drake & Hawkins*. Cambridge: Cambridge University Press, 1972.

———, N. P. Canny, and P. E. H. Hair, eds. *The Westward Enterprise: English activities in Ireland, the Atlantic, and America 1480–1650*. Liverpool: Liverpool University Press, 1978.

Archer, John Michael. *Citizen Shakespeare: Freemen and Aliens in the Language of the Plays*. New York: Palgrave Macmillan, 2005.

Armitage, David. *The Ideological Origins of the British Empire*. Cambridge: Cambridge University Press, 2000.

———. "The New World and British Historical Thought: From Richard Hakluyt to William Robertson." In Kupperman, ed., *America in European Consciousness*, 52–78.

———, and Michael J. Braddick, eds. *The British Atlantic World, 1500–1800*. Houndsmills, U.K.: Palgrave Macmillan, 2002.

Arnold, Oliver. *The Third Citizen: Shakespeare's Theater and the Early Modern House of Commons.* Baltimore: Johns Hopkins University Press, 2007.

Ayres, P. J. "The Revision of *Lust's Dominion.*" *Notes and Queries,* n.s., 17 (1970): 212–13.

Barker, Francis. "Treasures of Culture: *Titus Andronicus* and Death by Hanging." In David Lee Miller et al., eds., 226–61.

Barroll, Leeds. "Mythologizing the Ottoman: *The Jew of Malta* and *The Battle of Alcazar.*" In Stanivukovic, ed., 117–30.

Bartels, Emily C. "*The Battle of Alcazar,* the Mediterranean, and the Moor." In Stanivukovic, ed., 97–116.

———. "Imperialist Beginnings: Richard Hakluyt and the Construction of Africa." *Criticism* 34, no. 4 (Fall 1992): 517–38.

———. "Improvisation and *Othello*: The Play of Race and Gender." In *Approaches to Teaching Shakespeare's* Othello, ed. James R. Andreas et al. New York: Modern Language Association, 2005, 72–79.

———. "Making More of the Moor: Aaron, Othello, and Renaissance Refashionings of Race." *Shakespeare Quarterly* 41, no. 4 (Winter 1990): 433–54.

———. "*Othello* and Africa: Postcolonialism Reconsidered." *William and Mary Quarterly,* 3rd ser., 54, no. 1 (January 1997): 45–64.

———. "Othello and the Moor." In *Early Modern English Drama: A Critical Companion,* ed. Garrett Sullivan et al. Oxford: Oxford University Press, 2005, 433–54.

———. "Othello on Trial." In *New Casebooks:* Othello, ed. Lena Cowen Orlin. Basingstoke, England: Palgrave Macmillan, 2004, 148–70.

———. *Spectacles of Strangeness: Imperialism, Alienation, and Marlowe.* Philadelphia: University of Pennsylvania Press, 1993.

———. "Strategies of Submission: Desdemona, the Duchess, and the Assertion of Desire." *Studies in English Literature* 36, no. 2 (Spring 1996): 1–17.

———. "Too Many Blackamoors: Deportation, Discrimination, and Elizabeth I." *Studies in English Literature* 46, no. 2 (Spring 2006): 305–22.

Barthelemy, Anthony Gerard. *Black Face, Maligned Race: The Representation of Blacks in English Drama from Shakespeare to Southerne.* Baton Rouge: Louisiana State University Press, 1987.

———, ed. *Critical Essays on Shakespeare's* Othello. New York: G. K. Hall, 1994.

Bartolovich, Crystal. "'Baseless Fabric': London as a 'World City.'" In Hulme and Sherman, eds., 13–26.

———. "Shakespeare's Globe?" In Howard and Shershow, eds., 178–205.

Bate, Jonathan. "Othello and the Other." *Times Literary Supplement,* October 19, 2001, 14–15.

Batman, Stephen. *Batman uppon Bartholome, his Booke:* De Proprietatibus Rerum. 1538. London: Thomas East, 1582.

Beazley, C. R. *Prince Henry the Navigator.* London: Hakluyt Society, 1895.

Beckingham, C. F. "The Near East: North and North-east Africa." In Quinn, ed., 176–89.

Beidler, Philip D., and Gary Taylor, eds. *Writing Race Across the Atlantic World: Medieval to Modern.* New York: Palgrave, 2005.

Belsey, Catherine. "Desire's Excess and the English Renaissance Theatre: *Edward II, Troilus and Cressida, Othello.*" In *Erotic Politics: Desire on the Renaissance Stage*, ed. Susan Zimmerman. New York: Routledge, 1992, 84–102.

———. *The Subject of Tragedy: Identity and Difference in Renaissance Drama.* London: Methuen, 1985.

Bentley, Greg W. *Shakespeare and the New Disease: The Dramatic Function of Syphilis in* Troilus and Cressida, Measure for Measure, *and* Timon of Athens. New York: Peter Lang, 1989.

Berger, Harry. "Impertinent Trifling: Desdemona's Handkerchief." In Orlin, ed., 103–24.

Bevington, David. *Tudor Drama and Politics: A Critical Approach to Topical Meaning.* Cambridge, Mass.: Harvard University Press, 1968.

Bhabha, Homi K. *The Location of Culture.* London: Routledge, 1994.

Blackburn, Robin. "The Old World Background to European Colonial Slavery." *William and Mary Quarterly*, 3rd ser., 54, no.1 (January 1997): 65–102.

Blair, Sara. *Henry James and the Writing of Race and Nation.* Cambridge: Cambridge University Press, 1996.

Blake, John William, ed. and trans. *Europeans in West Africa, 1450–1560.* Vol. 1. 1942. Nendlen/Liechtenstein: Kraus Reprint, 1967.

Boemus, Johannes. *The Fardle of Façions.* Trans. William Waterman. 1555, London; New York: Da Capo Press, 1970.

Boito, Arrigo. *The Libretto* to Verdi, *Otello.* New York: RCA Records, 1978, 29.

Boose, Lynda. "'The Getting of a Lawful Race': Racial Discourse in Early Modern England and the Unrepresentable Black Woman." In Hendricks and Parker, eds., 35–54.

———. "'Let it be Hid': The Pornographic Aesthetic of Shakespeare's *Othello.*" In Orlin, ed., 22–48.

———. "Othello's Handkerchief: The Recognizance and Pledge of Love." In Barthelemy, ed., 55–67.

Bovill, E. W. *The Battle of Alcazar: An Account of the Defeat of Don Sebastian of Portugal at El-Ksar el-Kebir.* London: Batchworth Press, 1952.

Bradley, A. C. *Shakespearean Tragedy: Lectures on* Hamlet, Othello, King Lear, Macbeth. 2nd ed. 1905. London: Macmillan, 1929.

Bratlinger, Patrick. "Victorians and Africans: The Genealogy of the Myth of the Dark Continent." In Gates, ed., 185–222.

Braude, Benjamen. "The Sons of Noah and the Construction of Ethnic and Geographical Identities in the Medieval and Early Modern Periods." *William and Mary Quarterly*, 3rd ser., 54, no. 1 (January 1997): 103–42.

Braudel, Fernand. *The Mediterranean and the Mediterranean World in the Age of Philip II.* Trans. Sian Reynolds. 2 vols. New York: Harper & Row, 1972.

Braunmuller, A. R. *George Peele.* Boston: Twayne Publishers, 1983.

Bray, Alan. "Homosexuality and the Signs of Male Friendship in Elizabethan England." *History Workshop* 29 (1990): 1–19.

———. *Homosexuality in Renaissance England.* London: Gay Men's Press, 1982.

Bredbeck, Gregory W. *Sodomy and Interpretation: Marlowe to Milton.* Ithaca, N.Y.: Cornell University Press, 1999.

Brenner, Robert. *Merchants and Revolution: Commercial Change, Political Conflict, and London's Overseas Traders, 1550–1653*. Cambridge University Press, 1993.

Bristol, Michael D. *Big-Time Shakespeare*. London: Routledge, 1996.

———. "Charivari and the Comedy of Abjection in *Othello*." In Orlin, ed., 78–102.

Brown, Leslie, ed. *New Shorter Oxford English Dictionary*. Oxford: Clarendon Press, 1993.

Brown, Paul. "'This thing of darkness I acknowledge mine': *The Tempest* and the Discourse of Colonialism." In Dollimore and Sinfield, eds., 48–71.

Bullough, Geoffrey. *Narrative and Dramatic Sources of Shakespeare*. 8 vols. London: Methuen, 1957–75.

Burckhardt, Jacob. *The Civilization of the Renaissance in Italy*. 1929. New York: Harper & Row, 1958.

Burke, Peter. "American and Rewriting of World History." In Kupperman, ed., *America in European Consciousness*, 33–51.

Burton, Jonathan. "'A most wily bird': Leo Africanus, *Othello*, and the Trafficking in Difference." In Loomba and Orkin, eds., 43–63.

———. *Traffic and Turning: Islam and English Drama, 1579–1624*. Newark: University of Delaware Press, 2005.

Calderwood, James L. *Metadrama in Shakespeare's Henriad: Richard II to Henry V*. Berkeley: University of California Press, 1979.

Callaghan, Dympna. *Shakespeare Without Women: Representing Gender and Race on the Renaissance Stage*. London: Routledge, 2000.

———, ed. *A Feminist Companion to Shakespeare*. Malden, Mass.: Blackwell, 2000.

Campbell, Mary B. *The Witness and the Other World: Exotic European Travel Writing, 400–1600*. Ithaca, N.Y.: Cornell University Press, 1988.

Candido, Joseph. "Captain Thomas Stukeley: The Man, the Theatrical Record, and the Origins of Tudor 'Biographical' Drama." *Zeitschrift für Englische Philologie* 105, nos. 1–2 (1987): 50–68.

Cartelli, Thomas. *Repositioning Shakespeare: National Formations, Postcolonial Appropriations*. London: Routledge, 1999.

Cawley, Robert Ralston. *The Voyagers and Elizabethan Drama*. Boston: D. C. Heath, 1938.

Champion, Larry S. *Thomas Dekker and the Traditions of English Drama*. New York: Peter Lang, 1985.

Chaplin, Joyce E. "Race." In Armitage and Braddick, eds., 154–72.

Chew, Samuel. *The Crescent and the Rose: Islam and England during the Renaissance*. New York: Oxford University Press, 1937.

Cohen, Walter. "The Undiscovered Country: Shakespeare and Mercantile Geography." In Howard and Shershow, eds., 128–58.

Corbett, Julian S. *Drake and the Tudor Navy: With a History of the Rise of England as a Maritime Power*. 2 vols. London, 1898; Aldershot, U.K.: Gower, 1988.

Crane, Mary Thomas. *Framing Authority: Sayings, Self, and Society in Sixteenth-Century England*. Princeton, N.J.: Princeton University Press, 1993.

Craton, Michael. *Sinews of Empire: A Short History of British Slavery*. London: Temple Smith, 1974.

Crosbie, Christopher. "Fixing Moderation: *Titus Andronicus* and the Aristotelian Determination of Value." *Shakespeare Quarterly* 58, no. 2 (Summer 2007): 147–73.

Curtin, Philip. "Epidemiology and the Slave Trade." *Political Science Quarterly* 83, no. 2 (June 1968): 190–216.

———. "The External Trade of West Africa to 1800." In *History of West Africa*, ed. J. F. A. Ajayi and Michael Crowder. 3rd ed. Vol. 1. 1971. New York: Longman, 1985, 624–47.

———, et al. *African History: From Earliest Times to Independence.* 2nd ed. London: Longman, 1995.

Daileader, Celia. *Racism, Misogyny, and the* Othello *Myth: Inter-racial Couples from Shakespeare to Spike Lee.* Cambridge: Cambridge University Press, 2005.

D'Amico, Jack. *The Moor in English Renaissance Drama.* Tampa: University of South Florida Press, 1991.

Daniels, Christine and Michael V. Kennedy, eds. *Negotiated Empires: Centers and Peripheries in the Americas, 1500–1820.* New York: Routledge, 2002.

Dasent, John Roche, ed. *Acts of the Privy Council of England.* N.s. 26 (1596–97). London: Mackie & Co., 1902.

Davies, Anthony. "Filming *Othello.*" In *Shakespeare and the Moving Image: The Plays on Film and Television*, ed. Anthony Davies and Stanley Wells. Cambridge: Cambridge University Press, 1994, 196–210.

Davis, Natalie Zemon. *Trickster Travels: A Sixteenth-Century Muslim Between Worlds.* New York: Hill and Wang, 2006.

De Azurara, Gomes Eannes. *The Chronicle of the Discovery and Conquest of Guinea.* Trans. Charles Raymond Beazley et al. Vol. 1. London: Hakluyt Society, 1896.

Dekker, Thomas. *Lust's Dominion; or, The Lascivious Queen.* Edited from the 1657 edition by J. Le Grey Brereton. Louvain, Belguim: Librarie Universitaire, Uystpruyst, 1931.

Diamond, Elin. *Performance and Cultural Politics.* New York: Routledge, 1996.

DiGangi, Mario. *The Homoerotics of Early Modern English Drama.* Cambridge: Cambridge University Press, 1997.

Dolan, Frances. "Revolutions, Petty Tyranny and the Murderous Husband." In *Shakespeare, Feminism, and Gender: Contemporary Critical Essays*, ed. Kate Chedgzoy. Houndsmills, U.K.: Palgrave, 2001, 202–15.

Dollimore, Jonathan, and Alan Sinfield, eds. *Political Shakespeare: New Essays in Cultural Materialism.* Ithaca, N.Y.: Cornell University Press, 1985.

Drakakis, John. "Afterword." In Joughin, ed., 326–37.

Elliot, J. H. *The Old World and the New, 1492–1650.* Cambridge: Cambridge University Press, 1970.

Erickson, Peter. *Citing Shakespeare: The Reinterpretation of Race in Contemporary Literature and Art.* New York: Palgrave Macmillan, 2007.

———. "The Moment of Race in Renaissance Studies." *Shakespeare Studies* 26 (1998): 27–36.

Everett, Barbara. "'Spanish' Othello: The Making of Shakespeare's Moor." In Alexander and Wells, eds., 64–81.

Fage, J. D. *A History of Africa.* 3rd ed. London: Routledge, 1995.

The Famous History of Captain Thomas Stuckley. 1605. Malone Society Reprints. Oxford: Oxford University Press, 1975.

Feerick, Jean. "Spenser, Race, and Ire-land." *English Literary Renaissance* 32, no. 1 (Winter 2002): 85–117.

Florio, John, trans. *Montaigne's Essayes.* 3 vols. London: Dent, 1965.

Floyd-Wilson, Mary. *English Ethnicity and Race in Early Modern Drama.* Cambridge: Cambridge University Press, 2003.

———. "Moors, Race and the Study of English Renaissance Literature: A Brief Retrospective." *Literature Compass* 3, no. 5 (September 2006): 1044–52, doi:10:1111/j.1741-4113.2006.00366x.

Forman, Valerie. "Transformations of Value and the Production of 'Investment' in the Early History of the East India Company." *Journal of Medieval and Early Modern Studies* 34, no. 3 (2004): 611–41.

Fryer, Peter. *Staying Power: The History of Black People in Britain.* London: Pluto Press, 1984.

Fuchs, Barbara. *Mimesis and Empire: The New World, Islam, and European Identities.* Cambridge: Cambridge University Press, 2001.

Fuller, Mary C. *Voyages in Print: English Travel to America, 1576–1624.* Cambridge: Cambridge University Press, 1995.

Fuller, Thomas. *The History of the Worthies of England.* Ed. P. Austin Nuttall. 3 vols. New York: AMS Press, 1965.

Gates, Henry Louis, Jr., ed. *"Race," Writing and Difference.* Chicago: University of Chicago Press, 1985.

Genster, Julia. "Lieutenancy, Standing in, and *Othello.*" In Barthelemy, ed., 216–37.

Gerzina, Gretchen. *Black London: Life Before Emancipation.* New Brunswick, N.J.: Rutgers University Press, 1995.

Gillies, John. *Shakespeare and the Geography of Difference.* Cambridge: Cambridge University Press, 1994.

Gilroy, Paul. *The Black Atlantic: Modernity and Double Consciousness.* Cambridge, Mass.: Harvard University Press, 1993.

Goffman, Daniel. *The Ottoman Empire and Early Modern Europe.* Cambridge: Cambridge University Press, 2002.

Greenblatt, Stephen. "Invisible Bullets: Renaissance Authority and Its Subversion, *Henry IV* and *Henry V.*" In Dollimore and Sinfield, eds., 18–47.

———. *Marvelous Possessions: The Wonder of the New World.* Chicago: University of Chicago Press, 1991.

———. "Psychoanalysis and Renaissance Culture." In *Learning to Curse: Essays in Early Modern Culture.* New York: Routledge, 1990, 131–45.

———. *Renaissance Self-Fashioning: From More to Shakespeare.* Chicago: Chicago University Press, 1980.

Greene, Robert. *Selimus, Emperor of the Turks.* In *Three Turk Plays from Early Modern England*, ed. Daniel J. Vitkus. New York: Columbia University Press, 2000, 55–147.

Greg, Walter W. *Two Elizabethan Stage Abridgements.* Oxford: Clarendon Press, 1923.

Griffin, Eric. "Un-sainting James: Or, *Othello* and the 'Spanish Spirits' of Shakespeare's Globe." *Representations* 62 (Spring 1998): 58–99.

Gurr, Andrew. *The Shakespearean Stage, 1547–1642.* 3rd ed. 1992. Cambridge: Cambridge University Press, 1993.

Habib, Imtiaz. *Shakespeare and Race: Postcolonial Praxis in the Early Modern Period.* Lanham, Md.: University Press of America, 2000.

Hair, P. E. "Guinea." In Quinn, ed., 197–207.

———. "Morocco, the Saharan Coast, and the Neighboring Atlantic Islands." In Quinn, ed., 190–96.

Hakluyt, Richard. *The Principal Navigations, Voyages, Traffiques & Discoveries of the English Nation.* 12 vols. Glasgow: James Maclehose and Sons, 1903–5.

———. *The Principall Navigations, Voiages and Discoveries of the English Nation.* Ed. David Meers Quinn. Cambridge: Cambridge University Press, 1965.

Hall, Kim F. *Things of Darkness: Economies of Race and Gender in Early Modern England.* Ithaca, N.Y.: Cornell University Press, 1995.

Hankey, Julie, ed. *Plays in Performance:* Othello. Bristol: Bristol Classical Press, 1987.

Hanson, Elizabeth. "Brothers of the State: *Othello*, Bureaucracy and Epistemological Crisis." In Orlin, ed., 125–47.

———. *Discovering the Subject in Renaissance England.* Cambridge: Cambridge University Press, 1998.

Harris, Jonathan Gil. "Rematerializing Shakespeare's Intertheatricality: The Occidental/Oriental Palimpsest." (Unpublished, part of current book project.)

———. *Sick Economies: Drama, Mercantilism, and Disease in Shakespeare's England.* Philadelphia: University of Pennsylvania Press, 2004.

Harrison, G. B. *A Second Elizabethan Journal: Being a Record of Those Things Most Talked of During the Years 1595–1598.* London: Constable & Co., 1931.

Heilman, Robert. *The Magic in the Web: Action and Language in* Othello. Lexington: University of Kentucky Press, 1956.

Helgerson, Richard. *Forms of Nationhood: The Elizabethan Writing of England.* Chicago: University of Chicago Press, 1992.

Hendricks, Margo. "'The Moor of Venice,' or the Italian on the English Renaissance Stage." In *Shakespearean Tragedy and Gender,* ed. Shirley Nelson Garner and Madelon Sprengnether. Bloomington: Indiana University Press, 1996, 193–209.

———. "Surveying 'Race' in Shakespeare." In Alexander and Wells, eds., 1–22.

———, and Patricia Parker, eds. *Women, "Race," and Writing in the Early Modern Period.* London: Routledge, 1994.

Hennessey, Oliver. "Talking with the Dead: Leo Africanus, Esoteric Yeats, and Early Modern Imperialism." *English Literary History* 71 (2004): 1019–38.

Hess, Andrew. "The Mediterranean and Shakespeare's Geopolitical Imagination." In Hulme and Sherman, eds., 121–30.

Heywood Thomas. *The Fair Maid of the West, Parts I and II.* Ed. Robert K. Turner, Jr. Lincoln: University of Nebraska Press, 1967.

————. *If You Know Not Me, You Know Nobody*. In *The Dramatic Works of Thomas Heywood*. Vol. 1. 1874. New York: Russell and Russell, 1964, 189–351.

Hodgdon, Barbara. "Race-ing *Othello*, Reengendering White-Out." In *Shakespeare, the Movie: Popularizing the Plays on Film, TV, and Video*. London: Routledge, 1997, 23–44.

Holderness, Graham, and Andrew Murphy. "Shakespeare's England: Britain's Shakespeare." In Joughin, ed., 19–41.

Honingmann, E. A. J. *The Texts of* Othello *and Shakespearian Revision*. London: Routledge, 1996.

Horden, Peregrine, and Nicholas Purcell. *The Corrupting Sea: A Study of Mediterranean History*. Oxford: Blackwell, 2000.

Horn, James. *A Land as God Made It: Jamestown and the Birth of America*. New York: Basic Books, 2005.

Howard, Jean E., and Scott Cutler Shershow, eds. *Marxist Shakespeares*. London: Routledge, 2001.

Hughes, J. L., and J. F. Larkin, eds. *Tudor Royal Proclamations*. New Haven, Conn.: Yale University Press, 1969.

Hulme, Peter. *Colonial Encounters: Europe and the Native Caribbean, 1492–1797*. London: Methuen, 1986.

————, and William H. Sherman, eds. *"The Tempest" and Its Travels*. Philadelphia: University of Pennsylvania Press, 2000.

————, and Neil L. Whitehead, eds. *Wild Majesty: Encounters with Caribs from Columbus to the Present Day: An Anthology*. Oxford: Clarendon Press, 1992.

Hunter, G. K. "Othello and Colour Prejudice." In *Dramatic Identities and Cultural Traditions: Studies in Shakespeare and His Contemporaries*. New York: Barnes and Noble Books, 1978, 31–59.

————. "Sources and Meanings in *Titus Andronicus*." In *The Mirror Up to Shakespeare: Essays in Honour of G. R. Hibbard*, ed. J. C. Gray. Toronto: Toronto University Press, 1984, 171–88.

————, ed. *English Drama, 1596–1642: The Age of Shakespeare*. Oxford: Clarendon Press, 1997.

Hyland, Peter. "Moors, Villainy and the Battle of Alcazar." *Parergon* 16 (1999): 85–99.

Iyengar, Sujata. *Shades of Difference: Mythologies of Skin Color in Early Modern England*. Philadelphia: University of Pennsylvania Press, 2005.

James I. *His Majesties Lepanto, or, Heroicall Song, being part of his Poeticall exercises at vacant houres*. London: Simon Stafford and Henry Hooke, 1603.

Jehlen, Myra. "History Before the Fact: or, Captain John Smith's Unfinished Symphony." *Critical Inquiry* 19, no. 4 (Summer 1993): 677–92.

————, and Michael Warner, eds. *The English Literatures of America, 1500–1800*. New York: Routledge, 1997.

Jones, Eldred. *The Elizabethan Image of Africa*. Charlottesville: University Press of Virginia, 1971.

————. *Othello's Countrymen: The African in English Renaissance Drama*. London: Oxford University Press, 1965.

Jones, Emrys. "Othello, Lepanto, and the Cyprus Wars." *Shakespeare Survey* 21 (1968): 47–52.

Jones, Nicholas. "A Bogus Hero: Welles's *Othello* and the Construction of Race." *Shakespeare Bulletin* 23 (Spring 2005): 9–28.

Jordan, Winthrop. *White Over Black: American Attitudes Toward the Negro, 1550–1812.* Chapel Hill: University of North Carolina Press, 1968.

Jorgenson, Paul A. *Shakespeare's Military World.* Berkeley: University of California Press, 1956.

Joughin, John J., ed. *Shakespeare and National Culture.* Manchester: Manchester University Press, 1997.

Kahn, Coppélia. *Roman Shakespeare: Warriors, Wounds, and Women.* Ithaca, N.Y.: Cornell University Press, 1997.

King, Florence. *Confessions of a Failed Southern Lady.* New York: St. Martin's Press, 1990.

Knolles, Richard. *General History of the Turks.* London: Printed by Adam Islip, 1603.

Kristof, Nicholas D. "Shrugs for the Dead." *New York Times*, August 8, 2006, A17.

Kupperman, Karen Ordahl. "The Beehive as a Model for Colonial Design." In Kupperman, ed., *America in European Consciousness*, 272–92.

———. *Indians and English: Facing Off in Early America.* Ithaca, N.Y.: Cornell University Press, 2000.

———. *The Jamestown Project.* Cambridge, Mass.: Harvard Univeristy Press, 2007.

———. *Settling with the Indians: The Meeting of the English and Indian Cultures in America, 1580–1640.* Totowa, N.J.: Rowman and Littlefield, 1980.

———. "Why Jamestown Matters." Talk at McNeill Center, University of Pennsylvania. June 29, 2006.

———, ed. *America in European Consciousness, 1493–1750.* Chapel Hill: University of North Carolina Press, 1995.

Lane, Frederick C. *Venice: A Maritime Republic.* Baltimore: Johns Hopkins University Press, 1973.

Larsen, Thorlief. "The Historical and Legendary Background of Peele's 'Battle of Alcazar.'" *Proceedings of the Royal Society of Canada* (1939): 185–97.

Lewkenor, Lewes, trans. *The Commonwealth and Government of Venice.* By Cardinal Gasper Contareno. London: Imprinted by Iohn Windet for Edmund Mattes, 1599.

Liebler, Naomi Conn. "Getting It All Right: *Titus Andronicus* and Roman History." *Shakespeare Quarterly* 45, no. 3 (Fall 1994): 263–78.

Little, Arthur L., Jr. *Shakespeare Jungle Fever: Nation-Imperial Re-Visions of Race, Rape, and Sacrifice.* Stanford, Calif.: Stanford University Press, 2000.

Loomba, Ania. *Colonialism/Postcolonialism.* London: Routledge, 1998.

———. "'Delicious traffick': Racial and Religious Difference on Early Modern Stages." In Alexander and Wells, eds., 203–34.

———. *Gender, Race, and Renaissance Drama.* Manchester: Manchester University Press, 1989.

———. "'Local-manufacture made-in-India Othello fellows': Issues of Race, Hybridity and Location in Post-colonial Shakespeares." In Loomba and Orkin, eds., 143–63.

————. "Sexuality and Racial Difference." In Barthelemy, ed., 162–86.

————. *Shakespeare, Race, and Colonialism*. Oxford: Oxford University Press, 2002.

————, and Martin Orkin, eds. *Post-Colonial Shakespeares*. London: Routledge, 1998.

Lovejoy, Paul E. *Transformations in Slavery: A History of Slavery in Africa*. 1983. Cambridge: Cambridge University Press, 1995.

Lupton, Julia Reinhard. *Citizen-Saints: Shakespeare and Political Theology*. Chicago: University of Chicago Press, 2005.

MacCaffrey, Wallace T. *Elizabeth I: War and Politics, 1588–1603*. Princeton, N.J.: Princeton University Press, 1992.

MacDonald, Joyce Green. "Black Race, White Ewe: Shakespeare, Race, and Women." In Callaghan, ed., *A Feminist Companion to Shakespeare*, 188–207.

————. *Women and Race in Early Modern Texts*. Cambridge: Cambridge University Press, 2002.

————, ed. *Race, Ethnicity, and Power in the Renaissance*. Madison, N.J.: Fairleigh Dickinson University Press, 1997.

Maley, Willy. " 'This sceptred isle': Shakespeare and the British Problem." In Joughin, ed., 83–108.

Marlowe, Christopher. *The Complete Plays*. Ed. Frank Romany and Robert Lindsey. London: Penguin Books, 2003.

————. *Edward the Second*. Ed. Moelwyn Merchant. 1967. New York: Norton, 1992.

Mason, Peter. *Deconstructing America: Representations of the Other*. London: Routledge, 1990.

Matar, Nabil. *Britain and Barbary, 1589–1689*. Gainesville: University Press of Florida, 2005.

————. *Islam in Britain, 1558–1685*. Cambridge: Cambridge University Press, 1998.

————. *Turks, Moors, and Englishmen in the Age of Discovery*. New York: Columbia University Press, 1999.

Matz, Robert. "Slander, Renaissance Discourses of Sodomy, and *Othello*." *ELH* 66, no. 2 (1999): 261–76.

Maus, Katharine Eisaman. *Inwardness and Theater in the English Renaissance*. Chicago: University of Chicago Press, 1995.

McCandless, David. "A Tale of Two *Tituses*: Julie Taymor's Vision on Stage and Screen." *Shakespeare Quarterly* 53, no. 4 (Winter 2002): 487–511.

McPherson, David C. *Shakespeare, Jonson, and the Myth of Venice*. Newark: University of Delaware Press, 1990.

Mela, Pomponius. *The Rare and Singular worke of Pomponius Mela*. Trans. Arthur Golding. London: Printed by I. Charlewoode for Thomas Hacket, 1590.

Menon, Madhavi. *Wanton Words: Rhetoric and Sexuality in English Renaissance Drama*. Toronto: University of Toronto Press, 2004.

Miller, Christopher L. *Blank Darkness: Africanist Discourse in French*. Chicago: University of Chicago Press, 1985.

Miller, David Lee, Sharon O'Dair, and Harold Weber, eds. *The Production of English Renaissance Culture*. Ithaca, N.Y.: Cornell University Press, 1994.

Miola, Robert S. *Shakespeare's Rome*. Cambridge: Cambridge University Press, 1983.

Moncrieff, A. R. Hope. *Classical Myth and Legend*. New York: William Wise, 1934.

Montaigne, Michel de. *Montaigne's Essayes*. Trans. John Florio. Intro. L. C. Harmer. 3 vols. London: Dent, 1965.

Moschovakis, Nicholas R. "Persecution as Pagan Anachronism in *Titus Andronicus*." *Shakespeare Quarterly* 53, no. 4 (Winter 2002): 460–86.

Munday, Anthony. *The English Romayne Life*. London: By Iohn Charlewoode for Nicholas Ling, 1582.

Munster, Sebastian. Cosmographia. Switzerland, 1544.

Nash, Gary. *Red, White, and Black: The Peoples of Early America*. 1974. Englewood Cliffs, N.J.: Prentice-Hall, 1982.

Neely, Carol Thomas. "Women and Men in *Othello*: 'What should such a fool / Do with so good a woman?'" In *The Woman's Part: Feminist Criticism of Shakespeare*, ed. Carolyn Ruth Swift Lenz et al. Urbana: University of Illinois Press, 1980, 211–39.

Neill, Michael. "'Mulattos,' 'Blacks,' and 'Indian Moors': *Othello* and Early Modern Constructions of Human Difference." *Shakespeare Quarterly* 49, no. 4 (Winter 1998): 361–74.

———. *Putting History to the Question: Power, Politics, and Society in English Renaissance Drama*. New York: Columbia University Press, 2000.

———. "Unproper Beds: Race, Adultery, and the Hideous in *Othello*." *Shakespeare Quarterly* 40, no. 4 (Winter 1989): 383–412.

Newman, Karen. "'And wash the Ethiop white': Femininity and the Monstrous in *Othello*." In *Shakespeare Reproduced: The Text in History and Ideology*, ed. Jean E. Howard and Marion F. O'Connor. New York: Methuen, 1987, 143–62.

———. *Fashioning Femininity and English Renaissance Drama*. Chicago: University of Chicago Press, 1991.

Newstok, Scott L. "*Touch* of Shakespeare: Welles Unmoors *Othello*." *Shakespeare Bulletin* (Spring 2005): 29–34.

Orkin, Martin. "Othello and the 'plain face' of Racism." *Shakespeare Quarterly* 38 (1987): 166–88.

Orlin, Lena Cowen, ed. *New Casebooks* Othello: *Contemporary Critical Essays*. New York: Palgrave, 2004.

Oxford English Dictionary Online. Oxford: Oxford University Press, 2007.

Pagden, Anthony. *Lords of All the World: Ideologies of Empire in Spain, Britain and France, c. 1500–c. 1800*. New Haven, Conn.: Yale University Press, 1995.

Parker, Kenneth. "Reading 'Barbary' in Early Modern England, 1550–1685." *Seventeenth Century Journal* 19, no. 1 (Spring 2004): 87–115.

Parker, Patricia. "Fantasies of 'Race' and 'Gender': Africa, *Othello*, and Bringing to Light." In Hendricks and Parker, eds., 84–100.

———. "Shakespeare and Rhetoric: 'Dilation' and 'Deletion' in Othello." In *Shakespeare & the Question of Theory*, ed. Patricia Parker and Geoffrey Hartman. New York: Methuen, 1985, 54–74.

———. "Sound Government: Morals, Murals, and More." Presented at the World Shakespeare Congress, Valencia, Spain, April 19, 2001.

Peele, George. *The Dramatic Works of George Peele*. Ed. John Yoklavich. Vol. 2. New Haven, Conn.: Yale University Press, 1961.

———. *The Works of George Peele*. Ed. A. H. Bullen. 1888. Port Washington, N.Y.: Kennikat Press, 1966.

Phillips, Susan. "Multi-lingual Wheeling and Dealing: Dictionaries and the Early Modern Marketplace." Presented at the Shakespeare Association of America Annual Meeting. San Diego, Calif. April 7, 2007.

Polyhistor, Julius Solinus. *The excellent and pleasant worke of Iulius Solinus Polyhistor*. Trans. Arthur Golding. London: Printed by I. Charlewoode for Thomas Hacket, 1587.

Pory, John, trans. *The History and Description of Africa*. By Leo Africanus. Ed. Robert Brown. 3 vols. London: Hakluyt Society, 1896.

Potter, Lois. *Shakespeare in Performance:* Othello. Manchester: Manchester University Press, 2002.

Preston, Thomas. "Cambyses, King of Persia." In *Drama of the English Renaissance I: The Tudor Period*, ed. Russell A. Fraser and Norman Rabkin. New York: Macmillan Publishing, 1976, 61–80.

Quinn, David Meers, ed. *The Hakluyt Handbook*. Vol 1. London: Hakluyt Society, 1974.

Raman, Shankar. *Framing "India": The Colonial Imaginary in Early Modern Culture*. Stanford, Calif.: Stanford University Press, 2002.

Rawley, James A. *The Transatlantic Slave Trade: A History*. New York: W.W. Norton, 1981.

Ray, Sid. " 'Rape, I fear was root of thy annoy': The Politics of Consent in *Titus Andronicus*." *Shakespeare Quarterly* 49, no. 1 (Spring 1998): 22–39.

Read, Piers Paul. *Alive: The Story of the Andes Survivors*. 1974. New York: Quality Paperback Book Club, 2000.

Root, Deborah. "Speaking Christian: Orthodoxy and Difference in Sixteenth-Century Spain." *Representations* 23 (Summer 1998): 118–34.

Rowe, Katherine A. "Dismembering and Forgetting in *Titus Andronicus*." *Shakespeare Quarterly* 45, no. 3 (Fall 1994): 279–303.

Rowley, William. *William Rowley: His* All's Lost by Lust *and* A Shoemaker, A Gentleman. Ed. William Storke. Philadelphia: John C. Winston Co., 1910.

Royster, Francesca T. "White-limed Walls: Whiteness and Gothic Extremism in Shakespeare's *Titus Andronicus*." *Shakespeare Quarterly* 51, no. 4 (Winter 2000): 432–55.

Ryle, John. "The Many Voices of Africa." *Granta: The Magazine of New Writing* 92 (Winter 2005): 2–15.

Rymer, Thomas. *A Short View of Tragedie*. London: Richard Baldwin, 1693.

Said, Edward W. *Culture and Imperialism*. New York: Vintage Books, 1993.

———. *Orientalism*. New York: Vintage Books, 1978.

Sargent, Ralph M. "The Sources of *Titus Andronicus*." *Studies in Philology* 46, no. 2 (April 1949): 167–83.

Sarti, Roland. *Italy: A Reference Guide from the Renaissance to the Present*. New York: Facts on File, Inc., 2004.

Schorsch, Jonathan. *Jews and Blacks in the Early Modern World*. Cambridge: Cambridge University Press, 2004.

Schwab, Raymond. *The Oriental Renaissance: Europe's Rediscovery of India and the East, 1680–1880.* Trans. Gene Patterson-Black and Victor Reinking. Oxford: Oxford University Press, 1984.

Schwarz, Kathryn. "'My intents are fix'd': Constant Will in *All's Well That Ends Well.*" *Shakespeare Quarterly* 58, no. 2, (Summer 2007): 200–27.

Shakespeare, William. *The Merchant of Venice.* Ed. M. M. Mahood. 1987. Cambridge: Cambridge University Press, 2003.

———. *The New Variorum Othello.* Ed. Horace Howard Furness. 1886. New York: Dover, 1963.

———. *The Norton Shakespeare.* Ed. Stephen Greenblatt. New York: Norton, 1997.

———. *Othello.* Ed. Edward Pechter. New York: Norton, 2004.

———. *Othello.* Ed. Norman Sanders. 1984. Cambridge: Cambridge University Press, 1995.

———. *Othello, the Moor of Venice.* Ed. Michael Neill. Oxford: Oxford University Press, 2006.

———. *The Riverside Shakespeare.* Ed. G. Blakemore Evans et al. Boston: Houghton Mifflin, 1974.

———. *The Tempest.* Ed. Stephen Orgel. 1987. Oxford: Oxford University Press, 1998.

———. *Titus Andronicus.* Ed. Jonathan Bate. London: Routledge, 1995.

———. *Titus Andronicus.* Ed. Eugene M. Waith. Oxford: Oxford University Press, 1994.

Shammas, Carole. "English Commercial Development and American Colonization, 1560–1620." In Andrews et al., eds., *The Westward Enterprise,* 151–74.

Shapiro, James. *Shakespeare and the Jews.* New York: Columbia University Press, 1996.

Shyllon, Foralin. *Black People in Britain 1555–1833.* London: Oxford University Press, 1977.

Simmons, J. L. "*Lust's Dominion*: A Showpiece for the Globe." *Tulane Studies in English* 20 (1972): 11–22.

Sinfield, Alan. "Cultural Materialism, *Othello* and the Politics of Plausibility." In Orlin, ed., 49–77.

Singh, Jyotsna. *Colonial Narratives/Cultural Dialogues: "Discoveries" of India in the Language of Colonialism.* London: Routledge, 1996.

———. "Othello's Identity, Postcolonial Theory, and Contemporary African Rewritings of *Othello.*" In Hendricks and Parker, eds., 287–99.

Slights, Camille Wells. "Slaves and Subjects in *Othello.*" *Shakespeare Quarterly* 48, no. 4 (Winter 1997): 377–90.

Smith, Bruce R. *Homosexual Desire in Shakespeare's England: A Cultural Poetics.* Chicago: University of Chicago Press, 1991.

Smith, Emma. *William Shakespeare* Othello. Hordon: Northcote House Publishers, 2004.

Smith Ian. "Barbarian Errors: Performing Race in Early Modern England." *Shakespeare Quarterly* 49, no. 2 (Summer 1998): 168–86.

———. "Those 'slippery customers': Rethinking Race in *Titus Andronicus.*" *Journal of Theatre and Drama* 3 (1997): 45–58.

Smith, John. *Captain John Smith: A Select Edition of His Writings.* Ed. Karen Ordahl Kupperman. Chapel Hill: University of North Carolina Press, 1988.

Spencer, T. J. B. "Shakespeare and the Elizabethan Romans." *Shakespeare Survey* 10 (1957): 27–38.

Stallybrass, Peter. "Patriarchal Territories: The Body Enclosed." In *Rewriting the Renaissance: The Discourse of Sexual Difference in Early Modern Europe*, ed. Margaret W. Ferguson et al. Chicago: University of Chicago Press, 1986, 123–42.

Stanivukovic, Goran V., ed. *Remapping the Mediterranean in Early Modern English Writings*. New York: Palgrave Macmillan, 2007.

Stolcke, Verena. "Invaded Women: Gender, Race, and Class in the Formation of Colonial Society." In Hendricks and Parker, eds., 272–96.

Taylor, Gary. *Buying Whiteness: Race, Culture, and Identity from Columbus to Hip Hop*. New York: Palgrave, 2005.

Thomas, William. *The History of Italy*. Ed. George B. Parks. London, 1549; Ithaca, N.Y.: Cornell University Press, 1963.

Thompson, Ayanna, ed. *Colorblind Shakespeare: New Perspectives on Race and Performance*. New York: Routledge, 2006.

"Titus Andronicus' Complaint." In *Titus Andronicus*, ed. Eugene M. Waith. Oxford: Oxford University Press, 1994, 204–7.

Tokson, Elliot H. *The Popular Image of the Black Man in English Drama, 1550–1688*. Boston: G. K. Hall, 1982.

The Tragedie of Solimon and Perseda. London: Edward Allde.

Vaughan, Virginia Mason. "The Construction of Barbarism in *Titus Andronicus*." In MacDonald, ed. 165–80.

———. *Othello: A Contextual History*. Cambridge: Cambridge University Press, 1994.

———. *Performing Blackness on English Stages*. Cambridge: Cambridge University Press, 2005.

———, and Alden T. Vaughan. "Before *Othello*: Elizabethan Representations of Sub-Saharan Africans." *William and Mary Quarterly* 3rd ser. 54. no. 1 (January 1997): 19–44.

———. *Shakespeare's Caliban: A Cultural History*. 1991. Cambridge: Cambridge University Press, 1996.

Vickers, Brian. *Shakespeare, Co-Author: A Historical Study of Five Collaborative Plays*. Oxford: Oxford University Press, 2002.

Vitkus, Daniel J. Introduction. In *Three Turk Plays from Early Modern England*, ed. Daniel J. Vitkus. New York: Columbia University Press, 2000.

———. *Turning Turk: English Theater and the Multicultural Mediterranean, 1570–1630*. New York: Palgrave Macmillan, 2003.

———. "Turning Turk in *Othello*: The Conversion and Damnation of the Moor." *Shakespeare Quarterly* 48, no. 2 (Summer 1997): 145–76.

Walvin, James. *Black and White: The Negro and English Society 1555–1945*. London: Allen Lane, 1973.

Wayne, Valerie. "Historical Differences: Misogyny and *Othello*." In Wayne, ed., 153–79.

———, ed. *The Matter of Difference: Materialist Feminist Criticism of Shakespeare*. Ithaca, N.Y.: Cornell University Press, 1991.

Wheeler, Roxann. *The Complexion of Race: Categories of Difference in Eighteenth-Century British Culture*. Philadelphia: University of Pennsylvania Press, 2000.

Willan, T. S. *Studies in Elizabethan Foreign Trade*. New York: Barnes and Noble, 1959.

Williamson, James A. *A Short History of British Expansion*. 2nd ed. 2 vols. New York: Macmillan, 1931.

———. "Richard Hakluyt." In *Richard Hakluyt & His Successors*, ed. Edward Lynam. London: Hakluyt Society, 1946, 9–46.

———. *Sir John Hawkins: The Time and the Man*. Oxford: Clarendon Press, 1937.

Willis, Deborah. "'The gnawing vulture': Revenge, Trauma Theory, and *Titus Andronicus*." *Shakespeare Quarterly* 53, no. 1 (Spring 2002): 21–52.

Wilson, Richard. "Voyage to Tunis: New History and the Old World of *The Tempest*." *English Literary History* 64, no. 2 (Summer 1997): 33–57.

Wynne-Davies, Marion. "'The Swallowing Womb': Consumed and Consuming Women in *Titus Andronicus*." In Wayne, ed., 129–51.

Young, Robert J. C. *Colonial Desire: Hybridity in Theory, Culture and Race*. London: Routledge, 1995.

Yungblut, Laura Hunt. *Strangers Settled Here Among Us: Policies, Perceptions and the Presence of Aliens in Elizabethan England*. London: Routledge, 1996.

Zhiri, Oumelbanine. "Leo Africanus's *Description of Africa*." In *Travel Knowledge: European "Discoveries" in the Early Modern Period*, ed. Ivo Kamps and Jyotsna Singh. New York: Palgrave, 2001, 258–66.

———. "Leo Africanus, Translated and Betrayed." In *The Politics of Translation in the Middle Ages and the Renaissance*, ed. Renate Blumenfeld-Kosinski et al. Ottawa: University of Ottawa Press," 2001, 161–74.

INDEX

Aaron (in *Titus Andronicus*, Shakespeare and
  Peele): as alien, 6, 9, 44, 45, 65–67,
  82–83, 87, 100; blackness, 6, 67, 73, 80,
  88–94, 96, 98, 160; cultural origins, 75,
  80–82, 93, 168; discrimination against,
  65–68, 79, 83, 88–91, 93–99, 126; versus
  Eleazar, 22, 67, 119, 126, 127–28, 130, 134,
  145; incorporation, 5, 14, 69–70, 73–74,
  79, 80–88, 92, 119, 145, 168; as infidel, 79,
  93, 96–98; versus Muly Mahamet, 45,
  66–67, 68; offspring, 88–89, 91–94, 96,
  98–99; versus Othello, 22, 119–20, 176;
  stereotype and, 87, 88–89; Tamora and,
  79–82, 85–94, 98–99
Abdelmelec (in *The Battle of Alcazar*): ethnic
  identity, 22, 30–32, 34, 43–44; global politics, 33–36, 38, 42; history, 29
Adams, John Quincy, 159
Aeneid, The, 78, 82, 94, 191
Africa: and Atlantic slavery, 11–13, 17–18, 20,
  50–51, 58–60, 104–8, 192–93; blackness,
  56, 60, 61–62, 131, 148–52, 153; Christianity, 48, 57, 144, 147–51; classical descriptions of, 58, 139; Commission for Africa,
  7–8; as "dark continent," 18, 46, 47, 51,
  63, 139; disease, 60–61, 147; Egypt, 5, 6,
  15, 17, 146, 148, 149, 153, 185; England
  and, 3, 6, 10, 16, 17, 24–28, 30, 45–64;
  Europeans and, 15, 28, 50, 54, 143, 147,
  149, 153; history of, 138–54; Moors in, 143,
  147, 149–51, 153–54; Negroes in, 143, 144,
  146–47, 149–50, 151; North Africa (Barbary), 16–17, 46, 48–49, 51–55, 57–63,
  149–50, 152; outside influences in, 14,
  143–48, 150–51, 153–54; and Portugal, 22,
  23, 24–27, 38, 47–48, 146–48; regions, 10,
  149–53; religions, 24, 53, 54, 57–58,
  139–40, 142–43, 144, 147–51; strangeness,
  10, 12–14, 16, 22, 58, 81, 152, 175; West
  Africa (Guinea, Benin), 10, 11, 15, 24,
  47–50, 55–63, 148. *See also* Alcazar, battle
  of; Barbary; *The History and Description
  of Africa*
Africans: Abassins, 149, 151; Ethiopians, 11,
  62, 146, 149–50, 151, 194; ethnicity, 13, 47,
  103, 106, 139, 143–46, 149–50, 153–54;
  Moors, 3–4, 6, 10–13, 15, 16, 143, 147,
  149–50, 151, 153–54; Negroes, 143, 144,
  146–47, 149–50, 151, 159; Othello as, 3, 4,
  9, 10–13; in Shakespeare, 10, 147, 191; skin
  colors, 147–52. *See also* Moors; Negroes
Africanus, John Leo (al-Hasan ibn Mo-
  hammed el Wezaz al-Fasi): as author of
  The Geographical History of Africa, 138;
  hybrid identity, 14, 138–41, 153; and *Oth-
  ello*, 139, 142–43; and Pory, John, 6, 19,
  139–43, 146, 147, 148–53. See also *The
  History and Description of Africa*
Alcazar, battle of, 17, 21–24, 27–28, 38
Alday, James, 24, 54
Algiers, 168
Aleppo, 187
Alleyn, Edward, 159
All's Lost by Lust (William Rowley), 193
Amurath (Murad Can), 32–33, 35, 36
Andrews, Kenneth, 105
Arabians: in Africa, 139, 143, 144, 145–46, 151;
  and the East, 15, 49; Moors as, 1–2, 5, 9,
  31–32, 153, 187
Armitage, David, 46, 62
assimilation, 18, 81, 168, 169, 175–76

Banes, Edward, 104
barbarism: in Africa, 150; and Barbarians, 5, 22,
  30–31, 34, 43–44, 119, 157–58; Goths and,
  72, 76; of Moors, 6, 45, 67–68, 69, 79, 180

Barbary: in *The Battle of Alcazar*, 19, 21, 22, 30–31, 33, 34, 37, 41, 43–44; and Eleazar, 5, 81, 119, 128, 134, 136, 168; and England, 16, 17, 24–28, 30, 46, 48–49, 53–55, 57, 63; as ethnic marker, 4, 5, 22, 30–31, 34, 43–44, 119, 157–58; geographical region, 21, 149–50, 152; history, 143–47; and *Othello*, 157–58, 169, 189

Barbary Company, 26, 46

Barroll, Leeds, 32

Bartels, Emily C., 26, 184, 225n.79

Barthelemy, Anthony, 11–12, 30, 31, 197n.34, 201n.75, 218nn. 18, 23

Baskerville, Thomas, 103–8

Batista Antoneli, Juan, 106

Battle of Alcazar, The (George Peele), 21–44; choric frame, 29–32, 34–35, 41; and dramatic tradition, 5, 6, 19–20, 22, 44, 68; England in, 5, 22, 29–30, 35–41, 43–44, 68, 130, 136; genre, 29–31, 41–42, 43; global politics in, 19, 29, 32, 33–34, 38, 41–42, 44, 68; Ireland in, 29, 36–37, 38–40; Moorish identity in, 5, 22, 30–32, 34, 43–44; nationalism and, 29–30, 35–36, 38–41; race in, 6, 22, 30–32, 43–44, 160–61; textual history, 22, 29; Turks in, 30, 32–34, 43, 68. *See also* Abdelmelec; Muly Mahamet; Muly Mahamet Seth

Belsey, Catherine, 40

Best, George, 61–62

blackamoors: blackness, 101–3, 106, 115–16; deportation from England, 6, 19, 100–117, 154; as infidel, 100–101, 112–13, 115–16; Moors as, 10, 56, 131, 149, 150, 159

blackness: and Atlantic slavery, 11–13, 20, 50–51, 58–60, 104–8, 192–93; in *The Battle of Alcazar*, 6, 22, 30–32, 44, 160–61; blackamoors and, 101–3, 106, 115–16; in Hakluyt, 56, 60, 61, 62; in *The History and Description of Africa*, 147–52, 153–54; in *Lust's Dominion*, 6–7, 119, 124–27, 128–32, 134, 136, 160; and Moors, 6–9, 10–13, 19, 20, 30, 56; in *Othello*, 7, 8–9, 90, 153–54, 159–61, 163, 165, 181–83; as race, 7–9, 10–13, 17–20, 101–2, 112–13, 192, 194; in *Titus Andronicus*, 6, 67, 80, 88, 89–94, 96, 98, 160. *See also* Moors; Negroes

Booke of Battailes, Second part of the (John Polemon), 22, 23

Bovill, E. W., 25, 202nn. 13, 23

The Boyes answer to the Blackmoor (Henry King), 103

Bradley, A. C., 156

Brazil, 48, 50, 179

"Brief description of Africke, A" (Richard Eden), 55–56, 57

Braunmuller, A. R., 28, 203n.36

Brusor (in *Solimon and Perseda*), 5, 15

Burbage, Richard, 159

Burton, Jonathan, 140, 142, 218n.9

Cabot, John, 62

Caliban (in *The Tempest*), 191–94

Cambyses, King of Persia (Thomas Preston), 14–15

Candido, Joseph, 30, 204n.62

cannibals, 59–60, 61, 142, 170, 175–76, 178–79

Cecil, Robert, 53

Ceuta, conquest of, 54

Cham, 62

Charles I, 50

Christian Turned Turk, A (Robert Daborne), 193

Chus, 143

Cinthio, Geraldi (*Gli Hecatommithi*), 156–58, 169, 179

Claribel (in *The Tempest*), 191–92

colonialism: discourse of, 26, 81; English, 17, 46, 50–51, 62–63; and Moors, 63, 75, 80–82, 87, 96, 168–69, 175–76; and race, 11–13, 17–18, 26, 46, 191–94

Columbus, Christopher, 51–52

conquest: and African history, 143–45; and Moors (dramatic), 68, 69–76, 80–81, 92, 127–29, 168–69

"Continuation of the Lamentable and Admirable Adventures of Don Sebastian, A," 22

culture, concept of, 17

Cyprus (in *Othello*), 167, 171–73, 176, 181

Daileader, Celia, 8, 225n.73

D'Amico, Jack, 28, 197n.36, 202n.13

Darfur, 8

Davis, Natalie Zemon, 139, 140–41, 147, 218n.11

Decades of the new worlde (Peter Martyr), 55

Degadillo de Avellaneda, Don Bernardino, 105

de Roales, Juan, 106

Diamond, Elin, 201n.72

Discourse concerning western planting (Richard Hakluyt), 52

Diverse voyages touching the discoverie of America (Richard Hakluyt), 52

"Dolorous Discourse of a most terrible and bloudy Battel fought in Barbarie, A," 22

Dominica, 61

Drakakis, John, 38

Drake, Francis, 16, 104–8

Dutch, 48. *See also* Van Senden, Casper

Dutch Church libel, 101

East, the: Cathay, 54, 61; East Indies, 5, 13; England and, 16, 18, 49–54; exoticism of, 2, 14–15, 49; Persia, 15, 143–46; Portuguese imperialism and, 48; race and, 13; Scythia, 69, 160

Eden, Richard, 55–58, 60

Egypt, 5, 15, 17, 146, 148, 153, 185

Eleazar (in *Lust's Dominion*): versus Aaron, 22, 67, 119, 126, 127–28, 130, 134, 138, 145; blackness, 6–7, 119, 124–32, 134, 136, 160; cultural origins, 5, 81, 119, 127–29, 134, 136, 168; discrimination against, 119–22, 125–28, 130, 132, 135–37; interracial marriage, 119, 126, 129–30; versus Muly Mahamet, 66–67; versus Othello, 22; and Queen Mother of Spain, 119, 120–21, 127–29, 131, 134–35, 136; as Spanish subject, 5, 19, 120, 124, 129–37, 145, 199; versus Thomas Stukeley (in Peele), 130, 136

Elizabeth I: conflict with Spain, 102–9, 111, 114; deportation of blackamoors, 19–20, 100–117, 118; inscription of race, 100–103, 111–17; letters patent, 103–4, 108–9, 113–14; nationalism, 6, 100–112, 114–16; negotiations with Moors, 24–27

el-Malek, Abd, 21, 22, 24–27, 28, 32. *See also* Alcazar, battle of

el-Mansur, Ahmed, 21, 24–27, 29. *See also* Alcazar, battle of

England, early modern: and Alcazar (battle), 21–23, 27–28; and Barbary, 16–17, 24–38, 46, 48–49, 53–55, 57–63; blacks in, 47, 102–3, 109–11; and the East, 16, 18, 49–50, 51–54; expeditions to Guinea, 24, 47–51, 53, 55–63; foreigners within, 100–101, 161; global investments, 3, 9, 13–14, 16–20, 32; and *The History and Description of Africa*, 139–42, 153–54; imperialism, 17, 45–51, 139, 140; and the Mediterranean, 13–14,

17, 24, 49, 192–93; and Rome, 40, 63–64, 67–68; trading companies, 16, 26, 32, 49–50, 53. *See also The Battle of Alcazar*; Elizabeth I; Hakluyt, Richard

English Myrror, The (George Whetstone), 22

Ethiopians, 11, 62, 146, 149–50, 151, 194

ethnicity: African, 13, 47, 106, 139, 143–46, 149–50, 153–54; of Moors, 4–5, 16, 20, 103, 151, 154; race and, 4, 9, 13, 43–44, 103; Spanish, 126. *See also* Aaron; Abdelmelec; Africanus, John Leo; Eleazar; Muly Mahamet; Othello (in *Othello*, Shakespeare)

Everett, Barbara, 156

Famous History of Captain Thomas Stukeley, The, 22–23, 36, 39

Fenner, George, 50

Fez, 35, 144, 146, 147–48, 153

"Flea, The" (John Donne), 90

Florentines, 8, 162, 166, 169, 172, 189

Floyd-Wilson, Mary, 13, 210n.13, 225n.71

Freud, Sigmund, 84, 159

Frobisher, Martin, 62

Fryer, Peter, 102

Fuchs, Barbara, 118

Gates, Henry Louis, 4

Geographical History of Africa, The. See The History and Description of Africa

Gomez, Ana, 108

Good Hope, Cape of, 47, 48, 51, 151

Goths, 65, 69–75, 79–83, 86, 91–93, 143–45

Granada, 153

Greenblatt, Stephen, 62, 159, 169, 176, 212n.51, 223n.49, 224n.64

Gregory XIII, Pope, 38

Guinea: England and, 24, 47–51, 53, 55–63; geographical region, 10, 11, 15, 148

Hakluyt, Richard, *The Principal Navigations of the English Nation*, 45–64; and Alcazar, battle of, 23; Barbary in, 46, 48–49, 51–55, 57–63; Baskerville voyage, 104–7; exoticism, 58, 152, 175; Guinea in, 47–50, 53, 55–63; and *The History and Description of Africa*, 139; imperialist agenda, 16, 45–47, 51–52, 60, 63; the Levant in, 25, 53; Moors in, 6, 19, 24, 25–27; Negroes in, 55, 58–59, 61, 63, 103; and the New World, 46, 50, 52–53, 58–63; organization, 52–54, 64; skin color in, 47, 56, 60–62, 152

Hall, Kim, 12–13, 103, 139, 218n.9
Hanson, Elizabeth, 168, 226n.83
Harris, Jonathan Gil, 5–6, 13, 101, 199nn. 47, 54
Hawkins, John, 50, 58–60, 104–8
Hawkins, William, 50
Hennessey, Oliver, 140
Henri II (of France), 38
Heywood, Thomas: *The Fair Maid of the West, Parts I and II*, 6, 20, 193; *If You Know Not Me, You Know Nobody*, 23, 39
History and Description of Africa, The (trans. John Pory), 138–54; Africanus versus Pory, 6, 19, 139–43, 146–53; Arabians in, 139, 143–46, 151; Barbary in, 143–47, 149–50; Christianity in, 144, 147–52; Moors in, 143, 147, 149–50, 151, 153–54; and multiculturalism, 14, 143–48, 150–51, 153–54; Negroes in, 143, 144, 146–47, 149–50, 151; and *Othello*, 139, 142–43, 175–76, 179; racism, 149–50; religion in, 139–40, 143, 144, 147–51; and skin color, 143, 148–54; textual history, 14, 138–39, 141–42, 153–54. *See also* Africanus, John Leo
History of Herodian, The, 71, 72
History of the Worthies of England, The (Thomas Fuller), 39–40, 204n.39
Hodgdon, Barbara, 160
Hogan, Edward, 24, 25–27
Hortop, Job, 58–59
Hunter, G. K., 10, 29, 34, 203n.33

Indians: in *Lust's Dominion*, 121, 124, 129, 131; Moors and, 1–2, 4, 49, 96; versus Negroes, 58–59
infidel, Moor as: on early modern stage, 30, 31, 42, 79, 93, 96–98; in historical record, 24, 53, 58, 118, 121
interracial marriage: in Africa, 147–49; in *Lust's Dominion*, 119, 126, 129–30, 136; in *Othello*, 169, 171–74, 181–89; in *Titus Andronicus* (Shakespeare and Peele), 74–79, 99
Islam. *See* Mohammedanism
Italy, 5, 17, 41, 43, 153. *See also* Rome; Venice

Jamaica, 61
James I, 50, 51, 161
Jamestown, 46, 191
Jehlen, Myra, 26
Jews: in Africa, 143–47, 151; as cosmopolitan

subject, 13, 15–16, 158, 162; as dramatic model, 5, 15–16, 66, 82, 87, 91, 135, 160, 162–63, 190; expulsion of, 101, 132, 147; and stereotype, 56, 96
Jones, Eldred, 3–4, 10–12, 202n.8, 209nn. 5, 7, 218n.18

The Knight of Malta (John Fletcher), 193
Kristof, Nicholas, 8
Kupperman, Karen, 51, 58, 206n.23, 219n.36

Larsen, Thorlief, 29–30, 203n.29
Leo X, Pope, 140
Lepanto, His Majesties (James I), 161
Lewkenor, Lewes, trans., *The Commonwealth and Government of Venice*, 158, 161
Little, Arthur, 136, 217n.5, 227n.25
Lok, John, 49
Loomba, Ania, 13, 75–76, 198n.40, 209n.2, 211n.21, 212nn. 48, 50, 224n.65, 225n.71
Lust's Dominion (Thomas Dekker), 118–37; conquest in, 127–29, 168–69; and dramatic history, 5–6, 19–20, 44, 119–20, 158–59; and *Edward II*, 122–24, 127; fantasies of banishment (of Moors), 6–7, 118–28, 130, 132, 135–37; intermarriage in, 136; and *limpieza de sangre*, 127, 131–36; miscegenation in, 129, 134; textual history, 4, 20, 118–19, 193. *See also* Eleazar
Lyster, Christopher, 23

Maynarde, Thomas, 106, 107
Manso de Contreras (governor), 104, 106, 198
Marlowe, Christopher, 38, 159; *Edward II*, 78, 122–24, 127; *The Jew of Malta*, 5, 33, 49, 66, 82, 87, 91, 162, 190; *Tamburlaine*, 15, 22, 33, 39, 69
Matar, Nabil, 13, 23, 27, 30, 103, 199nn. 51, 52
Mauritania, 4, 146, 169
Mediterranean world: Africa and, 147; Cinthio and, 158; England and, 13–14, 17, 24, 49, 192–93; Moors and, 13–14, 18, 30, 43–44, 185; multiculturalism, 13–14, 18, 30, 43, 146–47, 158
Menon, Madhavi, 179
miscegenation: Africa and, 62, 147–48; England and, 17; in *Lust's Dominion*, 129, 134; in *Titus Andronicus* (Shakespeare and Peele), 79, 80, 88–94, 96, 98–99
Mohammed, Mulai, 21, 24, 25, 27, 31, 38

Mohammedanism: in Africa, 57, 143, 144, 147–51; and Africanus, John Leo, 6, 19, 139–41; and Moors, 4, 6, 13–14, 16, 31, 57, 118, 151; and Othello, 14

Montaigne, 22, 28, 179

The Moor's Revenge (Aphra Behn), 20

Moors: as African, 3–4, 10–13, 15–16, 143, 149–50, 153; as Barbarian, 5, 22, 30–31, 34, 43–44, 119, 157, 168; as blacks, 6–13, 19, 20, 30, 56, 103, 194; and Christianity, 138; critical approaches to, 3–4, 9–14, 17, 20; emergence as dramatic character, 3, 5–6, 16–20, 22–24, 29, 45, 194; in England, 17, 24; Europe and, 5–6, 14–16, 18, 29, 44, 138, 142, 159; as infidel, in historical record, 24, 53, 58, 118, 121; as infidel, on stage, 30, 31, 42, 79, 93, 96–98; Jews versus, 5, 15–16, 66, 82, 87, 91, 101, 135, 160, 162–63, 190; as Mediterranean subject, 13–14, 18, 30, 43, 158, 185; miscegenation and, 79, 81, 88–90, 93–94, 129; multiple identities of, 1–7, 16, 20, 31, 151, 154; as Muslim, 4, 6, 13–14, 16, 31, 57, 118, 151; Negroes and, 10–11, 103, 149–50, 159; non-European others and, 14–15, 29, 160; postcolonialism and, 12, 81, 140; racism and, 6–9, 10–13, 20, 44, 101, 192; relevance (current), 4–9, 18–19; skin color, 4, 149–50, 154; in Spain, 4, 16, 118–20, 147; Turks and, 5, 13–14, 15, 32–33, 53, 66, 96, 194; as villain, 19, 22, 66–68, 82, 86, 91, 96, 119, 136, 142, 160. *See also* Aaron; Abdelmelec; blackness; Eleazar; Muly Mahamet; Muly Mahamet Seth; Othello (in *Othello*, Shakespeare)

Morocco. *See* Barbary

Morocco (city of), 54

Muley Abdala Melek, The Tragicall Life and Death of (John Harrison), 22

multiculturalism: Africa and, 14, 143–51, 153–54; Africanus, John Leo, and, 14, 138–41, 153; Jews and, 13, 15–16, 158; the Mediterranean and, 13–14, 18, 30, 43, 158; Moors and, 1–7, 16, 18, 30, 43, 92, 136, 151–54, 158; in Venice, 158, 161, 168. See also *The Battle of Alcazar; Othello* (Shakespeare)

Muly Molocco, 22

Muly Mahamet (in *The Battle of Alcazar*): versus Aaron, 45, 66–67, 68; alienation,
29, 32–34, 37, 40–44; Edward Alleyn as, 159; versus Eleazar, 66–67; versus Othello, 176; as negro, 5, 22, 30–32; as stereotype, 19, 31, 33–34, 66–68, 142, 160

Muly Mahamet Seth (in *The Battle of Alcazar*), 29, 30, 33, 36, 41–42

Muscovites, 189

Muslim. *See* Mohammedanism

Naples, 147, 162, 191

Negroes: in Africa, 143, 144, 146–47, 149–50, 151, 159; and Atlantic slavery, 11–13, 58–60, 104–8; in *The Battle of Alcazar*, 5, 22, 30–32; in Elizabeth I's letters, 100–103, 113–15; and Indians, 107; in *Lust's Dominion*, 125–27, 132; versus Moors, 10–11, 103, 149–50, 159; in West Africa, 55, 58–59, 61, 63, 103. *See also* blackamoors; blackness

Neill, Michael, 4, 13, 67, 161–62, 199n.51, 214n.9, 220n.1, 222n.37, 224n.61

New World: Atlantic slavery, 11–13, 20, 50–51, 58–60, 192–93; colonialism, 11–13, 17–18, 26, 46, 191–94; Hakluyt and, 46, 50, 52–53, 58–63; Negroes in, 104–8

Nombre de Dios, 105, 106, 108

North Africa. *See* Barbary

"oil of hell," 135, 160

O'Neill, Shane, 38

Otello (Giuseppe Verdi), 163

Othello (dir. Orson Welles), 160

Othello (in *Othello*, Shakespeare): versus Aaron, 22, 119–20, 176; and Africanus, John Leo, 139, 142–43; as Arabian, 1–2, 5, 9, 187; and Christianity, 178; as colonial subject, 175–78; discrimination against, 82, 90, 159, 161–68, 169, 171, 180–84, 187, 190; versus Eleazar, 22; elopement, 155, 162–67, 170, 174, 176; ethnic identity, 1–4, 5, 187; exoticism, 1–5, 7, 58, 153–54, 170, 176–80, 184–90; as hero, 142, 159–61, 175; interracial marriage, 143, 169, 171–74, 181–89; as "Moor of Venice," 90, 99, 142–43, 153–54, 156–59, 161, 168–80, 187–90; versus Muly Mahamet, 176; as negro, 10; and shaping of Venice, 175–80, 184–89; status (in Venice), 106, 167–70, 171, 175–76; as stranger, 155–56, 169–71, 175, 181, 184

Othello (Shakespeare), 155–90; blackness in, 7, 8–9, 90, 153–54, 159–61, 163, 165, 181–83; versus Cinthio, 156–58, 169, 179; Cyprus in, 153, 158, 161, 167, 171, 172, 173, 176, 181; dramatic tradition and, 5–6, 19–20, 44, 159, 160–61, 168, 189–90; Florentines in, 162, 166, 169, 172, 189; handkerchief in, 185–87, 188; historical context, 10, 18, 29; and *The History and Description of Africa*, 139, 142–43, 175–76, 179; interracial marriage in, 169, 171–74, 181–84; lodging in, 171–74; versus *The Merchant of Venice*, 15–16, 161–63, 166; performance, 159–60; racist discourse in, 82, 90, 159, 161–68, 169, 171, 180–84, 187, 190; Spanish resonances, 169, 187; textual issues, 156, 166; Turks in, 1–3, 5, 68, 99, 163, 174, 180, 187, 190; Venice in, 1–3, 7, 82, 90, 99, 142, 153–59, 161–64, 166–90. *See also* Othello (in *Othello*, Shakespeare)
Othellophilia, 8–9, 182
Ovid, 71, 75, 89
Owsley, Nicholas, 107–8

Parker, Patricia, 165, 223n.42
Peele, George, 22, 45, 66
Philip II (of Spain), 28, 36, 38, 122
Philip III (of Spain), 118, 119, 122, 138
Philips, Miles, 58–59
Philomel, 71
Phrysius, Gemma, 58
Pinteado, Antonio, 49, 56–57, 60
Pliny, 58
Portuguese: in Africa, 22–27, 38, 47–48, 146, 148; Alcazar and, 22, 23, 27–28, 38; in *The Battle of Alcazar*, 5, 29, 30, 33–38, 40–43, 68; England and, 16, 47–58, 60, 100, 108–9; in *Lust's Dominion*, 132; in *Othello*, 188
Pory, John, 6, 19, 139–42, 147, 149–53, 154. See also *The History and Description of Africa*
postcolonialism, 12, 81, 140
Prestor John, 48, 57, 151
Prince of Morocco (in *The Merchant of Venice*), 5, 15, 162

Quintilian, 178

race: and Christianity, 96–97, 112–16; colonialism and, 12–13, 17–18, 26, 46, 63,

191–94; economics and, 27, 47–48, 102, 108, 109–17, 143; in Elizabeth I's letters, 101–2, 106, 112–13; as ethnicity, 4, 9, 13, 43–44, 103; gender and, 12, 62, 75–76, 178, 182–83, 188–89, 193; genre and, 12; instability of, 4–5, 9, 12, 194; as lineage, 9, 91–92, 132; miscegenation, 91–92, 129, 134, 147–48; nationalism and, 101–2, 109–12, 114–15; New World slavery and, 11–13, 17–18, 20, 50–51, 58–60, 192–93; and performance, 12, 136; and postcolonialism, 12, 81, 140; as religion, 12, 13, 43, 101; as skin color, 6–13, 30–32, 101–3, 143, 148–52, 153–54. *See also* blackness; racism; tawniness; whiteness
racism: in England, 100–103, 111–13, 114, 117, 118; and law, 126, 148, 161–62; in *Lust's Dominion*, 67, 119–21, 125–28, 130, 132, 135–37; against Moors, 5, 6–13, 18–20, 44, 101, 140, 192; in *Othello*, 82, 90, 159, 161–68, 169, 171, 180–84, 187, 190; Pory and, 149–50; in *Titus Andronicus*, 65–68, 79, 83, 88–91, 93–99, 126. *See also* Aaron; Eleazar; Muly Mahamet; Othello (in *Othello*, Shakespeare)
Ralegh, Walter, 63, 175
Ramusio, Gian Battista, 139
religion: in Africa, 24, 48, 53, 57–58, 139–40, 142–43, 144, 147–51; of Moors, 4, 6, 13–14, 16, 19, 31, 57, 118, 139–41, 151. *See also* infidel, Moor as
The Renegado (Philip Massinger), 193
Rio de la Hacha, 104–5, 108
Robeson, Paul, 160
Rodrigues, Francisco, 49
Rome: Africa and, 45, 143, 144; England and, 40, 63–64, 67–68; Moors and, 5, 14, 138, 139, 141. See also *Titus Andronicus* (Shakespeare and Peele)
Root, Deborah, 118
Ryle, John, 8
Rymer, Thomas, 159

Said, Edward, 11
Santa Cruz, 54, 105, 106
São Tomé, 48, 50, 61
Savile, Henry, 105
Scythia, 69, 160
Sebastian (king of Portugal), 21–23, 27–28. *See also* Alcazar, battle of
Selimus, Emperor of the East (Robert Greene), 15

Shakespeare, William, 81, 90, 97; *Coriolanus*, 95; *Cymbeline*, 8–9; *Hamlet*, 2, 40, 42, 43, 84, 159, 184; *Henry IV, Part 2*, 32; *Julius Caesar*, 42; *King Lear*, 77, 159, 184; *Macbeth*, 79, 83, 159, 184; *Measure for Measure*, 15, 159; *The Merchant of Venice*, 5–6, 15–16, 20, 134, 161–62; *A Midsummer Night's Dream*, 126; *Much Ado About Nothing*, 8, 84, 189; *Richard II*, 37; *Richard III*, 41; *Romeo and Juliet*, 126; *The Tempest*, 10, 17, 68, 147, 191–93; *The Winter's Tale*, 8, 189. See also *Othello* (Shakespeare); *Titus Andronicus* (Shakespeare and Peele)

Shammas, Carole, 51

Shirley, Anthony, 60–61

Sierra Leone, 10

Sinfield, Alan, 170, 223n.52

slavery, Atlantic, 11–13, 17–18, 20, 50–51, 58–60, 104–8, 192–93

Smith, Emma, 169–70, 171, 196nn. 25, 30, 221n.13, 223n.55

Smith, Ian, 67

Smith, John, 46

sodomy, 56–57, 151

Solimon and Perseda, 5

Solinus, 58

Spain: Africa and, 24–28, 49, 53, 54–55, 146–48; Alcazar and, 21, 22, 36, 38; armada, 102; in *The Battle of Alcazar*, 30, 35–36, 40, 41, 43; and English constructions of race, 100, 102–16, 124; in *Lust's Dominion*, 118–37; Moors in (dramatic), 5, 6, 118–37, 168, 193; Moors in (historical), 6, 14, 118–20, 147; Negroes and, 58–59, 63, 103–9, 111

The Spanish Moor's Tragedy, 119. See also *Lust's Dominion*

Stanley, Henry, *Through the Dark Continent*, 47

stereotypes: in *The Battle of Alcazar*, 19, 31, 33–34, 66–68, 142, 160; gender and, 183; in *Lust's Dominion*, 119, 124; of Moors, 138; in *Othello*, 162–66, 180–81, 183–84; in *Titus Andronicus* (Shakespeare and Peele), 66–68, 87, 88, 96–97; of Turks, 66, 96. *See also* blackness; infidel, Moor as; Moors; racism

Strachey, William, 46, 191

"Strangest Adventure that Ever Happened, The" (trans. Anthony Munday), 22

Stukeley, Thomas: dramatic character, 22, 29–30, 35–44, 130, 136; historical figure, 21–23, 37–40

Suarez, Pedro, 107

Tamora (in *Titus Andronicus*, Shakespeare and Peele): discrimination against, 65–67, 96, 98; incorporation within Rome, 74–81, 83; racial identity, 69, 72, 73, 89, 90; relation to Aaron, 79–82, 84–94

tawniness, 92, 129, 143, 148–52

Thomas, William, *The History of Italy*, 158, 161, 162

Titus (dir. Julie Taymor), 75, 89

Titus Andronicus (Edward Ravenscroft), 20

Titus Andronicus (Shakespeare and Peele), 20, 65–99; blackness in, 6, 67, 73, 80, 88–94, 96, 98, 160; and classical history, 63–64, 71–72; colonial politics in, 75, 80–82, 87, 96; conquest in, 68–75, 80–81, 92, 95, 99; cross-cultural incorporation, 69–70, 73, 75–88, 90, 92–94, 96, 98–100, 145; and dramatic tradition, 5–6, 19–20, 44, 68, 119, 158–59; interracial marriage in, 74–79; miscegenation, 79, 80, 81, 88–94, 96, 98–99; Muly, 81, 88, 89, 93; racial discrimination in, 65–68, 83, 88, 93–99, 126; Roman purity in, 45, 63–64, 66–70; textual history, 66–67, 85, 90; whiteness in, 73–76, 80, 89, 93. *See also* Aaron; Goths; Tamora

"Titus Andronicus' Complaint," 98

Titus Andronicus, The History of, 71

Tokson, Elliot, 11–12, 20, 201n.75, 203n.37, 218n.19

Towerson, William, 49, 55

trading companies, English, 16, 26, 32, 49–50, 53

Tripoli, 168

Troy, 69, 94

Troughton, John, 106

Tunis, 147, 168, 191–92

Turks: Africa and, 27–28, 32, 143, 145, 146; in *The Battle of Alcazar*, 30, 32–34, 43, 68; England and, 15, 17, 25, 32, 49; in Hakluyt, 52–54, 58, 63; Jews and, 5, 33, 66; in the Mediterranean, 13–14, 50, 158, 161, 168; Moors and, 13–14, 15, 16, 32–33, 53, 66, 96, 194; *Othello* and, 1–3, 5, 68, 99, 153, 156, 163, 174, 180, 187, 190; as stereotype, 66, 96

Van Senden, Casper, 100, 108–15
Vasques de Gama, 51
Venice: as dramatic setting, 1–3, 7, 82, 90, 99, 142, 153–54, 157–59, 161–64, 166–90; history, 2, 156–57, 158, 161–62, 168
Verde, Cape, 61, 151
Vitkus, Daniel J., 13, 199nn.52–54, 225n.71

West Africa. *See* Guinea
The White Devil (John Webster), 20, 193
whiteness: Africa and, 47, 146–52, 160; in *Lust's Dominion*, 133; Moors, and 4, 12, 19; in *Othello*, 163, 183; in *Titus Andronicus* (Shakespeare and Peele), 62, 73–76, 80, 89, 93

Williams, John, 24
Williamson, James A., 58, 199–200n.55
Willoughby, Hugh, 52
Wolley, John, 161
The Wonder of Women; or, The Tragedy of Sophonisba (John Marston), 193
Wyndham, Thomas, 24, 48, 49, 56, 60

Yeats, William Butler, 140
Yungblut, Laura Hunt, 100

Zhiri, Oumelbanine, 142

ACKNOWLEDGMENTS

Portions of this book have been published previously. A version of Chapter 1 appeared as "*The Battle of Alcazar*, the Mediterranean, and the Moor," in *Remapping the Mediterranean World in Early Modern English Writings*, ed. Goran V. Stanivukovic (New York: Palgrave Macmillan, 2007) and is reproduced by permission of Palgrave Macmillan. A version of Chapter 2 appeared as "*Othello* and Africa: Postcolonialism Reconsidered," *William and Mary Quarterly*, 3rd series, 54, no. 1 (January 1997) and is reprinted by permission of the Omohundro Institute of Early American History and Culture. Chapter 4, "Too Many Blackamoors: Deportation, Discrimination, and Elizabeth I," is reprinted by permission of *SEL Studies in English Literature 1500–1900* 46, no. 2 (Spring 2006).

It has been a great pleasure working with Mariana Martinez, Erica Ginsburg, John Hubbard, and especially Jerry Singerman at the University of Pennsylvania Press, and I am grateful to the anonymous readers as well as to the anonymous copyeditor, all whose suggestions have strengthened this book. Thanks, too, to AnnaLee Pauls, John Delaney, and Charles Greene at Princeton University Library for their assistance and enthusiasm in helping me access the Special Maps Collection for the cover illustration.

My research for this project has been enabled by a Solmsen Fellowship from the Institute for Research in the Humanities at the University of Wisconsin, Madison, and I am happily indebted to Paul Boyer, Susanne Wofford, Jacques Lezra, and Heather Dubrow, who served as generous hosts, as well as to Renée Baernstein and Wietse de Boer, who offered invaluable friendship and feedback. The project has been supported additionally by a fellowship from the Rutgers Center for Historical Analysis, for participation in the Black Atlantic Project, and by the input of my seminar colleagues, especially Herman Bennett and Jennifer Morgan. Crucial too have been opportunities to share my work with early modernists in the seminar "Constructing Race," run by the Institute of Early American History and Culture, and in the English departments at the University of Chicago, the University of Pennsylvania, Pennsylvania State University, Tufts University, the University of Massachusetts at Amherst, and the University of Miami–Ohio, where David Bevington, Kevin Dunn, Deborah Carlin, and Arthur Kinney have been gracious hosts.

I am extremely grateful to the many other friends and colleagues who have offered their support. Mary Crane has been endlessly available as a mentor, friend, and critic. Laura Knoppers, Jim Siemon, Rob Watson, Miriam Hansen, Dianne Sadoff, Beth Durkee, Linda Meyers, and Mary Bartels have shared their friendship, intelligence, and encouragement with me all along the way. The community of the Bread Loaf School of English (Middlebury College) has given me an inviting occasion to present parts of this book as well as an extraordinary place every summer to write it, and I am especially grateful to Jim Maddox, Isobel Armstrong, Margery Sabin, Jonathan Strong, Michael Armstrong, Lucy Maddox, Jim Sabin, Michael Cadden, Arthur Little, and Jeri Johnson for their generous interest, support, and love. At Rutgers University, Barry Qualls, Chris Chism, Cheryl Wall, Marianne DeKoven, Richard Miller, Paul Clemens, Richard Dienst, Leandra Cain, Cheryl Robinson, and Eileen Faherty have cheered me invaluably along, as have my colleagues in early modern studies, Ann Baynes Coiro, Jackie Miller, Ron Levao, and Tom Fulton. My graduate and undergraduate students have helped me think and rethink *Othello*, and I am indebted in particular to Colleen Rosenfeld and Scott Trudell for assistance on the manuscript, to Ed Kranz for the gift of *Trickster Travels*, and to Matt Cinotti for great conversations about *Titus*. I am grateful too for the work and support of Michael Neill, Karen Kupperman, Gil Harris, Tom Cartelli, Jyotsna Singh, Eric Griffin, Jonathan Burton, Peter Erickson, Larry Danson, Shankar Raman, David Riggs, Lena Cowen Orlin, Garrett Sullivan, and Kathryn Schwarz.

I dedicate this book to my dear friend Emma Smith, who has generously read and commented on multiple drafts and who, with her inimitable wit and wisdom, has spurred on this project and its author at the most crucial stages.